To Marie

SIDNEY GREIDANUS

SOLA SCRIPTURA

Problems and Principles in Preaching Historical Texts

WEDGE PUBLISHING FOUNDATION   Toronto—Canada

Typeset by J. H. Kok, Kampen, The Netherlands
Printed by General Printers, Oshawa, Ontario, Canada
Third printing 1979

ISBN 0-88906-103-3

Table of Contents

III. OBJECTIONS TO THE EXEMPLARY APPROACH

IV. THE REDEMPTIVE-HISTORICAL APPROACH

V. CRITIQUE

VI. PRINCIPLES FOR PREACHING HISTORICAL TEXTS

Introduction

Every preacher of the Word is faced with certain problems when he prepares a sermon on a historical text of Scripture. A preacher standing in the tradition of the Reformation realizes that he must preach the Word and only the Word. He professes with the *Belgic Confession* (art. VII): "Neither may we consider any writings of men, however holy these men may have been, of equal value with those divine Scriptures, nor ought we to consider custom... as of equal value with the truth of God...." He realizes that the Reformation's *sola Scriptura* remains the fundamental criterion also for his preaching. No matter how sound a church's doctrine of Scripture may be, when her preachers use the texts of Scripture as launching pads for dogmas or their own ideas, the profession of *sola Scriptura* is undermined by those who should be its exponents. Preachers are ministers, servants of the Word, also when preaching historical texts. Perhaps the awareness of this responsibility and of the problems involved in preaching historical texts has resulted in the *dis*use of many Scripture passages as preaching-texts. On the other hand, an insufficient awareness of the problems involved may be the cause for the frequent *mis*use of historical preaching-texts. But whether it be disuse or misuse, in neither case do we honor the Bible for what we profess it to be: God's Word to his people.

The Nature of this Study

Central in this study is a hermeneutical-homiletical controversy concerning the preaching of historical texts. This conflict, known as the exemplary – redemptive-historical controversy ("exemplarisch – heilshistorisch"), raged in the Gereformeerde Kerken in Holland during the 1930's and early 1940's. Although it brought many minds and pens into action, its fruit lies buried beneath the rubble of a world war and a church schism. Our major object will be to uncover this past controversy, to gain a clear view of the two opposing theories, to gather and systematize their arguments, in short, to recover the issues of the controversy. From that point of view, this dissertation may be termed a historical study.

We do not wish to stop, however, at a mere historical analysis of the theories presented some thirty years ago. The controversy offers a stimulus for re-thinking our present practice of interpreting and preaching historical texts, for it exposed many weaknesses in the traditional, "exemplary" approach — weaknesses which are, in the main, still with us today. We shall try, therefore, to carry into the present the fruitful themes of this past controversy, to show its contemporary relevance, and, with the aid of present-day insights, to formulate a few guidelines for interpreting and preaching historical texts.

Mode of Presentation

For the sake of orientation and to show the contemporary relevance of the controversy, we shall begin our presentation with a brief introductory chapter (I). Starting out on the broad base of homiletics and hermeneutics, it leads via a section on past and present exemplary interpretation and preaching to the Dutch controversy. Chapter II sketches the historical context of the controversy and offers a bird's-eye view of its course. The core of this study consists of chapters III and IV, which present the issues of the controversy. Although one could follow the debate historically by tracing the development of the issues, either individually or collectively, or by tracing the development in the view of each individual author, all these procedures would be cumbersome, would lead to needless repetition, and would fail to bring the issues sharply into focus. We have, therefore, decided to follow another course. To disclose the connection of the seemingly diverse issues and to show clearly the pros and cons of each individual issue, we have opted for a topical presentation which retains the style of the debate between two camps. Chapter III contains the redemptive-historical side's objections to the exemplary approach together with the exemplary side's defense, while chapter IV presents the redemptive-historical approach together with the exemplary side's objections. These two chapters have been developed in parallel fashion. The reader thus has an option either to read through each chapter in its entirety in order to discern the interrelationship of all issues, or, by referring to the Table of Contents, to skip from one chapter to the other in order to take in the pros and cons of each individual issue. In chapter V we critically examine several key assumptions of the redemptive-historical approach, drawing into our evaluation the exemplary approach as well. In conclusion, we round off this study with a brief chapter (VI) suggesting a few guidelines for preaching historical texts.

Language, Sources, Documentation

Since we desire to acquaint English-speaking preachers with the hermeneutical-homiletical insights which sprang up on Dutch soil, we have chosen to use only the English language in the text and to relegate all other languages to the footnotes. This choice has made it necessary to translate most of the quotations used in the text. Although several of our Dutch sources have been translated into English, these translations proved to be less than satisfactory for our purposes because often they fail to get across the specific point of the original Dutch text. For the sake of comparison, we frequently make a secondary reference (E) to these existing translations. When the note refers first to the original source, however, the translation of the quotation is entirely our responsibility. To avoid unnecessary duplication, the original Dutch quotation is cited in the footnotes only when this duplication is deemed of sufficient importance. We have tried to make the translations as literal as possible, retaining the liberty, however, to make stylistic changes in the interest of readability. One of these changes is the omission, without notification, of word emphasis. (In the pre-war Dutch text, it ranges from italics and letter-spacing through boldface type to normal and italicized capital letters). We have further taken the liberty of capitalizing the prefix before Dutch and German names and have entered these names accordingly in the alphabetical order of the bibliography.

The nature of this study requires that the original date of certain statements be immediately apparent. To achieve this, we have frequently entered these dates in the footnotes. When the date appears immediately behind the author's name, it indicates the date when the statement was first made or published, while the reference is to a later, more readily available publication, such as a subsequent compilation. When the reference is to the earliest publication, the date has been entered in the usual manner, behind the title of the book or periodical. In general, however, the footnotes have been cut down to a bare minimum. Except for references to books and articles not entered in the Selected Bibliography, the notes usually will not repeat the information which can be found in the bibliography, such as: titles of articles, initials of authors, names of editors, compilers, or translators, and facts of publication. We have further reduced the size of the footnotes by freely abbreviating the titles of books and periodicals. Abbreviations which may present problems for locating the intended publication in the bibliography are explained in the List of Abbreviations. Finally, except for adding initials to identical names, both in the text and in the notes, all authors will be designated by their last name only.

Chapter I

HOMILETICS AND HERMENEUTICS

Central in this study is a controversy pertaining to the preaching of historical texts. Although this conflict can be called a *homiletical* controversy, it will soon become apparent that *hermeneutics* plays a major role. We do not consider this an illegitimate intrusion on the part of hermeneutics; on the contrary, it demonstrates once again that it is impossible to reduce homiletics to some formal technique concerning the art of communication.

Communication

In America much research has been done of late in the area of communication.[1] The research clearly indicates that this discipline cuts right across the fields of psychology and sociology. One must also recognize, however, that there are various kinds of communication: a father communicates with his child, a teacher with his pupil, a chairman with his board, a senator with the senate, a preacher with his congregation. All of these are forms of communication; all have one thing in common: all use words to carry a message from the sender to the receiver. And yet each is distinct: the father speaks differently than does the teacher, the teacher than the chairman, the chairman than the senator, the senator than the preacher. The difference lies not so much in the fact that the senders are different (it may be one and the same person) nor in the fact that the receivers are different (they too could be the same). The difference lies rather in the different *relationship* between sender and receiver in each instance. In other words, it is the specific social structure — whether it be home, school, industry, state, or church — that determines the specific kind of communication.

---

1   See, e.g., W. Schramm (ed.), *The Science of Human Communication* (1963).

Homiletics deals with the communication taking place in the church. Because it is communication, homiletics cannot do without the aid of psychology and sociology. On the other hand, because homiletics deals with a special kind of communication — communication in the *church* — there is much more to it than a formal description of "how to get the message across." It is equally (if not more) concerned with "how to *get* the message."

This conviction is not new, of course: witness the traditional distinction between formal and material homiletics. In contrast to most English books on homiletics, however, this study places the accent on the material side. Our subject itself leads us in this direction, for we are dealing with a concrete controversy within the church — a controversy which refuses to be confined to anything like "formal homiletics." And rightly so, for, as we shall see, the root of the problem lies much deeper than the formal "how to get the message across"; it lies at the level of "how to get the message from Scripture." Although the distinction between formal and material homiletics may not be entirely fortunate, it does demonstrate that homiletics is concerned with the content of the sermon and its relation to Scripture at least as much as with the rules of rhetoric. It is by way of "material homiletics" that homiletics is firmly linked with the central concern of biblical hermeneutics.

The Preacher a Hermeneutist

Paul tells Timothy: "Do your best to present yourself to God as one approved, a workman who has no need to be ashamed, rightly handling the word of truth."[2] It requires effort to preach the Word "rightly"; it entails great responsibility, for the preacher does not speak for himself but is the spokesman for Another.[3] The preacher is in the original sense of the word a trans-lator, that is, one who transfers, who carries over the message of God. Furthermore, since he finds this message in Scripture in a foreign language, he must be a translator in the usual sense of the word. But he cannot begin to translate until he has understood the meaning, until he has interpreted the text. Thus the word "translator" shows something of the unity of the preacher's variegated task. A better but less common word is "hermeneutist." The preacher as hermeneutist expresses the fact that: (1) he interprets the Word, (2) he translates the Word, (3) he proclaims the Word, and (4) that these activities cannot be separated.[4] If the name "hermeneutist" accentuates

2 II Tim. 2 : 15. Unless otherwise indicated, the Revised Standard Version will be quoted throughout.
3 Cf. *TWNT*, III, 682-717, on "kerux."
4 Cf. *TWNT*, II, 659, on "hermeneuō." We find this three-fold usage also in N.T.

5

that interpretation is part and parcel of proclamation, it might be well to call the preacher a hermeneutist. We shall continue to use the common term "preacher," however, with the understanding that this word, too, implies the unity of the task of him who would preach the Word and that its consequences will be drawn for homiletics.[5]

Homiletics Today

It is gratifying that, on the European continent at least, homiletics is coming into its own. "Preaching is central in the theological discussions," Bakker says. "Every prominent debate touching, say, Barth, Bultmann, Von Rad, Pannenberg, Tillich, and Van Buren concerns the question of the content and relevance of preaching. Whereas one could hardly speak of a theology of proclamation in former days, and homiletics seemed to be a toolshed for tricks of the trade, today everything seems to center around preaching: theology of the Word, theology of proclamation, the redemptive event as *Sprachgeschehen* — you name it."[6] We might say that hermeneutics has been the key that unlocked the door of the toolshed in which homiletics had long been imprisoned. For "the new hermeneutical discussion centers on the question of the relevance of the Bible,"[7] and that is particularly the concern of the preacher. Although this new hermeneutical discussion gives a tremendously broad base to homiletics, at the same time it threatens to erase the borders between the various theological disciplines. For if Jonker is right that "trans-

Greek. Concerning (1), e.g., I Cor. 12 : 10, "the interpretation of tongues," and Luke 24 : 27, Jesus "interpreted to them." These instances also make clear that we are in the habit of distinguishing that which is a unity (4) in "hermeneuō": "the interpretation of tongues" might equally well be rendered "the translation of tongues," while "he interpreted to them" might, with the King James Version, equally well be rendered "he expounded to them." The act of interpreting entails translating and voicing as much as the act of proclaiming entails translating and interpreting. Concerning (2), e.g., I Cor. 12 : 10 (above), John 1 : 38, 41, 42, and Acts 9 : 36. Concerning (3), e.g., Luke 24 : 27 (above); cf. Acts 14 : 12: "Paul, because he was the chief speaker, they called Hermes" (the Olympian god Hermes was considered to be a herald and messenger of the gods).

5 Hoekstra says of homiletics: "Zij heeft tot object van onderzoek het ambt van den dienaar des Woords, en speciaal die functie van het ambt, welke werkzaam is in de *diakonia tou logou* te midden van de vergaderde gemeente des Heeren." *Gereformeerde Homiletiek* (1926), p. 12.

6 *Hom*, XXIV (1965), 253. In 1959 the name of this periodical was changed, significantly, from *Homiletica* to *Homiletica en Biblica* in order to give expression to the increased range of subjects covered. See also M. Doerne, "Homiletik," *Die Religion in Geschichte und Gegenwart*, III, 440, on recent developments in Germany: "Die Predigt wird also zur methodischen Perspektive der christlichen Theologie durchweg...."

7 Koole, *Hermeneutische Oriëntatie* (1962), p. 4.

lating the gospel for the present is really the main motive of the theological inquiries of men like Barth, Von Rad, Bultmann, Bonhoeffer, Ebeling, Fuchs, Tillich, and Frör,"[8] we have not only a company of theologians of different stripes but dogmaticians, O.T. scholars, and N.T. scholars — all scrambled together. The connecting link is hermeneutics.[9] We may fret about the obliteration of clear-cut borders, but it is a healthy development in that it shows both the unity of the theological disciplines and their subservient nature (no theological discipline is an end in itself) to their common goal — preaching.

The idea that homiletics covers such a broad area is quite in line with the conception of the Reformed homiletician Hoekstra. He defined homiletics as "that theological science whose object of investigation is the administration of the Word in the assembled congregation of Christ."[10] Although Hoekstra's definition might perhaps allow for a conception of homiletics which is purely formal, the greater part of his book deals with material homiletics. For "the administration of the Word" entails that "the minister must translate the Word of God as purely as possible."[11] Here hermeneutics must of necessity enter the picture, and Hoekstra goes so far as to speak of "the homiletical interpretation"[12] and, elsewhere, of "homiletical exegesis."[13] The adjective "homiletical" is meant to give expression to the fact that the objective of this interpretation or exegesis is to serve the administration of the Word in the church of Christ[14] — a goal for which we hardly require an adjective today.

We have tried to give some impression of the tremendous size of the field of investigation for those working in the area of homiletics. Countless are the avenues which open up to the investigator.[15] Unlike most others, this disser-

---

8 *Actuele Prediking* (1963), p. 60.

9 The connection, by way of hermeneutics, of O.T. and N.T. disciplines with homiletics is expressed by Frör, *Biblische Hermeneutik* (1964), p. 15: "Es gehört zu den wesentlichsten Ergebnissen der theologischen Hermeneutik der Gegenwart, dass sie mit besonderem Nachdruck die notwendige Einheit des hermeneutischen und des kerygmatischen Dienstes betont. Beides kann nicht voneinander getrennt werden, wie es in der vom positivistischen Historismus bestimmten Theologie lange Zeit der Fall war. Die hermeneutische Arbeit zielt letztlich auf den Vollzug der Predigt heute und kommt erst darin zu ihrer letzten Erfüllung." For the relation between dogmatics and preaching by way of hermeneutics, see, e.g., Kuitert, *De Mensvormigheid Gods* (1962), pp. 8f., 301f.

10 *Homiletiek* (1926), p. 12.

11 "Vertolken." *Ibid.*, p. 281.

12 *Ibid*, pp. 287–298.

13 "Homiletische Exegese," *GTT*, XXXII (1932), 505–519. This exegesis is called "homiletical" to distinguish it from and to encompass other kinds, such as grammatical, historical, psychological, pneumatical, and theological exegesis.

14 "Ge kunt dus by de homiletische exegese van verschillende soorten exegese gebruik maken, wanneer ge maar bedenkt, dat alles dienstbaar wordt aan de bediening des Woords, in de gemeente des Heeren." *Ibid.*, p. 512.

15 See, e.g., the broad range of subjects covered by Müller, *Die Lewende Woord*

tation will not analyze a small area in detail: to gain an over-all-view has its own peculiar advantages.[16] Nevertheless, lest we get sidetracked, it is imperative that we restrict ourselves from time to time. We do so now as we narrow our focus to the still broad area of exemplary interpretation and preaching.

EXEMPLARY INTERPRETATION AND PREACHING

The controversy which we shall analyze in this study has gone down in history as the "exemplary – redemptive-historical controversy." It has *literally* gone down in history: confined to one church[17] (among many) in a small country, it did not have the earth-shaking effect that many lesser controversies in other countries have had; and even in Holland itself, though the name may still be known,[18] the issues have for all practical purposes (preaching) been forgotten. Though there may be explanations for this (the war, the secession, the bitterness and complexities, the altered theological climate), there is hardly an excuse. We have no desire to break open old sores, but it should be possible to recover the controversy's worthwhile considerations for the practice of preaching without raising the hostility and antagonism of a former day.

In the 1930's a number of men in the Gereformeerde Kerken raised objections to the usual practice of preaching in that church. Simply put, their complaint was that the preachers, in preaching historical texts, would display the persons mentioned in the texts as models to be imitated, as examples to be followed — hence the term "exemplary preaching." The question arises where

---

aan die Mens van die Hede: 'n Bespreking van die Vrae rondom die Aktuele Woord-verkondiging (1961).

16 We might just mention that one doesn't lose sight of the forest for the trees, while, in addition, the trees can be seen in proper perspective. A disadvantage, of course, is that one cannot examine each and every tree in detail. Worth considering in this connection is Marshall McLuhan's definition of a specialist: "The specialist is one who never makes small mistakes while moving toward the grand fallacy." *Understanding Media*, p. 124 (cited by P. Schouls, *Man in Communication* [CP 1968], p. 64).

17 We have not been able to find evidence that members of denominations other than the Gereformeerde Kerken took an active part in the controversy, though they often struggled with some of the same problems. See, e.g., I. Kievit, *Voorwerpelijke Onderwerpelijke Prediking*: Eisch der Heilige Schrift (2nd ed., 1939), and C. Graafland, *Verschuivingen in de Gereformeerde Bondsprediking* (1965). In 1961, *Die Kerkblad* of the Gereformeerde Kerk in South Africa did carry a miniature debate on "Eksemplariese Prediking" without, however, breaking any new ground. On an even more reduced scale the Christian Reformed *De Wachter*, April 15, 1969, carried one article on the subject.

18 On at least four occasions a proposition regarding this controversy was defended at a promotion at the Free University: Ph. J. Huyser (1941), L. Batelaan (1942), L. Praamsma (1945), and R. H. Bremmer (1961).

this way of preaching originated. Although we do not hear this charge in the controversy, our first inclination might be to suspect the influence of 19th century Liberalism with its personality idea. Does not Schleiermacher's school see history as the depiction of the religious consciousness in individual persons, and the biblical texts as witnesses to cases of pious consciousness which, in being proclaimed, are beneficial to the religious consciousness of the congregation?[19] And does not Troeltsch attempt to salvage something from the complete relativism of historical criticism by pointing in the same direction? The personality idea is used as the bridge to relevant preaching. "The great personalities in the Bible are conceived of as the visible embodiment of the religious-ethical ideas which are to affect the inner life of the hearers."[20] The biblical persons are models deserving imitation.[21] Liberal theology and exemplary preaching go hand in hand — and yet, to look for the roots of exemplary preaching in Liberal theology is anachronistic. No one less than Bultmann calls attention to the fact (and that, as we shall see, not accidentally) that the exemplary approach was already practiced in the first century.

From Clement to the Present

I Clement, says Bultmann, generally uses the O.T. as a "book of ethical models,"[22] or, in Koole's words, as a "picture gallery."[23] Good examples are the patriarchs, Lot, Moses, Job, Rahab, David, Elijah, Elisha, and Ezekiel. All these are worthy of imitation. In addition to these good examples, the O.T. also contains many bad examples — e.g., Cain, the wife of Lot, Esau — whose actions must be shunned.[24]

Although Clement clearly uses the exemplary approach, it is doubtful that he is its originator. One could point beyond him to the Greek or Roman tradition,[25] or, as Bultmann intimates, to the homiletical tradition of the syna-

---

19   See Frör, p. 28.

20   *Ibid.*, p. 30.

21   Cf. Hoekstra, *Homiletiek*, p. 94, on F. Niebergall: "De bijbelsche persoonlijkheden dienen als modellen, welke we moeten navolgen. Men eischt tegenwoordig Erlebnispredigt, maar daar onze eigen Erlebnisse spoedig uitgeput zijn, worden de Erlebnisse van de historische typen en gestalten voor ons van beteekenis."

22   "Als ethisches Musterbuch." *Theologie des N.T.* (1953), § 55, 2, p. 476. The term is used already by Wrede in his *Untersuchungen zum Ersten Klemensbriefe,* 1891, p. 76: "Die Schrift ist das grosse ethische Musterbuch." Quoted by Koole, *De Overname van het O.T. door de Christelijke Kerk* (1938), p. 68, n. 4.

23   "Het OT is voor Clemens een beeldengalerij." *De Overname*, p. 68.

24   *Ibid.*, and Bultmann, *Theologie,* § 10, 2, p. 95.

25   Lord Chesterfield (1735), e.g., appeals to Dionysius, a Greek rhetorician (30 B.C.), for his thesis that "History is [moral] Philosophy teaching by examples." Quoted by Richardson, *History Sacred and Profane,* p. 87, n. 3. See also below, chapter III, n. 176.

gogue.[26] I doubt that the origin of the exemplary approach can be located in any one source; it seems to spring up wherever men are searching for the meaningfulness of past events, the relevance of history. It is this that gives the exemplary approach an almost universal appeal, and it is this that gives our topic such broad relevance.

Clement viewed the Bible as a "book of ethical models," a "picture gallery." This exemplary approach to Scripture leads, almost of necessity, to exemplary preaching. In reporting the liturgy of the worship services, Justin Martyr relates that preachers liked to choose a historical text and urge the hearers to follow the good examples sketched.[27] In the Middle Ages preaching the O.T. was recommended because "its stories fascinate people and mirror their lives."[28] And so it went, century after century, exemplary preaching of historical texts; not even Luther and Calvin managed to elude this traditional way of preaching.[29] According to Huyser: "All the subsequent Reformation-minded preachers — orthodox Lutherans, Calvinists, Puritans, Pietists, Methodists, and Baptists — walked in the footsteps of Luther and Calvin.... They saw it not only as their right but also as their bounden duty... to interpret and apply biblical history in an 'exemplary' way and thus to draw the line from the past to the present."[30] It is not our intention to present a history of exemplary preaching but merely to give an impression of its long-lasting reign — a factor which ought to caution us against a hasty condemnation of the exemplary approach. It is too easy to say: "The question whether Abraham's offer or Elijah's slaying of the priests of Baal are examples for us is typically Western, rationalistic, and 'moralistic.' "[31] Moralistic it may be, but the history of exemplary preaching seems to belie that it is typically Western and rationalistic.

In addition to this vertical, historical sampling, we can also take a horizon-

---

26   *Theologie*, § 10, 2, pp. 95f., and § 54, 2, p. 468. Others, often to sanction their own exemplary preaching, point to the existence of the exemplary approach in certain Bible passages, such as I Cor. 10, Hebrews 11, and James 5. These will be discussed in chapter III.

27   See Koole, *De Overname*, p. 69.

28   Hoekstra, *Homiletiek*, p. 68.

29   Reu, *Homiletics*, p. 278, quotes Luther: "This is the right understanding of the whole O.T., — to keep in mind the fine sayings in the prophets concerning Christ, to comprehend and mark the fine examples, and to use the laws according to our good pleasure and turn them to our profit." Regarding Zwingli and Calvin, Reu writes (p. 280): "Zwingli's and especially Calvin's sermons on the O.T. have the following features in common with those of Luther. They present the O.T. saints as patterns and warning examples ...." Cf. Huyser, *GTT*, L (1950), 208ff.

30   *GTT*, L (1950), 211. See pp. 205–212 for a brief history of exemplary preaching from Chrysostom to Spurgeon. On the Pietists, see also Hartvelt, *Over Schrift en Inspiratie*, p. 26. On Roman Catholics by a Roman Catholic, see Weterman in *Levende Zielzorg*, pp. 176, 179; by a Protestant, see H. H. Miskotte, *Sensus Spiritualis* (1966), which gives a survey, from a dogmatic point of view, of discussions among Roman Catholic authors of many of the problems we confront in this study.

31   K. H. Miskotte, *Als de Goden Zwijgen* (1966), p. 189.

tal, geographic sampling to show the extensive use of the exemplary approach today.

Germany

We have already had occasion to mention Bultmann. Bultmann is struggling with one of the central problems in theology today: the relevance of past events. He states very frankly that "the history of Israel is past and finished" for the Christian: "The events which were meaningful to Israel... have nothing to say to us."[32] And yet Bultmann cannot do away with the O.T. as easily as Marcion and Harnack could. There is still a "theological relevance," namely, when we see this O.T. history as "a history of deterioration," of "miscarriage."[33] For in its miscarriage it is a promise, "and we get the right to interpret that conflict... as one which belongs to human existence as such — the conflict of being created for God and called to God, and yet of being imprisoned in secular history."[34] Aside from the law–gospel dialectic, the secular–eschatological dualism, and various other motifs, we are confronted here with what Bultmann calls the "existentiale Interpretation" ("interpret that conflict [historical events] as one which belongs to human existence as such"). Though highly refined, this too is a form of the exemplary approach; as Bultmann says: "We can see our image mirrored in the O.T."[35] Westermann observes:

The history of God's people, recorded in the O.T., is to Bultmann ultimately only an illustration, an *exemplum* of human existence; the events which are recorded do not have the character of uniqueness. The "theological relevance" does not lie in the happening as such, but rather in this: that here an example of the failure of the history of salvation meets the believer just as the false way of salvation is shown to him by the

32 "Wer in der Kirche steht, für den ist die Geschichte Israels vergangen und abgetan," and, "Die Ereignisse, die für Israel etwas sagten... sagen uns für uns nichts mehr." *Glauben und Verstehen*, I, 333. This essay, "Die Bedeutung des A.T. für den christlichen Glauben," has been translated into English by B. W. Anderson, *The O.T. and Christian Faith* (London: SCM, 1964), pp. 8–35.

33 "Eine Geschichte des Scheiterns." *Ibid.*, II, 186. This essay, "Weissagung und Erfüllung," has been published in English in *Essays on O.T. Hermeneutics*, pp. 50–75.

34 Bultmann in *Essays*, p. 74. In this article, Bultmann attacks the redemptive-historical theory presented by J. C. K. Hofmann, *Weissagung und Erfüllung* (1841-44). Although different from the opposing theories we are dealing with, it gives us a view of the universality of the conflict: exemplary *vs.* redemptive-historical. This also becomes evident in Cullmann's *Christ and Time*, p. xxiv. "My new book... will attempt to rescue the term 'redemptive history' from being abused .... Many scholars ... feel that redemptive-historical thinking has nothing to say to modern man who understands himself existentially."

35 *Glauben und Verstehen*, I, 336.

law, so that he does not fall victim to this temptation.... The course of events within which God has truly given promise and fulfillment is replaced by the two realms of a false and a true way of salvation.[36]

A similar observation might be made regarding the position of the O.T. scholar Friedrich Baumgärtel. Even though he specifically rejects an understanding of the O.T. "in an exemplary sense, as if the O.T. religious-ethical ways of behavior are to serve the Christian as an example,"[37] the cause for this rejection lies not in the deficiency of the exemplary method but in the deficiency of the *Old* Testament. For "the O.T. is a witness out of a non-Christian religion"; "the O.T. is a witness from a religion outside the gospel and therefore from a religion strange to us."[38] Baumgärtel subsequently tries to rescue the O.T. from complete irrelevancy for the Christian by means of the basic promise "I am the Lord thy God." But in order to bring out this relevance concretely, he resorts to the exemplary approach — not in the sense of finding good examples worthy of imitation (it is, after all, the *Old* Testament), but more in the line of deterrent examples.[39] For instance, Baumgärtel rightly rejects the positive example Vischer deduces from Judges 3 (Ehud killing Eglon is a "cogent contribution of the Bible to the right of killing a tyrant") only to posit the negative example: "This murder becomes immediately relevant for our faith, when we... begin to realize that *we* desire to act just like the brave Ehud.... Indeed, we are Ehud." We should, therefore, understand "this story of Ehud as the judgment of God on my revolt against the holy God, on my evil desire to sovereignly change the course of history by murder...."[40] Elsewhere he asks: "Do not we ourselves again and again step into the conditioned situation of the O.T....? Are not we ourselves Jehu, who was a fighter for his church?" "We see ourselves as in a mirror. Thus we are 'Old Testament' men in the fore-court of the gospel...."[41]

Bultmann and Baumgärtel — two leading German theologians — cannot preach relevantly on an O.T. historical text except by way of the exemplary approach. Preaching being relevant by definition, it speaks for them that they seek to bridge the gap between the past event and the present audience, that they search for relevance. Here the whole German discussion around *Vergegenwärtigung* enters the picture. But whether exemplary preaching — positive or negative — is the answer remains to be seen. In any event, we cannot reject

---

36 *Essays*, p. 127.
37 *Verheissung*, p. 145.
38 Baumgärtel, *Essays*, pp. 135 and 145.
39 Cf. *Verheissung*, p. 84: "Die genannten Aussagen werden dadurch für uns relevant, dass wir sie als unsere eignen Aussagen erkennen... und so unter dem Evangelium zur Erkenntnis unserer Sünde kommen und dann doch mit Israel zusammen das Wahrwerden der Verheissung Gottes an uns erfahren dürfen."
40 *Ibid.*, pp. 94f. W. Vischer, *Das Christuszeugnis des A.T.*, II, 89, speaks of "dieser kräftige Beitrag der Bibel zum Recht des Tyrannenmordes."
41 *Essays*, p. 153.

their exemplary approach simply because we detect Lutheran, Pietistic, or Existentialistic overtones, for the exemplary approach reigns in a broader area than Lutheran, Pietistic, or Existentialistic circles. To demonstrate this, we move briefly to our home church — a church which prides itself in its *Calvinistic* heritage — and to the American scene in general.

America

The Christian Reformed Church periodically publishes books of sermons which, though not intended for this purpose, enable us to gain a general notion of the kind of sermons preached. The most recent, available books, dating from 1954 and 1955, contain a total of 43 sermons[42] (although date and number are a bit of a handicap, this sample is adequate for our purposes). To determine how many of these sermons are on historical texts and, of this number, how many are exemplary presents a few difficulties. All texts, of course, can be called historical because they arise in and are addressed to a specific historical situation. Generally, though, the term "historical text" signifies a text which, in distinction from, e.g., a prophetical, poetical, or dogmatical text, gives an *account* of a certain historical event. This does not alleviate all difficulties, however, for a prophetical book may be said to give, in its totality, an account of a certain historical event, and most do contain historical passages, while, vice versa, a historical account may contain prophetical, poetical, or dogmatical texts. And not only do our categories break down here and there, but the strange, yet common, practice of selecting a few words as text adds to the difficulties in classification. Where does one place a sermon which is supposedly based on a N.T. dogmatical text but which, because of a reference in the text to an O.T. person, turns out to be a sermon on an O.T. historical text? And where does one place a sermon which is based on a historical text but which, by abstracting a few words of direct discourse from the account, turns out to be a dogmatical sermon? We also encounter difficulties in the category "exemplary sermons": Must a sermon be totally exemplary to be included in this category? Here we shall follow the procedure used in the controversy of calling "exemplary" all sermons which contain an exemplary element. Because of the above-mentioned difficulties, the following figures intend to convey only a general notion of the kind of sermons preached.

Of the 43 published sermons, then, only 8 are on the O.T., and of these 8, only 2 sermons are on historical texts. Does this perhaps indicate some hesitancy on the part of Christian Reformed ministers to preach the O.T., and particularly its historical texts? Of course, the N.T. also contains many his-

42 *Book of Sermons,* X and XI (Grand Rapids: Christian Reformed Publishing House, 1954 and 1955).

torical texts, so that, all told, we have 15 sermons on historical texts in our sample. Three of these do not lend themselves to exemplary preaching — one cannot be preached that way ("The Story of the Temple Veil"), while two need not be treated that way because of the immediate relevance of Jesus' birth and death. Of the remaining 12 sermons, all are exemplary — Saul, John the Baptist, the thief on the cross, the N.T. church, Levi, Israel, Abraham, the women at the sepulchre (twice), Lot's wife, Cain, and the disciples are either good examples, warning examples, or both. The result of our analysis looks as follows in percentages:

O.T. text	(8 out of 43) . . .	19%
O.T. historical text	(2 out of 43) . . .	5%
O.T. and N.T. historical text . .	(15 out of 43) . . .	35%
Exemplary on historical text . .	(12 out of 15) . . .	80%

However interesting these figures may be, we must not infer too much from our extremely small sample. But it does demonstrate to some extent the prevalence in the Christian Reformed Church of exemplary preaching on historical texts.[43]

This result is not overly surprising when one considers that exemplary preaching is quite common in the English-preaching world. One can pick up English works on homiletics almost at random to find the exemplary approach either advocated or presupposed. We shall give a few excerpts from some rather recent books in the field of homiletics. Stevenson states:

> The universal appeal of the O.T. lies close to the realm of art. It has little to do with dates and places but much more to do with the ageless yearnings, struggles, guilts, expiations, and aspirations of the human spirits.... When a Jacob or a Jonah comes marching out of the pages of the O.T. and begins to live before our eyes in the living element of his own throbbing times, the years that separate us begin to melt away, and, as in any work of art, we identify ourselves with our hero or discover ourselves in our villain — waking at Bethel in shuddering awe at the uncomfortable nearness of God, or fleeing to Joppa with bag packed for faraway places to escape divine mandates that call us out of our narrowness to the wideness of God's mercy.[44]

Not only O.T. texts but also N.T. historical texts can be made relevant by means of the exemplary approach.[45] Davis says:

43 This is also true for the meditations, which, because of their brevity, show the exemplary structure even more starkly. More of the same may be found in the booklets for catechumens; cf. the excerpts in De Graaff, *CP 1969*, pp. 21ff.

44 *Preaching on the Books of the O.T.* (1961), p. 3. Somewhat differently, Reu, *Homiletics* (1922), p. 272: "The preacher who wishes to illustrate the nature of faith by living biblical examples must go to the narratives of the O.T." Note also p. 282, however: "The progressiveness of divine revelation... forbids... the portrayal of O.T. saints as direct patterns of Christian faith and life."

45 See, e.g., *The Theory of Preaching*, pp. 159 and 162, where Phelps (1881)

Listening to this story, if it is well told, people will first meet a human being. The truth of existence will confront them... in the concrete form of a person so like themselves that they may compare and also identify themselves with him. They can sit with him in the presence of Jesus and go with him to the moment of supreme possibility and supreme testing.[46]

The exemplary approach is so common in the English-speaking world[47] that Holwerda uses an English book to further illustrate for his Dutch students the (rejected) exemplary approach. He quotes from Driver:

The importance and real significance of the narrative lies in the *types of character* which they exhibit, and in the moral and spiritual lessons which, whether they are strictly historical or not, may be deduced from them. The patriarchs are *tupoi hèmoon;* and in their biographies examples of faith and goodness — and also, sometimes, of unworthiness and moral failure — are set vividly and expressively before us.[48]

These quotations should be sufficient to show the relevance of our topic for the American homiletical tradition. For good measure we conclude this section with quotations from Perry and Koller — quotations which speak for themselves:

Preaching on Bible Characters gives the minister an opportunity to set forth in a clear fashion the modern counterpart to the experience of a Biblical person. The use of this type of subject matter helps to make the Scriptures come alive with real persons who faced real situations, and with whose lives, difficulties, hopes and relationships God was immediately concerned and intimately involved.

There is an inexhaustible supply of material in the Scriptures from which to preach biographical sermons. This is seen when we realize that there are 2,930 different Bible characters.[49]

Another effective type of expository preaching is that of preaching on Bible characters. Faris D. Whitesell, in his excellent book on this subject [*Preaching on Bible Characters*], gives many reasons for placing this type of preaching in high priority. He points out that this is perhaps the easiest way to preach the Bible, the most likely to appeal to people and to hold

suggests for an O.T. text (Daniel 1 : 8) the exemplary topic: "An Ancient Model of Youthful Temperance," while the reviser of this book, Whitesell (1947), adds the equally exemplary topic on a N.T. text (Acts 6 : 3 – 8 : 2): "Stephen's Life Illustrates Three Ways by which we Can Glorify God."

46   *Design for Preaching* (1958), p. 181.
47   Cf. the approach Seerveld gleans from various English commentaries. *CP 1969*, pp. 55ff., and his critique, pp. 67ff.
48   Driver, *The Book of Genesis*, p. 247, quoted by Holwerda in his Dictaten *Historia Revelationis*, p. 21.
49   Perry, *A Manual for Biblical Preaching* (1965), p. 106.

15

their attention,... and the most likely to be remembered. And, for fresh-
ness and variety, there are approximately four hundred Bible characters
from which to choose![50]

Holland

We make a final stop at the Gereformeerde Kerken in Holland.[51] We can be
brief here, for in the sequel we shall be confronted with the arguments of
the defenders of the exemplary approach. But because those are, in the main,
voices of thirty years ago, it might be well to point out the prevalence of
exemplary preaching in this church today. Again, for our purposes a small
cross section will suffice.

At the time of writing, the most recent book of sermons, dating from 1966,
contains 27 sermons.[52] In classifying these sermons we encounter the same
difficulties we mentioned earlier. Here too, then, one must allow for some
latitude in the classification. Of the 27 sermons, 11 are on an O.T. text,
but only 2 sermons are on an O.T. historical text. Happily, the N.T. provides
12 sermons on historical texts so that we have a total of 14 in our sample.
Of these 14 sermons, 10 are exemplary — the Galileans, the paralytic, the
thief on the cross, Peter, the N.T. church, the Canaanite woman, Mephibosheth, Adam, Philip, and the ten lepers are in one way or another held up as
good or bad examples. To express our findings in percentages:

O.T. text	(11 out of 27) . . .	41%
O.T. historical text	(2 out of 27) . . .	7%
O.T. and N.T. historical text . .	(14 out of 27) . . .	52%
Exemplary on historical text . .	(10 out of 14) . . .	71%

We print these figures neither to present them as an adequate cross section
of the thousands of sermons preached nor to prejudge this kind of preaching,

---

50   Koller, *Expository Preaching without Notes* (1969), p. 32. Cf. p. 25 on the two
approaches for a "biographical sermon": "(1) Under the first main point, tell the
story of that life, preferably in chronological order; and under the second main point,
draw out the lessons; or (2) tell the life story, and indicate each phase by a main point,
followed by the lessons derived ...." (The book of Whitesell, *Preaching on Bible Characters*, appeared in Grand Rapids: Baker, 1955.)

51   We confine ourselves to the Gereformeerde Kerken though similar observations
could be made regarding other denominations. Opposing theories often exist side by
side, even within the covers of a single book: see, e.g., Hoenderdaal's exemplary
approach and Frederikse's anti-exemplary approach in *Wegen der Prediking*, respectively pp. 417f. and 73. In the Hervormde Kerk one is confronted with exemplary
preaching in the conservative wing (the Gereformeerde Bond) as well as the modernis-
tic wing (e.g., B. van Ginkel in Jonker's *Actuele Prediking*, p. 217: "Wij kunnen ...
in de lijdensweken preken over: Petrus, Kajafas, Pilatus, de vrouw van Pilatus, Herodus
en Judas als spiegel van onze relatie met onze eigen innerlijke 'schaduw' èn van onze
relatie tot de omgeving.").

52   *Menigerlei Genade*, LIII (Kampen: Kok, 1966).

but merely to give an indication of the prevalence of exemplary preaching in the Gereformeerde Kerken.[53]

In a way this prevalence is surprising, not only because there was such a battle in this church less than a generation ago against this kind of preaching, but also because of the present, increasing recognition of the time-conditioned character of the Bible: the words of Scripture are addressed to people living in a different time, culture, social structure, etc., and therefore cannot be read as if they were addressed to us *directly*. This historical awareness has led to a re-evaluation of several traditional interpretations and ecclesiastical practices such as barring women from holding office in the church. But if the time-conditioned character of specific *commandments* is thus recognized,[54] it is difficult to see why this time-conditioned character is not equally honored when it comes to the described conduct of certain persons — a conduct which lacks even the normativity of commandments. And yet, Sunday after Sunday, many Reformed preachers take these persons with them on the pulpit and invest their conduct, in one way or another, with perpetual, normative authority — as if these people did not live in a different time, culture, social structure, etc.

But we are getting ahead of ourselves. Let us merely ask at this point, Is there an alternative to exemplary preaching? What other method of interpretation gives such freedom, makes preparation so easy, leads to so relevant an application? Can preachers really do without the exemplary approach?

* * *

We have tried to give some indication of both the meaning of "exemplary approach" and its widespread influence in the history of preaching and in present-day hermeneutics and homiletics. No one should impose a certain method of interpretation and preaching upon others, but neither should preachers be imposed upon by the tradition and relative ease of exemplary preaching. Every preacher must be satisfied in his own heart and mind that he is doing justice to the text. And how else will one attain this than by thoroughgoing study of the problems involved?

Because the Dutch controversy brought many such problems to light, it retains its relevance. Huyser, a defender of the exemplary approach, says: "Even

53 The Dutch meditations reveal the same approach. "Een willekeurige christelijke scheurkalender ... bewijst dat het exemplarisme ook via kalenderblaadjes nog altijd zijn duizenden verslaat.... Niet alles is goud wat er blinkt. Exemplarische stukjes blinken van stichtelijkheid. Maar het goud ligt dieper." Thus H. J. Schilder, *Rachels Troost* (1960), pp. 13ff., n. 6.

54 This, of course, has long been recognized regarding certain commandments (e.g., I Cor. 11: "A man ought not to cover his head, ... A woman ought to have a veil on her head ...."), though it is not nearly as self-evident as we often take for granted today. J. Ridderbos calls attention to Calvin's appeal to the O.T. to justify killing a heretic and to the attempts of Knox and the Pilgrim Fathers to introduce into their respective countries the O.T. civil laws. *De Beteekenis van het O.T. voor de Christelijke Religie* (1913), pp. 29f.

though the issues have retreated to the background in present-day discussions, they continue to be important both for the theory and for the practice of preaching. Every minister of the Word is constantly confronted with them in the explication and application of O.T. and N.T. historical texts. How may and how must he draw the lines from the past to the present, from the then and there to the here and now?"[55] This is a world-wide problem: we could point to Frör's warning in Germany: "Moses is no moral example and the stories about him are no instances of exemplary behavior,"[56] or to Runner's appraisal in America: "All such preaching, for all its remaining good qualities, is essentially unsound, and does not build up in the congregation a rich and meaningful knowledge of the *Word* of God."[57] But once more we must narrow our focus, for, though the same issues play an important role in every country, they often arise in different contexts. It would only confuse matters, therefore, to try to treat all countries jointly.[58] From time to time we shall have occasion to use the wide-angle lens again, but we must now concentrate on a close-up of Holland, more specifically, on the Gereformeerde Kerken of some thirty to forty years ago.

THE DUTCH CONTROVERSY "EXEMPLARISCH–HEILSHISTORISCH"

Even when we confine ourselves to the Gereformeerde Kerken, the picture that presents itself is rather obscure. It is difficult to get the two opposing positions clearly into focus and to present them in a unified way. The cause for this lies in the complexity of the controversy and the lack of well-defined terminology.

Complexity

The complexity of the controversy is due, first of all, to the "interwovenness" of this controversy with simultaneous controversies in the area of dogmatics and philosophy. We might point, secondly, to the fact that the stand-

---

55 *GTT*, XLIX (1949), 232. Supporters of the redemptive-historical approach consider the issues equally relevant today. Cf. Trimp, *Petah-ja*, XV (1961), 86: "Het debat daarover en de studie daarvan is reeds gedurende vele jaren onder ons gestremd; maar de zaak, toén aangeroerd, blijft actueel." Cf. C. J. Breen, *De Poortwake*, XXII (1967), 176: "Het belangrijke werk, dat Prof. Schilder in zijn dagen mocht beginnen, is vandáág nóg brandend actueel."

56 P. 187.

57 *CP 1960*, p. 100.

58 One need only think of "Heilsgeschichte" which, in the Bultmannian sense, means practically the opposite of "heilsgeschiedenis" as used in the controversy. See further below, I, n. 72.

ard works in homiletics and hermeneutics[59] were so ambiguous that both sides were able to quote them in their favor. Thirdly, the proponents of redemptive-historical preaching had neither the time to develop into a homogeneous group nor an exhaustive, authoritative presentation of their viewpoint around which they could rally. They have left us a host of articles, often overlapping in content, from which we must glean their position. This also means that there are variations within either group depending on the author's personal view and the arguments he counters in his writing. Obviously, we cannot go into all the individual divergencies and skirmishes if we are not to lose sight of the major line of battle. Finally, we should mention the general confusion, the torrent of charges and counter-charges, and the misinterpretations of each other's positions — all in no small measure due to the fact that the controversy was, by and large, fought out before the general public in the church papers.[60] Yet, when all is said and done, two opposing positions crystallize: the exemplary and the redemptive-historical approach.

Terminology

It took some time before the terms "exemplary" and "redemptive-historical" were generally adopted. Holwerda coined the word *exemplarisch* in 1940: "This method I would call the exemplary method because it dissolves biblical history into various independent histories which are examples for us."[61] Not all his opponents were happy with the label stuck on their method, however: Streefkerk preferred to speak of a " 'typological' or 'analogical' element in redemptive history,"[62] while Huyser favored "deductive redemptive-historical exemplification," though he also recognized that "the term 'exemplary' preaching (or method) has gained currency and for that reason we shall continue to use it."[63] As for *heilshistorisch*, Holwerda initially labelled his own approach "Christocentric."[64] But here too there were various opinions about the proper name for this approach: Van 't Veer preferred "Christological";[65] Feenstra favored "revelational historical,"[66] and Van Dijk spoke of "revelational historical-Christocentric."[67] It was the term "redemptive-historical," how-

---

59   Hoekstra's *Homiletiek* (1926) and Grosheide's *Hermeneutiek* (1929).

60   Without underwriting all of Huyser's charged words, I am inclined to agree with him that this is not the right place to fight out a *theological*, i.e., scientific controversy. *GTT*, XLIX (1949), 240f.

61   *Gereformeerd Mannenblad*, XVIII (1940), 27.

62   Quoted in *Pro-Ecclesia*, VII (1941), 39.

63   *GTT*, XLIX (1949), 246.

64   *GM*, XVIII (1940), 27.

65   *Van den Dienst des Woords* (1944), p. 138.

66   *De Wachter*, XXXIX (1941), No. 38.

67   *PE*, VII (1942), 137.

ever, that was most frequently used and became the accepted term for this particular approach. It is not our purpose to act as arbiter in the Dutch terminology, nor to invent still other terms.[68] It is quite impossible to catch the whole of a multi-pronged attack in one word. Besides, as Holwerda later observes, not the terms but the issues at stake are of primary importance.[69] In settling for a literal English translation of these terms, however, some clarification may be required.

In the English-speaking world we have, to my knowledge, never been confronted with a similar controversy. As a result English technical terms for these two approaches are lacking. The fact that the term "exemplary" is not known in English theological jargon can be considered an advantage in so far as it is not freighted with wrong connotations. If we keep in mind the above-mentioned instances of exemplary preaching and the definition of Webster — "serving as a pattern; deserving imitation; serving as a warning" — we have caught its central thrust.

The term "redemptive-historical" offers more problems because it is not an unknown concept in English. We are troubled here by all sorts of connotations which the word has attained in its many-sided usage and its German origin. "Redemptive-historical," as the Dutch "heilshistorisch," is a literal translation of the German "heilsgeschichtlich," which is connected especially with Hofmann and the Erlangen school but no less with Cullmann today.[70] The terminological connection between Dutch and German words should not lead to the inference, however, that the redemptive-historical approach in Holland found its source of inspiration in the earlier German approach. On the contrary, we find that Hegel's philosophy of history, influential in shaping the redemptive-historical approach of the Erlangen school, was rejected by the Dutch theologians.[71] More recently, Barth and especially

---

68 Fortunately, we are not burdened with the more cumbersome terms and shall take the warranted criticism into the bargain. For critique on "exemplarisch," see Huyser, *GTT*, XLIX, 246ff.; on "heilshistorisch," see Grosheide, *GTT*, XLVI, 72ff.

69 "Opnieuw zij nadrukkelijk gezegd, dat de termen mij weinig interesseren; ze mogen wat mij betreft, vandaag de dag door andere vervangen worden. Doch de kwestie die ermee bedoeld wordt is van grote importantie." *Historia Revelationis*, p. 114.

70 Cullmann is also struggling to find a word which won't a priori place him in a certain corner. He settles for "redemptive history" but suggests that "revelational history" may be more comprehensive. *Christ and Time*, p. 27, n. 10. On the usage of "Heilsgeschichte" in Germany, see Steck, *Die Idee der Heilsgeschichte*: Hofmann–Schlatter–Cullmann.

71 A case for Hegelian influence on Schilder could perhaps be made by way of Schilder's dependence on Kuyper and Bavinck who, in turn, were influenced by Hegelianism via their teacher Scholten and German theologians such as Hofmann. (On Kuyper and Bavinck, see J. Veenhof, *Revelatie en Inspiratie*, pp. 259ff.) At the same time, it must be recognized that Schilder was radically opposed to Hegel's philosophy of history. See, e.g., *Wat is de Hemel?* (1935), pp. 22ff., 59; and *Heidelbergsche Catechismus*, III (1950), 275f., 280ff. The influence of Coccejus further complicates matters.

Bultmann have made use of "redemptive history" in such a way that not much history is left in redemptive history.[72] Again, the content they poured into the term should not be transferred to the term as used by the Dutch theologians who were, as we shall see, radically opposed to dialectic theology. Unfortunately, the many-sided use of "Heilsgeschichte" has filtered through in the literal English translation, making the term "redemptive history" less than ideal. Any substitute, however, would be equally prone to wrong connotations. If possible, we should divest ourselves of all a priori connotations and allow the term to speak in its own context. With this qualification we can use "redemptive history" ("redemptive-historical") in spite of its drawbacks.[73]

Before setting forth the disputed issues, we shall use the next chapter to present the historical context of the controversy and to give a bird's-eye view of its course.

---

72 Cf. Trimp, *Om de Oeconomie van het Welbehagen*: Een Analyse van de Idee der "Heilsgeschichte" in de "Kirchliche Dogmatik" van K. Barth, e.g., pp. 159, 193. This study indicates further that several other words which we must use in the sequel, such as "Christocentricity" and "einmalig," should not simply be filled with a Barthian or Bultmannian content.

73 In addition to the weakness that the word connotes different things to different people, we might also mention that the term "redemptive history" is somewhat misleading in that it is not history but *God* who redeems. Moreover, this history is not a separate category from ordinary history (as Bultmann, e.g., would have it), but God makes his redemptive history in ordinary history. See Mickelsen, *Interpreting the Bible*, p. 245, and Koole, *GTT*, LXV, 101f. Finally, we add with reservations Koole's observation (*Ibid.*, p. 102) that "the historiography of the Deuteronomist with its theme of apostasy and doom might better be called damnatory history (onheilshistorie) than redemptive history."

Chapter II   *Survey of the Exemplary—Redemptive-Historical Controversy*

THE BACKGROUND OF THE CONTROVERSY

As one delves into the history of the Gereformeerde Kerken between World Wars I and II,[1] one is struck by the ascendence of a new school of thought. According to J. H. Bavinck, "We can speak of a 'new spirit' or a 'new direction'.... In the totality of our church life in which various elements of earlier pietism and mystical subjectivism persist, this new spirit reveals itself as a rejuvenating and disquieting force."[2]

The "New Direction" in the Gereformeerde Kerken

It has been intimated by some that this "new direction" was a "theology of reaction,"[3] but this is an inadequate description on at least two counts: first, the word "reaction" fails to account for the independent positive contributions, and second, the word "theology" is a misnomer for a movement which is far broader than theology. Here we touch on what we called earlier the "interwovenness" of the homiletical controversy with simultaneous controversies in the area of dogmatics and philosophy. As S. J. Popma put it aptly in 1945: "In the reformational pursuit of the last number of years two motives go hand in hand: the struggle for a real Calvinistic philosophy which strives to do justice to the scriptural ground-motive of creation, fall, and redemption through Jesus Christ, and the struggle for an authentic ecclesiastical life," which includes issues in dogmatics and homiletics.[4] To disclose something of the nature and interrelationship of philosophy, theology (dogmatics), and homiletics in this new movement, we shall briefly discuss each in turn.

---

1 To limit our survey, we shall present primarily the immediate background of the controversy. J. Veenhof, *Revelatie en Inspiratie*, pp. 11–140, offers a fine survey of the theological background prior to World War I.

2 *De Toekomst van onze Kerken* (1943), p. 9.

3 E. g., Praamsma, *Het Dwaze Gods* (1950), p. 361, who also speaks of "absolutistische theologie" on p. 363.

4 *De Psychologie van een Schisma*, pp. 17 and 16.

Philosophy

The period under discussion saw the rise of a new, Calvinistic philosophy. Founded by Dooyeweerd and Vollenhoven, professors at the Free Reformed University in Amsterdam, it was called the *Wijsbegeerte der Wetsidee* (Philosophy of the Law-Idea, hereafter referred to as WdW). Dooyeweerd's systematic presentation of this philosophy was published in a three volume work in 1935/36.[5] In his foreword he stated:

> The great turning point in my thought was marked by the discovery of the religious root of thought itself, whereby a new light was shed on the failure of all attempts, including my own, to bring about an inner synthesis between the Christian faith and a philosophy which is rooted in faith in the self-sufficiency of human reason. I came to understand the central significance of the "heart," repeatedly proclaimed by Holy Scripture to be the religious root of human existence. On the basis of this central Christian point of view I saw the need of a revolution in philosophical thought of a very radical character.[6]

The same year 1935 saw the formation of the Association for Calvinistic Philosophy ("De Vereniging voor Calvinistische Wijsbegeerte"). Most of those whom we shall come to know later as proponents of the redemptive-historical approach were members of this Association. This was not just a mere coincidence; it indicates rather that there was a definite relationship between this new direction in philosophy and the new direction in preaching. It would be a mistake, however, to seek this connection in the first place in a common adherence to a particular philosophic system; the connection is to be found first of all at the pre-philosophic level. This basic, pre-philosophic commitment is already apparent in Dooyeweerd's above-cited words and is clearly voiced by Vollenhoven at the inauguration of the Association: "It is not philosophy that brings us together here — for philosophy is not first in our life — but the attachment to God's Word, because by grace we have learned the desire to live only out of the Christ, and religion, as a matter of the heart, has become the core of our entire existence...."[7]

To describe the connection between the WdW and the proponents of the redemptive-historical approach at the philosophic (theoretic) level is much

5 *De Wijsbegeerte der Wetsidee.* A second, revised edition in English was published between 1953 and 1958 under the title *A New Critique of Theoretical Thought.*

6 *New Critique*, p.v. Cf. Vollenhoven, *Het Calvinisme en de Reformatie van de Wijsbegeerte* (1933), p. 16: "Synthese tusschen het Christelijk geloof eenerzijds en de gangbare wijsbegeerte aan den anderen kant is onmogelijk."

7 Inauguration speech of Dec. 14, 1935, printed in *Mededeelingen*, I (1936), No. 1. This quotation is also found in C. Veenhof's *Om de "Unica Catholica"* (1949), p. 56, where one can find a more elaborate treatment of the role of the WdW in this new movement (pp. 51–375) than we can give here.

more difficult. The fact that such a connection does exist is evident from the writings of the redemptive-historical school. Men like Holwerda, Spier, and Veenhof reveal a marked influence of and commitment to the WdW. Their contributions to homiletics could not have been what they are without this influence.[8] The same cannot be said, however, for Schilder, the originator of the redemptive-historical approach. It is true that there were many points of agreement: witness the fact that Schilder joined the Association in 1939 and, in the same year, together with Vollenhoven submitted a minority report to the Synod of the Gereformeerde Kerken.[9] But, as Vollenhoven noted, "from the beginning there was more than one point at which we didn't see eye to eye."[10] For example, Schilder attacked the WdW on its view that faith is a function operative, positively or negatively, in *all* men, whether believers or unbelievers.[11] A related difference of still greater consequence was the place assigned to the church institute. Schilder "saw the church as universal, world encompassing and world dominating. With him the church could neither be pushed into any given corner nor restricted to a certain area. For that reason," Van Reest opines, "he collided with the WdW."[12] One final difference we might mention concerns the biblical ground-motive which the WdW formulated as creation, fall, and redemption through Jesus Christ.[13] In Schilder's work this ground-motive breaks through time and again, but, according to Stellingwerff, "time after time this ground-motive also disappears again behind other motives."[14] Enough to show that Schilder and the WdW were not in agreement on all issues. These differences were not accentuated in the period under discussion, however, and when it came to polemics, Schilder and the WdW tended to operate on the same wave length.

---

8 See, e.g., Spier, "Wijsbegeerte en Prediking," *Wijsbegeerte en Levenspraktijk*, pp. 40–59, and K. J. Popma, "Wijsbegeerte en Prediking," *Med*, Dec., 1941.

9 *Van "Oorzaken en Redenen"* (1939).

10 "In Memoriam K. Schilder," *Phil Ref*, XVII (1952), 149.

11 Schilder, *Heidelbergsche Catechismus*, I (1947), 355, II (1949), 410–435, 451–456.

12 R. Van Reest [K. C. Van Spronsen], *"Opdat Zij Allen Eén Zijn"*, I (1962), 126. We have deviated from the original by not capitalizing "church" in both instances, as Van Reest does "Kerk," because in our estimation the WdW would agree with this quotation if the Church (cap.) as the Body of Christ is meant. The divergence arises, however, on the place of the institutional church as one societal structure among many (cf. Schilder, *Ref*, XXV (1950), pp. 330ff., 339ff., 346f., 354ff.). On this point Holwerda, too, clashed with Dooyeweerd and Vollenhoven (see below, p. 51).

13 For the intent of this formulation, see Dooyeweerd, *New Critique*, I, 173ff. For further literature, see De Graaff, *The Educational Ministry*, p. 43, n. 140.

14 "Kritiek op K. Schilder als Filosoferend Dogmaticus," *Phil Ref*, XXVII (1962), 108. Cf. pp. 113, 122.

Theology

The connection between theology and homiletics is probably more readily apparent. The period under discussion saw an upsurge in biblical studies. In 1909 Herman Bavinck had demonstrated in word and in deed the poverty of Reformed exegetical studies — in deed by introducing a Dutch translation of Matthew Henry's Commentary; in word by writing in the introduction: "It would be too much to expect this commentary of Henry to satisfy the present needs in all respects. But in this area we are still extremely poor.... However much we may lament it, we must still live from what the past offers us."[15] Bavinck's wish for a "popular, short, sound, practical, and up-to-date" commentary was fulfilled after 1922 with the publication of an indigenous commentary series, the *Korte Verklaring*. At the same time other exegetical works rolled off the presses: the series "Bottenburg," Schilder's *Christus in Zijn Lijden* (1930), J. Ridderbos' *Het Godswoord der Profeten* (1930-1941), and de Graaf's *Verbondsgeschiedenis* (1936). In hermeneutics the standard work was written by Grosheide in 1929 and in homiletics by Hoekstra in 1926. All in all, compared with the beginning of the century, it was a productive period.

The "new direction" made its impact especially in dogmatics. The resulting unrest in the churches caused the Synod of 1936 to appoint a committee to investigate "views being propagated in our churches which deviate from the teachings accepted up till now."[16] Synod selected six subjects: common grace, the covenant of grace, the immortality of the soul, the pluriformity of the church, the natures of Christ, and self-examination. Because of much unpleasantness the committee did not function well: in 1938 Greijdanus left the committee, followed in 1939 by Schilder and Vollenhoven who sent a separate report to Synod.[17] This report shows how difficult it was to determine precisely what were the "accepted teachings" and what the new, for in the old as well as the new there existed little unanimity of opinion. It is clear, however, that there were differences between old and new — only, one wonders whether these should have been investigated at the level of formulated dogmatic propositions in all their diversity. As Van Teylingen pointed

15 Matthew Henry, *Letterlijke en Practicale Verklaring van het N.T.* with Introduction by H. Bavinck (Kampen: Kok, 1909), p. vii. Cf. Schilder's evaluation in *Ref*, IX (Oct. 19, 1928), 22: "... al is zijn boek voor den tijd, waarin hij leefde (1662-1714) natuurlijk veelszins prijzenswaardig, de kommentaar [is] voor onzen tijd vrijwel onbeteekenend. Over wezenlijke moeilijkheden huppelt het boek haast altijd heen; dwaasheden staan er genoeg in; veel omslachtig geredeneer verdringt de plaats van een heusche exegese; de allegorie raakt soms kant noch wal."

16 *Acta 1936*, Art. 212.

17 For their report on proceedings within the committee and the doctrines under discussion, see *Oorzaken*. For the other side, see the earlier published brochures by V. Hepp, *Dreigende Deformatie* (Kampen: Kok, 1936/37).

out: "The conflict is not of such a nature that it can be solved with a formula. There is a difference in spiritual insight and, as a result, a difference in the way theology is developed."[18] As matters stand, the selection of these six subjects seems somewhat arbitrary: faith, revelation, and redemptive history might equally well have been included. And why not redemptive-historical preaching? This preaching was, after all, a source of unrest and even of factionalism within the church.[19] Moreover, as we shall see later, several of the investigated dogmatic topics have a direct relationship with the homiletical controversy.[20] In any event, one cannot maintain with Grosheide that the new way of preaching and the doctrinal differences had nothing to do with each other.[21]

A more encompassing view of the issues is expressed in the observation, "In the end it is different ways of viewing redemptive revelation that determines the character of these doctrinal differences."[22] Seen in this broad perspective the connection with the homiletical controversy is evident, for here too the view of revelation is a central issue. Van Teylingen also attempts to gain a more encompassing view of the doctrinal differences. He takes the covenant of grace to be "*the* sector of the front where the major battle is being fought."[23] Historically, from the viewpoint of dogmatics this judgment is correct, even though it remains a *sector*. J. H. Bavinck also points at the renewed emphasis on the covenant as one of the marks of the "new direction": "They have discerned the covenant in its central thrust; they have understood that the covenant dominates, as it were, the whole scriptural revelation and that thus it should also have a central place in our faith life and preaching."[24]

In this connection we should mention one man whose name is almost synonymous with the renewed emphasis on the covenant: S. G. De Graaf.[25] As early as 1925 he wrote: "We must refrain from interpreting God's Word as if every word in the Bible immediately concerns the individual." He called this custom a "misuse of God's Word" which contributes greatly to

---

18 *Aard en Achtergrond van het Geschil in de Gereformeerde Kerken* (1944), p. 3.

19 Cf. Dijk, *OB*, XXII (1943), 2986, and D. J. Couvée, *De Bazuin*, CIII (March 18, 1960), No. 12. In 1936, of course, the homiletical controversy had not yet reached its peak.

20 Cf. Holwerda (1944), *Populair Wetenschappelijke Bijdragen*, p. 10: "Want in de prediking komen eigenlijk al die kwesties tegelijk aan de orde."

21 "... dat vele jonge predikanten toch anders preeken dan vele oudere.... staat evenmin in verband met de leergeschillen, die onder ons aan de orde zijn. Ook daarmede heeft het niets te maken." "Actualisme," *Noord-Hollandsch Kerkblad*, April 4, 1941. But see also his *Leerverschillen in de Geref. Kerken* (1941), p. 59: "... deze kwestie [zelfonderzoek] is van zeer veel belang voor de prediking."

22 Quod Testor [K. C. Van Spronsen], *PE*, VI (1941), 239.

23 *Aard en Achtergrond*, pp. 3ff.

24 *De Toekomst*, p. 15.

25 De Graaf, too, was a member of the Association for Calvinistic Philosophy.

the rise of individualism within the church.[26] In its stead De Graaf advocated more emphasis on the covenant both in interpreting and preaching the Word, and in 1936 he published his *Verbondsgeschiedenis* — an elaborate, practical demonstration of his hermeneutic principles for the historical texts of Scripture. We shall not be dealing extensively with De Graaf in the sequel, however, if for no other reason than that he did not play an active role in the specific controversy which concerns us. Moreover, his method is not to be identified with the redemptive-historical method.[27] De Graaf did share the same distaste for exemplary preaching, however, as is most strikingly illustrated by his admonition in introducing his *Verbondsgeschiedenis*: "We must not tell chiefly of people, of their faith as an attracting example and of their sins as a repelling example, but we must tell of the revelation of the grace of God in Christ."[28] On this note we turn out attention to homiletics.

Homiletics

At various points we have called attention to the impact the "new direction" had on preaching. The positive contributions made in the field of homiletics will be set forth in chapter IV, "The Redemptive-Historical Approach." Our concern at this juncture is merely to elucidate the background.

Despite the studies in philosophy and theology, despite biblical studies, commentaries, standard works on hermeneutics and homiletics, the preacher still had problems — particularly with historical texts. "The man who had to preach was faced with the question, What is the revelational content, the message of God for the church here and now?"[29] The "new direction," stimulated by its counterpart in philosophy and theology, sought the answer in a new method of interpretation and preaching: the redemptive-historical approach.

The word "new" should not be taken in an absolute sense, of course. No historical movement comes about without having roots in the past. Popma sees a "very intimate connection" between the "new direction" and the thought of Kuyper, Bavinck, Woltjer, and Geesink. "The *first* thing that strikes one is that connection, *next* the expansion on the basis of their thought, whereas the critique of their labor usually takes the form of pointing out and

26 *Het Woord Gods en de Kerk*, p. 21.
27 See, e.g., Holwerda's criticism of De Graaf's "way of allegorizing," *Begonnen*, p. 113. Cf. Van 't Veer, *Van den Dienst*, p. 154, on his typologizing.
28 P. 11.
29 Holwerda, *Begonnen*, p. 81. Cf. Veenhof, *Almanak 1953*, p. 170, who speaks of "de armoede van de toen gangbare exegese. Litterair-historisch werd knap werk verricht. Maar waar, speciaal in de verklaring van de 'historische' gedeelten van de Heilige Schrift, het eigenlijke, het wezenlijke, waar de theologische of, misschien beter gezegd, de *profetische* exegese beginnen moest, daar hield men plotseling op of maakte men er zich met een paar algemene opmerkingen van af."

attempting to correct the incongruous elements detected — rightly or wrongly — in the great predecessors."[30] One can observe this trend of both building on and correcting the conceptions of the predecessors throughout the broad range of the movement — philosophy,[31] theology,[32] and homiletics. Veenhof wrote an elaborate work on Kuyper's views of preaching,[33] and even Douma, a defender of the exemplary approach, observed: "The idea that sacred history... is a unity, is borne by one thought, and has Christ as its center is certainly not a discovery of the last few years" — an observation which he substantiates by quoting from J. Van Andel, Kuyper, and Sillevis Smitt (all writing around the turn of the century).[34] This link with the predecessors can be observed not only in the positive contributions of the redemptive-historical approach but also in its criticism of existing practices.[35] Already in 1895 Kuyper objected to the practice of tacking a few practical remarks onto an occurrence in the life of a Bible saint,[36] and in 1918 Fabius militated against the notion that the Bible is "a textbook for morals which sketches the lives of others with a view to deterring us from evil and coaxing us to imitate the good."[37]

Notwithstanding these links with the past, however, the redemptive-historical method must be seen as the new approach on the homiletical horizon. This becomes evident, for example, when we hear Van Dijk say: "Happily, a great many preachers are no longer satisfied with the way in which the historical sections of Scripture have usually been preached among us."[38] As is frankly admitted, the "new direction" departs from the usual way of preaching historical texts. This "usual way" may be called exemplary preaching. Its supporters defend the *status quo*. Indeed, one of their major arguments is: The fathers always preached this way! Douma writes: "Calvin

---

30 Quoted in Veenhof, *Om de Unica*, p. 154.

31 Dooyeweerd concluded his article "Wat de W.d.W. aan Dr Kuyper te danken heeft" with the words, "En in dit licht gezien, komt Kuyper ten volle toe de eeretitel van grondlegger der Calvinistische wijsbegeerte." *Ref*, XVIII (Oct. 29, 1937), 65. See this commemorative issue of Kuyper also for other instructive articles. Further, Vollenhoven, *Med*, I (1936), No. 1 ("... geboren uit een buigen voor de Schrift, ook als een doortrekken van de lijnen door Kuyper aangegeven."), Veenhof, *In Kuyper's Lijn* (1939), and especially Dooyeweerd, "Kuyper's Wetenschapsleer," *Phil Ref*, IV (1939), 193–232.

32 See, e.g., Schilder and Vollenhoven in *Oorzaken*, especially section I, "Algemene Genade."

33 *Predik het Woord*: Gedachten en Beschouwingen van Dr A. Kuyper over de Prediking (*ca.* 1943).

34 *De Heraut*, 1941, No. 3292. In similar vein Grosheide contends that "het naar voren brengen van de geschiedenis der openbaring allerminst gerekend mag worden tot de nieuwe dingen van onze tijd." *Heraut*, 1941, No. 3327.

35 That this link was cherished is indicated, e.g., by the frequent use made of quotations from Kuyper for the front page of *De Reformatie*.

36 *Heraut*, Sept. 8, 1895, quoted in *Ref*, XVIII (1938), 313.

37 Quoted by Van Reest, *Opdat Zij Allen*, I, 71.

38 *PE*, VII (1942), 137.

considered himself to be called by God to preach sacred history also in an exemplary manner. And not only Calvin but all Reformed preachers held that conviction."[39] Van Dijk does not disagree on this score. "Douma," he says, "has shown irrefutably and clearly that the method which many of us condemn was the method of the great reformer... and great preacher of Geneva."[40] But in spite of its solid tradition and honored practitioners, the "new direction" leveled a scathing critique on traditional, exemplary preaching — a critique which gave rise to the homiletical controversy. This critique will be presented in detail in chapter III, "Objections to the Exemplary Approach." But first this negative aspect, too, must be seen in its proper setting.

The Critique of Contemporary Trends

Above we took exception to the intimation that the new movement was a "theology of reaction." This characterization does contain an element of truth, however. Bavinck complains of the movement's "negativism," of its "preference for thinking in polemical patterns. The new spirit is forever busy setting itself off against something, fighting other trends."[41] This polemical attitude, as we prefer to call it,[42] is evident all along the line. For the sake of clarity we must make a distinction between the criticism directed mainly at trends *outside* the Gereformeerde Kerken and the criticism leveled at trends *within* that church.

Outwardly Directed Criticism: Dialectic Theology

Since the homiletical controversy was confined to the Gereformeerde Kerken, the polemics aimed at trends outside that church do not have a direct bearing on the controversy as such. Nevertheless, this criticism is an essential part of the background of the controversy. We limit ourselves to the theological movement that struck closest to home: dialectic theology.

Dialectic theology made an impact in Holland almost from the start.[43] In some circles Barth was hailed as the corrective to Kuyperian theology;

39 *Heraut*, 1942, No. 3336.
40 Van Dijk continues: "Dat dit een ding is van groote beteekenis, behoeft niet nader te worden aangeduid; wie nu zich opmaakt om aan te toonen, dat deze methode toch niet de juiste is, zal dat niet kunnen doen zonder groote schuchterheid." *PE*, VI (1941), 271.
41 *De Toekomst*, p. 12.
42 If only because "negativism" may imply that nothing positive is produced.
43 For the reception of Barth in Holland and literature of that time, see Berkouwer, *Karl Barth* (1936), pp. 14–21, 215–301.

others desired to combine Kuyper and Barth.[44] Small wonder that Reformed theologians took an active part in the discussions around Barth.

Schilder was among the first to attack dialectic theology.[45] He saw it as an internal threat[46] and wrote his polemical articles, "De Paradox in de Religie," in 1926 with a view to persuading "several 'young' neo-Calvinists" to return to their Calvinist starting point.[47] This was followed in 1928 by "Calvijn over de Geloofsparadox,"[48] and in 1933 by his dissertation, *Zur Begriffsgeschichte des "Paradoxon."* As can be surmised from the titles, Schilder's polemics against Barth converged on the latter's notion that "the paradoxical character of a religious truth disregards the fundamental law of logical thought $(A=A)$."[49] Referring to publications of Dooyeweerd and Vollenhoven, Schilder contends that Calvin saw redemption as the re-establishment of the creation order; hence, redemption can only really be redemption if it also maintains the laws of thought as original creation laws.[50] Schilder notes that in practice dialectic theology all too often tends to identify creation and sin (the implication being that redemption tends to be seen as redemption *from* rather than *of* creation). "But Calvin saw sin as *privatio boni* and for that reason redemption as *restitutio in integrum creationis.*"[51] This restitution holds also for the laws of thought and has its consequences for the doctrine of revelation. "To ascribe to God an *anti*rational (Brunner) act of revelation which violates the laws of thought (Haitjema) is, according to Calvin, to accuse God of the sin of infringing upon his own law. With his revelation God does not break the *laws* of thought [creation] but our *sins* of thought."[52]

We notice that Schilder's rejection of dialectic theology proceeds from the ground-motive of creation, fall, redemption. This is even more evident in 1935 when he writes: "We do not accept the [dialectical] antithesis between God and nature, God and history, God and the creature, for between nature and God as well as between nature and grace there is no conflict. The conflict

---

44 *Ibid.*, pp. 16f., 250.

45 By no means the only one: we mention only Grosheide (1923) and Schilder's later opponent Hepp (1925).

46 *Bij Dichters en Schriftgeleerden* (1927), p. 76: "Ook onder ons wint de nieuwe theologie haar discipelen," and he speaks of "gereformeerde leidslieden" and "neo-calvinisten" who desire a synthesis between Kuyper or Bavinck and Barth (pp. 129ff.).

47 *Ibid.*, pp. 65–147. Cf. p. 140: "Hier vroeg het polemische element meer ruimte dan het thetische. Het was opzet. Het is in dezen tijd noodig dat enkele 'jongere' neo-calvinisten eerst weer op hun *eigen* plaats komen, *daarna* kunnen ze pas vooruit."

48 Collected in *Tusschen "Ja" en "Neen"* (1929), pp. 233–305, and directed against a major promotor of Barth in Holland, Haitjema. See also pp. 307–359.

49 *Ibid.*, p. 235.

50 *Zur Begriffsgeschichte*, p. 465. The "Denkgesetze" specifically mentioned are the laws of identity, contradiction, and excluded middle.

51 *Ibid.*, p. 464.

52 *Ibid.*, p. 465.

is elsewhere. It is between sin and grace, sin and God, sin and God's Word...."[53] Driven by the ground-motive of creation, fall, redemption, there can be no question of any dualism between nature and grace.[54] Rather, grace permeates nature, redeems it so that it becomes what it was intended to be.

From here we gain a perspective on history, for in dialectic theology history, as part of "nature," stands in antithetical relation to God — the wholly Other.[55] The nature – grace dualism declares history unfit for God's redemptive acts;[56] to speak of *redemptive history* is a contradiction in terms: "Revelation means the end of history."[57] It is true that God's revelation does enter history, but vertically, like lightning. "For Barth revelation is always an intersecting." "The vertical line (God's) intersects the horizontal line (man's) — that is an encounter. But as soon as these two lines have encountered each other, they part again. And that's the sorry plight; that's... Barth's big heresy."[58] For "God, also as the God who reveals, is not only transcendent but also immanent. He does not only reach down to us but also walks with us. Revelation is not merely a continual intersecting of our horizontal plane but also a patient accompanying on that horizontal plane."[59] Barth does justice neither to the covenant[60] nor to the history of revelation. In Schilder's words: "Barth has 'murdered' a splendid Reformed discipline — the *historia revelationis*, the history of God's (special) revelation."[61]

We must keep in mind that this attack was directed against the early Barth and preceded the homiletical controversy proper. Nevertheless, already at this stage the implications for preaching came to the fore. In 1931 Schilder remarked: "Dialectic theology will never arrive at sound exegesis and will never learn the A B C of healthy hermeneutics as long as it fails to make room for the *historia revelationis* (and as soon as it does that, dialectic theology will

53   *Wat is de Hemel?*, p. 60. Cf. Van Teylingen, "Over den Wijsgeerigen Achtergrond der Dialectische Theologie," *Phil Ref*, X (1945), 2–24.

54   See Schilder, *HC* (1939), pp. 171ff. The same fear of dualism is noticeable in the controversy on common grace when the question is put whether there is talk of a "'terrein van gemeene gratie,' en daarnaast een 'terrein van bijzondere genade,'" and the conclusion is "de volstrekte noodzakelijkheid der afwijzing van het dualisme tusschen 'natuur' en 'genade.'" Schilder and Vollenhoven, *Oorzaken*, I, 4 and 22. See also Vollenhoven, *Het Calvinisme*, pp. 46f.

55   Cf. Schilder, *Bij Dichters*, pp. 104ff.; *Tusschen*, pp. 343ff.; and Berkouwer in *Beproeft de Geesten* (ed. N. Buffinga, 1934), pp. 82ff., and *Karl Barth*, pp. 49ff.

56   Schilder, *HC* (1939), p. 172.

57   Schilder, *Wat is de Hemel?*, p. 31.

58   Schilder, *Bij Dichters*, pp. 108 and 106.

59   *Ibid.*, p. 106. Cf. p. 109.

60   Schilder, *Wat is de Hemel?*, pp. 28ff. Cf. Berkouwer, *Karl Barth*, pp. 93–98, e.g., p. 94: "Zoo verslindt ook hier op dit zoo vitale punt van theologie en Christelijk leven de Goddelijke *actualiteit* alle *continuiteit* van het werk Gods in deze wereld en de dragende werkelijkheid van Zijn verbond."

61   *Bij Dichters*, p. 106. Cf. pp. 134ff.

cease to exist) ...."[62] At the same time this outwardly directed criticism could take an inward turn as when Schilder found fault with those Reformed preachers who didn't draw on the Reformed heritage, who failed to bring out the progressive character of revelation in their sermons, who didn't provide their congregation with the biblical antidote against dialectic theology.[63]

In view of this strong opposition to dialectic theology, it should come as no surprise that later, at the height of the controversy, Holwerda and Van 't Veer, followers of Schilder, clashed with those under the influence of Barth.[64] For by that time Vischer had written his *Das Christus Zeugnis des A.T.* (1934) and exegetical works of Barthian stamp were flooding the market. Again the critique centered on redemptive history. Holwerda wrote: "Although Vischer may speak of a history of revelation, in the final analysis he fails to do justice to it. Basically it amounts to a docetic dissolution of redemptive history."[65] And Van 't Veer observed: "Reading the books and sermons of the Barthians, it seems sometimes that the allegory of the first centuries and the typology of the Middle Ages have sprung to life again in new form.... Everywhere they want to see the 'witness' to the Word incarnate(!). Thus all of Scripture becomes a tautology.... The 'signs' may differ, but the thing signified is everywhere the same. In this way the *history* of revelation is slighted."[66]

As the renewed emphasis on redemptive *history* may be seen in part as a reaction against the a-historical, if not anti-historical, thrust of dialectic theology,[67] so the plea for redemptive-historical *preaching* may be seen, at least in part, as a reaction against the hermeneutical-homiletical solutions proposed by dialectic theologians.[68] This does not mean, however, that dialectic theologians became directly involved in the exemplary – redemptive-historical controversy. There is no evidence that they entered the debate at any point. Only indirectly, by way of the books it deposited also in Reformed parsonages, did dialectic theology become a factor in the controversy; as Holwerda says: "Our preachers had to face the question in how far this literature could be used for their preaching."[69] The controversy itself, however, was strictly confined to the Gereformeerde Kerken.[70]

62 *GTT*, XXXII (1931), 64.

63 *Ref*, XI (1931), 382.

64 Holwerda (1942), *Begonnen*, pp. 96ff.; Van 't Veer (1943), *Van den Dienst*, pp. 123ff.

65 *Ibid.*, p. 100, with credit to Herntrich.

66 *Van den Dienst*, p. 130. Cf. also Berkouwer, *De Persoon van Christus* (1952), pp. 87ff. (*E*, 113ff.).

67 So, e.g., Popma, *De Psychologie*, p. 39.

68 See, e.g., Schilder's call for redemptive-historical preaching to arm the congregation against "dergelijke filosofémen" as dialectic theology. *Ref*, XI (1931), 382.

69 Holwerda, *Begonnen*, p. 82.

70 The fact that dialectic theologians did not enter the controversy directly did not, of course, keep the Reformed from taking account of their writings (see above and chapter IV, *passim*).

In one way this simplifies analyzing the controversy because, for now, it enables us to assume a fundamental consensus regarding the conceptions of God, revelation, and Scripture.[71] This, after all, is the time of which Berkouwer writes: "The Gereformeerde Kerken... have accepted the isolation of the Reformed view of Scripture as a calling."[72] "We must be well aware of the fact," Holwerda amplifies, "that isolation in the view of Scripture also means isolation in exegesis, hermeneutics, and homiletics."[73]

In one way, we said, this consensus simplifies analyzing the controversy. On the other hand, it makes matters more complex because it becomes more difficult to discern clearly the demarcation line dividing the two camps in the controversy. We shall meet some of this complexity in the next section.

Inwardly Directed Criticism: "Subjectivism"

It is difficult to describe in a few words the foe within the Gereformeerde Kerken which drew the fire of the "new direction." The difficulty lies primarily in the fact that these churches, notwithstanding fundamental agreement, were not nearly as homogeneous as could be expected of a rather small church in a small country. Even disregarding the A and B direction which continued for a good while after the Union of 1892, the differences are plentiful. Dijk attempts to locate these geographically as well as historically. The geographical borders do not concern us since we are considering the church as a whole, but something should be said of the historical roots. Dijk mentions four religious currents which left their mark on the Gereformeerde Kerken: (1) Dutch Pietism (or Mysticism as Huyser prefers) with the following characteristics: "*subjectivism*, which accentuates the 'experience of the Christian'; *individualism*, which has no eye for the significance of covenant and church; and *spiritualism*, which reduces Christian living to the inner life." (2) The continuation of Anabaptist errors, to wit, the dualism matter − spirit, nature − grace, earth − heaven — a dualism which leads to subjectivism and spiritualism. (3) Objectivism with its rationalistic overtones resulting in an overestimation of the "things which are believed." (4) Spinozism which lends its support to either rationalism or mysticism.[74]

71   Contrasting it with Germany, Holwerda says: "Gelukkig is onder ons deze kwestie niet actueel geworden door verschil van meening over het gezag van het O.T." *GM*, XVIII (1940), 27.

72   *Het Probleem der Schriftkritiek* (1938), p. 294.

73   *Begonnen*, p. 97, with references to Berkouwer (foregoing note) and Grosheide (*Hermeneutiek*, p. 115).

74   *Dienst der Prediking* (1955), pp. 120ff. Cf. Huyser, *De Ouderling en de Prediking* (1959), pp. 130ff., and already in 1914, Van Schelven, *De Bewerking van eene Pietistisch-getinte Gemeente*, pp. 26ff.

We have reproduced Dijk's findings in some detail to show both the complexity of the theological picture[75] and to warn against any hasty pigeonholing. Huyser, for example, oversimplifies matters considerably when he switches the "new direction" onto track No. 3: "objectivism."[76] In so doing he perpetuates an erroneous view which Popma refuted already in 1945.[77] In its simplicity this scheme, objectivism vs. subjectivism, certainly is tempting, but the fact of the matter is that the "new direction" also attacked objectivism. Although its fire was directed at what was called "*subjectivism*,"[78] this term — surprising as it may seem — encompasses the concept objectivism. When Popma, for example, says that the "new direction" strikes also at "the fancied objectivism which is really subjectivism,"[79] he can subsume objectivism under "subjectivism" because the latter has been defined as that theory or tendency which takes to *be* the law that which is actually *subject* to the law. Hence, it makes little difference whether one makes the faith experience normative or the intellect: either case is "subjectivistic." Nor does it make much difference whether one thinks individualistically or collectivistically: in either case one has absolutized that which is (individually or collectively) subject to the law of God.[80]

This "subjectivism" in its many possible forms was considered to be diametrically opposed to *sola Scriptura*. Hence the call for a return to the Scriptures — a call to a philosophy without synthesis with non-Christian thought,[81] a dogmatics freed from unscriptural fetters, a proclamation which would truly be preaching of the Word. This is a program, a goal to strive for; no one has attained it.[82] Nevertheless, the goal — as well as the obligation to help each other reach it by mutual correction — remains.

75   Cf. the varied influences Vollenhoven detects among the theologians opposing the new movement, *Med*, Dec., 1965, p. 3.

76   "Een typisch voorbeeld" of objectivism. *Ouderling*, p. 134.

77   *Psychologie*, pp. 31ff., a refutation of Bavinck who mentioned objectivism as *one* of the marks of the "new direction" in *De Toekomst*, pp. 13f.

78   "In de situatie, waarin de Kerk verkeerde, werd dat een strijd tegen het subjectivisme." Popma, *Ibid.*, p. 17.

79   *Ibid.*, p. 36.

80   *Ibid.*, pp. 34f. Cf. De Graaf, *Het Woord Gods* (1925), p. 16, to the effect that 19th century subjectivism entered the church as collectivism but soon degenerated to individualism because subjectivism is predisposed to judge the value of the experience of the congregation by one's own experience. On the subjective – objective problem in German theology, see Berkouwer's *Geloof en Openbaring in de Nieuwere Duitsche Theologie* (1932). Berkouwer, too, prefers to speak of "subjectivism" in the sense of "normsubjectiveering." But this also means: "Daarom kan dit subjectivisme optreden in verschillende vormen, al naar gelang de normen, die gesubjectiveerd worden." *Ibid.*, p. 135. Cf. his *Op de Tweesprong* (*ca.* 1950), pp. 88ff.

81   See, e.g., Dooyeweerd's criticism of the "traditioneele subject–objectschema" taken over by Kuyper. *Phil Ref*, IV (1939), 220.

82   "De 'nieuwe geest' ... beweert allerminst zelf de zonde van het subjectivisme overwonnen te hebben." Popma, *Psychologie*, p. 34.

Objectivism. — We shall first take a closer look at the criticism of what is normally called objectivism. This word usually connotes an overestimation of faith objects, the *fides quae creditur,* doctrines. Consequently, it is often associated with scholasticism — the attempt to capture the fulness of God's revelation in a closed theological system of logical categories and distinctions. Through it all runs a rationalistic streak,[83] for only reason can discover these objects, distil the doctrines from Scripture, and fit them into a systematic (logical) whole. Whatever one may say of the WdW in its early years, it is clear that it put the *ratio* in its proper place.[84] Veenhof says that the supporters of the WdW "were of a radically anti-scholastic spirit,"[85] and Van Reest opines that Schilder "attacked the scholasticism in Kuyper in order to retain him as a reformer of the church."[86]

In homiletics objectivism is usually associated with dogmatic sermons. Van Reest judges that many sermons in the thirties were steeped in "dead dogmatism."[87] Van Dijk analyzed the sermons of the fathers and came to the conclusion that the "biggest mistake" in their style of preaching was that their sermons turned into lectures on one or more doctrines. "Their usual method was to dissolve the text into various elements, and to speak separately on each element. Since these elements could easily be linked with the loci of dogmatics, the sermon would become a lecture about some dogmatic subjects."[88] Thus "the disintegrated text was a means to display dogmatic truths."[89] Van Dijk continues: "I see in this an immense wrong. It testifies to a lack of respect for God's Word.... Although such preaching seems to adhere closely to the text by dealing with it word for word, basically it is nothing other than the supposedly detested 'motto-preaching' in which the text is used as a peg on which to hang one's own thoughts."[90] The question is not whether the fathers personally acknowledged the authority of Scripture but

83 "De invloed van rationaliserende stromingen." Dijk, *Dienst der Prediking,* p. 121. Huyser prefers to use the phrase, "een sterk intellectualistische inslag." *Ouderling,* p. 133.

84 One need only think of the distinction between theoretic and pre-theoretic, and the view of the analytical function as by no means the highest of some 15 functions of man.

85 *Om de Unica,* p. 61.

86 *Opdat Zij Allen,* I, 167. Note, however, that K. J. Popma, granting that Schilder fought scholasticism, also states: "Doch menigmaal is hij in scholastieke valstrikken vastgeraakt," particularly in his "filosoferen over God" and his speculation in the "toepassing van de analogia entis." *Phil Ref,* XXII (1957), 27ff.

87 "Het dorre dogmatisme." *Ibid.,* p. 107. See also Schipper's "oorlogsverklaring aan de opvatting, dat de prediking 'waarheden' brengt, waarover men warm debatteeren kan met 'andersdenkenden.'" *Van den Dienst* (1944), p. 39.

88 *De Preektrant* van de Dominé's in de Kerken der Afscheiding, in de Jaren 1835-1869 (1935), p. 8. N.B. Van Dijk is not to be confused with Dijk.

89 *Ibid.,* p. 12. Cf. Schilder, *Ref,* X (1930), 212f.

90 *Ibid.*

whether their way of preaching was in accord with this confession.[91] Schilder wrote: "We can dauntlessly deride motto-preaching, but I'm sure that a large part of the orthodox preachers in Holland follows the selfsame, purely liberal method every Sunday — with only this difference: the orthodox preachers fit certain particulars of the historical text into an orthodox framework, into certain chapters of dogmatics."[92] Preaching, however, is not presenting doctrines but letting the text speak. The goal that beckons the preacher is *sola Scriptura.*[93]

Subjectivism. — More prevalent than objectivism — at least in the sense that it drew more fire from the "new direction" — was subjectivism. Kamphuis characterizes the style of Schilder's dogmatics as "anti-subjectivistic."[94] Vollenhoven makes a similar evaluation and notes that the common foe of subjectivism first brought Schilder and the WdW together.[95] This foe did not present itself as a clear systematic theory, however;[96] it could not be localized in any one district or person. Here both the influences of the past[97] as well as contemporary influences[98] entered the picture to form a complex synthesis. We gain the clearest view of this elusive enemy when we hear him described as pietism and mysticism.

The opposition to *pietism*, better, pietistic tendencies, as such was nothing new. In a 1914 address to Reformed preachers, "The Pastoral Approach to a Pietistically Colored Congregation," Van Schelven mentioned four false motifs basic to pietism: (1) individualism, (2) a faith life without Christ because of its search for certitude in self-examination, (3) an unscriptural notion of the church, and (4) a simplistic psychology.[99] All of these and the resultant multitude of wrong practices he considered to be still present, in greater or lesser degree, in the Reformed churches of his day.

Over the years the picture did not change a great deal. Especially in rural areas people clung tenaciously to pietistic emphases. According to Popma, writing in 1945, there are still "pietistically colored congregations; there is a lack of joyful assurance of faith; there is a striving to reach that assurance

---

91   *Ibid.*, p. 34.

92   *Ref*, XI (1931), 374.

93   At times this return to the Scriptures, taken as a "thing out there," is described as "objectivism." Cf. Dijk, *Dienst der Kerk*, pp. 87f. The crux of the matter is, however, whether or not Scripture was thought of as a "thing out there."

94   *Almanak 1953*, p. 100.

95   *Phil Ref*, XVII (1952), 149.

96   "Het blijft bij praktijken, en bij voorzichtige aanduidingen, of naieve demonstratie van subjectivistische inslag." Schilder and Vollenhoven, *Oorzaken*, II, 18.

97   See Dijk's analysis above. Particularly on Zeeland, A. Janse, *Lourens Ingelse* (1932).

98   Mainly, it seems, the "Buchmanbeweging" and dialectic theology. Van Reest also makes mention of Weatherhead and Stanley Jones. *Opdat Zij Allen*, I, 110.

99   *De Bewerking*, respectively pp. 13, 20, 31, 37.

36

by grasping at certain marks within oneself as the ground of certitude...."[100]

What did change over the years was the nature of the opposition from rather unorganized, occasional attacks to a widely supported, concentrated attack upon these pietistic tendencies. The battle concentrated itself on three related fronts. In the first place, the "new direction" objected to the *anthropocentric* viewpoint: "The mistake of many people is that their lives are ruled by a cultus of their own salvation instead of a cultus of God."[101] The attention is focussed on man, not God and his redemptive work. Janse characterized "the dominant interest in man, placing man central in religion" as "a serious sin of our fathers"; he called for the abandonment of "this self-willed religion" and a return to Scripture which places central not the "marks of the Christian or 'the faith of the congregation' but the grace of God through Christ."[102] The anthropocentric viewpoint was not only considered unbiblical,[103] but its excessive emphasis on self-examination, it was felt, also forced people into an introspection which led to *introversion*. And introversion can never give certitude in Christ and joy in being a Christian: "Let us cease searching for our own certitude in self-analysis, and let us stop teaching others to grope in that way. Let us seek certitude in the only way it can be found: the simple acceptance of God's promises, the acceptance of the Christ of God's promises, by faith, by immediate, unconditional faith."[104] Introversion, in turn, was taken to be practically synonymous with the attendant *individualism*. But "in the covenant God always approaches his entire people, never merely individual persons," De Graaf says.[105] This emphasis on the covenant was not so much a collectivistic reaction to rampant individualism as a re-assertion of the biblical notion of the covenant which breaks through the individualism—collectivism dilemma by seeing the individual ever in organic relation with the community: the tree and the branches, the body and the members.[106]

Thus, these pietistic tendencies — the anthropocentric view, introversion, and individualism — were deemed to be at odds with biblical revelation and to slight God the Creator and Redeemer as well as his work in creation and re-creation throughout the ages. Against this background the emphasis on a theocentric viewpoint, on God's covenant, on redemptive history, comes into more prominent relief.

From a slightly different angle we notice the same objections in the oppo-

---

100 *Psychologie*, p. 37.

101 De Graaf (1936), *Verbondsgeschiedenis*, I, 10.

102 *Lourens Ingelse* (1932), p. 18; cf. pp. 9 and 60. Also Van Dijk, *De Preektrant* (1935), p. 24.

103 "Het is te allen tijde ongeoorloofd anthropocentrisch te spreken." Schilder, *HC* (1939), p. 13. Cf. *Wat is de Hemel?*, pp. 150, 170.

104 Van Dijk, *De Preektrant*, p. 45. Cf. Janse, p. 4. On self-examination and subjectivism, see Schilder and Vollenhoven, *Oorzaken*, VI, 12–17.

105 *Verbondsgeschiedenis*, I, 12. Cf. *Het Woord Gods*, pp. 18ff.

106 See Holwerda, *Begonnen*, pp. 108ff.; and *Populair*, pp. 15ff.

sition to *mysticism*. The term as such was used rather loosely[107] and practically synonymously with "pietism."[108] Under the heading of "mysticism" one can hear the same charges: anthropocentric, introversive, individualistic.[109] Under the same heading one can also hear charges of neglecting history: only the internal counts; "the attention is turned away from the world outside and the eye is closed to what God has wrought and will work on the broad highways of redemptive and revelational history; all that remains is God and the soul embracing each other."[110]

The specific flavor of the charge "mysticism" must be sought in Schilder's description of mysticism as "a commendation of a specific way of knowledge. Over against the knowledge of God which one receives from the Word revelation deposited in Scripture... the mystic asserts that he can know God by 'feeling'.... This 'feeling' is usually nothing other than 'the capability of coming to immediate knowledge' — im-media-te, that is, without media, without reflection, without Scripture study, without books, letters, concepts, etc."[111] But in this way Scripture does not receive its due; in Van Schelven's words, the Bible becomes a "(by)bell next to the chiming of the Spirit in the soul."[112] But the Bible and the Spirit are not two opposite poles existing in tension;[113] there is never any antithesis between God's external speaking and his internal speaking, between letter and Spirit.[114]

At this point the criticism of the tendencies towards mysticism detected within the Gereformeerde Kerken blended with the criticism of dialectic theology. If this seems strange because dialectic theology had itself attacked mysticism, it must be remembered that the critique of dialectic theology converged on its dualism: nature—grace. The very same accusation was leveled at mysticism: "Mysticism makes opposites of nature and grace."[115] At this basic level the two join hands. Thus Schilder accuses dialectic theology of the very error it fights: mysticism. He writes:

> The anti-mystical arguments from Barthian side have likewise robbed the continuous line of revelation and confession of their value in order to glorify again, over against this continuity, the "moment" in which the listener hears the voice of God. Although they began with strong polemics

---

107   "Het blijkt, dat in ons praktisch kerkelijk-geestelijk leven termen als 'mystiek,' 'bevinding,' 'onderwerpelijkheid,' 'ervaring,' 'geloof,' 'gemeenschap met God,' enz. kriskras dóór elkaar gebruikt worden." Schilder, *Tusschen*, p. 168.

108   Where Dijk speaks of "pietism," Huyser wants to speak of "mysticism" (see above), and Van Schelven, p. 23, sees pietism as giving rise to mysticism.

109   E.g., Schilder, *Tusschen*, respectively pp. 185ff., 174ff., 192ff.

110   Schilder, *HC* (1939), p. 27. Similarly, *Tusschen*, pp. 174ff.

111   Schilder, *Ref*, XVIII (1938), 226.

112   P. 21. The play on the word is better in Dutch: De Bijbel als bij-bel.

113   See Holwerda, *Populair*, pp. 11–15, and Schippers, *Van den Dienst*, pp. 46–48.

114   Schilder, *Tusschen*, p. 178. Cf. pp. 183f.

115   Schilder, *College Verslagen* (1939), p. 38.

against mysticism, the typical expressions of the latter soon appeared in their own constructions. Mysticism was anti-historical, at least suprahistorical; the Barthian view is similar. Mysticism desired the unification of the speaking God and listening man, and also from the Barthian camp came statements declaring the speaking God and listening man to be "one."[116]

Whether they carried a pietistic, mystic, or other stamp, over against these subjectivistic tendencies the "new direction" stressed the *sola Scriptura*. As far as the preaching of historical texts was concerned, this translated into an emphasis on redemptive history. In 1931 Schilder wrote: "Experience teaches us that the preaching of historical texts often reveals the tendency to present results of psychology by describing various 'soul conditions,' to picture types of godliness, to present illustrations for the well-known 'doctrine of salvation,'" and he spoke of a "menacing and almost automatic psychologizing of historical texts."[117] To break out of this vicious circle which gets out of the text what it reads into it, Schilder wrote his series of articles, "Concerning the Unity of 'Redemptive History' in Connection with Preaching."[118] Redemptive history with all it entails was seen as the scriptural answer to subjectivistic preaching, as the biblical way of entering the hermeneutic circle in order to do justice to the historical text both in interpretation and preaching.

THE CONTROVERSY ITSELF

With this background in mind we can now zero in on the homiletical controversy. The issues involved will be set forth in detail in the next two chapters. At this juncture in our survey our purpose is merely to introduce the two sides taking part in the controversy.

The Redemptive-Historical Approach

We have already come across the names of the defenders of the redemptive-historical approach, but it might be helpful to list them together. We list only those who took an active part in the debate in the various publications. They

---

116 Schilder, *Ref*, XVIII (1938), 227. Cf. *College Verslagen*, p. 36. As to Barth and subjectivism, Hoekstra charges "dat hij inderdaad Schleiermacher, die door hem de voordeur is uitgestuurd, heimelijk door de achterdeur weer binnenlaat, en dat het subjectivisme bij Barth nog sterk nawerkt." *Het Woord Gods in de Prediking* (1931), p. 7. Later, p. 44, he speaks of "het echt Luthersche anthropologische stempel."
117 "Een dreigende en vaak voorhandene verpsychologiseering van 'historische stoffen.'" *Ref*, XI (1931), 373.
118 *Ref*, XI (Sept. 11 – Sept. 25, 1931), 365ff.

were: B. Holwerda, K. Schilder, H. J. Spier, D. Van Dijk, M. B. Van 't Veer, and C. Veenhof.

Schilder might be called the initiator of the redemptive-historical approach. Huyser calls him the "auctor intellectualis" and the "'Urheber' [spiritual father] of this novelty in Reformed homiletics."[119] We can agree here, provided this characterization does not obscure the personal contributions of and variations between each of the above-named authors, and provided the word "novelty" is not taken in an absolute sense.[120] It is true, however, that the articles of Schilder in the early thirties stimulated the search for an approach to Scripture different from the traditional one. He wrote, for example: "Here and there we still encounter Lenten sermons in which the figures around Christ receive the primary attention. There is talk of Judas, Peter, Pilate, Herod, the Sanhedrin, Mary, etc.... (their inner conflict, their comfort, their hardening hearts), while the first and foremost question is forgotten, namely, what *Christ* has done, what *God* has let his Son experience, what the *Son* has experienced in and through the actions of those figures around him."[121] Christ should be central, not man. It took Schilder more than 1500 pages to demonstrate this theme in his trilogy of 1930, *Christus in Zijn Lijden*. In a review Greijdanus judged that Schilder had attained his goal: "Not the various persons met on the road of suffering should attract the main attention but Christ himself."[122] These books of Schilder filled a real need,[123] but were only the beginning. It was particularly between 1939 and 1942 that a lively interchange took place.

To the redemptive-historical approach we can ascribe the basic motive of *sola Scriptura*. We must be careful, however, to understand this correctly. We do not intend to suggest that the exemplary approach was anti-*sola Scriptura*. The opposing sides cannot neatly be categorized as pro and contra Scripture. Huyser, for instance, gives voice to the profession of *sola Scriptura* from the exemplary side when he writes: "Basically the only thing to which the minister of the Word is bound in his preaching is the Word of God revealed in the Scriptures of both the Old and the New Testament."[124] Nor do we wish to suggest a simple identification between this basic motive and Luther's call for *sola Scriptura* at the time of the Reformation, though the two certainly

---

119 *GTT*, L (1950), 214.
120 See above, pp. 27f., on the continuity with tradition.
121 *Ref*, X (1930), 204.
122 A review of Vols. I and II in *GTT*, XXX (1930), 560.
123 See Veenhof, *Almanak 1953*, p. 171.
124 *Ouderling*, p. 80. Cf. p. 105: "Het Woord Gods is de zaak, waarom in de prediking alles draait; het is er de kern, de pit en het merg van, de eigenlijke substantie. Is dat niet zo, dan is heel de preek daarmee geoordeeld, dan is ze niet geweest een ware bediening van het Woord...."

are not unrelated. It has been noted that the point at issue for Luther was not in the first place the formal recognition of *sola Scriptura* as such, but the functioning of this profession within the church.[125] This is also the case in the controversy under discussion: at stake is not the *formal* acceptance of *sola Scriptura* but whether or not this profession is functioning fully (the *sola*) in the interpretation and preaching in the Gereformeerde Kerken. In this light we must see the call of the thirties to "return to Scripture."[126]

The redemptive-historical approach wishes to apply the *sola Scriptura* consistently in hermeneutics and homiletics. Holwerda says: "The Bible does not contain many histories but *one* history — the one history of God's constantly advancing revelation, the one history of God's ever progressing redemptive work. And the various persons named in the Bible have all received their own peculiar place in this one history and have their peculiar meaning for this history. We must, therefore, try to understand all the accounts in their relation with each other, in their coherence with the center of redemptive history, Jesus Christ."[127] This, in a nutshell, is the program of the redemptive-historical school. If their attack on the opposition is at times overbearing, it is fed not by self-complacency but by a zeal for the Word of God. "It is only deserving of the Word of God, isn't it, that we force our thoughts to submit to the norms for preaching which the Word itself presents?"[128]

The redemptive-historical approach is a program, an ideal, a goal to strive for. No one suggests that this goal has been attained: "Everyone knows that many sermons constructed according to the redemptive-historical method can be criticized.... The discussion, however, is not about practical results but about the *proper method* for reaching ever better results."[129]

This desire to do justice to the Scriptures in preaching must be honored. In spite of the animosities, we meet evidence of this underlying motive constantly. "Let our opponents at least recognize," Holwerda pleads, "that monotonous and clumsy introductions such as these ['Not Abraham or David...

125 Rossouw, *Klaarheid en Interpretasie*, p. 154: "Luther het begryp dat dit nie in die eerste plek gaan om 'n formele stryd oor die Skrif of sy gesag as sodanig nie, maar wel om 'n stryd oor die *uitleg* daarvan, oor die wyse waarop dit in die kerk verstaan word en oor die wyse waarop die inhoud daarvan aktief in die kerk funksioneer."

126 "... onder ons werd ook begeerd en geijverd om weer de weg terug naar de Schrift te vinden. Menigeen zag in onze kring deformatie. Men was van oordeel, dat de prediking te veel het accent legde op de subjectieve ervaring van de Christen.... dat het Woord Gods in het gedrang kwam ...." Dijk, *Dienst der Kerk*, p. 87.

127 *GM*, XVIII (1940), 27.

128 Schilder, *Ref*, X (1930), 203.

129 Holwerda, *Begonnen*, p. 80; cf. *ibid.*: "Dezelfde gebreken en ellendigheden bederven ook heel veel van onze preken." So also Schilder, *Ref*, X (1930), 219: "Niemand zal de pretentie voeren, dat hij ooit een prediking geven kan, die aan al deze dingen volkomen uitwerking geeft"; and Van Dijk, *De Preektrant*, p. 32.

but Christ is central here'] testify to a serious struggle to catch the precise content of the text."[130]

From this foundational motive the assault is launched on the traditional way of preaching historical texts. This manner of preaching, it is felt, does not allow the *sola Scriptura* to function fully. "No justice is done to Scripture when the deeds of persons who figured once upon a time in a particular historical episode occasion some stimulating, warning, or edifying remarks in the sermon."[131] Van Dijk goes as far as saying: "It is my conviction that exemplary treatment of historical texts cannot rightly be called 'ministry of the Word.'"[132] Again, it is not the doctrinal soundness of the opponents that is called into question but their way of treating and preaching historical texts. And with regard to the content of that preaching, the point at issue is not primarily whether the truths proclaimed are biblical, but whether these truths are actually revealed in the preaching-text. "Ministry of the Word," Van Dijk insists, "is to proclaim to the congregation that message which God gives in the text." Hence, "when one studies the text, he must try to discover its special content." That specific content must be preached, not notions — however beautiful — which could equally well be tacked onto other texts.[133]

This homiletical principle has implications for all preaching-texts, of course, whether they be historical, dogmatic, poetic, or whatever. In the controversy the attention is focussed exclusively on the O.T. and N.T. historical texts, however. Here the deficiencies of the traditional method of preaching are particularly evident. In this preaching, it is felt, the shortcomings of objectivism and subjectivism, of pietism and mysticism mingle in various degrees to form a questionable mixture — "exemplary preaching."

The Exemplary Approach

We shall also list alphabetically those who responded to the challenge by actively defending, in one way or another, the traditional way of preaching historical texts. The names we shall meet most frequently are: J. H. Bavinck,[134] K. Dijk,[135] J. Douma, Ph. J. Huyser, J. Schelhaas, and N. Streefkerk.

---

130   *Ibid.* Cf. one of Holwerda's own introductions: "We zijn hier gekomen om het Woord des Heeren te hooren 'naar den zin en de meening des Gééstes,' en niet naar den smaak en de traditie van ménschen." *Tot de Dag Aanlicht*, p. 246.

131   Van Dijk, *PE*, VII (1942), 137.

132   *Ibid.*, VI (1941), 279.

133   *Ibid.* So also Schilder, *Ref*, XI (1931), 365: "Een aaneenrijging van op zichzelf, blijkens andere Schriftgedeelten, wel ware beweringen, die dan, hetgeen zeer brutaal is, vastgeknoopt worden aan een tekst, dien men eigenlijk ook ergens anders had kunnen kiezen" is "eigenlijk *volstrekt* geen bediening des Woords."

134   To be distinguished from Herman Bavinck whose name will be written in full.

135   Not to be confused with Van Dijk on the redemptive-historical side.

It hardly needs saying that these men are not willing to defend the excesses in traditional preaching,[136] but they do desire to show the legitimacy of the exemplary approach and the illegitimacy of an exclusively redemptive-historical approach. As Douma says: "Our fathers knew very well that redemptive history is a unified structure with Christ at its center, but they still felt free to treat separately (using biblical givens) certain persons described in Scripture, to picture them psychologically, to speak of their struggles and trials, their strengths and weaknesses, and then to draw parallels between the experiences of the Bible saints and the struggles of believers today. Without any hesitation our fathers held up the virtues of the biblical persons as an example to all, but also their sins and weaknesses as a warning."[137] It is this tradition which the exemplary side wishes to uphold.

On the exemplary side one meets, at times, a reverence for the fathers bordering on deference, an uncritical acceptance of tradition, a fear of anything new. Though this may have been a motive in their defence of the status quo, we would prefer to describe their basic motive as a concern for the *relevance* of the sermon. This concern comes to expression, for instance, in the frequent charges that the exclusive use of the redemptive-historical method leads to objective sermons, mere explication, lectures on redemptive history, sermons without tangible relevance. To ward off this danger, the exemplary side desires to uphold the legitimacy of the exemplary "element." They want not merely the objective but also the subjective, not merely explication but also application, not merely God's acts but also man's response. They are not against the redemptive-historical method as such, but they are opposed to the use of this method to the exclusion of the exemplary "moment."

At this point we are faced with a complication. Till now we have been able to speak of "redemptive-historical" and "exemplary" as the two sides in the controversy, the approximation of two horns of a dilemma; but at this juncture the picture is complicated by the fact that the exemplary side does not recognize this as a dilemma. They are perfectly willing to accept the "redemptive-historical," thus combining the two horns of the dilemma. It is not a question of "either-or" for them but of "both-and." Bavinck,[138] Dijk,[139]

---

136   E.g., Huyser, *GTT*, **XLIX** (1949), 243: "Wij nemen het natuurlijk niet op voor de uitwassen, die door een moralistische toepassing van deze methode in de practijk zijn ontstaan."

137   *Heraut*, 1941, No. 3292.

138   "Ik mag [de historische boeken] lezen als één doorloopende geschiedenis, maar ik mag ze ook lezen als een bundel van geschiedenissen (meervoud), geschiedenissen waarin ons allerlei personen geteekend worden." *De Bijbel*: het Boek der Ontmoetingen (1942), p. 55.

139   "Tegen de probleemstelling *heilshistorisch* of *exemplarisch*, waarbij het een naast het ander niet bestaanbaar is, [zijn] zeker ernstige bezwaren... in te brengen." *OB*, **XXII** (1944), 3035. "Ik...accepteer niet het òf-òf." *Ibid.*, p. 3036. Cf. *Dienst der Prediking* (1955), pp. 109f.

Douma,[140] Huyser,[141] Schelhaas,[142] and Streefkerk[143] — all feel perfectly free to combine the "redemptive-historical approach" with the exemplary approach.[144] Given this combination on the exemplary side, where is the dilemma? Add to this the exemplary side's desire to uphold the *sola Scriptura* and the redemptive-historical side's obvious wish to be relevant,[145] and the question becomes urgent: Where is the dilemma in the controversy? or at least, Where is the point of divergence between the two sides? Dijk suggests that there might be "something common in the terms which eliminates them as alternatives and makes of the two methods a twofold treatment proceeding from a different aspect or motive."[146] Overduin states that "there is no question of a contrast" between redemptive-historical and exemplary, providing one first give these terms an "appropriate content."[147]

But is it only a question of semantics? Granted that the terminology is not always clear, granted that there are many misinterpretations of each other's position, it is too farfetched to say that the controversy is just a gross misunderstanding. Huyser has perceived something of the dilemma — though he overstates the case — when he speaks of "these new, anti-'exemplary' notions which intended to bring about a radical revolution in material and formal homiletics."[148] From the other side we recall Van Dijk's assessment that exemplary preaching "cannot rightly be called 'ministry of the Word.'"[149] This is not merely a difference of emphasis; there is definitely a dilemma here — only, it is difficult to lay the finger on the precise point of divergence because of the proxim-

140 "Ik [moet] afwijzen de *tegenstelling* tusschen de christocentrisch-heilshistorische opvatting en de exemplarisch-practische. Het is hier geen kwestie van òf-òf, maar van èn-èn.... Het gaat ons om het goed recht, de geschiedenis *óók* exemplarisch te mogen behandelen ...." *Heraut*, 1941, No. 3334. Cf. No. 3335; also No. 3338 about "de hoogere synthese."
141 "De voorstanders van de 'exemplarische' methode... [willen] deze methode volstrekt *niet exclusief*... stellen en slechts ruimte opeisen voor een 'exemplarisch' *moment* in de prediking over historische stof ...." *GTT*, XLIX (1949), 236.
142 "Historische boeken bieden geschiedenis van Gods werk.... Maar de historische stoffen mogen en moeten ook als voorbeelden worden gebruikt." *GTT*, XLII (1941), 126. Cf. p. 113 for redemptive-historical followed by "tevens" exemplary.
143 "Het exemplarisch *element* mag niet vergeten worden. Het is hier geen kwestie van òf-òf, maar van èn-èn ...." Quoted in *PE*, VI (1941), 349.
144 See also Overduin's warning against an "overwaardering" of redemptive history on the part of some, which destroys the good cause for which they fight. *Ref*, XVIII (1938), 311, 335, 350f.
145 E.g., Holwerda, *Begonnen*, p. 86: "... de prediking over historische stoffen moet práctisch zijn .... Anders zou het immers geen prediking meer zijn."
146 *OB*, XXII (1944), 3036.
147 "Wanneer men maar weer goed luistert naar de Schrift, dan zal men allereerst aan deze termen een goede inhoud geven en vervolgens zal men ontdekken dat hier geen sprake is van een tegenstelling." *Opdracht en Dienst*, XXXIX (Nov., 1964), 23.
148 *GTT*, XLIX (1949), 240.
149 See above, II, nn. 132, 133.

ity of both sides doctrinally and especially the accommodating attitude on the exemplary side. In fact, the precise location of the dilemma became itself a point of dispute.

The Dilemma

For our purposes the precise location of the dilemma is largely an academic question — that the difference in approach touches a broad spectrum of issues will become evident in the next two chapters. Still, it might clarify matters if we take a moment to try to localize the point of divergence in hermeneutics and attempt to show some of the implications for the practice of preaching historical texts.

If we take the exemplary side's statements that they desire no "either-or" but a "both-and" at face value, we should not search for a dilemma between a redemptive-historical method and a *pure* exemplary method. In theory at least there is no pure exemplary method. The prevalent theory on the exemplary side agrees with Grosheide's rule for historical texts: "One can first investigate the meaning of a certain part of redemptive history within the totality of revelation. Here it is especially the Christocentric that comes up for discussion.... After this one must, in the second place, also take every complete history, every unit, large or small, in and by itself. Apart from its place in and its meaning for the totality of divine revelation, it proclaims something to us.... One can ask, which virtue is praised here, which sin is punished."[150] Grosheide warns that these two may not be separated, but continues: "The first will no doubt point more to the *historia revelationis*, the second to the application."[151]

This gives us an idea of what is meant by the combination: redemptive-historical *and* exemplary. The existence of such a combination, however, does not mean that there is no dilemma in the controversy; it only means that we ought to look for the dilemma first of all in another place, that is to say, between the redemptive-historical and this redemptive-historical — exemplary synthesis. We find confirmation for this in the charges of "exclusivism" leveled at the redemptive-historical camp. Typical of the exemplary side is Douma's assertion: "Not one of us is opposed to the redemptive-historical method as such; what we object to is the *exclusive* redemptive-historical method."[152] Van 't

150   *Hermeneutiek* (1929), p. 193. Appeal to this rule is found, e.g., in Douma, *Heraut*, 1941, No. 3334, and Streefkerk, in *PE*, VII (1941), 39.
151   *Ibid.*, p. 194.
152   *Heraut*, 1942, No. 3337. Cf. Huyser, *GTT*, XLIX, 243: "Wat de nieuwe heilshistorische ideologie voor ons totaal onaannemelijk maakt, is haar *star exclusivisme....* Men wil dit ['exemplarisch'] moment uit de homiletische interpretatie van historische stoffen geheel *verbannen....* Dit extremistisch standpunt is voor ons onaanvaardbaar."

Veer, from his side, correctly observes that the difference between him and Streefkerk is that the latter, "besides trying to find the meaning of a particular history by reading it as a part of the one integrality of revelation, in addition desires to see each history as a rounded-off whole so that every part may also be taken in and by itself. However much I would like to," Van 't Veer adds, "I cannot go along with this."[153] Hence, the two sides pitted against each other in the controversy should be seen first as exclusivism vs. synthesis.

The question next arises whether or not this synthesis is a live option for the practice of preaching. Grosheide wants to maintain the synthesis but readily admits: "Whereas the central redemptive events will speak especially in their significance for the totality of God's work [the redemptive-historical], the surrounding facts will speak more in a comforting, admonishing manner [the exemplary]."[154] Continuing in this line Douma seems to have no qualms about taking examples from Scripture without seeing the persons concerned within the context of redemptive history.[155] What is left then of the synthesis? And does not the dilemma in fact (in practice) tend to become a dilemma between redemptive-historical and pure exemplary preaching?

We can also approach it from another angle. Holwerda suggests: "The fact that they warn against 'exclusivism,' that they desire a 'synthesis,' shows that they want to combine two contradictory methods." He fears that this will lead to dualism in preaching, in that the redemptive-historical method will be used for the explication and the exemplary method for the application. But "it will not do to account for the historical moment in the explication, only to neglect it in the application."[156] Van 't Veer adds: "A combination of these two methods is certainly not possible if one desires to preserve the unity of the sermon, for each has a different view of the historiography of Scripture and will thus interpret that history according to different rules."[157]

Here we touch upon the fundamental difference: divergent conceptions of the historiography of Scripture, that is to say, of the nature of historical texts. This basic divergence, in turn, leads to different methods for interpreting and preaching such texts. Although Huyser and others protest that they

---

153 *PE*, VII (1941), 60.

154 *Hermeneutiek*, p. 194. The attempt of Holwerda to save Grosheide for the redemptive-historical method (*Begonnen*, pp. 86f.) is not overly successful; the opposition can and does appeal to him with more reason. We must remember, however, that Grosheide as well as Hoekstra wrote before the controversy and that both are ambiguous on these matters.

155 "Het gaat ons om het goed recht... elk onderdeel *afzonderlijk* van alle zijden, bijv. ook psychologisch, te mogen belichten." *Heraut*, 1941, No. 3334 (emphasis added). Cf. No. 3335: "We zouden de prediking verarmen, indien wij de 'omkleding,' die God om het 'zaad' geeft, ook niet meer afzonderlijk behandelden, zonder de juiste plaats in het geheel der Godsopenbaring te kunnen aanwijzen." Cf. Bavinck, *De Bijbel* (1942), pp. 53ff. For Huyser, see below, IV, n. 90.

156 *Begonnen*, p. 86.

157 *Van den Dienst*, p. 159.

do not want to use another method but merely desire to safeguard the exemplary element, the question is put how they acquire such elements. Van 't Veer answers: "One can obtain an exemplary element only by abstracting a particular history from the one history of redemption and then drawing a parallel between the abstracted situation and a similar situation in our time."[158] Here the two methods stand in stark contrast to each other. Though they can be combined in theory perhaps, in the practice of preaching the combination is infelicitous because of the inherent dualism. Once that dualism is considered a drawback for preaching, it can most easily be overcome by simply bypassing the redemptive-historical method. Clearly, then, in *practice*, the dilemma does tend to become one between the redemptive-historical method and the pure exemplary method. This is substantiated by the fact that the controversy originated in the opposition to sermons which were considered to be so completely exemplary that Van 't Veer's first category in classifying sermons of the thirties is: "purely exemplary."[159] But whether "pure" or "combined," both were attacked for not doing justice to the historical text.

Summarizing, we might put it this way: in *theory* the dilemma is: either exclusive redemptive-historical interpretation and preaching or a combination of redemptive-historical and exemplary; in *practice*: either exclusive redemptive-historical preaching (barring lapses) or the combination which often leads to exclusive exemplary preaching.

Representatives of both sides might object to this way of putting the dilemma. To begin with the exemplary side, Dijk might object that he would choose neither the one horn nor the other. Holwerda had tried to delineate the differences in three ways: (1) viewing redemptive history either as the foundation of dogma and ethics, or as illustrative of dogma and ethics; (2) interpreting the historical text either in its organic context and as part of the historical development, or as a fragment and abstracted from history (timeless); and (3) interpreting the historical text either synthetically (thematically, according to the main thought), or atomistically.[160] Dijk readily agrees that when the alternatives are formulated so sharply, any combination of the two methods is out of the question.[161] "But," says Dijk, "if we

---

158 *Ibid.*

159 *Ibid.*, pp. 140f. Cf. p. 145: "Het blijkt uit de practijk toch overduidelijk, dat het niet juist is, als men tegenover de voorstanders van de heilshistorische methode opmerkt, dat niemand onder ons het in zijn hoofd krijgt 'de Gewijde Geschiedenis zuiver en alleen exemplarisch te behandelen.' Zeker, in *theorie* zal niemand de zuiver exemplarische methode willen verdedigen, maar de *practijk* is hier sterker dan de theorie."

160 *Begonnen*, pp. 87ff. The meaning of these terms will become clear in chapters III and IV.

161 "Wanneer Holwerda zo het alternatief stelt: óf dogmafunderend óf illustratief, óf synthetisch óf atomistisch, óf organisch óf fragmentarisch, is het antwoord niet moeilijk .... We stemmen hem terstond toe, dat er geen enkele combinatie van deze

put the problem differently and view the exemplary biblically, purged of all atomistic and illustrative extravagance, then there is room for this way of treating the text, while paying attention also to the course of redemptive history."[162]

But Dijk's way of putting the problem is hardly a way out of the dilemma. To speak of an exemplary element purged of all extravagance means, in fact, a swing in the direction of the redemptive-historical camp. Van 't Veer, too, is willing to speak of an "exemplary element," be it in quotation marks: "I believe... that the 'exemplary element' which they want to *add* to the redemptive-historical method comes out best by the correct utilization of that method."[163] But this "correct utilization" entails that one may never obtain that "exemplary element" by abstracting it from its historical context.[164] Although this comes close to Dijk's statement, "purged of all atomistic and illustrative extravagance," it is not quite the same. We don't want to fall over words or their absence, but it may be significant that Dijk leaves out the "fragmentary." In any event, Dijk remains opposed to Holwerda's "one-sided emphasis on redemptive-historical preaching,"[165] and Holwerda from his side would never agree with Dijk that "the exemplary element may not be forgotten," for here a non-historical, fragmentary interpretation is *added* to the redemptive-historical interpretation.[166] Granted that Dijk and others defending the exemplary method are averse to exemplary excesses, methodologically they can hardly disqualify these excesses because they themselves have opened the door to them by their insistence on an exemplary element, by their insistence on viewing each episode *also* as an isolated unit.[167]

As to the redemptive-historical school, its members might object to the word "exclusive" as we used it to characterize their method. Didn't we just hear Van 't Veer speak of an "exemplary element"? Huyser calls this "ambiguous (equivocal?)" and a "puzzle."[168] A still greater puzzle might be Holwerda's statement: "The question is not whether one may use a certain

---

beide mogelijk is." *Dienst der Prediking* (1955), pp. 109f. = *Dienst der Kerk,* pp. 105f. Cf. *OB,* XXII (1944), 3036.

162 *Ibid.,* p. 110. Cf. *OB,* XXII, 3036.

163 *Van den Dienst,* p. 159. Cf. p. 167: "Het is juist zoo, dat dit 'exemplarisch element' alleen heilshistorisch... kan worden gevonden."

164 "Een bepaalde trek uit een historische episode verkrijgt juist haar rechte en zuivere beteekenis door het geen oogenblik los te maken uit die historie, door het geen oogenblik apart, zelfstandig te nemen, maar steeds in zijn historisch verband te zien." *Ibid.*

165 *Dienst der Prediking,* p. 74.

166 *Ibid.,* p. 254. E.g., "Elke geschiedenis... heeft niet slechts een plaats in de historia revelationis maar komt ook met een applicatie tot ons."

167 When one observes the seemingly limitless arbitrariness to which this opens the door in preaching, one may well wonder in how far it is still possible to speak of a *method* here.

168 "Dubbelzinnig." *GTT,* LI (1951), 4.

episode as an example, but the *way* in which one may do this,"[169] or, still stronger: "We don't forget that these things are written as examples for us;[170] on the contrary, that is our starting point which enables us to show *why* these things are examples."[171] At first sight these statements don't seem to fit the exclusive redemptive-historical scheme. But here the question of semantics enters the picture. The quotation marks Van 't Veer places around "exemplarisch element" in appropriating the term[172] should warn us that he uses it in a different sense than his opponents. As appears from the context he means by this "the practical character of the sermon," the applicatory character of the text.[173] The same goes for Holwerda: the context shows that he means by his use of the word "example" that "a particular history is meaningful for us," that it has "practical significance."[174] In addition, both Holwerda and Van 't Veer use the word "voorbeeld" (example) in a more technical sense, the redemptive-historical sense of *tupos*, namely as "vóórbeelding," pre-figuration.[175] Accordingly, far from signifying a concession to the exemplary side and, thus, a toning down of the dilemma, the redemptive-historical use of "example" indicates rather a concentration of the dilemma in this one word which can be filled with either redemptive-historical or exemplary content.[176] The exclusiveness is retained even in appropriating the opposition's favored word. Instead of a denial of the charge of exclusivism, one finds violent opposition to any kind of synthesis.

So the two sides stand over against each other on the validity of an exemplary element — a narrow point (and, as we shall see, by no means the only one) with broad implications. For it involves differing conceptions of the nature of historical texts and hence differences in methods of interpretation and preaching. Given the presuppositions on both sides, there is no way out of this dilemma: one must choose one horn or the other; there is no third possibility. Only a modification of these presuppositions would open the way to another choice.

---

169 *Begonnen*, p. 94.

170 "Tot voorbeelden voor ons" — an allusion to the *tupoi* of I Cor. 10 : 6 and 11, which the K.J.V. translates as "examples" and "ensamples," the R.S.V. as "warnings" and "as a warning."

171 *GM*, XVIII (1940), 27, quoted in *Begonnen*, p. 82. Cf. (1939) *Een Levende Hoop*, IV, 5f.

172 This seems to have escaped Huyser's notice (*GTT*, L, 4). See above, II, n. 163.

173 See *Van den Dienst*, pp. 158f.

174 *GM*, XVIII, 27 and 28.

175 *Begonnen*, pp. 94ff., and *Van den Dienst*, pp. 162ff.

176 Holwerda, *Ibid.*, p. 94: "... 'voorbeelden'... in de heilshistorische dan wel in de exemplarische zin van het woord." Cf. p. 96: "De heilshistorische methode handhaaft dus volledig de betekenis van het voorbeeld, maar dan in de bepaalde zin, die dit woord in de Schrift heeft."

THE FADE-OUT OF THE CONTROVERSY

We speak of the fade-out of the controversy rather than its end inasmuch as the latter might suggest an abrupt end, the issues resolved, a peace treaty signed. Such was not the case: no consensus was ever reached, and even to this day the issues at stake keep cropping up here and there. Still, we *can* speak of the fading of the controversy: the zeal subsided, the interest waned. The fade-out set in around 1940, reaching a low point after 1944. From then on articles further clarifying the positions appeared sporadically from either camp but drew no reaction from the other. Huyser's apologia for the exemplary approach (1949-1951) received no reply. The element of dialogue was lacking to such an extent that one can hardly speak of a continuation of the controversy. Some reasons that suggest themselves for the rather sudden fade-out of a controversy carried on with so much fervor only a few years earlier are: World War II, the doctrinal differences and secession, the retreat of the redemptive-historical approach, and the altered theological climate.

World War II

In May, 1940 the German armies invaded Holland and occupied it till 1945. The disruptive influence of this occupation on the normal pattern of life was hardly conducive to carrying on the controversy. Schilder, for example, was arrested on August 22, 1940 for his anti-Nazi polemics, and in the same week the publication of *De Reformatie*, the major voice for the redemptive-historical approach, was forbidden. Schilder was released again on December 6 of that year, but others were not so fortunate. In view of the increasing suffering, it is hardly surprising that the interest in a theoretical debate waned as the War progressed.

Doctrinal Differences and Secession

By general agreement, the war was hardly a suitable time to resolve doctrinal differences either.[177] But the issues taken up by Synod in 1936 were not resolved by the next Synod (commencing in 1939) before the War set in, and a speedy solution seemed advisable to restore peace at least in the churches. The unanimous acceptance of the pronouncements of this Synod on the six

---

177 See, e.g., the "bezwaarschrift" of Dooyeweerd and Vollenhoven in Veenhof, *Om de Unica*, pp. 219–232, *passim*, and Grosheide, *Leerverschillen* (1941), p. 61: "We moeten erkennen, dat het thans geen tijd is om rustig Synode te houden en over leer-geschillen te handelen."

doctrinal issues in 1942[178] seemed to reach the desired goal. But dissent soon raised its head again, and in the measure that these grievances[179] became the focal point of discussion after 1942, the homiletical controversy receded into the background.

In 1943 Bavinck wrote of the ascendency of "factionalism" which, he predicted, "in the long run can become fatal."[180] It did not take long. On March 23, 1944, Schilder was suspended, on August 3 excommunicated, and on August 11, 1944, the fatal schism in the Gereformeerde Kerken became a reality with the "Acte van Vrijmaking of Wederkeer."[181]

This ecclesiastical secession spelled a severe blow for the new movement as a whole. In 1944 Schilder resigned from the Association for Calvinistic Philosophy because of his "disappointment"[182] that Dooyeweerd and Vollenhoven, though they had supported him against Synod in various ways,[183] refused to leave the Gereformeerde Kerken. In 1946 a membership meeting was arranged to discuss the differences of opinion within the Association regarding the Secession.[184] At this gathering, Holwerda's notion of church-sovereignty[185] clashed with the Association's notion of sphere-sovereignty. In itself this need not have led to any resignations, but Holwerda insisted that a break in the church implies a break everywhere.[186] The result was that Holwerda and several others resigned from the Association.

Ecclesiastically, meanwhile, the redemptive-historical and exemplary camps

---

178 To be found in *Acta 1939*, Art. 682. (The discrepancy in dates is the result of the extension of Synod of 1939 till 1943).

179 See, e.g., the "Verklaring van Gevoelen" of 1943. Reprinted in Veenhof, *Om de Unica*, pp. 441–446.

180 *De Toekomst*, pp. 17ff.

181 Hence the name "Vrijgemaakten" (literally, the Liberated). Both churches claimed the name "Gereformeerde Kerken in Nederland." For the sake of convenience we shall designate the "Vrijgemaakten" as the Geref. Kerken (31) — a common designation in which the "31" has reference to Article 31 of the Church Order (Dordtsche) to which Schilder appealed to repudiate the decisions of Synod. In contrast, the other side was called a "synodocratie" and received the appellation "Geref. Kerken (Synodaal)" — an epithet for which we have no need.

182 G. Puchinger in *Perspectief* (Kampen: Kok, 1961), p. 62.

183 See Veenhof, *Om de Unica*, pp. 219–232.

184 Holwerda spoke for one side (published in *Ref*, XXI [Sept. 28, 1946], No. 51; XXII [Oct. 5 and 12, 1946], Nos. 1 and 2), Van Teylingen for the other (summarized in *Correspondentie-Bladen*, XII [April, 1947], 28–31). See the latter also for the emotional discussion following these speeches (pp. 31–67).

185 Not to use Van Teylingen's stronger, "kerkelijk absolutisme." *CB*, XII, 28. Holwerda stated, e.g.: "Ik... wil met hand en tand die bevoegdheid der kerk [een bindend oordeel uit te spreken over de voorwetenschappelijke grondslagen o.a. van de wijsbegeerte] vasthouden en verdedigen." *Ref*, XXII (Oct. 5, 1946), No. 1.

186 In the discussion Holwerda said, e.g.: "De leden der vereeniging werpen in de *kerk* ons uit als staande buiten het Koninkrijk Gods. Daarmee werpen ze ons uit *alle* verbanden uit." And later, "Is de band in de kerk kapot, dan overal." *CB*, XII, pp. 40 and 65.

had become two churches. We are not suggesting that the breach ran neatly along the line of demarcation between these two camps, and yet, we are faced with the fact that Holwerda, Schilder, Van Dijk, and Veenhof (Van 't Veer died in 1944) ended up in the Gereformeerde Kerken (31),[187] while Bavinck, Dijk, Douma, Huyser, Schelhaas, and Streefkerk remained in the Gereformeerde Kerken.[188] If a meaningful dialogue had been difficult before the secession, after the secession it became a virtual impossibility.

Retreat of the Redemptive-Historical Approach

The secession also meant that other issues became preponderant: the front had changed. Furthermore, when Greijdanus, a close associate of Schilder, advocated in his hermeneutics of 1946 that one must not neglect the examples in Scripture,[189] the conviction of the legitimacy of the exclusive redemptive-historical approach must have received a severe blow.

A greater blow was yet to come when Schilder himself, after the secession, introduced an exemplary element in his meditations. Berkouwer called attention to the fact that Schilder "detected in the O.T. the distinct contours of a 'synodocratic'[190] community and of a group which liberates itself from the bunglers behind the gilded temple doors...."[191] Berkouwer correctly observed that, "in this manner, one can appeal to Malachi's call for revolt and speak of bunglers behind the gilded temple doors in *every* schism."[192] But Huyser gets carried away when he declares that the exemplary method has now been swallowed hook, line, and sinker,[193] and his call for an "amende honorable"[194]

187 On "31," see above, II, n. 181. For a partial description of this black chapter in the history of the Geref. Kerken, see Van Tongeren, *Bewaard Bevel* (1962), pp. 156–194.

188 On Sept. 8, 1967, the Geref. Kerken from their side confessed that they themselves "in het geheel van de schuldige broedertwist... niet vrijuit gaan," and asked for forgiveness of "al wat in die conflictsituatie en met name in haar tuchtmaatregelen in haar houding en optreden niet was naar de Geest van Christus en niet beantwoordde aan de katholiciteit van de kerk." *Acta 1967/68*, Art. 130.

189 He speaks among other things of the goal of the O.T. as "het geven van bemoediging en voorbeelden van standvastigheid of volharding." *Schriftbeginselen ter Schriftverklaring*, p. 86. Cf. p. 119: "Er ligt waarschuwing in aan een ieder, om toch zóó niet te doen en te spreken, als die daar vermelde zondaren." More broadly, see the rule given on p. 30, worked out on p. 31 that, e.g., in Gen. 12 : 1 ("Go from your country....") there is also a "Godsgedachte" for us, "n.l. van losmaking van alle banden aan zondige wereld en omgeving, en eventueel zelfs van verwijdering of vertrek."

190 See above, II, n. 181.

191 The latter alludes to a meditation on Mal. 1 : 10. Berkouwer mentions several other meditations (not all on historical texts). *Geref. Weekblad*, II (Feb. 28, 1947), 273. Again about "'exemplarische' meditaties," *Ibid.*, III (Feb. 6, 1948), 250.

192 *Ibid.*

193 The figure of speech had to be changed from, "dat juist van die zijde... thans

is preposterous. For Huyser should have seen, in the first place, that Schilder did not introduce an exemplary element of an individualistic, subjectivistic type, and this, after all, was the major bone of contention. Nevertheless, it is true that Schilder introduced an exemplary element: the historical interpretation does not receive its due; the uniqueness is passed by. With the secession uppermost in their minds, it is understandable that Scripture tended to be read in the light of that event.[195] This is no justification, however: methodologically, Schilder reopened the door to exemplary preaching of whatever kind. But — and this Huyser should have seen in the second place — it is precisely this *neglect* of the historical interpretation that Berkouwer called the "*decay* in exegesis."[196] "In this way," he wrote, "one loses completely the benefit of the debate about exemplarism, and exegesis ends up in a swamp."[197]

Schilder's inconsistency underscores the difficulty of practicing the redemptive-historical approach consistently. This difficulty was recognized right from the start. There was no long tradition which would lend support — as Schilder put it in 1933: "We must put the plow in virgin soil";[198] or Van Dijk later: "As yet there has been but little produced in this direction."[199] That mistakes were and would be made was readily admitted.[200] But neither the difficulties nor the mistakes were (nor need they be) conceived of as detracting from the value of the redemptive-historical approach itself. On the other hand, both the difficulties of and lapses from this approach may well be reasons for its retreat. Retreat, however, does not mean defeat: Holwerda, for one, continued to defend the redemptive-historical approach to his dying day; in 1961 Trimp still rejected any synthesis,[201] and today its implications for exegesis are still being worked out in the Gereformeerde Kerken (31).[202]

met grote vrijmoedigheid in exegese en Schriftmeditatie de 'exemplarische' vlag mèt wimpel wordt uitgestoken." *GTT*, XLIX (1949), 244.

194   *Ibid.*, p. 245.

195   For the change in Holwerda's post-secession meditations and sermons, see, e.g., *De Wijsheid*, pp. 128f.; *Populair*, p. 173; *Een Levende Hoop*, II, 12, 14f., 55f., 61, 79, 119, 127.

196   The title of the article, "Verval der Exegese." *Geref. Weekblad*, II, 273.

197   *Ibid.*: "Zoo gaat het voordeel van het debat over het exemplarisme volledig verloren en geraakt de exegese in het slop." Huyser has seen it, he even quotes it, but somehow he misses the point.

198   *Ref*, XIV, 27. Cf. *Ref*, XI (1931), 365.

199   *Van den Dienst* (1944), p. 190.

200   *Ibid.* Cf. *PE*, VI (1941), 287; and Holwerda, *Begonnen*, p. 80, and p. 112: "... ook wie naar deze methode werkt is van gevaren omringd. Dat ligt niet aan de methode, maar aan onze zwakheid."

201   *Petah-Ja*, XV (June, 1961), p. 86. Not so pronounced is H. J. Schilder's position in *Rachels Troost* (1960), e.g., p. 13: "Over voorbeelden, exempelen, valt te praten: laat dat in elk geval opnieuw worden bezien (en maar niet te vlot bijbelpersonen als 'voorbeeld' behandelen!). Maar het kwaad zit in het exempla*risme*."

202   E.g., *De Geschiedenis der Godsopenbaring* in Hoofdlijnen Beschreven, eds. I. de Wolff and G. Van Dooren (3 vols. completed; 1947-1955).

We might surmise other reasons for the fade-out of the controversy, such as the difficulty in precisely locating the dilemma (see above), the sense of futility and frustration, and a general weariness of quarrels. But with respect to the Gereformeerde Kerken there is particularly one reason that stands out: the changed theological climate.[203]

At the risk of oversimplifying matters, we might describe the change as the breakdown of "the isolation of the Reformed view of Scripture."[204] It is really broader than this: there is a change in mentality, which is reflected, e.g., in the general lack of interest today in the doctrinal differences which loomed so large only 25 years ago. Nevertheless, the heart of the matter is the view of Scripture. Not without merit is Runia's designation of the change as a switch from a "deductive approach," which reasons from the inspiration and infallibility of Scripture to the parts, to an "inductive approach," which begins with the parts and may or may not end with the inspiration and infallibility of Scripture.[205] It would be fairer, however, to see the contrast not so much between deductive and inductive[206] as between the deductive approach[207] and today's approach which, recognizing Scripture's own claim of inspiration, sets out to study the parts to determine the meaning, the content of this claim. In this endeavor the historical text is again central in the investigations — differently, however, than in the thirties. What was assumed then is investigated now, namely, the historical accuracy, better, the historical nature of historical texts.[208] This is such a decisive change that it prevents a return to the controversy of the thirties on the latter's terms.

This shift to "a new way of approaching Scripture"[209] has not come about without tension: not everyone has kept pace with the change, and the resulting

---

203   To mention just two books on the subject: G. Puchinger, *Is de Gereformeerde Wereld Veranderd?* (1966); and Van Teylingen, *Tussentijdse Balans* van het Heroriëntatieprocess in de Gereformeerde Kerken (1964).

204   See above, II, nn. 72, 73.

205   " 'New' Views of Scripture," *Torch and Trumpet*, XVII (Oct. 8, 1967), p. 11. See also his *Karl Barth's Doctrine of Holy Scripture* (1962), pp. 111ff., however, where Runia criticizes both Warfield's "deductive method" and James Orr's "inductive method." Cf. *CRC Report*, pp. 41ff. (*Agenda 1961*, pp. 158ff.).

206   Cf. Koole, *Verhaal en Feit* [1966], p. 42, about "Schriftonderzoek" and "zelfgetuigenis der Schrift": "In ieder geval kan het één niet aan het ander opgeofferd worden."

207   What Berkouwer today might call "aprioristische beslissingen." *Heilige Schrift*, II (1967), 244.

208   "Mét de literaire genres is het vraagstuk van de *aard* der historiciteit meegekomen, en men kan zonder overdrijving zeggen dat hier thans het zwaartepunt van alle theologische discussies is gelegen." Hartvelt, *Over Schrift en Inspiratie* (1967), p. 61.

209   "Een nieuwe wijze van omgang met de Schrift." *Ibid.*, p. 11.

dissent has given rise to a great deal of discussion.[210] One could speak of a new controversy — new because the question "exemplary or redemptive-historical" lies beyond its scope. And yet the newer controversy, like the older before it, is primarily concerned with historical texts. Add to this the fact that exemplary preaching seems to be on the increase again, and there is every reason to reconsider today the findings of the earlier controversy. And, vice versa, the results of today's investigations may aid us in breaking out of the dilemma: *either* exemplary preaching (including the synthesis) *or* redemptive-historical preaching.

* * *

This concludes our historical survey of the exemplary — redemptive-historical controversy. In the next two chapters we shall treat this controversy topically and in greater detail. Chapter III deals with the exemplary approach, Chapter IV with the redemptive-historical approach. For the sake of unity in the presentation we have taken the liberty of viewing both from the redemptive-historical standpoint,[211] being at great pains, meanwhile, to avoid straw men from being set up and knocked down and to hear out the exemplary side as well by allowing its supporters ample opportunity to defend themselves and to attack the redemptive-historical method. These two chapters have been constructed in parallel fashion to bring the differing opinions on each issue into better focus and to facilitate grasping the pros and cons of any one particular issue.[212]

210   And even the formation of "De Vereniging van Verontrusten in de Geref. Kerken in Nederland."
211   To take one's stance on the exemplary side is not very suitable because it lacks a well-defined method and its compromising attitude would not bring the issues sharply into focus. To take the stance of a neutral observer, even if possible, would be analogous to giving a running commentary on several ping-pong matches simultaneously. That leaves the stance on the redemptive-historical side, which is quite suitable to enter and get involved in the controversy because it continually takes the initiative.
212   See Table of Contents, pp. x, xi.

Chapter III   *Objections to the Exemplary Approach*

The objections to the exemplary approach range far and wide. We shall attempt to bring some order into the many and varied objections by arranging them under different headings. It will be understood that what is offered in this chapter is not a complete description of the exemplary approach, if for no other reason than that the polemics focus our attention particularly on the weaknesses. Nor should we think that every objection raised is applicable in the same degree to every person in the exemplary camp. On the other hand, it will become clear that these objections do not merely concern some excesses in Reformed preaching, but that they hit the main stream of Reformed homiletics at many crucial points.[1] It is the traditional way of preaching that comes under scrutiny here, and as such, these objections should be a stimulus to critical self-reflection for every preacher of the Word.

OBJECTIONS TO THE EXEMPLARY VIEW OF SCRIPTURE

The Primacy of Scripture as Source of Illustrations

Because of the ambiguity of the word "voorbeeld," which, as the word "example," can mean either a model to be imitated or an illustration to elucidate, the impression may be given that in attacking exemplary preaching, the proponents of the redemptive-historical method were in effect attacking the use of illustrations (examples) in the sermon. This, however, is not the case. Both sides would agree with Huyser that illustrations are useful in the sermon in that they gain attention, clarify, convince, stimulate, and aid recollection.[2]

---

1 To make this clear and to show the exemplary approach in proper perspective we shall frequently refer to Hoekstra who, though himself not actively involved in the controversy (he died Jan. 20, 1936), carried the Reformed homiletical tradition forward into the 1930's.

2 *Het Exempel*, pp. 211ff. Because J. G. Woelderink in his review of this book, *Hom*, XII (1952), 12, leaves the impression that the controversy was about illustra-

Nevertheless, the first sign of disagreement appears at this rather superficial level, namely, as soon as one asks which of the various sources of illustration material has the priority. Huyser states as a matter of course: "Naturally, Holy Scripture has the primacy."[3] But is this really so self-evident? Why should the stories in Scripture hold a prerogative position for purposes of illustration? Huyser can appeal to Hoekstra,[4] Calvin,[5] and even Paul: "Everything recorded in Scripture about persons and other matters is indisputable truth, profitable for teaching, for reproof, for correction, and for training in righteousness."[6] But does Paul teach the primacy of Scripture as *source for illustrations*? Or do Hoekstra and Calvin, even if they should teach this kind of primacy, have the final word? This issue, the primacy of Scripture as source for illustrations, never gave rise to a direct confrontation, but we should observe that Holwerda, e.g., takes quite a different tack.

In 1939 Holwerda wrote an article, "Bijbelse Voorbeelden,"[7] for those engaged to be married. He wished to show the couples what the character of Christian marriage is, and for this he used examples of marriages mentioned in the Bible. At a later date Holwerda would probably have made his presentation somewhat differently,[8] but already at this stage he writes: "Naturally, it would also have been possible to illustrate everything with examples from church history."[9] And in 1942 he says concerning sermons: "We don't deny, of course, that one may illustrate a certain 'truth' with a biblical story," but again, "as long as one is looking for illustrations he need not limit himself to Bible stories;[10] he can in certain instances also elucidate by taking illustrations from church history...."[11]

Opinions do not differ, therefore, on the questions of whether illustrations in general may be used in the sermon, or whether illustrations may be taken from redemptive history, but on the question of the *primacy* of the biblical narratives over, say, church history as a source of illustrations. The difference

tions, we stress that the controversy had nothing to do with illustrations as such. Schilder's attack on the homiletical use of anthropomorphic illustrations of God ("Anthropomorphe Prediking," *Bij Dichters* [1927], pp. 392-411) has no *direct* bearing on the present controversy. See Chapter V.

3 *Ibid.*, p. 177.

4 In his *Homiletiek* (1926), p. 342, Hoekstra says that it is "aanbevelenswaardig de personen, die tot exempla dienen, te kiezen uit de H. Schrift."

5 "Erkennende de juistheid van de classieke stelregel, dat de geschiedenis in het algemeen een *magistra vitae* is, slaat Calvijn toch de paedagogische waarde der bijbelse geschiedenis veel hoger aan dan die der profane.... Zij is de exempelbron bij uitnemendheid...." Huyser, *GTT*, L (1950), 209.

6 *Het Exempel*, p. 177, with a partial quotation of II Tim. 3 : 16.

7 See *De Betekenis*, pp. 23-65.

8 E.g., p. 40, but cf. pp. 53ff. for a different emphasis.

9 *Ibid.*, p. 23.

10 N.B.: Huyser does not say this either; we are still discussing "het primaat."

11 *Begonnen*, p. 88.

may hardly seem worth mentioning except that the seemingly innocent state-ment of the primacy is part and parcel of the exemplary approach. For behind this primacy view lies not the (legitimate) pedagogic consideration that these stories are better known (or the concern that they become better known), but a certain view of the historical texts of Scripture which holds that one of the specific purposes for which these stories have been recorded is to exemplify certain "truths": a dogmatic "truth" which must be believed, or an ethical "truth" which must be lived. Holwerda, on the other hand, feels that exemplification is not the specific purpose of historical texts, though these texts may be used for this just as well as church history and other sources may be. "But," and this is the point, "once one has taken a historical text as preaching-text, he must take that text in accord with its own nature and no longer as illustration."[12] The controversy centers, therefore, on *the historical text as preaching-text*.[13]

The Persons in the Historical Preaching-Text as Examples

The point at issue boils down to this: May the preaching-text itself be used as an illustration? More precisely formulated, may the persons mentioned in the preaching-text be set forth in the sermon as good examples to be imitated or warning examples to be shunned? Appealing to, among others, Hoekstra[14] and Grosheide,[15] the proponents of the exemplary approach would answer the question in the affirmative. What this answer entails we might make clear by referring to some sermons of the thirties: a sermon on I Sam.20 sets forth the friendship between David and Jonathan as the ideal friendship to which Christians today must attain; another on I Sam.1 sets forth Hanna's praying for a child as the example we must follow in our every need; essen-tially the same message is presented on the basis of II Kings 4 because the widow asking Elisha to help her is also answered miraculously by God; the fleeing Hagar becomes a picture of all sinners; we see ourselves por-trayed in Lot; Jacob's struggle at Peniel becomes our spiritual struggle; we

---

12 *Ibid.*

13 Huyser seems to forget this when he speaks of the "principiële noodzake-lijkheid" to preach "exemplarisch" on II Peter 2 : 6, Rom. 9 : 10-13, and James 5 : 17-18. *GTT*, L, 213. Even though these texts mention occurrences from redemptive history, they are not "historical texts." See further below, pp. 113–119. Overduin also misses the point when he speaks of "Christus als Borg én Voorbeeld" as supposedly representing the redemptive-historical *and* exemplary which are combined in I Peter 2 : 21-25. *Opdracht*, XXXIX (1964), 24.

14 See *Homiletiek* (1926), e.g., pp. 334, 342, 348f., 357.

15 *Hermeneutiek* (1929), e.g., pp. 193f.

flee from God as Jonah did; the Bartimaeus in us should cry out, "Jesus, Son of David, have mercy on me."[16]

If it be objected that these are excesses of the thirties which no one would care to defend, we must remember not only that these examples are taken from actual sermons preached but also that Huyser in 1951 defends similar examples. Among others, he mentions and endorses the examples of the sick woman (Luke 8 : 44), the blind men (Matt. 9 : 27-31), and Pilate (Matt. 27 : 24): as the woman reached to touch the border of Jesus' garment, so we must touch the Savior, if only the border of his garment; as the blind men called for the Lord's help in faith, so we must call for his help in faith and he will heal our spiritual blindness; Pilate, on the other hand, is a warning example: as Pilate washed his hands in innocence, so our "Pilate-natures" often deny our guilt.[17]

Over against this exemplary use of the historical preaching-text, the re-demptive-historical side claims that this is not only an illegitimate use of the preaching-text but also a degradation of redemptive history to the level of "profane" history. Van Dijk remarks: "This preaching method degrades sacred history and places it on a par with profane history.... Appealing to the normative pronouncements of Scripture, I could as well preach on the death of Prince William I in this exemplary manner as I could on, e.g., the death of Jacob; I could as well hold up Napoleon as a deterrent example as, e.g., Nebuchadnezzar because in both cases the normativity must be carried in from elsewhere."[18] This is a telling argument against the Reformed exempla-ry preachers who, less consistent than some of their English colleagues, would oppose Burrell's view "that the death of a great man [of our time] may... be made a profitable theme for homiletic treatment."[19]

We shall have occasion later to come back to this norm which in exemplary preaching must be placed in judgment over the text in order to determine whether the person concerned is a good or bad example. The point we want to note at this introductory stage is that as late as 1951 Huyser, as one result of his upholding the special character of redemptive history over "profane" history, gives Scripture "the primacy" as source of illustrations, while his opponents reject the primacy at this level. To this Van Dijk adds that, as a matter of fact, the exemplary approach degrades redemptive history to "pro-

16 These and more examples from sermons of the thirties were collected by Van 't Veer, *Van den Dienst*, pp. 140-145.

17 *GTT*, LI, pp. 7 and 9. See pp. 5-9 for additional examples with references to the particular sermons.

18 *PE*, VI (1941), 295.

19 *The Sermon* (1913), p. 97. Similarly in French, A. Vinet, *Homiletiek*, tr. E. Moll (1875), pp. 74ff. and in German, with qualifications, A. Eckert, *Die Ge-meindepredigt der Gegenwart* (1914), pp. 134ff. For the opposition to Burrell's notion that "the use of the text is purely conventional," see, e.g., Hoekstra, *Homiletiek*, pp. 226f.

fane" history. Both sides wish to honor the *sola Scriptura*; both sides desire to uphold the special character of redemptive history, but they go about it in quite different ways. Even at this stage it is evident that the controversy concerns not merely some practical aspect of preaching, but that it is rooted in a different view of Scripture, particularly of its historical sections. This, in turn, gives rise to a different hermeneutical and homiletical approach to the historical texts in Scripture.

OBJECTIONS TO THE EXEMPLARY METHOD OF INTERPRETING HISTORICAL TEXTS

Because of the synthesis discussed previously and the freedom in the exemplary approach, it is difficult to speak of one particular exemplary method, let alone analyze the hermeneutic principles by which it is guided. We do gain some solid ground, however, when we recall Grosheide's "rules for historical texts," namely, to see the text first as part of the whole, and secondly to take the text in and by itself.[20] Grosheide may plead for the unity of this approach,[21] but he cannot help speaking of "two procedures"[22] because he perpetuates a basic dualism in his hermeneutical approach. This dualism is eagerly embraced by the exemplary side:[23] to see the historical text as part of the one redemptive history is fine, but it is essential to view it also in and by itself, especially if one wants a relevant application. It is against this second way of treating the text that the objections are raised. We shall present these objections under three headings according to the scheme provided by Holwerda: illustrative, fragmentary, and atomistic.[24]

The Illustrative Interpretation

In objecting to the illustrative interpretation, Holwerda raises the question of the nature and purpose of historical texts. "Everyone knows," he says, "that every genre of literature has its own rule of interpretation: a historical report is different from a section of the prophets or epistles; a psalm has still other characteristics, and wisdom literature, in turn, bears its own unique

---

20 See above, p. 45; for the "synthesis," above, pp. 43ff.
21 *Hermeneutiek*, p. 194: " ... het tweede is de verbijzondering van het eerste. Het ééne mag dan ook niet van het andere worden losgemaakt."
22 "Twee handelwijzen," *Ibid.*
23 See above, II, n. 148 and nn. 136-142.
24 See above, p. 47. Note that Holwerda introduces these terms not as scientifically exact replacements of "exemplary" but as a condensation of his objections. *Begonnen*, p. 88.

stamp."[25] Each of these genres, thus, has its own specific rules of interpretation.[26] To determine the specific rules for a historical text, one must know its distinctive nature. And this is, in Grosheide's words, that it "describes facts, events": "The distinguishing mark of history is that it relates what once happened."[27] From this (at that time) common basis Holwerda proceeds: "The object then is to treat a historical text as a *fact* of history and not as, e.g., a parable. Whoever thinks it possible that God let a certain history be recorded in order to give 'teaching in pictorial form,' loses sight of the difference between a parable and a piece of history."[28] The phrase "teaching in pictorial form" refers to Schelhaas who had written: "It is very well possible that the Lord did not have a certain history recorded in order to illuminate his progressing revelation, but in order to picture the human response to his words and deeds, or ... to present teaching in pictorial form and in concrete reality."[29] Holwerda feels, however, that to allow for the illustrative purpose of a historical text is to overlook its uniqueness, namely its factual character. For if a historical text serves to "illustrate and depict concretely a certain 'truth,' then the factual character of such an event is not overly important since that illustration can equally well be given in a parable or allegory."[30]

Given the presuppositions of all concerned, Holwerda has a point. In, e.g., Bavinck's *Mensen Rondom Jezus* of 1936, one is hard put to find any difference in approach to a parable and a historical text except for the acknowledgement with a parable that "the man in our text has never lived." But just as with historical texts, "there are numerous people in the world much like this man, and for that reason an attentive contemplation of his conduct is worthwhile."[31] Huyser, too, does not deny that an exemplary sermon on a historical text might be essentially the same as a sermon on a parable.[32] For the exemplary side it is not a question of "either-or," however, but of "both-and." To the present day Schelhaas maintains the factuality of all

25 *Ibid.*, p. 87.
26 Cf. Grosheide, *Hermeneutiek*, pp. 192-215 for the rules for "historische stoffen," "betoogende stoffen," "profetische stoffen," and "gelijkenissen." Even Hoekstra, striving for an all-inclusive "indeeling der stoffen" is forced to discuss separately "stoffen van bizonderen vorm," among which "de historische stoffen." *Homiletiek*, pp. 352–377.
27 *Ibid.*, pp. 192 and 193.
28 *Begonnen*, p. 87.
29 (1939) *GTT*, XLII (1941), 126f.
30 *Historia* (1954), I, 21. Cf. Schilder, *Ref*, XI (1931), 381: "Onze 'leering' komt zo toch ook eigenlijk los van het objectieve feit te staan; die objectiviteit was enkel maar memoriepost."
31 P. 98. Cf. pp. 142f. On historical texts see, e.g., p. 93: "De man, van wie ons dit vers ... vertelt, is een man, zoals wij ze als het ware dagelijks rondom ons zien ...." Further, the introduction, p. 5, and pp. 19, 97, 127, 155, 166f.
32 See below, p. 133.

historical texts: "It goes without saying that every genre of literature must be taken and interpreted in accordance with its own character. A fable is no historical narrative, a historical narrative no fable."[33] But Holwerda feels that it is precisely the exemplary approach which, in practice, neglects this factuality — partially or completely. With relentless logic he argues: "Whoever interprets historical texts in an exemplary manner need no longer be concerned about their historicity. He has, without knowing it, gone over to the camp of the enemy" — the enemy being men like Driver who deduce their "moral and spiritual lessons" from the biblical narratives "whether they are strictly historical or not."[34] If, however, the conviction of the factuality of the biblical narratives is to function fully in the hermeneutical approach to historical texts, then the illustrative interpretation must be avoided. For in preaching, justice must be done to the nature and specific purpose of the preaching-text. If the text is historical, it will call for a historical method of interpretation which accounts for its historical (factual) character at every step of the interpretive process.

The Fragmentary Interpretation

While the objection to the illustrative interpretation is that the factuality of the historical text does not function (sufficiently) in the hermeneutical approach, the objection to the fragmentary interpretation is that it shatters redemptive history into many fragments: the unity of the one redemptive history is broken up into many (his)stories by treating the text in and by itself. As early as 1930 Schilder attacked those in whose view "the Bible is not a unity in which one continuous, progressive history of God's special revelation is recorded. They dissolve Holy Scripture into a series of spiritual, edifying fragments. The one Word of God is shattered into many words about God, and the one work of God is dissected into many separate works which are related somehow to God and religion."[35]

Again, for the exemplary side it is not a question of "either-or," but of "both-and." In the words of Bavinck: "I may read the historical books as a unity, but I may also break them apart; I may read them as one continuous

33 Schelhaas' minority report to Synod 1967 in defense of Assen, 1926. *Bijlagen Acta 1967/68* (bijlage 48a), p. 261. = *De Val van Assen*, p. 78.

34 *Historia*, I, 21. For the full quotation from Driver, see above, p. 15. See, e.g., the poor case Grosheide makes for retaining the historicity of Gen. 20 after interpreting it as a warning against lying. *Het Belang van de Historiciteit der Bijbelsche Verhalen* (1926), pp. 8ff.

35 *Christus in Zijn Lijden*, I, 29 (E, p. 39). Runner calls this "biblicism, viz. the effort not so much to live in the light of the one Word of God as integral directing Principle of our lives as to imitate specific situations or apply particular texts *directly*, i.e. lifted out of the Word taken as a whole." *CP 1962*, p. 156.

history, but I may also read them as a collection of histories (plural) — histories in which various persons are pictured for us."[36] Somehow Bavinck still tries to hold together these two ways of reading the text: "While it is true that one may never lose sight of its connection with the entire Scripture, nevertheless, it is not illicit to focus one's attention separately on one part of the totality." The consequence of this is that historical texts are approached with the question: "What is God telling us in all these stories about those divers individuals?"[37] Thus the end result is a separation of the two ways of reading Scripture, with the major, if not total, emphasis falling on the second, fragmentary way.[38] Bavinck is quite in line here with the fathers, who, as Douma expresses it, "knew very well that redemptive history is a unified structure with Christ at its center, but this did not inhibit them from treating separately certain persons described in Scripture...."[39] Van 't Veer replies, however: "The knowledge that this history is a unified structure should have kept them from this [fragmentary] approach. For the realization of that unity must so fill us with respect for the unity of the building that we no longer treat one small subdivision as an independent entity."[40] Holwerda is like-minded: "If one does not see the historical text as a member of the larger unit, if one does not observe the organic connection but views things fragmentarily, it is impossible to arrive at a sound interpretation and, hence, impossible to present a good sermon."[41]

The Atomistic Interpretation

The atomistic interpretation is to be distinguished from the fragmentary interpretation. Whereas "fragmentary" refers to the isolation of the text (event, person) from the totality of Scripture (redemptive history), "atomistic" refers to the isolation of certain "atoms" *within* the text from the inner coherence, the central thrust of the *text*. Holwerda claims that the result of an atomistic treatment is one of two things: "Either all kinds of practical remarks are tacked onto the several parts of the text with the result that the sermon, because the main thought was not caught, does not exhibit any unity and the hearers complain that it sticks together like sand — either that, or the sermon centers around one particular 'atom' which has been abstracted from the totality of the text."[42] More often than not such an "atom" is a part

36 *De Bijbel: Het Boek der Ontmoetingen* (1942), p. 55.
37 *Ibid.*, p. 56: "Wat zegt God ons in al die verhalen over al die menschen-levens?"
38 See the references to *Mensen Rondom Jezus*, above, III, n. 31.
39 *Heraut*, 1941, No. 3292.
40 *GM*, XIX (1941), 66.
41 *Begonnen*, p. 91.
42 *Ibid.*, p. 92.

of a person, a part of his character, a part of his experience, a part of his conduct. Huyser's "exemplary element" represents just such an "atom." When he says: "Adam's flight from God, Abraham's white lie, Lot's worldliness, Jacob's slyness and deceit, Moses' hot-temper and impatience, ... and numerous other things are character traits which are found again in contemporary Christianity,"[43] he has isolated certain "atoms" from the texts. Should any of these "atoms" be treated independently in the sermon, the result would be atomism — making absolute that which is a dependent part — and a loss of the central thrust of the text. Should one, for the sake of a unified sermon, place *one* "atom" central, the central thrust is displaced by that which is not central.[44] In either case the meaning of the text will be distorted.

Moreover, sermons tend to become monotonous because the uniqueness of each and every text is not caught. Interpreted atomistically, Holwerda says, "one can preach the same sermon on, e.g., Matthew 11 : 1-6 (the doubt of John the Baptist) and John 20 : 24-29 (the doubt of Thomas): 'Jesus Delivers from Doubt.'" One can apply Genesis 22 (Abraham's faith tested) in the same way as Matthew 15 : 21ff. (the Canaanite woman's faith tested). "But in this way the uniqueness of these texts is not preached."[45] As a matter of fact, the exemplary approach cannot possibly do justice to the uniqueness of the text because it seeks an analogy between the person(s) in the text and people today. "That analogy is subsequently found between John the Baptist/Thomas and us in the doubting, between Abraham/the Canaanite woman and us in the testing of faith. But because no one can ever doubt in exactly the same way as Thomas did, because no one can be tried in his faith exactly as Abraham was, the uniqueness of their doubt and testing must of necessity be disregarded."[46] In other words, the "atom" (doubt, testing) is lifted out of its textual (historic) environment into another realm where, though still called "doubt" or "testing," it has lost its unique connections and therefore its special meaning. Thus generalized, the application to people today is readily made. But in so doing, "justice is not done to the text,"[47] and that, certainly, should be the first concern of the minister of the Word.

Unfortunately, the defense of the exemplary approach at the hermeneutic level consisted almost entirely of, "the fathers did it this way," and "the preachers in the Bible interpreted redemptive history in this way" (the latter will be discussed later). This lack of defense points up the shortcomings of the exemplary approach as a hermeneutic *method*, and that, in turn, is bound to have its repercussions in preaching.

---

43   *Het Exempel*, p. 178.

44   Thus Holwerda's critique of Aalders: "Hij neemt een bijkomstigheid als het centrale, en groepeert daar de rest omheen." *Historia*, I, 22.

45   *Begonnen*, p. 92.

46   *Ibid.*, p. 93.

47   *Ibid.*, p. 92.

OBJECTIONS TO THE EXEMPLARY PREACHING OF HISTORICAL TEXTS

The objections to exemplary preaching range over a broad area. In this section we confine ourselves to the objections in the area of hermeneutics-homiletics: objections having to do with the way in which the *text* is treated in the sermon. Roughly analogous to the fragmentary and atomistic interpretations, two main subjects come to our attention: (1) biographical preaching, and (2) the historical equation mark.

Biographical Preaching

Holwerda characterizes the exemplary approach as that method which "dissolves biblical history into various independent histories." "The exemplary preacher," he says, "finds in the Bible the biographies of Abraham, of David, of Elijah — biographies which are analogous to our biographies and therefore full of instruction."[48] In the English-speaking world sermons constructed according to this method have been named "biographical sermons."[49] Burrell recommends this kind of preaching as follows:

> There is an inexhaustible supply of material [for biographical sermons] in the Scriptures. The worthies whose memories are there embalmed were intended to serve for our profit and admonition. Abraham and David, John, Peter, Paul and the Marys have passed in pretty constant review before the churches; but there are multitudes of less familiar names. And it is singular how the nobodies of Scripture repay the preacher for unearthing and the congregation for listening to their story.[50]

The first objection raised against this biographical preaching is that it is anthropocentric.

Anthropocentric Preaching

In 1918 Hoekstra wrote a booklet in which he names as one of the criticisms on sermons of that time that they were not Christocentric.[51] He then gave in a nutshell what was to become one of the major issues in the later controversy: "Our preaching may not be preaching of Peter or Mary but

48   *GM*, XVIII (1940), 27.
49   Cf. Burrell, *The Sermon*, pp. 95ff., and more recently, e.g., Perry, pp. 106ff., and Koller, pp. 25ff.
50   *Ibid.*, p. 97.
51   *De Tegenwoordige Critiek op onze Preeken*, pp. 14ff.

must be preaching of Christ."[52] Hoekstra tries to work this out later in his *Homiletiek*,[53] but his presentation is so ambiguous that those who are subsequently charged with anthropocentric preaching are able to appeal to Hoekstra himself. For, although he says that "one may never forget that Christ must be central and that the ministry of the Word may never degenerate into a character analysis of Mary, Thomas, or Peter,"[54] at the same time he recommends for "the warm summer months...a series of texts grouped around a personage in the history of revelation." "A look at the heights and the depths in the lives of the Bible saints is stimulating for the faith life of God's children."[55] Hoekstra is but continuing in the line of the fathers,[56] and the same may be said for all those defending the exemplary approach. We should emphasize at the outset that there can be no doubt that all desire to preach Christocentric sermons.[57] Nevertheless, the objection to these exemplary, biographical sermons is that they are in essence *anthropocentric.*

In their striving for Christocentric sermons the exemplary preachers are hampered by the dualism we noticed earlier. Bavinck recognizes that Moses has meaning only in his own particular place in redemptive history,[58] and yet he writes: "Nevertheless, I may also break that same Moses out of those historic connections for a moment; I may view him in and by himself."[59] "I disregard for a moment all those relations in which he stands; I view him alone and reflect on the language emanating from his life....I see but one man...in whom sin wells and bubbles but in whom grace is also powerfully at work."[60] To call this "anthropocentric" without qualification is too simplistic, however. In the concept "grace" Bavinck retains the connection with God, and he wants to view the lives of these men only from the perspective of their relation to the Word of God that came to them.[61] Perhaps we might

---

52 *Ibid.*, p. 16. Interestingly, in the same year, Grosheide wrote a booklet in which he called for "Christocentric" exegesis because in preaching "wordt er nog zooveel ... gedraaid en geknoeid." *De Eenheid der N.T. Godsopenbaring* (1918), p. 33.

53 *Homiletiek* (1926), e.g., pp. 164ff., 172ff., 221f., 291f.

54 *Ibid.*, p. 264.

55 *Ibid.*, p. 268. See also, e.g., pp. 296, 308, 359.

56 On Calvin, see, e.g., Nixon's *John Calvin, Expository Preacher*, p. 84: "Let us contemplate, then, in the person of Peter, that it is very necessary that God strengthen us each minute of time." Peter's three falls are "a dreadful example," p. 85.

57 As is recognized by Van 't Veer: "Hier is ons gemeenschappelijk uitgangspunt.... In Oud en Nieuw Testament hebben wij Gods openbaring in Christus Jezus. En daarom *moet elke* preek christologisch zijn." *Van den Dienst*, p. 137.

58 "Alleen op dat moment heeft zijn leven zin." *De Bijbel*, p. 53.

59 *Ibid.*

60 *Ibid.*, p. 54.

61 "Het levensgedrag van al die menschen wordt ons altijd beschreven in verhouding tot het Woord; die verhouding is het wezenlijke geweest in hun aller bestaan." *Ibid.*, p. 57. Cf. p. 66.

circumscribe the difference between, e.g., Holwerda and Bavinck in this way: whereas Holwerda's approach centers on God in his relation to man at a certain stage of redemptive history, Bavinck's fragmentary, biographic approach centers on man in his relation to God. But however we delineate the difference, "anthropocentric," as here used, should not be conceived of as completely divorced from God.

The problem we confront here in the ideal of Christocentric preaching of historical texts is clearly put into words by Schelhaas: "Although it is true that the text is above all about God's revelation and his work in and through Christ, yet certain specific men appear in the text and surely they too may, yes they must...be pictured and portrayed. The text is most certainly also about them."[62] Dijk admonishes: "Let the preacher present neither Simeon nor Mary nor the rich young man as the main character around whom everything turns; let him preach Christ!"[63] At the same time Dijk does not want to forget the "exemplary element,"[64] and he ends up by suggesting at least one anthropocentric theme: "Peter's Believing Perplexity about Jesus."[65]

The dualism in the exemplary approach is clearly expressed by Huyser. Say that one preaches on David being pursued by Saul or Absalom: "After a description of the historical situation a line can first be drawn to the believers today...— that is the 'exemplary' line; next a connecting line can be drawn to Christ, the Son of David, in whom all anguish and suffering for the sake of righteousness reaches a climax — that is the Christological line...."[66] We notice that Huyser wants a sermon which is both Christological and relevant. These two aims need not necessarily lead to dualism, but they do in Huyser because he searches, in this instance, for the relevance *outside* the Christological: he searches for the relevance in the exemplary, in the analogy between the man in the text and the man in the pew. But in this way the result, far from being Christocentric, can at best be Christological *and* anthropological, at worst, anthropocentric. While exemplary theory may call for Christological, even Christocentric sermons, the sermons it inspires are all too often anthropocentric[67] — anthropocentric in the sense that Moses, David, Peter, or Mary becomes central.

---

62 *GTT*, XLII (1941), 127f.

63 *Dienst der Prediking*, p. 254. Cf. (1937) *Dienst der Kerk*, p. 111: "... niet anthropocentrisch de mens, de zondige of de vrome mens prediken maar theologisch-christocentrisch God geopenbaard in Jezus Christus."

64 *Ibid.*: "Het exemplarische element [mag] niet worden vergeten."

65 *Ibid.*, p. 260. Similarly in preaching on Acts: "daarbij mag niet Paulus, maar moet Jezus Christus in het middelpunt staan" (p. 275), followed by the suggested "theme": "Agrippa en Paulus en... een Christen te zijn" (p. 280). Cf. pp. 161-163.

66 *GTT*, LI, 17.

67 Cf. Van 't Veer's analysis of Reformed sermons. *Van den Dienst*, pp. 140ff.

In contrast to this anthropocentric, biographic preaching detected in the Gereformeerde Kerken, Holwerda first called the approach he represented "the Christocentric method."[68] He fully recognized that the exemplary side also aimed at Christocentric sermons but maintained that somehow they missed the mark.[69] "They can say many true and fine things about what God in the coming Christ was for Abraham and then make a parallel with what God in Christ Incarnate is for us. But unintentionally and unnoticed they have switched from the *historia salutis* to the *ordo salutis*. The question is no longer: What meaning, what task, did Abraham, Elijah, etc. have for God's one, ever advancing work in Christ, but the reverse: What meaning does God in Christ have for those men. Though it is not intended, in fact the Christ*ian* takes center stage here."[70]

Schilder's trilogy of 1930 is meant as an alternative to this anthropocentric, biographic approach. "In our opinion it is a requirement of the first order that on the road which Christ travels as the Man of Sorrows, not one single subsidiary figure may dominate our thoughts because Christ is always the only one around whom, from whom, and to whom everything moves."[71] The polemical note is present all through this work: whoever would preach Christ and not Peter "must take his starting-point in Christ."[72] "It doesn't matter whether we can fathom Pilate, but whether we can see Christ."[73] "It is not Mary's maternal grief but the passion of her Son, of God's Son, her Lord, which is proclaimed.... The moment we put Mary and her grief at the center of our thinking, we have insulted the Son, and with that, fortunately, also Mary herself."[74] At one point Schilder goes so far as to call upon the Heidelberg Catechism (L. D. XXXV) that God "will not have his people taught by dumb images but by the living preaching of his Word." This statement in the Catechism was first of all directed against the images in Roman Catholic churches, but, says Schilder, "it would be the height of arrogance if we were to claim that the basic fault... in Christian thinking which designed all these images remained entirely outside the confines of Protestantism. On the contrary, also the Protestant spirit, even the orthodox spirit, has never completely emancipated itself from this characteristically human tendency towards visual, pictorial representation."[75] The Protestant

---

68 *GM*, XVIII (1940), p. 27. For some unmentioned reason Van 't Veer, *Van den Dienst*, p. 138, preferred "christologisch." For the switch to "heilshistorische methode" see below, IV, n. 80.

69 "Daar is heel wat prediking, die oprecht bedoelt 'christocentrisch' te zijn, en het toch niet is." *Begonnen*, p. 90.

70 *Ibid.*

71 *Christus in Zijn Lijden*, I, 157 (E, p. 163).

72 *Ibid.*, II, 183 (E, p. 198).

73 *Ibid.*, p. 328 (E, p. 342).

74 *Ibid.*, III, 323 (E, p. 340).

75 *Ibid.*, p. 24 (E, p. 37).

church which cast the images out the front door takes them in again via the back door through which the preacher enters. The sculpture of stone is replaced by a sculpture of words — and Christ is dishonored.

Scripture Optional

Biographical preaching also misjudges the historical text and therewith dishonors Scripture. For the fragmentary interpretation extracts the Bible "saint" from the total context of redemptive history and is thus left with a man. That same man, say Abraham, will also be found in the Koran, the Talmud, the Book of Mormon, the writings of the Church Fathers. "Now if the overall context," Schilders asks, "if the connection of that person in the one history does not concern me, why don't I take the text from the Koran, the Book of Mormon, etc.?"[76] Why pretend to preach from the Bible when the Koran serves the purpose equally well?

Naturally, all Reformed preachers want to preach from the Bible; they would never agree that contemporary man may be "a profitable theme for homiletic treatment."[77] But what prevents them? "When one preaches about Samson, David, or Thomas and treats of their spiritual struggles,... he makes use of the (in that case) completely accidental fact that these men happen to appear in the Bible.... In their personal spiritual life these men are similar to thousands of others whose names... are not mentioned in the Bible. What possible reason could there now be to preach about David or Samson and not about those anonymous people, not about people in my neighborhood, a man in the Koran or in the latest novel?"[78]

By asking these questions Schilder wants to drive home the point that biographic preaching has in effect left the Reformed starting point and has no real defense against liberal theology. This is true even where the connection with Christ is made. One could preach about Thomas' doubt, Thomas who is found by Christ and brought to believe. "But Christ does that even today. That means that one has only looked for an *illustration* for the general topic of the ongoing work of the good Shepherd. The same illustration, however, could equally well have been chosen from apocryphal, 'profane,' or contemporary history.... In principle there is then no difference in method from the liberal preacher who (frankly exposing his method) announces a series of sermons on Faust-motifs: e.g., Doubt."[79]

76 *Ref*, XI (1931), 374.
77 See above, III, n. 19. Huyser says: "De Goethe-, Schiller-, Wagner-, Shake-spearepreken, die men in het buitenland heeft aangedurfd, verwerpen wij als homiletische *extravagantie*." *GTT*, L, 217, with references.
78 Schilder, *Ref*, XI, p. 374.
79 *Ibid*.

The *sola Scriptura,* so ardently confessed in theory, barely functions in the practice of exemplary preaching: one hardly needs the Bible for exemplary sermons. Ironically, the exemplary preacher, earnestly toiling to portray the man in the text in his personal struggles, therewith the better to draw a line to the man in the pew, could, methodologically, have saved himself the trouble and sketched merely the man in the pew, for, motivated by the search for analogy (relevance), he loses precisely that distinctiveness which occasioned the appearance in the Bible of the man in the text.

We shall hear more on this in the next complex of objections which are raised against the way exemplary preaching seeks relevance in the analogy, in the parallel between the man in the text and the man in the pew.

The Historical Equation Mark

Huyser states forthright: "The specific distinguishing mark of the exemplary method is that it desires to draw a parallel between then and now."[80] Holwerda does not deny that a relevant sermon will have to draw a parallel at some point ("Whoever makes an application draws a parallel between then and now."), but at the same time he warns against various illegitimate parallels.[81] That is why he, for one, would object to Huyser's statement: "The characters of the biblical persons, however far separated from us by the ages, are mirrors for us. In them every Christian can see himself more or less clearly reflected.... This is concrete pictorial instruction accessible also to the uneducated and children."[82] We need not repeat the previously mentioned objections to a statement such as this, but now we must add the objection: when this conviction becomes a principle for interpreting historical texts, it is bound to short-circuit that interpretation by overlooking the historical discontinuity between the person(s) then and people today, by placing an equation mark between past and present so that "then" = "now."[83] The reality of the historical gap is undeniable, however, and this may not be concealed for the sake of a relevant application. The people in the text live at a different stage of redemptive history than we do today. To neglect this in preaching is to slight the nature of the historical text which records events of the *past.* This is true not only for the O. T. (where the problem seems to be concentrated for Lutherans) but equally so for the N.T.

We can elucidate concretely the difference between an exemplary sermon, which places a historical equation mark, and the redemptive-historical approach, which wants to account for the historical discontinuity. A sermon of

80 *GTT,* L, 218.
81 *Begonnen,* pp. 112f.
82 *Het Exempel,* p. 178.
83 Holwerda, *Begonnen,* p. 85.

the thirties on the wedding in Cana contains the following application: As the bridal couple invites Jesus to the wedding, so we must invite Jesus into our house daily; and as Jesus makes the water into wine, so he will make our ordinary water into delicious wine.[84] Holwerda, on the other hand, takes the progress in redemptive history into account in addressing engaged couples on the same text: "It is impossible for you to invite Jesus as they did because He is no longer on earth as to his human nature. Therefore He will never be the guest at your table as He was at theirs. He is not here; He is risen. Moreover, you are not allowed to invite Jesus as they did, for at that time they only knew him as Jesus, the son of the carpenter from Nazareth.... But He has been preached to you as the Christ." And the "application" far from being a historical equation, "then" = "now," is rather a contrast, "then" is *not* "now": "You are richer by far."[85] If the redemptive-historical side thus accounts for the historical gap separating us from the people in the N. T., how much the more will this be accentuated when they deal with people mentioned in the O. T.

Whether the text is from the O.T. or the N.T., exemplary preachers employ a historical equation mark in one way or another. This does not mean that they propose an indiscriminate imitation of the examples given by the persons in Scripture.[86] This is already evident from the category "warning examples." And even the good examples cannot be copied indiscriminately. Douma refers to Calvin's observation that we "end up in an immense labyrinth of lamentation" if we do not use discretion in following the good examples, and he goes on to show from church history what great tragedies the simple copying of examples can lead to, such as the Anabaptist Munster tragedy and the action of the iconoclasts.[87]

How then are we to judge if and in how far an example given in Scripture is normative for us today? Douma, following Calvin, answers: "We must first apply the criterion of God's Word to their deeds, for even the best children of God can stumble. And only that deed which answers to the requirement of God's Word can be an example worthy of our imitation."[88] But this hardly solves the problem. Van Dijk correctly observes: "Someone's conduct may have been good in a certain specific situation, whereas every attempt to imitate that conduct in general would most certainly be wrong."[89] Take, e.g., Samuel hewing Agag to pieces, Samson committing suicide, Jere-

84 A sermon mentioned by Van 't Veer, *Van den Dienst*, p. 145.
85 *De Betekenis*, p. 55.
86 At least in theory; as to the practice of preaching Van 't Veer seems t have a different opinion. *GM*, XIX (1941), 81.
87 *Heraut*, 1941, No. 3296. Cf. Huyser, *GTT*, L, 210f., on Calvin's rejection of imitation of offerings (as practiced in the Roman Catholic Church), of dancing before the ark like David, of possessing like David more than one wife.
88 *Ibid.*, No. 3297.
89 *PE*, VI (1941), 279.

miah preaching treason[90] — every one of these deeds is a good deed in the sense that it "answers to the requirement of God's Word" at that time. But which preacher today would recommend that his congregation follow these good examples? Which preacher would recommend that the poor deposit their last pennies in the collection plate (Luke 21 : 2), that Christians have all their possessions "in common" (Acts 2 : 44f.), that all must have an eye-blinding conversion experience (Acts 9 : 3ff.), that women must be veiled when praying (I Cor. 11 : 6)?

One feels instinctively that "the requirement of God's Word" must somehow be taken in a more general sense than the requirement of God's Word at that particular time. Huyser expresses this when he writes: "For a correct treatment of the deductive example it is required that one keep in touch with the religious-ethical norms of Scripture and their restricted or more general validity."[91] Concretely, this means for Huyser that, although the poor widow of Luke 21 and the early Christians of Acts 2 "are examples of liberal giving and of devotion to the Lord and to each other, this must not be stretched to the point that we would be required to imitate these examples literally."[92] Dijk warns similarly against "exemplary equation marks": "In a sermon on Saul's conversion, the application should not be that we, too, must have an identical experience, but rather that Christ smashes the most stubborn hearts and that we, too, by nature are such enemies of Him."[93]

Whether this switch from the specific to the general does not blunt the text and whether these general "religious-ethical norms" may be imposed on the preaching-text we must save for later in our discussion. The point we want to note at this time is that we are confronted here with one of the major hermeneutical-homiletical problems facing the preacher: How does one bridge the historical gap?[94] Even those favoring exemplary preaching cannot avoid this question because, as we have seen, they do not want to

90 Dealing with this problem, Clowney mentions these examples in his *Preaching and Biblical Theology*, p. 80.

91 *GTT*, LI, 14. Cf. Hoekstra, *Homiletiek*, pp. 336f.

92 *Ibid.*, p. 15.

93 *Dienst der Prediking*, p. 276. Cf. Bavinck, *Mensen Rondom Jezus*, p. 155: "Ieder mens heeft zijn eigen aard en wij kunnen onszelf niet tot Zacheüssen maken. Maar we kunnen wel dit doen, we kunnen ons uit Gods Woord laten onderwijzen, dat bekering... onder andere ook inhoudt, dat we andere mensen worden, ook in ons dagelijks gedrag." Thus, both Saul and Zacheus become, as Schilder would put it, an illustration for the doctrine of conversion, or, in Holwerda's words, a switch is made from the *history* of salvation to the *order* of salvation.

94 The same question is asked by Müller, *Die Lewende Woord*, p. 152: "Hoe word die 'garstige breite Grabe' (Lessing) tussen die tyd en die situasie van die teks en die tyd van die hoorder oorbrug? Waar lê die gelykblywende kontinuum, die bemiddelende instansie, die hermeneutiese prinsiep wat die teks en die hoorder verbind?" See here for further literature.

be *strict* imitators of the persons in Scripture.[95] They simply *cannot* be strict imitators[96] because the *reality* of the historical gap impinges upon their starting point that the persons in the text are examples and mirrors for us today: the force of history cracks the exemplary mirror. That is where the tension arises in exemplary preaching. On the one hand, a historical equation mark is employed: "the deeds of people in the past are transported into our time";[97] they are our examples. On the other hand, the historical discontinuity intrudes on this ideal scheme: the persons in the text do not fit our situation exactly; we cannot literally do the same things they did. The only way out of the ensuing difficulties is to delimit, to restrict the exemplary use of the person in the text: not the total person, not all his deeds, but a few particulars in him are exemplary for us. The impinging historical gap thus moderates the exemplary preacher to drawing but a few parallels, we could say, to transporting but a few "atoms" into our time. This can be done in a variety of ways. In the controversy we meet with psychologizing, spiritualizing, and moralizing.

Psychologizing

Psychologizing is closely related to what was called "psychological exegesis." To counteract those who consider psychological exegesis the end all and be all of exegesis and who "see in Scripture only pious and important people who can be our example," Grosheide links psychological exegesis very closely to grammatical and historical exegesis.[98] Hoekstra similarly subsumes psychological exegesis under "homiletical exegesis,"[99] thus indicating that it is but a component of the interpretative process. The danger is, of course, that in the practice of preaching, psychological exegesis will begin to lead an independent life. Consider the challenge: "The minister must try to fathom the motivations and character of the persons involved; he must penetrate

95 See also Douma's quotations of Calvin's rejection of "dwaze imitatie." *Heraut*, 1941, No. 3296.

96 Even Bavinck, who in his book *De Bijbel* proceeds as far as anyone on the road of the historical equation, of identity ("Wij moeten ons als het ware met hen *vereenzelvigen* .... Wij zelf worden er beschreven."), must admit, "De menschen over wie het gaat, staan ... op een ander niveau dan wij" (p. 66). But in this book at least the identity wins out. The major distinction is: "Zij hebben het Woord rechtstreeks ontvangen, wij ontvangen het door hen heen" (p. 66), "maar als mensch waren ze mij gelijk" (p. 67). "Alles is anders geworden. En toch, in diepste wezen is alles gelijk gebleven" (p. 71).

97 Van 't Veer, *Van den Dienst*, p. 141.

98 *Hermeneutiek* (1929), p. 174. Cf. p. 168.

99 "De homiletische exegese maakt naast de grammaticale ook gebruik van de historische en psychologische exegese," and also "pneumatische en theologische exegese." *GTT*, XXXII (1932), 509 and 510.

through the external actions to the psychical processes taking place beneath the facts."[100]

Both Grosheide and Hoekstra caution against the inadequacies of psychological exegesis,[101] and both sides in the controversy seem to have been aware of its pitfalls. Bavinck admits that other explanations than those he proposes may be possible, that a subjective element enters in,[102] though he does not go as far as Van 't Veer and Holwerda who speak of "fantasy."[103] Huyser agrees that the givens of Scripture are not sufficient "to enable us to construct a complete psychological picture of the persons appearing in redemptive history," but, he says, "that is not the point at issue."[104] Perhaps not, but it is significant that as early as 1931 Schilder called attention to the fact that "the preaching of historical texts often reveals the tendency to present the results of psychology by describing various 'soul conditions,' to picture types of godliness, to present illustrations for the well-known 'doctrine of salvation.' " He spoke further of the preaching custom, the habit, "which seemingly justifies this desire to make of church and revelation history a history of souls."[105] Apparently the subsidiary nature of psychological exegesis often tends to assume a rather independent function in practice.[106]

In his own practical exposition Schilder is continually on guard against psychologizing, that is to say, against the emphasis on and independent functioning of psychological exegesis: "When we speak of Christ, there is no room for a psychological treatise on Judas and his remorse"; we must "turn from the *psychology* of Caiaphas and Pilate and turn (convert) to the *theology* of Christ."[107] We notice again the Christocentric – anthropocentric polemic.

---

100 *Ibid.*, p. 510. Cf. *Homiletiek*, p. 357: "Nauwkeurige kennis is noodig van de speciale psychologie .... Deze kennis wordt gebruikt om de in de heilige historie optredende personen te beschrijven in hun ziellijk beweeg, de verborgen motieven bloot te leggen die tot de daden hebben geleid, en den rijkdom van emoties te beschrijven die de personen bezielden...."

101 "De psychologische verklaring kan dus slechts met alle voorbehoud worden gegeven." *Hermeneutiek*, p. 175. "Bij de analyse van het geestelijke leven houde de prediker steeds in het oog, dat de menschelijke ziel nooit tot in haar diepste diepte te peilen is...." *Homiletiek*, p. 357.

102 "In zielsbeschrijving ligt nu eenmaal altijd iets subjectiefs...." Introduction, *Mensen Rondom Jezus*, p. 5. Cf. Popma, *De Psychologie*, p. 33.

103 "Zielkundig teekenen .... moet leiden tot phantasie, die de grenzen van gezonde en geoorloofde exegese overschrijdt." *GM*, XX (April, 1942), 1. Cf. Holwerda's evaluation of a sermon outline: "M'n collega is toch over Achan en over de stemming in het volk aan het fantasééren geslagen...." *Hom*, III (1942), 39.

104 *GTT*, LI (1951), 3.

105 *Ref*, XI, 373.

106 See, e.g., Bavinck, *Mensen Rondom Jezus*, pp. 96f.: " ... wij schrikken van de zielkundige juistheid van deze beschrijving [van Lucas]. Ja, zo zijn de mensen en zo zijn ze nog.... Om ons tegen zulk een gedrag te waarschuwen, heeft ons het evangelie deze man ten voeten uit getekend." Cf. p. 145.

107 *Christus*, II (1930), pp. 232 (E, p. 244) and 330 (E, p. 343).

"He who would preach the suffering Christ must not present psychological sketches based on Peter's denial, for then he is not preaching Christ but a subdivision of the doctrine of redemption, the stages of grace in the soul, which he illustrates with the dramatic story of Peter's denial of Christ."[108] In Dijk, on the other hand, we again meet the "both-and": "Although the men around Jesus...may not be discussed in a one-sided psychological manner, one may not dispense with a psychological analysis; in the story of Peter's denial the figure of the suffering Christ... must certainly occupy the main place, but Peter's own psychological processes may not be disregarded; it is the same Peter of Matthew 16: 16, 22; 26: 51, and of John 21: 20, and in his 'fall and rise' there are also lines which, without placing equation marks, extend to us."[109]

Let us grant Huyser that, at least in theory, the point at issue is not whether one can construct a complete psychological picture of the Bible "saints." Let us assume further that in the psychological interpretation, only biblical givens will be used, so that there is no question of "fantasy."[110] Given the difficulties and pitfalls of this procedure, given the scanty results in terms of indubitable motivations and character traits, plus the fact that one is admittedly dealing with secondary figures, the question arises *why* exemplary preachers tend to emphasize psychological exegesis. The answer to this question is already evident in Dijk's statement above, but we can give it a better perspective by quoting Hoekstra to whom an appeal is often made. Having set forth both the necessity and the limitations of psychological exegesis for historical texts, Hoekstra continues:

> Upon closer analysis of the religious utterances it becomes evident that, even though the men and women pictured in Scripture are ages removed from us,... they were nevertheless people like us — sinners who must live by grace, believers involved in the same struggle that we face. And precisely because they are on the same spiritual plane as we are, they can be examples for us to imitate.... In the psychological treatment of figures like Saul, Ahab, Herod, and Judas, we must bear in mind that they...were people with whom we are related — our psyche harbors by nature the seeds of the same wickedness.[111]

---

108 *Ibid.*, p. 183 (E, p. 198).

109 *Dienst der Prediking* (1955), p. 255. Cf. pp. 107, 127ff.

110 Cf. Dijk above, and Huyser, *GTT*, LI, 3: "Wel kan men bepaalde karaktertrekken, die de Schrift ons in het doen en laten van een of andere figuur aanwijst, psychologisch trachten te verklaren, eventueel met gebruikmaking van andere desbetreffende Schriftgegevens ...."

111 *Homiletiek*, p. 358. Note that Hoekstra wrote before the controversy came to a head (1926), that this is not his sole emphasis (cf. pp. 353-362), and that he is but carrying forward an element which had its place in Reformed preaching from Calvin onward (cf. Douma, *Heraut*, 1941, No. 3292).

In the controversy Douma similarly desires to defend the right to treat "separately (using biblical givens) certain persons described in Scripture, to picture them psychologically, to speak of their struggles and trials, their strengths and weaknesses, and then to draw parallels between the experiences of the Bible saints and the struggles of believers today."[112] In answer to our question, I don't think we are far off the mark (this, too, being a piece of psychological exegesis) when we say that the motivation for the emphasis on psychological exegesis is that it enables the preacher to make his sermon more readily relevant: it allows him greater facility in drawing certain parallels between "then" and "now." This motivation for relevance is certainly not to be scorned; but what is its cost? Does psychologizing do justice to the text?

Holwerda observes: "The warning against 'psychologizing' in preaching was...in reality opposition against a method which buried the real content of the text under an avalanche of edifying remarks."[113] Van 't Veer says: "The question is whether Scripture itself presents us a psychological description of the persons included in its historiography. If this is not the case, then I may not picture them psychologically. The historiography of Scripture must be respectfully treated according to its own method, and that is not the psychological method."[114] Elsewhere he wonders why "the exemplary element is always sought under the aspect of religious experience or in the psychical life." Since the text presents much more than a description of what happens to or in the soul of the person concerned, the exemplary method *abstracts* the psychical element from the total picture. The text may speak, e.g., of Elijah's body, his physical posture in prayer, his clothes, and many other elements; and "no one" would think of abstracting, say, the information about his clothes in order to deliver a sermon on fashion.[115] "But why, then, do some preachers feel (as we see in many sermon themes) that they *are* allowed to lift Elijah's soul and faith struggle, his quest and pains and doubt out of the total complex of ideas which together constitute this one episode in the one redemptive history, and use these elements for a discourse on 'doubt,' 'testing,' 'unbelief,' etc.?"[116]

Having isolated the Bible "saints" from the one redemptive history (the

---

112 *Heraut*, 1941, No. 3292.

113 *Begonnen*, p. 91.

114 *GM*, XX (April, 1942), 1. Cf. Schilder (1933), *Preken*, I, 478: "De Schrift is er niet, om ons de karakters en de zielsgesteldheid van *mensen* te verhalen, doch om ons te doen zien, hoe God zich heeft geopenbaard in Jezus Christus."

115 Van 't Veer's "niemand" is too strong. If Willem Teellinck in 1620 managed to present four sermons on fashion in connection with the information in Matthew 3 about John the Baptist's clothes (see Schippers, *De Gereformeerde Zede*, p. 75.), it is not entirely inconceivable that someone might preach similarly on Elijah's clothes.

116 Van 't Veer, *Van den Dienst*, pp. 159f.

fragmentary interpretation), thereby losing "the *historical* tie between David, Abraham and us," the exemplary preacher is forced to find another connection in order to make an application. At this point the "atomistic interpretation" comes to his aid and the connection is often found in "the *psychical* resemblance."[117] Promising as it may seem, this psychologizing slights redemptive history,[118] and since its "atomism" finds no warrant in the text, it must be qualified as an arbitrary and subjective choice on the part of the preacher.

Spiritualizing

Another, perhaps even more common way to solve the problem of the historical gap is by spiritualizing. This eliminates the hazardous expedition into the motivations of persons from the distant past and "the psychical processes taking place beneath the facts." By spiritualizing the events in the text it is much easier to throw a bridge across the then — now gap, thereby opening the way for instant application.

Some instances of this we have come across earlier: Jacob's physical struggle at Peniel becomes our spiritual struggle; the physical blindness of the two men in Matthew 9 becomes our spiritual blindness; the woman's reaching to touch the border of Jesus' garment becomes our spiritual reaching to touch the spiritual Jesus; and the Cana wedding invitation to the earthly Jesus becomes our invitation to the heavenly Jesus. Regarding the wedding in Cana Holwerda asks how the application can speak of (1) a life-long invitation, (2) to Jesus only, (3) in his divine nature, (4) as the Christ, since the text speaks of an invitation (1) for the wedding day only, (2) including the disciples, (3) directed to the earthly Jesus, (4) as friend. "The parallel we draw appears to be no parallel at all. And when, in spite of this, we continue to apply the text in this manner, we have disregarded the actual text, and the Word has remained closed."[119]

Other examples of spiritualizing abound. "Matthew 8:23ff. (the storm on the sea) often receives an application having to do with 'spiritual' storms on the 'sea of life'; Luke 24:29 ('Stay with us, for it is toward evening') is applied in the style of the well-known 'Abide with me'; John 21:7 ('It is the Lord!') often becomes a sermon on providence: in all puzzling experiences we must learn to see that 'it is the Lord.'"[120] It is not

117 "Veelal doet men dat zo, dat men, inplaats van de *historische verbinding* te erkennen, de eenheid zoekt in de *psychische overeenkomst.*" Holwerda, *Begonnen*, p. 89.

118 *Ibid.*, "de grote nivellering."

119 *GM*, XVIII, 36.

120 Holwerda, *Begonnen*, p. 90. Other examples of this are given by Van 't Veer, *Van den Dienst*, pp. 144f.

denied that "proper, even edifying remarks are made, but they have nothing to do with the text."[121] This procedure is sometimes dignified by the term "the deep sense," but Holwerda calls it "violation of the Word."[122]

In essence spiritualizing is nothing other than allegorizing — a method rejected by both sides. Holwerda claims: "Allegory is by no means dead,"[123] and the sermons of the thirties bear him out. For, with whatever name it is disguised, when "the historical *fact*...completely evaporates in the style of Alexandria," it is allegory.[124] We prefer to speak of spiritualizing rather than allegorizing, however, if for no other reason than that Reformed preachers generally recoil at the very thought of allegorizing. It must, further, be granted that most of the exemplary sermons which attain the parallel by spiritualizing do not completely ignore the historical facts. Rather, for the sake of application, a few elements ("atoms" again) are lifted out of the text and context, spiritualized and applied.

Often this parallel is sought in the sphere of "Jesus and the soul." Holwerda finds this "mystical spiritualizing," as he calls it, in Bavinck's exposition of Matthew 2: The long journey of the wise men "is transformed into a mystical meeting between the soul and Christ, a road without camels, without miles, without halting places...."[125] Again, what right does one have to neglect the historical, to select a few particulars, and to develop the parallel in this fashion? In spiritualizing the choice of elements and the direction the parallel will take is largely up to the preacher. As such it is subjective and can hardly be distinguished from overt allegory.[126] Moreover, since the text gives no warrant for it, spiritualizing, too, is an arbitrary way of making the text relevant for the hearers today.

Moralizing

A third objection strikes at moralizing. Van 't Veer warns that the exemplary method, consistently carried through, "'treats' us to a piece of moralism."[127] Van Dijk, too, calls attention to the fact that "exemplary treatment

---

121 *Ibid.*

122 "Verkrachting van het Woord," *GM*, XVIII (1940), 28. Schilder speaks of "wanbedrijf." *Ref*, XI (1931), 382.

123 *Begonnen*, p. 90.

124 Holwerda, *Hom*, III, 42.

125 *GM*, XVIII (1940), 36, in opposition to Bavinck's exposition in *Geschiedenis der Godsopenbaring*, II (1938), 43ff.

126 In America, Hartill also rejects allegory, but via spiritualizing (every man is lame on both feet as Mephibosheth) he arrives at a kind of allegory that would have done Philo honor. *Principles of Biblical Hermeneutics* (1947, tenth printing 1960), pp. 44ff.

127 *Cursus*, I (1943), No. ii, 4.

of historical texts easily degenerates to moralistic preaching."[128]

Huyser is well aware of this danger. In tracing the history of exemplary preaching he himself links "exemplary" with "moralistic": "The thematic and textual preaching of the Middle Ages became more and more an 'exemplary'-moralistic monstrosity."[129] And in dealing with Chrysostom's preaching he remarks: "A large drawback in this 'exemplary' preaching is that the obligation to imitate is one-sided and receives too much emphasis....The *moralistic* feature is very much to be regretted."[130] These quotations indicate that Huyser clearly sees the danger of moralizing in exemplary preaching and that he wants nothing to do with it. Nevertheless, the exemplary preaching he continues to advocate can still be labelled "moralistic" by his opponents. The suspicion arises that in their use of the word "moralistic" the two sides miss each other; and they will certainly miss us if we don't examine its meaning more closely.

As early as 1941 Huyser expressed his aversion to "moralistic preaching," but, as appears from the context, he uses the word in a different sense than is usual.[131] Huyser means by "moralism" the (semi)Pelagian tendency which denies the *sola gratia*, a tendency which he discovers, for instance, among the Remonstrants and in the rationalism of the 18th and 19th century.[132] Moralistic preaching is legalistic; it issues imperatives without the divine indicative; it makes of the gospel a moral law; it seeks to accomplish by works what can only be accomplished by grace.[133] Although this is a legitimate way of circumscribing "moralistic preaching," it is hardly likely that in a Pelagian sense it would become an issue among Reformed preachers.

There is another use of the word, however, which strikes closer home. N. Ridderbos writes: "The danger is certainly not imaginary that we preach essentially moralistic sermons on O.T. historical texts by paying undue attention to the virtues and vices, the noble or base character of the persons

---

128 *PE*, VI (1941), 287. J. W. Smit in *Ons Kerkblad* (Zeeland), April 27, 1946, speaks of "een zedepreekje."

129 "Een 'exemplarisch'-moralistisch gedrocht." *GTT*, L, 207.

130 *Ibid.*, p. 205.

131 If we can speak of a "usual sense." For various ways in which "moralism" is used see, e.g., Troost, *Casuïstiek en Situatie-Ethiek*, pp. 48, 50, 68 (115f. on "moraal"); on "ethical," e.g., Olthuis, *Facts, Values and Ethics*, pp. 197ff. Clowney's use of "ethical preaching" in distinction from "moralistic preaching" (pp. 78ff.) is a variation but no solution.

132 "Men legde een ander fundament, dan hetwelk God gelegd heeft in het kruis en de opstanding van Jezus Christus.... Zo kwam het tot moraalprediking." *De Paraenese* (1941), p. 86. Cf. *De Reformatie der Prediking* (1955), pp. 8-18, for Huyser's deep aversion of the anthropocentric and moralistic preaching in the Middle Ages.

133 *Ibid.*, respectively pp. 107, 86, 87, and 45. Apparently using the word in the same sense, Douma writes: "Calvijn heeft, evenmin als andere Gereformeerde predikers, een soort moraalprediking bedoeld ...." *Heraut*, 1942, No. 3336.

concerned."[134] This may indeed lead to a denial of the *sola gratia*, but that need not be the essential consideration for calling a sermon "moralistic." A sermon may be termed "moralistic" simply when the preacher places an undue emphasis on morals, when he doesn't consider the sermon complete unless it contains admonitions, exhortations for conduct, when, in season and out of season, imperatives form the capstone of the sermon. It is in this sense that Huyser advocates moralistic sermons. "We dare posit the thesis," he says, "that every Bible text that can be preached... contains a hidden exhortative stimulus whose sharpness the congregation must feel."[135] At one point he finds fault with a sermon of Wielenga on II Samuel 18 : 31-33 (David receiving word of the death of Absalom).[136] Huyser complains: "In vain does one anticipate a practical remark in this sermon, such as: the example of this lamenting father is a warning call to all Christian parents to take the upbringing of their children seriously as long as they have the opportunity, lest they too must cry out their despair in a similar bitter lament when the grave of their children is being dug and it is too late. One can hardly claim that such an applicatory remark is too farfetched; it is ready at hand in the text!"[137] This is a perfect example of what we call moralizing: it does not deny the *sola gratia* necessarily, but it tacks an imperative onto an element in the text — in this case the lament of David — in order to have a "practical" remark for people today. It may not be farfetched because it lies on the very surface, but it is so superficial and "cheap" that anyone who lives into the story at all must experience this "practical" remark as a foreign element which misses the point and completely disrupts the moving story.

The assumption that *every* text contains exhortations for proper behavior[138] forces the text a priori into a moral mold which may or may not suit the text. The text is approached with (among others) the question: What conduct is advocated here? But suppose it is not the intent of the text to answer that question? Historical texts are particularly stubborn on this point, but if the question is put to them anyway, the answer must somehow be deduced from the conduct of the person in the text. This is no easy matter, however, because the text frequently neither approves nor disapproves that conduct; and even where it does approve, the problem remains in how far we can imitate that conduct today (think again of Samuel hewing Agag to pieces, etc.).[139] At this point Hoekstra introduces the concept of progression in the

134 *GTT*, LVI (1956), 151.
135 "Een verborgen paraenetische prikkel," *De Paraenese*, p. 119.
136 To be found in *Menigerlei Genade*, XXIX (1939), 65-80, under the theme: "Christus' worsteling met David om de erkenning van Gods recht in Absalom's dood."
137 *GTT*, L (1950), 216.
138 Cf. Huyser's definition of "paraenese," *De Paraenese*, p. 4.
139 See Koole on the struggle of the early church with the question "in hoe-

history of revelation. We must, he says, "investigate at which level revelation was at the time in which the events took place in order to evaluate the persons and their actions from that perspective.... And only after the persons have been thus evaluated according to the right criteria can lines be drawn from the past to the present...."[140] In similar fashion Huyser wants to take into account "the difference between the old and the new dispensation and the level of revelation in the epoch concerned."[141] In itself this is indispensable for understanding the actions of persons then; at the same time it calls attention to the "shifts in normativity"[142] and the distance we today are removed from those actions. In other words, taking account of the epoch does help in understanding the past actions, but it fails, just as does direct approval in the text, to bridge the then — now gap: it only accentuates it.

Nevertheless, the "ought," supposedly hidden for us in every text, must be uncovered. But how? Huyser suggests that "for a correct treatment of a deduced example one must keep in touch with the *religious-ethical norms* of Scripture and their restricted or more general validity."[143] But this begs the question, for the problem is precisely to determine what is "restricted" and what is "more general." Hoekstra seeks the answer to this in what he calls "the analogia fidei,"[144] and Douma says simply: "Holy Scripture offers... general rules for evaluation so that we are able to know which deeds we should imitate and which we should shun."[145] It is all rather vague, but the tenor is that Scripture presents general norms which must be used to evaluate the conduct of the man in the text. And only after this has been done can the moral be applied to people today.

It is at this point that Van Dijk sets in the attack: "The major objection to the exemplary treatment of sacred history is... that on account of it preaching so easily ceases to be truly ministry of the Word because (except for a few instances in which the narrative itself relates God's approval or disapproval) the text itself does not indicate whether a certain deed is good or bad. So I must first determine how that deed should be evaluated on the basis of other, normative parts of God's Word. Having done this, however, I have

verre het gedrag van de bijbelheiligen *per se* normatief is." *De Overname*, pp. 272f., and 74f.

140   *Homiletiek*, pp. 358f.

141   *GTT*, LI (1951), 15.

142   "De verschuivingen in de normativiteit" regarding vengeance, slavery, polygamy, etc. Schippers, *De Gereformeerde Zede* (1954), pp. 24ff.

143   *GTT*, LI, 14.

144   "Door nauwkeurige exegese van den tekst en gebruikmaking van de analogia fidei moet vastgesteld, wat voor alle personen, tijden en omstandigheden, en wat slechts voor een individu op een bepaald oogenblik geldt." *Homiletiek*, p. 336. On the term *analogia fidei*, see Grosheide, *Hermeneutiek*, pp. 54ff., 247.

145   "Algemeene regelen ter beoordeeling," with an appeal to Calvin. *Heraut*, 1941, No. 3295; cf. Nos. 3296, 3297. Cf. Grosheide, *Hermeneutiek*, p. 95: "Maatstaf is hier de zedewet."

lost the right to say: 'This is what God says here; this is revealed to us in this text.' "[146] Huyser tries to refute this argument by claiming that no one is able to treat a historical text without "the aid of other, normative parts of Scripture." As evidence he points to a sermon by Van Dijk which mentions that Samson transgressed God's will by wanting to marry a non-Israelite.[147] But Van Dijk does not propose that a text should be interpreted independently of its context (this being one of the grievances against exemplary preaching), but that the selected preaching-text should be preached and not some other "truth," however scriptural. As Schilder might have put it, the historical text should not be treated as a concrete illustration of some moral "truth" found elsewhere; it has its own message.

The danger of treating the text as an illustration of some moral "truth" is inherent in the assumption that every text contains an "ought" and that this "ought" must be the capstone of the sermon. The exemplary preacher usually tries to discover this "ought" in the attitude or conduct of the person in the text, but he also realizes that he cannot present this example as normative per se. Is it a good or bad example? And if good in that epoch, is it still normative today? In answer to these questions Huyser presents the rule "that one may never detach a historical text from the religious-ethical norms of Scripture."[148] And only after the person in the text has been judged by that code can he receive a place in the sermon — either as theme or, more likely, as a sub-point.[149]

It is to this custom in exemplary preaching that Van Dijk responds: "The truth which is herewith presented to the congregation God teaches in another text and must be carried back from there into the preaching-text. But then that part of Scripture which was announced as preaching-text is in fact not preached. At best one may say that a few good, scriptural remarks were occasioned by the text, but that is, strictly speaking, no longer ministry of the Word.... For then the content of the sermon is determined not by the text itself but by the preacher's ingenuity."[150] This ingenuity may tack a moral onto David here, another onto Jacob there; the sermon will be very "practical" indeed, but also very subjective in that the choice of morals to be presented is largely

146 *PE*, VI (1941), 287.
147 *GTT*, L (1950), 214f.
148 *Ibid.*, p. 216.
149 See Huyser, *GTT*, LI, 13.
150 *PE*, VI, 279. Van Dijk continues with "een heel frappant voorbeeld daarvan" from Calvin for whom the words of Peter, "these men are not drunken" (Acts 2 : 15), become the occasion for a tirade against the sin of drunkenness. "Hier wordt zelfs niet een voorbeeld der gemeente voorgehouden; een, door een der handelende personen gesproken woord, dat daar, heel duidelijk, in een bepaald verband voorkomt, wordt eenvoudig uitgelicht en tot een kapstok gemaakt, waaraan de prediker zijn eigen gedachten ophangt."

left up to the preacher. And in the process the first and foremost question is forgotten: Is this the intent of the text?

Typologizing

Side by side with the objections to the above-mentioned parallels we find objections to the arbitrary use of the typological parallel. The objections tend to confine themselves to the Christological parallel: then – Christ.[151] This parallel is often drawn when the preacher has an O.T. text and feels obliged to refer in his sermon to the person of Christ. Not the attempt to find Christ in the O.T. but the arbitrary manner in which this is done is the subject of criticism.

A few samples of typologizing in sermons of the thirties are: Joseph's obedience in looking for his brothers is a prophetic type of Christ's obedience; his sale to the Ishmaelites prefigures Christ's being sold by Judas; his good fortune in Egypt is in its deepest sense God's blessing of Jesus who is led to Egypt; his imprisonment and subsequent crowning shows the humiliation and crowning of Christ to save his people; Jacob's wrestling at Peniel points to Christ's wrestling at Calvary; Naomi's care of Ruth becomes Christ's care for his people; Ichabod ("the glory has departed from Israel") is a type of the baby Jesus, born humbly because the glory of man has departed; the homage the women paid David is a shadow of the homage the baby Jesus received in Bethlehem, while Saul's hatred foreshadows Herod's hatred; the silence in which God comes to Elijah is fulfilled in "Silent Night"; Esther and Mordecai take turns in being types of Christ, etc.[152] Though not as forced as some of the typologizing practiced in the early church and the Middle Ages,[153] there is obviously reason for Holwerda's warning against "forcing parallels": "When one magically produces a line in every text to the cross or the incarnation, one cannot escape schematism."[154] Sometimes the forced nature of the parallel is recognized and eased by means of combining the typological with a spiritualizing and moralizing parallel. Such is the case in a sermon on the wood which Moses cast into the bitter water at Mara: the wood is not directly a type of the cross, but it does take the bitterness out of the water just as the cross takes the bitterness out of our Mara waters. We must therefore believingly cast the wood of the

---

151 In distinction from certain other types such as: sabbath – eternal rest, crossing the Red Sea – baptism, and the less technical use treated above, O.T. believer – Christian.

152 These and more samples were collected by Van 't Veer, *Van den Dienst*, pp. 142ff.

153 See, e.g., those mentioned by Van 't Veer, *Ibid.*, p. 139, and by Koole, *De Overname*, pp. 110ff.

154 *Begonnen*, p. 112.

cross into the Mara waters of our suffering and death. Thus it becomes drinkable.[155]

Van 't Veer seeks the "negative cause and explanation" for typologizing in "the fact that the Christological character of the historical text is not perceived." When one disengages a text from the totality of redemptive history, he has "robbed it of its Christological character and retains, at best, an edifying moral which contains nothing particularly Christian. Because of the overriding desire to preach Christ, one must then resort, unintentionally, to some artifice or other in order to 'make the sermon Christocentric.' The easiest way to do this is to call in the aid of typology, thus opening the way for making an almost limitless number of 'types.'"[156] "But," Van 't Veer contends, "the Christological character of a historical text is not salvaged by the discovery of a type."[157]

Typology in and by itself cannot make a sermon Christocentric. If that were the case, Schilder points out, one could preach a Christocentric sermon on Joseph from a text in the Koran or the Book of Mormon, or, for that matter, one could dispense with a text entirely and preach a Christocentric sermon on any Christian who was ever persecuted. "But when the Bible speaks of Joseph, he appears... as a certain particular believer who on the 'road' and in the framework of the one redemptive history had his unique place and significance."[158] One can hear in the objections to typologizing the fear of losing the *sola Scriptura*. One can feel the fear of losing the progressive revelation in *history*, the fear of dissolving the *lines* of history into *points* of typology (the fragmentary approach): "A series of little lights here and there is not yet a beam of light, presents no line of light, doesn't show the advent of the approaching light."[159] One can sense the fear that the historical equation mark will be introduced by means of typology: "A. becomes a type of Christ,... B. a few centuries later... ditto, and of C., more centuries later and in a different environment, the same thing holds true.... A Messianic glimmer in a dark or dusky environment seems so becoming, but we do not get to see the great evolution of the Messianic self-revelation and self-preparation of the Logos."[160]

In his opposition to typologizing Schilder even appeals to the second commandment of the decalogue to show that *making*, creating types of Christ is illegitimate: "Let Reformed preachers refrain from that practice if they really respect... this lofty and compelling prohibition of all licen-

---

155 Mentioned by Van 't Veer, *Van den Dienst*, p. 143.

156 *Ibid.*, p. 153.

157 *Ibid.*, p. 154.

158 *Ref*, XIV, 42.

159 Schilder, *Ref*, XI, 381. Cf. *Ref*, XIV, 51. In *HC*, II (1949), 310, Schilder speaks of typologizing as "knabbel-hermeneutiek."

160 *Ibid.*

tiousness in the sphere of 'making images.'"[161] Van 't Veer agrees: "We do not have the right to make and multiply 'types.' God has given them, and we must confine ourselves to the ones he has given."[162] This restriction does not nearly solve all the problems connected with typology, but it must be seen as an attempt to check the unbridled fantasy of those who insist on drawing "a line to Christ," an attempt to cut off at its roots the arbitrariness of this typologizing which is hardly distinguishable from allegorizing.[163]

*　*　*

To recapitulate the foregoing: We have seen that the underlying objection to exemplary preaching is that the unity of the one redemptive history is broken up into many (his)stories. This fragmentation severs the historical connection with Christ — subsequently forcing the preacher to discover that connection in an (unhistorical) analogy — but the person in the text has at least been salvaged from the past and can function as a positive or negative example. Biographical preaching is anthropocentric, however, and if one wants to preach on the lives of men, Scripture, in effect, is optional. Moreover, other problems loom on the horizon: the examples simply don't fit our situation today; the historical gap defies all attempts to apply them directly; apparently there is still too much historical debris clinging to the examples. The solution is found in the "atomistic interpretation": not the whole person, not all his actions, but certain "atoms" are exemplary. At this point psychologizing, spiritualizing, and moralizing enter the scene. But the selection of just these "atoms" is arbitrary and subjective. In addition, it constitutes a further "de-historization" of the text (the historical equation mark), for all these attempted parallels, including typologizing, have one thing in common: the tendency to lift that "atom" out of the stream of history into a realm of timeless structural similarity. We see this in the attempt to make a sermon Christocentric by means of typologizing (an analogy in structure),[164] and again, only extended two thousand years farther, in the

161　*Ref*, XIV (1933), 35. Cf. *College Verslagen* (1939), pp. 30f.
162　*Van den Dienst*, p. 154. Similarly Hoekstra, *Homiletiek*, pp. 297f., 359f.
163　Cf. Holwerda's rejection of the allegories presented by Vischer and Hellbardt ("dwaasheid," "willekeur"). "Maar uit eigen literatuur óók zijn tientallen voorbeelden aan te wijzen...." *Begonnen*, pp. 112f. E.g., Dijk, *Dienst der Prediking*, p. 208, accepts Samson's carrying away the gate of Gaza as a legitimate type of Christ carrying away the gate of death. In America, typology turns into allegory in, e.g., Hartill, p. 47: "Jericho is a type of the world under the curse of God. Rahab was a bad character," and as such analogous to all mankind. "The men said: 'Our life for yours.' Here is substitution as portrayed at Calvary." Cf. Hulst, *Hoe Moeten wij het O.T. Uitleggen*, pp. 111ff., to the effect "dat het streven overal in het O.T. een getuigenis van den Christus te vinden, tot allegorese leidt." See further Berkouwer, *De Persoon van Christus*, Chap. VII, pp. 87ff. (E, pp. 113ff.), and Wright, *God Who Acts*, pp. 65f.
164　Cf. Pannenberg, "Redemptive Event and History," in *Essays*, p. 327. Mis-

attempts to make the text relevant for today by means of psychologizing (the soul of man remains the same),[165] spiritualizing (timeless truths), and moralizing (a timeless ethical code).[166] In his laudable concern to bring out the relevance of the text the exemplary preacher does injustice to the text by "de-historizing" certain of its elements. This attempt to gain immediate application is a homiletical short cut resulting in a hermeneutical short circuit. "We don't see concrete situations anymore; we typologize, spiritualize,...psychologize everything, and, in spite of all our fine tirades against those evil moderns who cut the Scriptures to bits with the 'knife of criticism,' we use the selfsame knife insolently to scratch all the dates off God's messages. In the 'world' that is punishable; in science you lose your credibility; but in the church it seems to be the prerequisite for false edification."[167]

OBJECTIONS TO EXEMPLARY-SUBJECTIVE PREACHING

Another complex of objections to exemplary preaching also concerns anthropocentric preaching, but now in the sense that the man in the pew becomes a major element in the sermon. This was not altogether lacking in the preceding section, of course: it was for the sake of the man in the pew that the man in the text had to function as an example. But in this section we move further away from the hermeneutical questions to concentrate on the man in the pew and the role he plays in the preaching process.

In 1931 Schilder wrote about the sermons of that time: "It struck me that many more themes were devoted to questions of the Christian's personal life — questions concerning suffering, comfort, pains, assurance of faith, submission, certitude, constancy, strength, armor, perseverance, etc. — than to the strict proclamation of God's 'objective' work *in history*...."[168] Later, Holwerda wrote in the same vein: "People ask for 'warmth,' 'something practical.' That seems legitimate enough, but often it is nothing other than a reduction of the content of Scripture to the theme: God and the soul."[169] Bavinck takes this polemic to be a "reaction against pietism and subjectiv-

kotte, *Sensus Spiritualis*, p. 129, speaks of an evaporation "tot een tijdloos spreken," and Cullmann, *Christ and Time*, p. 133, speaks of "hidden, timeless truths" that would make the N.T. "superfluous." Schilder contends that "een bloote vergelijking...onmiddellijk den Goddelijken zin van het evangelie miskent, als men staan blijft bij de vergelijking. Gods werk gaat altijd verder...." *Christus*, I, pp. 29f. (E, p. 40).

165 "De verbinding tussen toen en nu [werd] veelszins gezocht en gelegd in de analogie van de zielsgesteldheid...." Trimp, *Petah-Ja*, XV (1961), 86.
166 "De kleurloze taal van de tijdloze moraal." *Ibid.*
167 Schilder, *Ref*, XI (1931), 382.
168 *Ref*, XI, 365.
169 *Begonnen*, p. 106.

ism": "The new spirit is averse to the 'soul,' religious experiences, the inner marks of the Christian,... all digging around within oneself...."[170] By calling this "the objectivism of the new spirit," Bavinck and others[171] seem to see the controversy as an extension of the infamous objective – subjective dilemma, which in the history of preaching continually causes the pendulum to swing from one pole to the other: from objective preaching to subjective preaching and back again.[172]

Because of the variety of connotations clinging to the terms "objective" and "subjective," it might be well first to consider their meaning. The terms as such bear the burden of a lengthy life in philosophy and theology.[173] "Objective – subjective" may indicate the contrast independent – dependent,[174] or reality – knowledge,[175] or impersonal – personal,[176] or again, passive – active, universal – individual, external – internal.[177] These various meanings are also more or less clearly reflected in homiletics when the terms "objective preaching" and "subjective preaching" are set over against each other. To make a long story short,[178] we proceed immediately to the meaning of these terms in the homiletical controversy under discussion. To give precise definitions is rather difficult because the participants in the controversy did not operate with precise definitions or identical meanings. But negatively, we can say that both sides rejected the extremes of either pole: objective preaching in the sense of a lecture in dogmatics as often associated

---

170   *De Toekomst* (1943), p. 13.

171   E.g., Dijk, *OB*, XXII (1944), 3019: "Terwijl aan de eene zijde...de schaal vaak doorslaat naar een subjectivistisch-ingestelde prediking, is aan den anderen kant de objectivistische instelling de rots waarop men strandt." Cf. Huyser, *De Ouderling* (1959), pp. 133f.

172   On this oscillation see Bakker, *Eschatologische Prediking bij Luther*, p. 39. Cf. Wingren, *Die Predigt*, p. 37, who observes: "Diese beiden Predigttypen sind oberflächlich betrachtet einander feindlich, aber in der Wurzel sind sie zusammengewachsen, und sie begünstigen einander in vortrefflicher Weise. Je subjektiver der erste Typ wird, und je mehr derselbe alles in einem frommen Seelenzustand auflöst, desto objektiver und massiver wird der andere Typ und mit desto grösserem Autoritätsanspruch reiht er Lehren aneinander, die geglaubt werden sollen...."

173   See, e.g., Berkouwer, *Heilige Schrift*, I, 61ff., and Kuitert, *De Realiteit*, pp. 156ff.

174   See Vollenhoven, *Geschiedenis der Wijsbegeerte* (Franeker: Wever, 1950), p. 236.

175   Cf. Olthuis, *Facts, Values and Ethics*, pp. 174f.

176   Interestingly, K. J. Popma, *Levensbeschouwing*, VI, 238, traces this usage of "subjective" to ancient rhetoric which, in connection with its "moralistische inslag," used a person as "subjectum" for his pedagogic value as "aanvurend en opwekkend voorbeeld." Cf. Huyser, *GTT*, XLIX, 248f., on *exempla virtutis* and literature.

177   See S. J. Popma, *De Psychologie*, p. 31, for the latter three sets.

178   See further Veenhof, *Prediking en Uitverkiezing*, pp. 167ff. for various connotations since Kuyper; see also above, pp. 33-39.

with dead orthodoxy,[179] and subjective preaching in the sense of a presentation of one's own religious experiences as often associated with Schleiermacher.[180] Between these extremes, however, there remains enough room in Reformed homiletics for the objective – subjective dilemma to maintain itself. To arrive at a working definition we might, positively, describe the two poles as follows: Objective preaching is concerned with the presentation of truths external to the hearer, dogmatic truths or redemptive facts as they occurred in history; subjective preaching, on the other hand, stresses the personal assimilation of these truths, the internal realization of redemption, the inner experience. The major contrast is, in Dijk's words, between "what happens *outside* us" and "what happens *inside* us."[181]

The exemplary preachers, then, are accused of an excessive concern with the *intra nos*. But this is not the most fundamental objection. The most basic objection against exemplary-subjective preaching, and with it against traditional Reformed homiletics, is that it fails to overcome the objective – subjective dilemma itself.

The Objective – Subjective Combination

In 1918 Hoekstra mentioned as one of the criticisms of the sermons that they were "too objective": "The objective redemptive truth is presented, but a description of the manner in which this truth is appropriated in our heart is neglected. The preacher... fails to sketch the condition of my soul; the sermon has little effect on me because I cannot discern whether my spiritual life is normal or abnormal."[182] Hoekstra's answer to this criticism was his advice that preachers should combine the two horns of the dilemma: "In the sermon the objective and the subjective element must be joined together."[183] He reiterated this solution later in his *Homiletiek*: "The preacher must not only present the redemptive truth objectively but must also see to it that this truth be subjectively appropriated by the congregation."[184]

Dijk, at a later date, is a little more wary of the terms "objective" and "subjective."[185] He suggests that "God's Word and that Word alone determines how we are to preach and whether the sermon is to deal with the

179 Cf. Hoekstra's rejection of "leerrede," *Homiletiek*, pp. 156f.
180 Cf. *ibid.*, pp. 87ff.; also Dijk, *Dienst der Prediking*, pp. 63ff. on "Mitteilung des religiösen Bewusstseins."
181 *OB*, XXII (1944), 3011.
182 *De Tegenwoordige Critiek op onze Preeken*, pp. 19f.
183 "Moeten samengaan." *Ibid.*, p. 21.
184 P. 300. See, e.g., p. 163 for the appeal to the Reformed tradition for this solution.
185 "We zijn soms zoo ellendig schematisch geworden." *OB*, XXII (1943), 2987.

objective work of Christ 'outside us' or the subjective work of the same Christ 'within us' through the Spirit."[186] "It all depends on the text!"[187] This is a worthwhile contribution, but it fails to overcome the objective – subjective dilemma. We see this clearly in Dijk's own writings. He writes, e.g.: "When the text speaks of Christ's work for us, the objective side must be brought out."[188] Obviously, the polarity remains: there is still one "side" (read: "pole") which is to be complemented in the same or another sermon by the other "side," namely, something more subjective.[189] This objective – subjective tension becomes clearer still when we focus our attention on the historical text, for here the preacher is confronted with something *extra nos*, so that "the objective side must be brought out." But the rules Dijk gives for preaching historical texts are alternately objective and subjective.[190] Dijk is caught in the dilemma just as much as Hoekstra, and like Hoekstra, he really offers no other solution than to combine the two poles in preaching historical texts.[191]

In Huyser's presentation we find the same tension, be it in a different form. Huyser certainly does not want a one-sided subjective sermon: "It is most certainly a primary requirement that the congregation be instructed in the redemptive truths." But proper edification of the congregation requires also that the sermon "evoke religious feelings"; and "the sermon is only truly effective when the faculty of the will begins to operate."[192] Faculty psychology or not, one needs both the objective and the subjective in an "effective sermon." This also holds for a sermon on a historical text. "In general it is desirable that an 'exemplary' admonition be preceded by a Christological

---

186 *Ibid.*, Dijk offers the same solution in 1952, *Dienst der Kerk*, pp. 104ff.: "Op deze vraag [objectieve, voorwerpelijke óf subjectieve, onderwerpelijke prediking] weet ik maar één antwoord: geen van beide; de Schrift moet gepredikt worden en geen dogma noch bevinding; of de prediking zich meer zal bewegen op het terrein van de ontvouwing der heilswaarheid of op dat van de voorzichtige vertolking der zielservaring hangt eenvoudig van de tekst af ....". Cf. *Dienst der Prediking* (1955), p. 119.

187 *Ibid.*, p. 3011. Cf. Schilder, *Ref*, XI (1931), 374: "Dáárvoor [preaching about "bevinding"] moeten we *andere* teksten zoeken"; and *College Verslagen* (1939), p. 23: "Willen we spreken over geloofsstrijd, laten we dan een tekst uit Paulus nemen."

188 *Ibid.*

189 Hence Dijk's concern that all of Scripture be preached, also the " 'subjectieve' stoffen." *Ibid.* Cf. *Dienst der Kerk*, p. 105: "Indien slechts het gehele Woord Gods wordt gepredikt ... komt in de prediking èn de leer des heils èn de bevinding tot haar volle recht."

190 See *Dienst der Prediking* (1955), pp. 200ff., 254f.

191 E.g., the preacher must preach "in die geschiedenis de komst van Jezus Christus" (*Ibid.*, p. 201) and "houde het historisch verhaal als een spiegel aan het kerkvolk voor" (p. 202).

192 *De Paraenese* (1941), p. 78.

proclamation [the indicative]," but the order may be reversed[193] — as long as both the objective and the subjective receive their due. Isn't this what, e.g., Moses does in Deuteronomy? "The preacher there is not merely concerned about the *objective facts*, but all the more about the *subjective teaching* which can be deduced from those facts for the present and the future."[194] Thus Huyser considers the objective – subjective combination to be the scriptural way[195] of preaching historical texts.

The redemptive-historical side, however, objects to this combination. Holwerda says: "It is true that one receives something for both the intellect and the heart in this manner; there is 'explication and application.' But this is not a sermon, for the truth is never a combination of two lies, and obedience in preaching is not attained by a combination of divergent preaching sins."[196] In similar fashion, Veenhof begins his criticism from the common conviction that neither subjective nor objective preaching by itself is correct (that is, after all, the reason for combining the two). "A subjective preacher is lame on one side, an objective preacher on the other side. But isn't then a preacher who preaches objective – subjective sermons lame on *both* sides? Is the combination of one one-sidedness with another one-sidedness ever the truth? Does the combination of two maladies ever produce health?"[197]

What with medical transplantations today, Veenhof's metaphor may be turned against him, for one would not join the lame side with a lame side but the healthy side with another healthy side. That, I believe, was the intention of the combination objective – subjective: not the extravagance of either side, but the good parts of each should be combined.

For Veenhof, however, this figure of speech is adequate because, in his opinion, neither objective nor subjective preaching has a healthy side which may profitably be joined with the healthy side of the other. There are no "good parts" in either one because both objective preaching and subjective preaching are permeated by a "fundamentally false view of Scripture." The objective preacher makes of Scripture "a theory, isolated information about God, Christ, sin, redemption, etc. This false view of Scripture cannot be corrected by any conceivable combination." The same is true for subjective preaching: "No conceivable combination can correct this sin in

---

193 *GTT*, LI (1951), 16.

194 *GTT*, L, 164. Cf. p. 167 on Psalm 78: "Ook hier is de toeleg duidelijk om niet maar de *objectieve feiten* weer te geven, doch de *subjectieve lering* ... het volk in te scherpen."

195 The appeal to Scripture will be treated in the last section of this chapter.

196 (1944) *Populair*, p. 21. Cf. Spier's criticism of I. Kievit, *Voorwerpelijke Onderwerpelijke Prediking*: Eisch der Heilige Schrift (2nd ed., 1939). Spier (1943), *Wijsbegeerte*, p. 56, writes: "Het is niet gemakkelijk in te zien, hoe de synthese van twee gevaarlijke uitersten, de harmonie tussen twee dwalingen, de waarheid kan opleveren."

197 *Bondsboekje 1940*, p. 59.

preaching. Here too it is not a combination with something else that is required but a fundamental *change* in attitude towards Scripture."[198]

It appears, then, that "objective" and "subjective" are not nearly as far apart as has often been supposed. The difference is often thought to exist in this: the objective is a matter of the head, the subjective of the heart. But is this subjective element really aimed at the heart? Is it not but another *objective* exposition, this time of the *ordo salutis*, aimed at the head? Is not this subjective element an explication of what our experience ought to be, and therefore in essence objective? "The subjective — to employ this miserable terminology — is as 'objective' as the objective."[199] "The subjective preacher really speaks about only one dogma: the order of salvation, the application of redemption,... whereas the objective preacher also 'deals' with other dogmas in his 'sermons.'"[200] "In both cases preaching is degraded to a treatment of loci, and the battle concerns the number of loci, especially if the *locus de salute* must come up for discussion in every sermon. But loci-treatment is not preaching; neither does it become preaching by a shot of 'de salute.'"[201]

Because of the underlying wrong view of Scripture and the resultant wrong view of preaching, any combination of objective and subjective as well as the whole dilemma is rejected outright.[202]

The Explication – Application Dualism

Closely related to the rejection of the objective – subjective combination is

---

198   *Ibid.*, p. 60.
199   Holwerda, *Populair*, p. 23. Cf. Schilder already in 1919: "Wie kan... loochenen, dat heel het samenstel van gemoedsleven en bevinding... weer wordt een formuleering van geijkte *dogma's* over des christens heilsweg? Hoeveel gemoedelijke menschen zijn er... voor wie al het subjectieve een objectieve theorie wordt?" *Om Woord en Kerk*, II, p. 30. Cf. *Tusschen* (1929), p. 207.
200   Veenhof, *Bondsboekje*, p. 60.
201   "Een scheut 'de salute,'" Holwerda, *Begonnen*, p. 107.
202   What was called "objective" above (including, therefore, "subjective") was philosophically attacked as "subjectivism." Vollenhoven wrote: "De probleemstelling 'subjectivisme – objectivisme' in den zin van een strijd tusschen de voorstanders van het beleven en die van het 'belijden' blijft... binnen het subjectivisme steken. Evengoed als de voorzichtige verbinding van die twee." *Correspondentie-bladen*, I (1936), No. 2, p. 8. The term "subjectivism" is introduced because "de menschelijke activiteit wordt normeerende instantie en men rust in het subject, niet in het volbrachte werk van Christus" (Popma, *De Psychologie*, p. 37). Better perhaps (we are moving to the denotations knower – reality, active – passive): "Heel die grond-onderscheiding van individu met zijn innerlijke activiteit [the (logical) subject] èn de passieve buitenwereld [the external, objective world] daartegenover is subjectivistisch, want ze neemt de wereld van eigen bewustzijn als maatstaf en principe" (Popma quoted by Veenhof, *Om de Unica*, p. 159). Cf. Spier, *Wijsbegeerte*, p. 56.

91

the rejection of the explication – application dualism. From the 17th century on, Reformed theologians had defined the sermon as *explicatio et applicatio verbi Dei*. Hoekstra, in making this traditional definition his own, concludes: "This correct view of the nature of the ministry of the Word [as explication *and* application] gives to both the objective and the subjective element its rightful place."[203] Evidently, there is a close relation for Hoekstra between objective – subjective and explication – application.[204] As a matter of fact, the prior distinction, objective – subjective, may lead directly to the explication – application dualism in preaching.[205]

When we speak of "dualism" here, we do not mean that the sermon is necessarily divided into two consecutive parts: first the explication and then the application. That may well be the case (and I imagine that the custom of liturgically dividing the sermon into two parts by congregational singing may have fostered this), but Hoekstra, though he calls this "the elementary or natural division," discourages the use of this division for each and every sermon.[206] A sermon might consist of three, four, or more parts; the application might come at the end of each major section or after every idea that is applicable — and yet that sermon can be called dualistic: not because it consists of two parts, but because it manifests a basic dualism. Hoekstra gives expression to this when he says: "However one may formally divide the parts between explication and application, materially the sermon always remains explication and application of the Word of God."[207] It is this tension between explication and application, between the Word and the congregation, that qualifies the sermon as basically dualistic. This tension is prominent in exemplary sermons where both the objective teaching and the "line to us" are of vital importance.

In spite of the long and distinguished tradition of the explication – application design, Holwerda says: "In my opinion the explication – application scheme must be rejected because it is connected with the objective – subjective dilemma, and because, unintentionally, it overlooks the nature of the Word of God and the nature of preaching."[208] As did the objective – subjective com-

203 "Komt tot zijn recht," *Homiletiek*, p. 163.

204 "Een preek zonder toepassing mist het karakter van *bediening* des Woords.... De prediker heeft niet alleen de heilswaarheid objectief voor te stellen, maar ook zich te beijveren, dat zij subjectief worde toegeëigend" (*Ibid.*, p. 300). "...op welk gebied van het geestelijk leven de objectieve tekstwaarheid hare subjectieve projectie zal vinden" (p. 303). Cf. p. 405.

205 Van Dijk found this to be the case in sermons delivered a century ago: "In de preek wordt de tafel toegedekt, worden de spijzen uitgestald [the objective explication] en dan komt altijd weer de vraag: 'Hebt gij daar nu deel aan...?' [the subjective application]." *De Preektrant*, p. 23.

206 The reasons are practical: repetition, lack of attention for the explication, one must still find a division for the explication. *Homiletiek*, p. 405. Cf. p. 417.

207 *GTT*, XXXII (1932), 506.

208 *Begonnen*, p. 108. Cf. Spier, *Cursus*, I, v, 12: "Daarom moet de preek

bination, so the dualism explication – application runs aground primarily on the conception of the Word of God. For does not this dualism arise because the Word of God is seen as an objective factor "out there," so that the preacher must *add* an application, or at least *direct* the objective factor into the appropriate subjective sphere? "Apparently the Word is viewed as a truth external to us, as a theory which must be made applicable.... It is seen as a statement, a pronouncement, not as speech, address.... In this way the nature of Holy Scripture is completely misjudged."[209]

The basic question is: What is Scripture? Is it but a passive object containing information of times-gone-by, possessing all kinds of truths which *I*, the active knower, must distill from it,[210] and which I, the preacher, must *make* applicable? Veenhof answers: "Scripture is not like that at all! It presents no truth divorced from reality, no theory, information, or doctrine which must be bent towards and applied to genuine life by preachers!"[211] With that the definition of preaching as explication *and* application falls into disgrace, and with it the exemplary sermons which constantly manifest this dualism.

The Subjective Preaching

From the rejection of the objective – subjective combination and its negative implications for the explication – application dualism, we move to the subjective pole where we find in particular an impassioned debate on "kenmerken-prediking" — the preaching of traits, distinguishing marks, by which a person may know whether or not he is in Christ. It is beyond our scope to follow the complete course of this debate since it would lead us straight into one of the doctrinal disputes: the question of self-examination ("zelfonderzoek"), which in turn is related to the conception of the covenant[212]

---

niet een combinatie zijn van een 'objectieve' uitlegging, en een 'subjectieve' toepassing." Veenhof, *Bondsboekje*, p. 58: "Wie gaat 'verklaren' en daarna 'toepassen,' loopt gevaar het karakter der Schrift aan te tasten, door eerst van haar een 'beschouwing' te *maken*, die dan, nà die verwringing, zeer zeker moet worden 'toegepast'!"

209 Holwerda, *Populair*, pp. 22f. Frör, pp. 25f., treats the same problem in Germany: "Die ursprüngliche Einheit von Geist und Wort wurde aufgelöst in ein Nacheinander von objektiv gültiger Lehrmitteilung und verselbständigter applicatio auf den Hörer." Frör considers this a post-Reformational development to rationally safeguard Scripture from all attack.

210 Cf. Popma in Veenhof, *Om de Unica*, p. 160: "Tegen dit 'objectivisme,' dat in den grond van de zaak 'subjectivistisch' is, heeft de 'nieuwe geest' zich met kracht verzet." See further, above, III, n. 202.

211 *Bondsboekje*, p. 58.

212 In the original motion at Synod these two were joined together: "het genade verbond (zelfonderzoek)." *Acta 1936*, Art. 152. Cf. *Acta 1939*, Art. 682:

and from there linked with the conception of the church, faith, and baptism.[213] But we should remove the possible misconception that the rejection of "trait preaching" involves the outright rejection of self-examination. "The necessity of self-examination is acknowledged by all," Schilder and Vollenhoven contend.[214] Even as ardent an opponent of "kenmerken-prediking" as Van Dijk says: "Continual self-examination cannot be dispensed with."[215] But "self-examination" for him does not mean a search for internal traits to determine whether one is in Christ (doubt in God's covenant promise being the point of departure here), nor does it mean a probing for marks to determine whether one's faith is genuine (this amounts to seeking a more certain foundation in marks within oneself than in the believing acceptance of God's promise).[216] "Faith is its own mark; it carries its own assurance."[217] In Van Dijk's view, true self-examination is to continually examine oneself "whether he *lives* out of that faith, whether he lives in sanctification and obedience."[218]

With this in mind, we turn specifically to "kenmerken-prediking." Van Dijk defines it as that preaching "which presents various marks of authentic spiritual life in order that the hearers may be able to determine their state: whether they do or do not partake of Christ."[219] Without any qualms Van Dijk repudiates this kind of preaching. Contrariwise, Impeta defends the proposition: "The sermon must repeatedly deal with the marks of faith and grace so that whoever lacks them be alarmed and whoever possesses them be encouraged."[220]

Restricting ourselves to that which pertains to our subject, we note first of all the connection with the objective – subjective combination. Impeta and others reject Van Dijk's position as being "one-sided" (read: "too objective") and desire instead to combine, to balance the objective and the subjective elements in preaching: "The preaching of self-examination, according to

"...dat dit zelfonderzoek ongetwijfeld in het verbond der genade zijn uitgangspunt behoort te nemen...."

213   Van Reest, at least, ties it in with "veronderstelde wedergeboorte." *Opdat Zij Allen*, I, p. 38.

214   The minority report to Synod, *Van Oorzaken*, VI, 24. Cf. p. 21: "Ten onrechte is derhalve...door sommigen aldus uitgelegd, dat zij...het zelfonderzoek *verwierpen*." The point at issue was, however, the manner in which it was carried out (cf. pp. 1ff., 18f.).

215   *Verbond en Belijdenis* (1939), p. 30. Cf. "Zelfbeproeving," *Ref*, XVI (1936), 293.

216   *Ibid.*, pp. 9ff., 23ff., 30.

217   Van Dijk, *De Preektrant*, p. 44. Cf. the quotations of Kuyper and H. Bavinck in Schilder's *HC*, II (1949), 504f.

218   *Verbond*, p. 30. Cf. *Ref*, XVI, 305.

219   *De Preektrant* (1935), p. 37. Cf. pp. 25ff. to the effect that this was "schering en inslag" a century ago.

220   "Kenmerken-prediking, in dezen zin... is nuttig en noodig." Proposition VII of *Zelfonderzoek Noodzakelijk!* (1936), p. 137.

the yardstick of the many marks of faith which Scripture offers in abundance, is the necessary reverse [of covenant preaching], the counterbalance required by the weight of the matter itself."[221]

Inasmuch as these marks are to be found primarily within the person, we are here at the "applicatory end" of our earlier discussion on psychologizing. The exemplary approach could freely search out these "marks" in the persons mentioned in a text and draw parallels to the hearers today. "One Sunday Abraham would be held up as the hero of faith, followed by the application: Do you have that faith also? ... The next Sunday we would be told that as Jacob we must know our 'Jabbok' or at least our 'Peniel'.... Then again it was the soul of Peter, of Judas, of Pilate, etc."[222] Schilder leaves no doubt regarding his aversion to this projection of mentioned or unmentioned elements in the text into the subjective sphere of the hearers. Concerning possible sermons on the healing of the lame man (Acts 3) he writes: "*Wrong*: every sermon about the man's misery, consolation, or conversion" with its subsequent application in those areas; on God's appearances to Abraham: "*Wrong*: a pious assurance of God's nearness to 'a' pilgrim, to 'a' wavering, lonely, or impatient person"; on Thomas: "*Wrong*: motifs concerning doubt or the cure, or concerning the aloofness of one who fails to attend the meetings of disciples."[223] The rejection of such preaching is not only based on the conviction that it misses the intent of historical texts and that it is anthropocentric (biographic) but also — viewing it from the side of the application — that it is anthropocentric-*subjective* preaching. There is such an excessive concern with the soul of man that it leads Janse to exclaim: "Surely the 'marks' of faith must be found in a Christian's wallet just as well as in his soul!"[224] There is such an excessive concern with the internal state of the man in the pew that the application colors the supposedly objective explication.[225] "Though it is not intended, the Christ*ian* in fact takes center stage here."[226] " 'Kenmerken-prediking' really draws man away from Christ and directs his attention to himself."[227] What is left then of the ideal of a Christocentric sermon?

221 *Ibid.*, p. 110. See p. 5 on "te eenzijdig" and "meer objectieve richting."
222 Van Reest, *Opdat Zij Allen*, I, pp. 40f.
223 *Ref*, XI (1931), 374. See here also for the proposed alternatives on these and other narratives.
224 *Lourens Ingelse* (1932), p. 55.
225 Our questions determine in a large measure the answers we receive.
226 Holwerda, *Begonnen*, p. 90. Cf. Van Dijk, *De Preektrant*, p. 24: "Heel de preek krijgt een sterk pietistische inslag, d.w.z. dat in de prediking de mensch in zijn vroomheid terugdringt God en Zijn openbaring."
227 Van Dijk, *De Preektrant*, p. 45. This is not only contrary the nature of preaching but also contrary the nature of faith. "Het ging ons er om, weer duidelijk als de grondgedachte der Reformatie te poneren, dat geloof is een vertrouwen in en op God, en niet een onderzoek, of we wel gelovig zijn. Vooral niet, wanneer men met dat onderzoek zou bedoelen het naar bínnen zien, ... want zulk een zelfonder-

Even when the text proclaims the central redemptive event of Christ's resurrection, some preachers cannot resist the subjective application: "Did Christ arise in your heart?" Very personal, very direct — but Holwerda calls it "the curse of mysticism that festers also in our circles. It imposes an entirely different problem on us than does the gospel. The gospel says: Easter is really a fact! Do you believe that? But mysticism says: That Jesus arose in Joseph's garden we believe all right, but the really important question is: Did he arise in your soul?... Decisive is the *repetition* of Easter in everyone personally."[228]

The rejection of this kind of subjective application may be symptomatic of objectivism, but such a diagnosis would be too simplistic. The view of the nature of Scripture, the sermon, redemptive history, the covenant, faith — all play a significant role in this rejection. K. J. Popma pointedly speaks of "faith-subjectivism" because the preacher, in making such a subjective application, operates with a "distinction between the truth and *my* conviction of the truth of the truth. That means that the truth of God becomes truth-for-me only when I assent thereto" or experience it.[229] Clearly, the objective – subjective dilemma is involved again. "In reality Scripture is considered to be insufficient: it is not the law of faith for us; we ourselves place that law... in our personal appropriation [or experience] which would subsequently *make* Scripture the law of faith."[230] In this way the *sola Scriptura* becomes dependent on the subjective pole and is in effect eliminated as norm.

The rejection of subjective preaching in general and "kenmerken-prediking" in particular did not proceed from a lack of concern for the spiritual well-being of the man in the pew; on the contrary, the pastoral concern is very much in evidence — on both sides, we might add. The Christian's certitude of salvation being at stake, it could hardly be otherwise. The question boils down to this: Should the Christian seek assurance in the marks of faith within himself? It is Van Dijk's conviction that the preaching of traits "can never accomplish what is expected of it: assurance for a child of God and the unmasking of hypocrites." As a matter of fact, "trait preaching" may have just the opposite effect: "The hypocrite may come to (false) assurance and

---

zoek leidt de aandacht van de hoofdzaak af, is eigenlijk in strijd met het karakter van het geloof, dat zich naar buiten richt... op God...." Vollenhoven, *Mededelingen*, Dec., 1965, p. 3.

228 (1939) *De Wijsheid die Behoudt*, p. 92. Cf. p. 176: "Hoogstens is Matth. 28 dan nog een illustratie, hoe dat feit zich in geestelijke zin bij ieder voltrekt." Van Dijk objects to this kind of applicatory question because "daardoor wordt weer elke hoorder gezet aan het begin van den weg en gebroken wordt de kracht der roepstem, die hier [John 10 : 16] de groote Herder tot Zijn kudde doet uitgaan." *De Preektrant*, p. 24.

229 *Levensbeschouwing*, VI, 241.

230 K. J. Popma, *De Vrijheid der Exegese* (1944), p. 256.

the true believer may become disquieted." "Both he who posits the traits and he who examines himself accordingly are subject to error. How in the world, then, could one ever expect to come to certitude in this way?" "The sad phenomenon of the scarcity of certitude also in our Gereformeerde Kerken is in no small measure due to the fact that these people have been taught to search for certitude where it cannot be found."[231] The answer to the problem is neither the proliferation of traits (with all the speculation involved in that[232]) nor the insistence upon preaching these traits, but "to return ever again to God's promise, to realize that promise in one's life, and to rest in that promise."[233]

The Multiple Application

In the foregoing we saw that one of the motives for "trait preaching" was to "alarm" the unbelievers in the congregation, to unmask the hypocrites, to urge them to repent, and at the same time to reassure and encourage the true believers. This motive led almost of necessity to what was traditionally called "onderscheidenlijk preken" — preaching with separate applications for each of the different categories of people in the congregation. The major division ran between the converted and unconverted, but within each of these groups there could also be sub-groups which rated a special application of comfort or admonition.[234]

Van Dijk rejects this dual or multiple application primarily because of its underlying assumption that the congregation is "a mixed lot."[235] Not that he denies that there may be hypocrites within the congregation, but the preacher, "who has accepted a confessional church which excommunicates all who demonstrate in their lives that they do not belong to the Lord's congregation, does not have the right to sift the people once more when addressing them. He may not reserve a separate place for hypocrites in his sermon." The preacher who does this, Van Dijk contends, "commits three wrongs": "He insults the church of Christ by addressing it as a mixed lot"; "he harms the church of Christ" because believers may begin to doubt and hypocrites tend to close their ears at the familiar refrain; and finally, "he retards the upbuilding of the church" because his view of the hearers

---

231 *De Preektrant*, pp. 43-45.
232 "Zooveel hoofden zooveel zinnen." Schilder, *Tusschen*, p. 207.
233 Van Dijk, *Verbond*, p. 25.
234 Among the converted were "bekommerden en verzekerden," among the unconverted "onverschilligen, openbare zondaars, werkheiligen, doodrechtzinnigen," etc. Van Dijk, *De Preektrant*, p. 16; see pp. 16ff. for examples of these multiple applications.
235 "Een gemengde hoop volks." *Ibid.*

is bound to distort the goal and content of his sermons.[236]

It is beyond our scope to treat all the ins and outs of this dispute. Clearly, the conceptions of the covenant and the church[237] once again play a major role in aligning the opposing sides. What interests us is the connection of this dispute with the homiletical controversy. We begin to sense this connection when we hear Hoekstra advocating "onderscheidenlijk preken" and linking it to the objective – subjective combination: "Through the multiple application the preacher causes the objective truth to be subjectively appropriated."[238] Hoekstra states as a general principle: "The Word of God must be held up as a mirror before the unconverted,... and also before those who already came to conversion.... The preacher should know and describe all the different varieties of spiritual life in order to illuminate that entire, rich area with the lamp of the Word."[239] We bypass the objection of anthropocentric-subjective preaching at this point in order to come straight to the question of whether *historical* texts might be an exception to the rule of multiple application. Hoekstra indicates no such restriction in 1918, but in 1926 he warns that "not every text is a 'locus' for all kinds of applications": the place where "the objective truth of the text will find its subjective projection" depends on, among other things, the content of the text. "It is not feasible to draw up rules for this," Hoekstra says; but he continues: "We can mention, however, that it is indispensable to preach *onderscheidenlijk* in order to achieve a proper method of application.... According to Scripture and experience, not all members of the congregation are true believers. It is necessary, therefore, ever again to make a distinction between the converted and the unconverted."[240] Apparently the historical text forms no exception to this rule — a fact which is borne out in his subsequent treatment of historical texts.[241]

Dijk is more careful in his presentation. He rejects, first of all, an application which is "an appendix with all kinds of differentiations for various spiritual conditions"[242] — an unambiguous statement that goes far in curbing the exuberant proliferation of sub-divisions in both congregation and application. Secondly, like Hoekstra, Dijk takes into consideration the specific

236 *Ibid.*, p. 19. Cf. pp. 35ff. See also I. De Wolff, *Verbondsmatige Zelfbeproeving* (Enschede: Boersma, 1936), pp. 54ff., and Holwerda, (1944) *Populair*, pp. 27ff.

237 Van Dijk, *Ibid.*, pp. 19, 37, counters the notion of a "volkskerk," and Holwerda, *Populair*, p. 29, contends, "De grote fout is, dat men de gemeente hier niet meer ziet als kerk van onzen Heere Jezus Christus; dat men er geen ernst meer mee maakt, dat allen de belofte toekomt en daarom de verantwoordelijkheid voor allen groot is."

238 *De Tegenwoordige Critiek* (1918), p. 23.

239 *Ibid.*, p. 22.

240 *Homiletiek*, p. 303.

241 See *ibid.*, p. 358.

242 "Zielsgestalten," *Dienst der Kerk* (1952), p. 106 = *Dienst der Prediking*, p. 110.

content of the text which simply cannot be bent every which way to treat a variety of conditions: "The distinctions in 'onderscheidenlijk preeken' are not to be arrived at, at least not primarily, on the basis of the congregation but on the basis of the richly varied Word of God."[243] The text decides the direction the application will take — at least "primarily." Dijk's slight hesitation seems to leave the door ajar for at least dual applications, and that is indeed the case. For Dijk contends: "The object of preaching is the church, the flock of Christ — a flock in which intruders are mixed with the sheep. For that reason the demand for self-examination and the call for faith and conversion should not be lacking in any service of the Word; the preacher should minister the Word of God *onderscheidenlijk*."[244]

Again we ask, Should there be a dual application with *every* text? The text decides, Dijk says, *but* "the warning may not be forgotten in any sermon — even if it is only one striking sentence. The message of God's 'covenant wrath'...must be heard in every sermon, even if it is but for a moment."[245] The historical text is no exception; as a mattter of fact, there is more latitude here than with some other texts: "The preacher should choose a form which grips the congregation, also the individual; he should hold the historical narrative as a mirror before the congregation."[246] This advice in conjunction with Dijk's view of the congregation as "sheep and intruders" makes it difficult to see how he can avoid a dual application of historical texts, much as he prefers to let the text itself decide matters. But rather than saying that Dijk does not let the text decide, it would be fairer to say that he conceives of the historical text as having more than one point so that multiple applications may be deduced from it. This, in turn, raises the question: In how far is this view of the historical text determined by the prior view of the congregation to which the text must be applied? In other words, does the conception of the congregation as divided into converted and unconverted somehow determine the view that the historical text has a dual message? The possibility of the existence of this kind of hermeneutic circle is as difficult to prove as it is to disprove.

In any event, it is striking to see how naturally exemplary preachers take to the dual application. In one sermon Abraham might be held up as a mirror for the converted, an example to be followed, while the unconverted might be warned; in another sermon Judas might be held up as a mirror for the unconverted, a warning example, while the converted might be comforted;

---

243 *OB*, XXII (1943), 2988. Similarly Impeta, *Zelfonderzoek*, p. 9: Whether hypocrites must be addressed "hangt van 'de gelegenheid,' van de tekstkeuze enz. af."

244 (1950) *Dienst der Kerk*, p. 37.

245 *Het Gericht Gods* (1952), p. 36. Here Dijk outdoes Impeta. The latter wants to warn hypocrites "geduring weer," but "overeenkomstig de tekstkeus." *Zelfonderzoek*, p. 117.

246 *Dienst der Prediking*, p. 202.

in still another sermon Jacob might function both as a good and a warning example — something for either group. There is nothing in the exemplary method as such that rules out "onderscheidenlijk preken" on historical texts. Quite the opposite is the case for the redemptive-historical method, which prohibits using the person in the text as an example for either one group or both and which, because of its stringent adherence to the message of the text, cannot allow for a multiple application when the text has but one message. "Let the preacher preach the gospel to *all*! Only then does he swing the ax of Christ. Woe to the preacher who *presupposes* divisions in the church and directs the word of the text to only one group. He must preach it to all and by that means Christ shall make the divisions.... The ax and the winnow are the emblems of the ministry of the Word. The stumbling block lies in the Gospel itself!"[247]

The Faculties of Man

Before concluding this section of objections to exemplary-subjective preaching, we should mention the opposition to the division of the individual hearer into various parts along the lines of faculty psychology and to the subsequent classification of texts and examples to correlate with these parts of man.

Hoekstra is still so enamored by faculty psychology that he uses its findings to classify the texts of Scripture into teaching ("didactische"), admonishing ("protreptische"), and stirring ("empoëtische") texts which are respectively aimed primarily at the intellect, the will, and the emotions of man[248] — *primarily*, because Hoekstra does not make the division absolute, neither in the texts ("Every text, after all, affects our entire soul."[249]) nor in the sermon ("Every sermon must influence the head, hand, and heart."[250]). The major reason why Hoekstra cannot make the division absolute is that in spite of his fascination with faculty psychology, he still conceives of man as a basic unity since the intellect, the will, and the emotions are functions of the "I."[251] Nevertheless, he tries to maintain this division "because it is made

247 Holwerda (1939), *De Wijsheid*, p. 77. Cf. *Populair*, p. 29: "De belofte wordt onmiddellijk een dreigement voor wie niet geloven. En zo brengt de prediking scheiding, en wordt het koninkrijk der hemelen tegelijk geopend en gesloten." Van Dijk, *De Preektrant*, p. 36: "De juiste, Schriftuurlijke prediking, die de gemeente wijst op haar rijkdom en roeping is vanzelf een veroordeeling van wie in de kerk niet waarlijk van de kerk zijn. Tot een andere vorm van bediening van dezen sleutel heb ik geen recht.... Ik heb heel die gemeente, als *geloovigen* op te wekken tot een leven van geloof en heiligmaking."

248 *Homiletiek*, pp. 320ff.

249 *Ibid.*, p. 321.

250 *Ibid.* Cf. pp. 325, 333, 346.

251 *Ibid.*, p. 320: "Het Ik is werkzaam in de kenfunctie, de streeffunctie en de emotioneele of gevoelsfunctie."

from one point of view, namely, the goal of preaching in relation to the main functions of the human psyche," and because "it shows the connection between classical rhetoric and homiletics."[252]

We shall bypass the many objections that could be raised against this classification[253] in order to come immediately to the historical text. Where, in Hoekstra's view, do historical texts fit into this classification? The answer is that "although they fit under one of the three categories, they have such a special form that they require a separate discussion...from a different point of view."[254] Hoekstra does not say explicitly which one of the three categories encompasses historical texts, but from the general trend of his argumentation and the examples given we might infer that it is, in the main, the teaching category.[255] In general, therefore, these texts are aimed primarily at the intellect. This presents a problem for the application because, "even though the teaching element dominates in a text, a sermon on it, though mainly teaching, should aim at all of man's faculties and should, therefore, contain volitional and emotional as well as intellectual moments."[256] At this juncture the exemplary approach comes to the rescue by allowing the preacher to go over the text once more to uncover the examples that will stimulate the will and fire the emotions. Consequently, depending on where the emphasis falls, Hoekstra is also able to fit certain historical texts under the categories of admonishing and emotion-stirring texts.[257] The examples, therefore, turn out to belong to two of the three categories: admonishing and emotion-stirring. Interestingly, Huyser outdoes Hoekstra by adding a third category:

252 *Ibid.*, p. 322.

253 See Dijk, *Dienst der Prediking*, pp. 116, 196ff., who calls this classification too psychological, too subjective, not clear-cut, and arbitrary – one of the few places where Dijk disagrees sharply with Hoekstra. See also Jonker, *Actuele Prediking*, p. 23, and p. 99: "De lijn [van deze indeling] loopt van Aristoteles, Cicero over Augustinus, Hyperius, Steinmeyer naar Hoekstra.... Het principe wordt gelegd in de *mens*, in zijn psychische gesteldheid en niet in de *Schrift*."

254 *Homiletiek*, p. 352.

255 Either as information of past events or conceived more dogmatically. "De historie des heils is van zoo hoog belang, omdat God in de feiten zijn raad verwerkelijkt en zijne gedachten openbaart. 't Zijn feiten, die spreken van de deugden Gods." *Ibid.*, p. 353. The examples of historical texts classified under "didactische stoffen" are to be found on p. 324.

256 *Ibid.*, p. 325. Cf. p. 302: "De applicatie projecteert de tekstgedachten... zoowel in de intellectueele en volitioneele als in de emotioneele sfeer." This leads Hoekstra to speak of a *usus didacticus,* a *usus protrepticus,* and a *usus empoëticus.* Cf. *Het Woord Gods,* pp. 59f. Similarly Huyser, *De Paraenese,* p. 78.

257 Cf. *Homiletiek*, p. 334: "Tot de protreptische stoffen zijn...te rekenen... ook historische gedeelten der H. Schrift, waaruit... vermaningen en waarschuwingen afgeleid kunnen worden," and p. 348: "Vooral de geschiedenis van de godsmannen des Ouden en des Nieuwen Testaments is een fontein van troost." In fact, the classification of a text may switch from one genus to another, depending on the angle from which the preacher approaches the text, "omdat in verband met het gezichtspunt de stof zich enigermate heeft gewijzigd" (p. 322).

"The example is not always ethical in nature.... It may also belong to the area of religious *logic* or the area of the emotions."[258] With this example for the intellect the scheme is complete: man has three faculties; corresponding to this the preaching-texts can be divided into three categories; in addition, the examples can be divided into three categories. Should the text now prove to address only one faculty of man, the examples it contains form a reserve battalion, as it were, to ensure that the other two faculties are also covered.[259]

The objection to this scheme is directed at the base on which the whole structure rests. Holwerda observes: "It seems to me that in this manner the Bible as well as man are cut in pieces. Apparently one can receive something for his intellect without receiving anything for his heart and vice versa. But what is left, in this view, of the one whole man whom God addresses? Does God speak only to the mind of man or merely to his emotions or will? If not, does He accost man on three disconnected fronts? Does God address himself to three parts of man in succession? ... The shoe pinches on all sides. Surely the question may be asked: Is this what Scripture says about man? Has justice been done here to the scriptural revelation regarding the heart?"[260] With the rejection of this "peculiar anthropology" which is "informed by a vain, unscriptural philosophy,"[261] the whole scheme of three faculties in the addressee and three corresponding categories of texts and examples collapses. The preacher need not forever be balancing intellectual, volitional, and emotional elements in the sermon, for the man in the pew is not a conglomerate of three parts each of which may be reached with a special text or example. Man is one, and he is addressed as a unity by the Word of God.

* * *

In this section we have considered the objections to certain homiletical principles underlying the exemplary approach. These principles (or their rejection) have consequences which reach much farther, of course, than the preaching of historical texts alone. The objective – subjective combination, the explication – application dualism, the subjective preaching, the multiple application, and the faculties of man — all these (or their rejection) play a role in the construction of a sermon on any text. The points of dispute mentioned are themselves informed by philosophy, theology, and psychology. One could pinpoint different views respecting a great many subjects, but central here

258   *GTT*, LI, 16, emphasis added.
259   Huyser does mention the example for the intellect, but he neither works with it nor needs it since, in his view, the redemptive-historical approach already addresses the intellect. To fill the vacuum it leaves with respect to the other two faculties he stresses examples for the emotions and especially for the will (see above, pp. 78ff. on "moralizing").
260   (1944) *Populair*, pp. 21f.
261   *Ibid.* Cf. Veenhof, *Bondsboekje*, p. 41.

too is the view of Scripture. In our final section on the objections to the exemplary approach we return once again to Scripture by considering the foundation of the exemplary approach: the hermeneutical-homiletical examples found in Scripture.

OBJECTIONS TO USING THE PREACHERS IN SCRIPTURE AS EXAMPLES

Huyser concludes his articles on exemplary preaching as follows: "We cannot do without 'exemplary' preaching. Holy Scripture leads the way. Even if there had been no one in the whole Christian church who had followed Scripture in this, we would still count it our duty to proceed in a deductive-'exemplary' manner in explicating and applying historical texts."[262] The final appeal for exemplary preaching is to Holy Scripture. This may seem to be the end of the matter, but it will be instructive to see how this appeal is made.

Examples for Homiletics and Hermeneutics

In one of his publications Huyser names the grounds for "the right and duty of exemplification." The major, "fundamental" ground is Scripture: "On principle the example of the preachers in the Old and New Testament is normative for everyone preaching the Word of God. Prophets, apostles, sages, psalmists, and especially Christ used 'exempelen' time and again in their preaching. We must conform ourselves to these examples."[263] Here again the exemplary approach reveals itself as more than a pragmatic method of preaching. This approach includes and proceeds from a certain fundamental view of Scripture: not only are the persons mentioned by the biblical preachers examples to be imitated, but the biblical preachers themselves are examples to be imitated by preachers today — their sermons are the norms for our sermons. In other words, whatever else the Bible may be, it is also an exemplary "textbook" for the science of homiletics.[264]

We find a little of this in Hoekstra's *Homiletiek* also. Holy Scripture is

---

262 *GTT*, LI (1951), 17. Cf. Schelhaas, *GTT*, XLII (1941), 126: "De historische stoffen mogen en moeten ook als voorbeelden worden gebruikt. Dat dit naar Gods wil is, wordt ons in het N.T. klaar voor oogen gesteld. Wij verwijzen hiervoor slechts naar I Cor. 10 en Heb. 11... waar historische personen en gebeurtenissen als exempelen worden benut." See also Douma, *Heraut*, 1942, Nos. 3336ff.

263 *Het Exempel* (1952), p. 174.

264 "De Gereformeerde homiletiek heeft er altijd prijs op gesteld uit de gegevens der H.S. aangaande de prediking te worden opgebouwd, zoowel wat het principieele, als wat het materieele en formeele aangaat." Huyser, *GTT*, XLII, 254. For Huyser, too, "de homiletiek is een theologische vakwetenschap." *GTT*, XLIX, 241.

the *principium*, the foundation of both material and formal homiletics.[265] But this starting point does not enable Hoekstra to deduce a scientific homiletics from Scripture. As a matter of fact, in material homiletics he rejects the classification of texts which Hyperius deduced from Scripture (II Tim. 3 : 16 and Rom. 15 : 4) and posits instead the classical (psychological) triad.[266] He states, moreover, that "the rules for an effective treatment of texts in preaching are deduced partly from Scripture and partly from Christian rhetoric and psychology."[267] As to formal homiletics, "the form of Scripture is, generally speaking, a model for preaching." Indeed, "Scripture points out by several examples the proper elocution of the ministry of the Word." Paul spoke "not in plausible words of wisdom, but in demonstration of the Spirit and power" (I Cor. 2 : 4), and Jesus spoke "as one who had authority" (Matt. 7 : 29). These are examples for the preacher today.[268] But the examples in Scripture are apparently not enough for formal homiletics, for Hoekstra continues with a list of five other items which shape the form of the sermon: logic, rhetoric, aesthetics, psychology, and the preacher's individual talent.[269]

For Huyser, however, the method to be followed in preaching is given without qualification in the example of the prophets and apostles: "We must take our bearing on their methodological example."[270] This presupposition explains the identical development in Huyser's publications. *De Paraenese in de Prediking* (1941) begins with a chapter on the "paraenese" in the preaching of the O.T. and the N.T.; the articles " 'Exemplarische' Prediking" (1949-1951) contain a chapter " 'Exemplary' Preaching in Scripture"; *Het Exempel in de Prediking* (1952) begins with the "exempel" in the preaching of Moses, the sages, the prophets, the psalmists, Jesus, Paul, James, etc.; and *De Ouderling en de Prediking* (1959) begins with "the elder in Scripture." This is not merely a way of starting every book by beginning at the beginning, Scripture, and from there tracing the developments in church history; for Huyser these chapters are basic and decisive: "The Fundamental Part," he calls them.[271] For, "this *example* [of the preachers in Scripture] is normative for every gospel preacher. He is tied to it. Where would he get the right and freedom to do it differently? The way in which we are to preach the Word of God to our contemporaries must be gleaned from the Word itself; we must copy Christ and the holy men who spoke that Word before and after Him."[272]

---

265 *Homiletiek*, pp. 56, 381.
266 *Ibid.*, p. 320.
267 *Ibid.*, p. 326.
268 *Ibid.*, pp. 381f.
269 *Ibid.*, pp. 382ff.
270 *Het Exempel*, p. 175. In similar vein Douma, *Heraut*, 1942, No. 3340.
271 See *De Paraenese*, pp. 6ff.; *Het Exempel*, pp. 46ff.; and *GTT*, L, 163ff. The latter chapter is called "de fundamentele zijde van de zaak" in *GTT*, XLIX, 245.
272 "Aflezen" and "afzien," *De Paraenese*, p. 77.

Concretely, this has negative as well as positive implications. Negatively, a political sermon, e.g., is contraband: "Did Jesus and the apostles ever concern themselves with politics in their sermons?" "Contemporary preachers must learn from the example of apostolic preaching in which there is neither semblance nor shadow of politics."[273] Positively, "the apostolic example teaches us that... admonitions in preaching must be given in a brotherly manner," that the sermon must contain illustrations as well as admonitions,[274] and, of course, that the exemplary element be brought out in preaching historical texts.[275]

The examples for exemplary preaching are given us throughout Scripture, but especially in I Cor. 10, Heb. 11, and James 5. This apostolic preaching is the norm for our preaching of the historical text. These passages do not mention all the persons we might meet in our text, of course, but in them the Examples (apostles) have given us examples of exemplary preaching which may be extended to all historical texts.[276] We shall return shortly to these prooftexts par excellence, but we should first take away some possible misconceptions and show the implications of this exemplary approach to Scripture which finds in Scripture exemplary preaching in the literal sense of the word.

Not all the defenders of the exemplary method would follow Huyser in his rigid consistency. Dijk observes that because of the essential difference between inspiration and illumination "the revelation in Scripture and *our* preaching are not parallel and may therefore not be compared with each other."[277] Huyser, of course, also recognizes this difference — "Indeed, there is a profound difference" — but he also feels that there is "a certain similarity and continuity." The way in which the prophets and apostles preached in their day is the *norm* to which "we must conform as much and as well as possible."[278] Dijk, in contrast, states explicitly: "Holy Scripture gives no model for the ministry of the Word and presents no exact rules for the technique of preaching."[279] He also offers a splendid alternative to the exemplary approach: "The elements in the sermons of the prophets and apostles do not tell us that we must preach like they did, but rather that these

---

273   Huyser, *Hom*, XXII (1963), pp. 100f. This, by the way, seems to contradict *De Ouderling* (1959), p. 98: "Wat door de predikkunde lijnrecht uit de Schrift en met name uit het apostolische voorbeeld der prediking gehaald is, heeft stellig bindende kracht; waar echter uit deze bron niet geput is of de getrokken consequenties twijfelachtig zijn, houdt de binding op en vertoeft men in de sfeer der vrijheid."

274   Respectively: *De Ouderling*, p. 115; *Het Exempel*; and *De Paraenese*.

275   "De exemplificerende behandeling is plicht t.o.v. alle historische stoffen... die door de Schrift, waar en hoe dan ook, 'exemplarisch' worden geinterpreteerd." *GTT*, L, 213.

276   See Huyser, *GTT*, LI, 9ff. on "generale exemplificatie" and "analoge exemplificatie" on the basis of these and other texts.

277   *Dienst der Prediking* (1955), p. 13.

278   *Het Exempel* (1952), pp. 174f.

279   *Dienst der Prediking*, p. 38.

elements are the material for and the object of our preaching. The application, including, e.g., admonitions, must be part and parcel of our preaching — not because Scripture happens to have admonitions in its sermons but because God's revelation brings not merely the message of his truth but also the message of his law and gospel demands...."[280]

In spite of this emphasis, Dijk asserts nevertheless: "We can learn much from the preaching of the apostles. The form of their preaching, as we know it from Acts 2 and 13, may not be normative for us, but this *is* normative: their preaching, however theocentric, was always preaching Christ and Him crucified, and they always tied themselves to the Scriptures which testify of Him. Their preaching tells us that we, too, should not seek our strength in plausible words of human wisdom but in the ministry of the Lord's Word alone, that we should not yield to the 'wisdom of the world' which considers the cross foolishness. It teaches us further that in this preaching of Christ we should feed the flock entrusted to us, admonishing, warning, and comforting, so that justice may be done to the administration of the keys of the kingdom."[281]

One cannot help wondering whether Dijk at this point re-introduces the exemplary use of Scripture for homiletics. He does not, to be sure, go into as many details as Huyser does, but is there any essential difference in approach? It should be clear that we are not questioning *what* is said about preaching but the *basis* on which this is said. For Huyser that basis is the exemplary approach — but, it seems, no less so for Dijk. Having made the apostolic sermons normative examples for these central elements in preaching, how can he deny Huyser the right of making the details normative as well? He can do this (and he does it in two instances[282]) only by rejecting the examples as basis (norm) and finding that basis instead in the nature of the Word which is to be preached.

Dijk's wavering on this score discloses the difficulty of completely discarding the exemplary approach. This exemplary use of Scripture seems to be ingrained in our very system. On what other basis than the exemplary approach can Nixon say, "The general form of [Paul's] letters, with about two-thirds of the space given to doctrine and the last one-third to ethics, illustrates the proper proportion for good expository preaching"?[283] On what other basis can Volbeda say, "God has not only issued pastoral precepts in His Word, but He also affords us pastoral examples in both the O.T. and the N.T.... The examples are normative as well as preceptive"?[284] Even Clowney, in his *Preaching and Biblical Theology*, appeals to James 5 and I Cor. 10

---

280   *Ibid.*, p. 13. Similarly, p. 20.
281   *Ibid.*, p. 32.
282   See above, III, n. 280.
283   *John Calvin, Expository Preacher*, p. 15.
284   *The Pastoral Genius of Preaching*, p. 84.

for his contention that no choice need be made "between ethical preaching and that which is redemptive-historical": "The New Testament... not only *sanctions* both but does not set them in opposition."[285]

One can discover the influence of the exemplary approach not only in homiletics but in any number of subjects. In *church order* (church law), the polemics against Rome forced the churches of the Reformation to re-examine the value of the biblical examples, Schippers points out, "for the forty days of Lent were intended as an imitation of the forty day fast of Moses, Elijah, and Christ. And what were they to say when the Roman polemicists directed the attention of those desiring to follow the apostolic examples to the fact that the first Lord's supper was celebrated at night, with unleavened bread, exclusively with men, who were all office bearers?" Although the exemplary approach was tempered in Reformed circles, it was not completely discarded: "The fact that women are not permitted to be office bearers according to the present Reformed church order... is connected with the method of the Reformed to deduce their church order from Scripture, paying close attention to the example of the apostolic churches."[286] In *liturgics*, the introduction of the processional hymn can be seen as an attempt to copy the example of Israel which went to the temple singing. In *missions*, who does not recall the heated debate whether and in how far Paul's missionary methods should be copied today?[287] These are just a few samples of the wide-spread influence of the exemplary approach,[288] but its problematical nature at this level is today most evident in *hermeneutics*.

Both Grosheide and Greijdanus base their hermeneutics, at least in part, on the exemplary approach. Although Greijdanus says plainly, "Scripture is no textbook for biblical hermeneutics," he merely means by this the obvious fact that Scripture "presents no systematically well-ordered totality of principles or rules for biblical hermeneutics." But the material for hermeneutics (as well as other theological sciences) "is contained in Scripture and spread throughout. We are to locate this material, bring it together, and order it into a transparent whole."[289] One of the major sources of this hermeneutical

---

285 P. 78, emphasis added.

286 Schippers, *De Gereformeerde Zede*, p. 152 and p. 251. Since this was written (1954), the Gereformeerde Kerken have opened the ecclesiastical offices to women. On the exemplary use of Scripture for church polity in general see, e.g., J. R. De Witt, *Jus Divinum*: The Westminster Assembly and the Divine Right of Church Government (Kampen: Kok, 1969), *passim*.

287 See, e.g., Roland Allen, *Missionary Methods*: St. Paul or Ours? (London: World Dominion, 1953).

288 See also the conception of Price that Jesus as Teacher is the example for the "assistant teachers" in the church today — a "model van pastoraal optreden" which Firet rejects. *Het Agogisch Moment*, pp. 78ff. See further the exchange between North and Troost on the exemplary use of Scripture for social ethics. *IRB*, Oct., 1967, pp. 46-56.

289 *Schriftbeginselen ter Schriftverklaring* (1946), p. 56.

material is "the way in which the organs of revelation viewed, interpreted, and applied the O. T."[290] For that reason Greijdanus analyzes the interpretations of Scripture passages given by Jesus, the evangelists, Paul, Hebrews, and Peter, and from these examples deduces rules for our hermeneutics.[291] "We must," he says, "pay close attention to the way our Lord, his apostles, and other organs of revelation ... view and interpret the preceding O.T. revelation in order that we may see how *we* should view and interpret Holy Scripture...."[292] In other words, their interpretation is the example for our interpretation; their "hermeneutics" is normative for our hermeneutics — the exemplary approach.[293]

One of the most obvious problems facing the exemplary approach in hermeneutics is that Jesus and the apostles do not interpret *every* O.T. text. To gain some *general* hermeneutic principles, one must, therefore, by inductive reasoning extend the offered examples of exegesis. For instance, on the basis of a few types presented in the N.T. one must, along with the church fathers, say that "the apostles have given us as an example several types with which to discover still more types."[294] This can be done in the same way Huyser extends the "exemplary element" to all historical texts, namely by generalization or analogy.[295] Unless some barriers are set up here and there, however, this method opens the way to the most extravagant typologizing. But having accepted the exemplary approach, what right does one have subsequently to raise barriers? It should come as no great surprise that there is a growing conviction today that "any justification of the use of typology within modern scientific exegesis cannot be simply derived from its use within the N. T."[296] This conviction, in turn, is connected with the current view of the nature of the "exegesis" contained in the N. T. The latter is, as Berkouwer puts it, "the fruit of a way of thinking which, methodologically and verbally, is not isolated from the Jewish use of Scripture but displays a great number of kindred features; this insight has become practically a *communis opinio.*"[297]

This presents another problem for the exemplary approach: Are the Jewish ways of thinking also exemplary, that is, normative for our hermeneutics?[298]

---

290 *Ibid.,* p. 63.
291 *Ibid.,* pp. 66-99.
292 *Ibid.,* p. 125.
293 Grosheide is a bit more restrained in his *Hermeneutiek*: "We hebben ons af te vragen, in hoeverre, wat het N.T. doet ... ons tot voorbeeld kan zijn" (p. 235). Nevertheless: "Wie de Schrift als het Woord Gods aanvaardt, zal juist in het N.T. het O.T. op volkomen juiste wijze zien gehanteerd" (p. 108).
294 So Schildenberger according to Miskotte, *Sensus Spiritualis*, p. 75.
295 See above, III, n. 276.
296 Eichrodt in *Essays*, p. 231.
297 *Heilige Schrift*, II (1967), 172. See there, n. 130, for literature and pp. 161ff. for extensive discussion. Cf. H. Ridderbos, *IRB*, Jan., 1968, pp. 38f.
298 This problem also plays a central role in German hermeneutical discussions.

Grosheide is forced to face this question when he discusses the "extremely curious way[299] in which Paul allegorizes" in Galatians 4. "The question," he says, "is this: If Paul allegorizes like that in Gal. 4 and we want to learn from Scripture itself how we should allegorize, why should we not follow the method which Paul uses here?"[300] This question, of course, is itself inspired by the exemplary approach, but we should give Grosheide credit for not evading the issue.[301] His solution consists of two parts: (1) Gal. 4 is unique in the N. T., and (2) Paul is speaking about a specific event, and "what is said of a specific event may not be made a general rule." On this basis Grosheide concludes: "We believe, therefore, that Gal. 4 does not teach us anything about the permissibility of the allegorical interpretation."[302] One could ask whether *one* N. T. example is less normative than two or three, and whether it is not precisely the presupposition of the exemplary approach that the interpretation of a specific event (text) may be made a general rule, thus making his conclusion (from the exemplary point of view) dubious, to say the least. And what to say about the N. T. use of the Septuagint:[303] Is this exemplary for us today? Because of its starting point, the exemplary approach is really in no position to make exceptions. If someone makes exceptions anyway, it is to the discredit of his own approach and it would seem to be high time to scrutinize the validity and value of that approach.

This is all the more urgent in view of the (stubborn) fact that we tend to fall back into the exemplary approach by force of habit. Koole is a case in point. He is well aware of the problems involved in applying the exemplary approach in hermeneutics. Already in 1938 he wrote: "One may highly value the N. T. exegesis of the O. T., but one may certainly not consider it entirely normative for our present-day exegesis."[304] In 1960 he added the

See, e.g., *Essays on O.T. Hermeneutics*: Bultmann, pp. 51ff.; Zimmerly, p. 120, n. 98; Westermann, pp. 125, 131; Baumgärtel, pp. 142f.; Pannenberg, pp. 324ff.

299 "Zeer merkwaardige wijze." Berkouwer, *Heilige Schrift*, II, 173, n. 130, notes that the word "merkwaardig" was formerly frequently used to denote a use of Scripture which today is called "Jewish" or "rabbinical."

300 *Hermeneutiek*, p. 188.

301 "We mogen aanvankelijk gevoelen, dat dit hier nu wel zoo gedaan is, doch dat dit geen algemeene regel kan zijn, met dit gevoel zijn we niet gereed." *Ibid.*

302 *Ibid.*, p. 188f. Earlier, p. 51, Grosheide used another argument: "Wat Paulus in Gal. 4 met de geschiedenis van Hagar doet, geeft ons op zichzelf nog niet het recht om andere geschiedenissen zoo te behandelen, juist omdat Paulus niet uitlegt, maar een bijzonder gebruik van de historische feiten maakt, waarbij hij als apostel onfeilbaar geleid werd door Gods Geest." Hence, "het is geen model."

303 See, e.g., E. E. Ellis, *Paul's Use of the O.T.* (1957), pp. 11ff.

304 *De Overname*, p. 11. Also Stelling VII: "De exegese van het O.T. mag niet van de wijze, waarop het in het N.T. aangehaald wordt, uitgaan." The two major reasons why this normativity is "onmogelijk" are: "Enerzijds staat het gebruik dat het NT van het OT maakt in het teken van zijn tijd; anderzijds verbiedt juist het geloof in de Inspiratie van het NT onze aanmatiging, als zouden wij op dezelfde wijze diepzinnigheden uit het OT te voorschijn kunnen brengen" (p. 14, cf. p. 306).

observation: "I would rather no longer speak here [e.g., Matt. 2 : 15] of an exegesis of the O. T. by the N. T. (as I did in my dissertation) but of a *usus*, a use of the O. T. by the N. T." — the implication being a further strengthening of his earlier conviction that we cannot, in our scientific exegesis, simply copy the "usus" the N. T. makes of the O. T.[305] In 1965, however, regarding exemplary *preaching*, Koole states as a matter of course that it is "clearly enough legitimated in I Cor. 10": "The exemplary sermon can appeal to the N. T. itself."[306] This is hardly different from Huyser's "We appeal to Scripture: the preachers in the Old and New Testament...."[307] One may well ask why a certain type of preaching should be any more legitimated by the N. T. than certain kinds of "exegesis."

Unfortunately, the controversy did not deal specifically with this exemplary use of Scripture for homiletics and hermeneutics. As a result, it is rather difficult to determine whether or not the redemptive-historical side extricated itself completely from this traditional way of thinking. Is the concern to show that the N. T. speaks of "examples" only in a redemptive-historical sense merely an attempt to beat the opponent on his own ground, or is it considered exemplary "proof" for the correctness of the redemptive-historical approach? We cannot completely rule out the latter possibility,[308] but the tenor of the redemptive-historical approach is such that it would at least seriously question the exemplary use of Scripture for homiletics and hermeneutics.

We note, in the first place, that the Bible does not give us complete information on how the prophets and apostles preached. Huyser himself admits that, as to external form, "no examples of preaching are to be found in the writings of the older prophets"; as for Paul, "there is not one single example of congregational (as distinguished from missionary) preaching." In order to gain examples, "one must, therefore, try to form a general picture of the preaching of the prophets from all kinds of fragmentary givens"; the same holds for Paul's preaching: "From the missionary letters one must conclude

---

305 *Hom*, XIX, 50. See already Grosheide, *Hermeneutiek*, pp. 50f., 108, and 236: "... van exegese van de plaats uit het O.T. is betrekkelijk slechts zelden sprake.... Veel vaker moet gesproken van gebruik, wil men van toepassing." Cf. *RES Report*, p. 20.

306 *GTT*, LXV, 101. Note that the subsequent "alleen kan de betekenis van de O.T.ische geschiedschrijving hiermee onmogelijk uitgeput zijn" equals the "both-and" of the exemplary side.

307 *De Paraenese*, p. 97.

308 E.g., Van 't Veer, *Van den Dienst*, p. 167, says "dat het N.T. ons er in voorgaat om de O.T.ische historie alleen naar heilshistorische methode te lezen. En alleen wie dat doet...." How much of the exemplary, if any, is expressed in "voorgaan"? More clearly exemplary is De Wolff's rejection of a separate application for the unconverted: "Laten wij daarin niet wijzer zijn dan God, Die ons ook te dien opzichte, de brieven der apostelen tot voorbeeld gegeven heeft." *Verbondsmatige Zelfbeproeving*, p. 56.

back to the apostolic preaching in the early Christian church."[309] Without denying that much of Scripture reflects and arises from the preaching at that particular time, one might well question the verity of the reconstructed examples: Does not the same hypothetical element enter into this reconstruction of the sermons of that time as into the (rejected) reconstruction of the psyches of that time?

In the second place, the rejected historical equation mark is introduced also at this level of the exemplary approach. The reconstructed sermons must somehow function as the normative examples for our preaching. Is not the uniqueness of the preaching of the prophets, of Jesus, of the apostles, disregarded in this way? In connection with the preacher's language Schilder remarks at one time: "Whoever chooses Jesus as a *model* dishonors Christ the Prophet. For Jesus, now taken as he appeared in history, belonged to his own century. The language he spoke was the language of his age, his country, his people...." Moreover, "Jesus' work was quite different from that of the preacher in Christ's church...."[310] Does not the exemplary approach compare persons who cannot be compared? We don't mean the difference divine – human, inspired – illumined — a difference which can readily be acknowledged in the exemplary scheme, example – imitator, in the sense of those revealing the norm and those trying to attain the norm — but the difference in task and time and place. How can the preacher in today's established church be called upon to follow the example of Paul in a mission situation 1900 years ago?[311] How can today's preacher be called upon to follow the example of the N. T. writers in their specific use of the O.T.?[312] Huyser acknowledges that the preachers in the Bible do not give textual, expository sermons.[313] This means that his reconstructed examples of ser-

309 *GTT*, XLII, 195f. Cf. *De Paraenese*, p. 29.

310 (1923) *Om Woord en Kerk*, III, 221. In this connection Schilder refers to an extreme in the exemplary approach, a dissertation by W. B. J. Van Eyk entitled: *Dissertatio Theologica de Jesu Christi eloquentia oratori sacro imitanda* (Utrecht: 1851).

311 We must give Huyser credit for opposing the exemplary approach of Beyer, *Das Wesen der christlichen Predigt nach Norm und Urbild der apostol. Predigt* (1861). Huyser contends: "De prediking in de christelijke kerk van thans heeft zich niet te conformeeren aan de missieprediking, maar aan de gemeenteprediking der apostelen." *De Paraenese*, p. 29. In *GTT*, XLIX, 242, Huyser also makes the distinction between Paul's missionary sermon in Acts 13 and the letters directed at congregations, but he completely ignores other differences. Which missionary today could imitate the example of Acts 13? and which preacher the example of Paul's letters?

312 Cf. J. Ridderbos, *Het O.T. in onze Prediking* (1922), pp. 6f.: "De prediker wordt van dezen eisch [to find first of all the historical context and the meaning of the text in that context] ook niet ontslagen door het voorbeeld der N.T. schrijvers, die dikwijls een O.T. tekst uitsluitend bij het licht der vervulling beschouwen, zonder van het historisch verband gewag te maken....Nu zou de Christelijke prediker stellig verkeerd doen wanneer hij deze methode [Matth. 2:15] ook wilde toepassen...bij het prediken over een O.T. tekst."

313 E.g.: "Hoe vrij deze toespraak, en hoe los het verband met de voorafgegane Schriftlezing zijn kon, is te zien uit Hand. 13:16vv." *GTT*, L, 177.

mons from Bible times fall into an entirely different category from our textual, expository sermons, and the examples turn out to be no examples for us because he compares two different ways of preaching. Specifically: the preachers in the Bible give no sermons on a particular historical text; hence, any appeal to their examples is simply not pertinent.

In the third place, we note the question of the appropriateness of this search for homiletical examples. At one point Schilder denounces those who completely miss the purpose of the historical text by distilling from it psychological preaching motives. This, he says, "is as reprehensible as it would be if, e.g., the geographer deduced his geography from the biblical narratives, or if the Freudian gleaned his material for sexual pathology from that source."[314] It is hard to say whether Schilder would extend this to the theologian who deduces his homiletics from the way they preached in sacred history, but the point to note is his concern to do justice to the purpose, the scopus of the text. Any questioning next to the central thrust of the text is suspect. Given this concern to do justice to the purpose of the text, the exemplary use of Scripture for homiletics must have been highly questionable for the redemptive-historical side. Has the Bible been given us to deduce the method of preaching in biblical times so that we might make this example our norm today? Is one of its purposes to provide us with homiletical models?

Although this question was not explicitly asked in the controversy, the evidence we have leaves little doubt as to the answer that would have been given had the question been asked. For nowhere do the proponents of the redemptive-historical method seek to back up their way of preaching with homiletical models from Scripture. Huyser is undoubtedly right when he says: "The number of prooftexts brought forward for exclusive redemptive-historical preaching is very scanty."[315] But instead of accusing his opponents of a deficiency on this score, he should have realized that if they *had* come with such model prooftexts, they would implicitly have granted him the validity of the exemplary approach. Moreover, Huyser is wrong in saying: "They have, in fact, been able to name no ground other than Acts 13,"[316] for Holwerda, to whom this refers, definitely does not posit Acts 13 as a "ground" for the validity of redemptive-historical preaching. Here we have a clear case of Huyser reading his own approach back into Holwerda's words.[317] It is Huy-

314 *Ref*, XVI (1936), 236.
315 *GTT*, XLIX (1949), 242.
316 *Ibid*.
317 We have another case later when Huyser summarizes Van Dijk's objections to exemplary preaching as: "4. Er is voor het 'exemplarisch' preken geen grond, noch voorbeeld te vinden in de H. Schrift" (*GTT*, L, 217). But Van Dijk says in fact: "Zij... meenen dat zij zich daarvoor kunnen beroepen op de Heilige Schrift. Hebben zij daartoe het recht? Naar mijn overtuiging niet" (*PE*, VI, 303). Neither here nor in the rest of the article does Van Dijk use "voorbeeld" as the ground that would decide matters. It may also be significant that this is the final part of Van Dijk's discussion, while for Huyser, being fundamental, it always comes first.

ser who sees, next to the example of the "fragmentary view of history" of I Cor. 10, the example of the "centripetal view of history" in Paul's sermon in Acts 13,[318] thus securing "grounds" for both exemplary and redemptive-historical preaching. Holwerda, however, is not looking for "grounds" to justify redemptive-historical preaching but tries to show merely that "redemptive-historical preaching does not eliminate the applicatory nature of the sermon," that it "draws" people, that it "brings a crisis." Instead of a long argumentation he illustrates this with Luke 24 and Acts 13.[319] Had not modesty prevented him, he could have illustrated this equally well with his own sermons. Huyser's subsequent charge of "the strange inconsistency that the redemptive-historians ... have placed a historical equation mark between the missionary preaching of Acts 13 and the regular preaching in our churches"[320] must, therefore, be dismissed as completely unfounded. We agree that it would have been a "strange inconsistency" indeed if the charge had been true. Consistency in the redemptive-historical approach would require one to be as critical of the presentation of normative examples for the conduct of the preacher as of the presentation of normative examples for the conduct of the Christian. Only when the example can lay claim to being the intent of the text can it lay claim to normativity.

Examples for Exemplary Preaching

To "prove" its legitimacy, Douma presented many N. T. examples of exemplary preaching.[321] The examples par excellence, however, were I Cor. 10, Hebrews 11, and James 5. After what has been said in the foregoing, it will be clear that the appeal to these examples could hardly put much weight in the balance. Indeed, Van 't Veer says: "The interpretation of these three texts cannot in the least decide the point at issue, that is, whether the exemplary or the redemptive-historical method should be used in preaching historical texts."[322] Nevertheless, these texts do reveal a certain use of O.T. history, and inasmuch as the exemplary side appealed to them, they were discussed at length. We shall touch upon only the highlights of this discussion.

---

318   *De Paraenese*, p. 107.

319   *Begonnen*, p. 107 = *GTT*, XLIII (1942), 396 to which Huyser refers. Note that Holwerda speaks here of "voorbeeld" in the sense of illustration, but Huyser reads it (automatically?) as "bewijsplaats" (*GTT*, XLIX, 242).

320   *GTT*, XLIX, 242.

321   "Laten we dan nu nagaan, wat de Schrift zelf ons inzake exemplarische prediking leert. Bij de Schrift als het onfeilbare Woord Gods ligt toch de beslissing." *Heraut*, 1942, Nos. 3336 and ff.

322   *GM*, XX (April, 1942), 1.

In distinction from Gal. 4, which speaks of a specific event, Grosheide feels that I Cor. 10 does give expression to a "hermeneutical rule" because "it concerns the total history of Israel in the desert."[323] Paul recalls certain events in the history of Israel, using them to warn the Corinthians: "Now these things were our examples, to the intent we should not lust after evil things, as they also lusted" (vs.6 K.J.V.); "Now all these things happened unto them for ensamples: and they are written for our admonition, upon whom the ends of the world are come" (vs.11 K.J.V.). This seems to be a clear-cut example of exemplary "preaching" on the part of Paul, and Huyser is quick to conclude: "The preacher may, therefore, utilize these historical narratives as examples and directly derive from them a 'sensus moralis.'"[324]

The redemptive-historical side raises the question, however, whether the word translated as "examples," *tupoi (tupikōs)*, is used in the exemplary or redemptive-historical sense. Appealing to Goppelt and Michel, Holwerda comes to the conclusion that for Paul *tupos* has a historical undertone: "Paul does not mean: these things are written 'illustratively, pictorially, pedagogically,' as an example for us in the exemplary sense, but: these things happened (!!) as a prefiguration of the events of the messianic age. 'Example,' therefore, has no exemplary but a purely redemptive-historical content."[325]

Huyser, appealing to Bindemann and the same Michel, comes to quite the opposite conclusion: "The root meaning of the word according to Acts 7 : 44 is: model, technical example. In I Cor. 10 it has a negative purport: a warning example that, in view of the disastrous consequences, would deter us from sin."[326] In Romans 5 : 14, Huyser admits, "example" has a "purely redemptive-historical content." But that means that "the coming of the antitype... is absolutely certain. As certainly as the person follows his preceding shadow, so certainly does the N.T. antitype follow the O.T. type. The type in redemptive history is prophetic in the strictest sense; it proclaims that

---

323 *Hermeneutiek* (1929), p. 189. Cf. his commentary in the K.V. series, *I Korinthe* (1933), p. 124: "In vs. 11 doet de Apostel een uitspraak... die van heel veel belang is, omdat ons hier gegeven wordt een stelregel voor het gebruik van het O.T. in de nieuwe bedeeling."

324 *De Paraenese*, p. 106. Cf. Douma, *Heraut*, 1942, No. 3337: "Hier leert ons God zelf in Zijn Woord, dat wij, omdat de feiten uit Israels geschiedenis voorbeelden zijn, ze ook zoo tot onze leering en waarschuwing *moeten* aanvaarden .... En *moet* dat niet in de prediking worden doorgegeven?"

325 *Begonnen*, p. 95.

326 *GTT*, L, 172. Cf. Eichrodt, *Essays*, p. 229: "Paul uses the word *tupos* only twice (Rom. 5 : 14 and I Cor. 10 : 6) to indicate typologically the prerepresentation of that which is to come. Moreover, in the latter of these two places, as with the adverb *tupikōs*... in I Cor. 10 : 11, the alternative explanation of a model or example in the moral sense... could perhaps be maintained."

certain persons, facts, and conditions which it prefigures, will necessarily appear and occur in the N. T. epoch."[327] With this definition of "type" Huyser comes to 1 Cor. 10: "If the sins of Israel and the judgments of God described by Paul in 1 Cor. 10:6ff. had this typological-prophetic meaning, that would mean that the Corinthians and the whole N.T. church were *predestined* to fall into sin and be destroyed by God's judgments. But this *necessity* to fall into similar evil ways does not exist." Hence, "the sins and judgments of the past...do not have the meaning of 'type' but of a warning and admonishing example."[328] Huyser thus excludes I Cor. 10:6ff. from typology by linking typology with prophecy and that conceived as requiring a necessary, literalistic fulfilment so that the typology – prophecy combination takes on a definite deterministic flavor. With this new definition Huyser has introduced an element which did not come up for discussion during the controversy proper.[329]

The redemptive-historical side rejected the appeal to I Cor. 10 as an example of exemplary preaching. "What is said here has nothing at all to do with exemplary preaching," Van Dijk says. The words "these things happened to them" should already caution us that Paul is not calling men, the Israelites, examples but is speaking of history and "has in mind what God is doing in the actions of men." It is in *history* that Paul sees a typological connection. "What happened in O. T. times finds its completion, its fulfilment, in what happens in the history of the N.T. congregation. It is basically one people of God, wandering through the desert there, treading the streets of Corinth here. It is one life that both peoples live, one law of life that rules both. The only difference is that what was shadow for the former finds its fulfilment among the latter. This meaning of 'types' in I Cor. 10 is entirely different from holding up the individual actions of certain persons in revelational history as an example for us."[330]

Holwerda expands on this by comparing Paul's interpretation with what he found to be the distinctive traits of the exemplary interpretation: illustrative, fragmentary, and atomistic. In contrast to the illustrative interpretation, Paul, in his use of "type" as a historical fact and a prefiguration of events of the messianic age, "retains history in its *factuality* and does not use it

---

327 *Ibid.*, p. 173.
328 *Ibid.*, p. 174.
329 Huyser wrote this in 1950, acquiring this element of necessity from A. Robertson and A. Plummer, *Commentary on First Corinthians* (1911), and J. Weiss, *Der erste Korintherbrief* (1910). But doesn't Paul in I Cor. 10 allude to the types (baptism in Moses, manna, water) from out of the reality of the fulfilment, the antitypes which he observes in Corinth (baptism in Christ, the Lord's supper)? Then the element of necessity, predestination, would not apply to vss. 1-5 where even Huyser admits the typology (*Ibid.*), and it is difficult to see why this element should be introduced in vss. 6-11.
330 *PE*, VI (1941), p. 307.

merely as pictorial teaching, as a concrete illustration of some proposition." In contradistinction to the fragmentary interpretation, Paul "interprets and applies this history *organically*; he will not hear of a 'historical equation mark' but says expressly: 'us, upon whom the end of the ages has come.'" And finally, in contrast to the atomistic interpretation, Paul "interprets '*synthetically*.' He does not speak about the vice of grumbling in general but the murmuring against God's redemptive benefits: 'the rock was Christ.' Accordingly, the application becomes (synthetically): 'Let us not tempt Christ.' "[331] On all three counts Holwerda sees I Cor. 10 as giving no support whatever to the exemplary approach.[332]

Hebrews 11

Another "example of exemplary preaching" is Hebrews 11. Does not the writer hold up the faith of person after person — Abel, Enoch, Noah, Abraham, etc. — as an example to us? And does not he himself say in vs. 32 that he lacks the time to speak of many others? "The preacher," Huyser concludes, "thus receives the right to treat analogous incidents in redemptive history as an extension of Heb. 11 : 3-31."[333]

Van Dijk observes, however, that the writer of Hebrews 11 does not preach on a historical text but deals with "faith": "He is not treating Genesis such and such; he preaches about faith, if I may put it that way, and for this uses illustrations from the O.T."[334] Van Dijk would have done better not to "put it that way" since this gives Huyser another occasion to superimpose his own exemplary structure on these words: According to the redemptive-historical side, he claims, "we must view Hebrews 11 as a *sermon*, a sermon which is a *prototype* of our sermons on dogmatic texts but not of our sermons on historical texts."[335] The redemptive-historical side is not concerned about "prototypes," however. They do not need a prototype to justify the use of illustrations from redemptive history (or any other history) in sermons on dogmatic texts. Besides, Hebrews 11 is not a sermon on a dogmatic *text*, so how could it possibly function as prototype for our sermons? The point is,

331 *Begonnen*, p. 94. See also (1939) *Een Levende Hoop*, IV, 5f. On Christ as the rock, see Clowney, p. 79, n. 11.

332 So also Van 't Veer, *Van den Dienst*, p. 165: "Wie zich deze beteekenis van het voorbeeld indenkt, moet wel zien, dat men aan I Cor. 10 geen recht mag ontleenen voor de aanwending van het voorbeeld, zooals dit in de exemplarische methode steeds weer geschiedt." And (p. 164), "Deze typologische verklaring [including the baptism in Moses as a type of the baptism in Christ] kan alleen heilshistorisch worden gefundeerd."

333 *GTT*, LI, 11. Cf. p. 7 for similar reasoning by H. Veldkamp.

334 *PE*, VI (1941), 303.

335 *GTT*, L (1950), 182.

as Holwerda expresses it more carefully: "In line with his discourse, which is dogmatical in character and not redemptive-historical, the writer *illustrates* from history the theme: 'by faith.' But that in itself says nothing about the way these historical texts themselves should be preached."[336]

More to the point is Huyser's following observation: "The writer certainly does treat 'Genesis such and such.' He draws out of the historical text something which is in it according to the intent of the Spirit. If, then, the example is in the text, a good homiletical interpretation requires that one extricate it when preaching on that text. One ought to adhere to the maxim, honored by all Reformed people always and everywhere: *Scripture interprets itself*; and he ought to grant straightforwardly the plain fact that Scripture in Hebrews 11 interprets the redemptive history of the O.T. in an 'exemplary' sense."[337]

The reply that was given to this argument will be discussed below (with James 5), but at this juncture a word should be said about the (mis)use of the maxim: "Scripture interprets itself." This maxim can serve as an argument only when the text to which one appeals does indeed intend to give an interpretation of the text under discussion. Ironically, it is Douma who, tracing the use of "examples" in the N.T., calls to our attention the fact that the N. T. writers occasionally use as "examples" persons who are not mentioned in the historical texts of the Bible. He mentions, e.g., the persons in Hebrews 11 : 35ff. for whom we have no corresponding O. T. text.[338] If the "examples" can thus be taken from *extra*-biblical as well as biblical sources, it would seem more probable that the intent of the writer (Spirit) is not so much to offer pieces of normative interpretation on several Bible texts as to present several concrete illustrations to drive home his point.

James 5 : 16-18

The final "example of exemplary preaching" we mention is James 5. Van Dijk approaches this text in the same way he approached Hebrews 11 : "The apostle speaks here of the power of the prayer of faith and illustrates this by pointing to the experience of Elijah. Naturally, one may use history in this way: when one preaches on the power of prayer he may elucidate this with illustrations.... But that is completely different from preaching on the history of Elijah as an illustration of the power of prayer."[339] James' use of

---

336 (1942) *Begonnen*, p. 95. See pp. 95f. for Holwerda's argument that the redemptive-historical view of history is also the foundation of Hebrews 11. Cf. Van 't Veer, *Van den Dienst*, pp. 166f.

337 *GTT*, L, 182.

338 *Heraut*, 1942, No. 3338. Further, No. 3340 on Jude, and No. 3342 on II Tim. 3 : 8 (Jannes and Jambres).

339 *PE*, VI (1941), 303. Similarly Van 't Veer, *Van den Dienst*, p. 158: "Jako-

Elijah as illustration and our textual preaching on I Kings are two distinct entities. Consequently, James' usage cannot possibly be normative for our preaching of this O.T. text. As a matter of fact, the expositor "who, in preaching I Kings 17 [*sic*], handles Elijah's prayer as an example for us, definitely does violence to the true sense of this chapter. He who desires to preach on the power of prayer should preach on James, not Kings."[340]

But Huyser objects: "If Scripture itself derives an example from I Kings 18 : 42ff., this is irrefutable proof that there is in fact an example in this history, otherwise it could not have been drawn from it." And this means that the preacher must bring out this example when he preaches on that text. "The preacher not only has the right to do this, but it is his biblical duty. He neglects this duty if he fails to bring out the 'exemplary' element.... Whoever refuses to interpret and apply this history in the light cast upon it by the Spirit through James 5, violates Scripture and purposely suppresses the truth. This does not mean, of course, that Elijah's significance as example should become the theme of the sermon as if that were the total meaning of the text. The 'exemplary' *element* in this history is not everything. But according to Scripture, which must be honored as its own interpreter, it is an integral ingredient of the content of the text and as such it should be plainly brought forward in the sermon."[341]

We might have been at a loss to know what the reply would have been (Huyser wrote this in 1950 and received no reply), had not Streefkerk raised essentially the same question in 1941. He wrote: "I am told that when I speak about prayer, I may think of Elijah. But am I not allowed to refer to the power of his prayer when I narrate or preach the *history* of Elijah? That seems extremely odd to me.... True, the revelational character of this history must be the main point, but I do not consider it illicit to make

---

bus 'preekt' dan ook niet over I Kon. 18, maar brengt als illustratie het gebed van Elia ter sprake bij een uiteenzetting over het gebed. Daarom zegt deze tekst niets ten gunste van de exemplarische methode."

340 *Ibid*. Van Dijk mentions 1 Kings 17 twice. Van 't Veer immediately corrects this to I Kings 18 : 42-45 (*GM*, XIX [1941], 73), which is clearly the prayer James has in mind. Van Dijk's slip does raise the question, however, why James did not use the prayer mentioned in the previous chapter (I Kings 17 : 20-24) as a more suitable illustration for his specific theme: the power of prayer for the restoration to health (James 5 : 14ff.).

341 *GTT*, L (1950), pp. 178f. In line with this, Dijk offers a "schets voor een biddagpreek over I Koningen 18 : 42b-46," in which he says in the introduction: "Over dit bidden onderricht ons het Woord Gods in onzen tekst"; and later: "Jakobus 5 : 16-18 ... geeft ons alle vrijmoedigheid om in Christus Jezus de lijnen van die gebedsworsteling te trekken tot onze gebedsure van vandaag." *Hom*, III (1942), pp. 54ff. A reminder may be in order that the exemplary preacher does not necessarily require a N.T. text for this "vrijmoedigheid" since he takes the liberty of extending a few N.T. examples to all suitable historical texts.

a side reference to the power of Elijah's prayer, all the more since Scripture (James) precedes us in this."[342]

In response, Van 't Veer acknowledges that the power of prayer is indeed an element in I Kings 18; but, he says, we should not overlook the fact that there are many other elements in this text: "e.g., that God exists, that He reveals himself, that He has established a relation between himself and man, that man can and may and must pray; the whole possibility, reality, and miracle of prayer meets me in this one prayer of Elijah." And that is only the beginning, for the prayer is a prayer for rain, which "reveals God's hand in nature, brings me to his providence." Further, the faith of Elijah, the vitality of his body after years of hardship, his posture in prayer.... "What a host of elements are contained in such a text," and what a multitude of directions the application could take if the text is seen as a number of elements. One could preach on all these (and more) elements in the text; he "would not be telling falsehoods, but he would *neglect* the revelation in this particular text." For these individual elements can be found in many another text. That is why many another text can also be used to illustrate the power of prayer. But the fact that one can use an element in a text as an illustration does not mean that that illustration is "the specific intent of the text." One can use the same text to illustrate the existence of God, but that does not mean that he must then speak about the existence of God when he *preaches* that text. "One could use every text to speak about the existence of God, and no one could say that it is not an ingredient of the text. But we can and do say that it is not the meaning, it is not the intention of this revelation here and now."[343]

With this we have come full circle: the question of the *intention*, the scopus of historical texts runs as a thread through the whole debate, and pivotal here and elsewhere is the notion that our preaching should do justice to the intention of the chosen preaching-text.

* * *

Before closing this chapter, it might be well to make a final observation. We have presented the attack on exemplary preaching by systematizing the rather desultory objections which were raised during the controversy. The arguments themselves, however, both pro and con, we gained largely from those involved in or associated with the controversy. A clear exception to this was the section on the exemplary use of Scripture for homiletics and hermeneutics: here, admittedly, we went beyond the controversy. We felt justified in this for three reasons. First, Huyser's post-controversy defense

342 Reprinted in *PE*, VI (1941), 349.
343 *GM*, XIX (1941), pp. 73f. Cf. Schilder, *Ref*, XI (1931), 374: "Dat iets in den tekst ter sprake komt, is toch niet genoeg voor den prediker."

of the exemplary method necessitated a rejoinder in terms of the redemptive-historical approach he attacked. Second, the questions we raised are but a natural extension of the redemptive-historical emphasis on the intention of the text. The Bible may not be forced to answer questions which it does not intend to answer.[344] And third, it enabled us to give some indication of the deep-seated nature of the exemplary approach in Reformed theology, from which "depth" it emerges in various theological and other disciplines. If one wants to reject exemplary preaching, he must be fully aware of the far-reaching implications involved in such a rejection; it implies the necessity to rethink our use of Scripture in all fields.

The other sections of this chapter, however, were cast in the thoughts and words of those involved in the debate some thirty years ago. From our vantage point today we cannot agree with each and every argument used; but who can deny that the exemplary approach, so often taken for granted, was quite thoroughly discredited — and that in its own theological setting? More importantly, the controversy brought to light many weaknesses of traditional Reformed homiletics — weaknesses which are still with us today. To recognize the problems is the first step in overcoming these weaknesses. In the next chapter we shall see how the redemptive-historical side tried to solve the problems they themselves brought to light.

344 What a strange inconsistency, for instance, when James 5 is used as scriptural proof for exemplary preaching, which is not the point at all, while, when it comes to the point James 5 makes — the power of prayer: "Is any among you sick? Let him call for the elders ... and the prayer of faith will save the sick man" — we tend to blunt this by introducing the unique apostolic situation.

Chapter IV   *The Redemptive-Historical Approach*

Parallel to the development of the foregoing chapter, we shall present in this chapter the positive contributions of the redemptive-historical side and the objections raised by the exemplary side. Though the two sides are thus being contrasted and their differences highlighted, we should not lose sight of the fact that there are many points of agreement between these Reformed theologians. We shall begin our presentation at the starting point shared by both sides: the conception of redemptive history.

REDEMPTIVE REVELATIONAL HISTORY

What is redemptive history? Both sides involved in the controversy are united in their opposition to the depreciation of redemptive history manifest in dialectic theology.[1] Both sides agree that redemptive history is not to be slighted. Hoekstra, for example, says: "The history of redemption is so extremely important because God realizes his counsel and reveals his thoughts in the historical facts."[2] The exemplary side earnestly desires to uphold the value of redemptive history. Dijk remarks: "This history is of such vital importance because God's revelation in this world... is neither a-historical nor suprahistorical but... enters history and works out God's plan in the facts of history."[3] Redemptive history is so significant because it is intimately related with God's revelation; in fact, redemptive history is itself *revelation*.

This may be the reason why no precise definition of redemptive history is given. Searching for a clear-cut distinction between redemptive, sacred, and revelational history, one finds instead that these terms are used practically synonymously[4] and that the features ascribed to the one are also ascribed to

---

1   See above, pp. 29–33.
2   *Homiletiek*, p. 353.
3   *Dienst der Prediking*, p. 199.
4   See, e.g., the quotations of Hoekstra and Dijk above, the quotations below, and on "heilshistorisch" and "openbaringshistorisch" as two words to describe the same method, above, I, nn. 66, 67, 70. In 1946 (*Ref*, XXI, 225) Schilder tried to

the other. The best we can do at this stage is to present the presuppositions regarding redemptive revelational history which both sides hold in common. Under separate headings we shall present the three postulates which function as the foundation on which the hermeneutical principles of the redemptive-historical approach are erected. At the same time we shall notice that below this foundation — like a pile supporting the foundation of a building — God's eternal decree, the Counsel of Peace, functions as the ultimate pillar of support.

Common Postulates

Redemptive History is History

To claim that redemptive history is *history* may seem tautological until we recall the rather common distinction between *profane* and *redemptive* history. Barth is castigated for following Kierkegaard in applying this distinction in such a way that a dualism between two realms results: history and suprahistory.[5] Schilder regrets that the Reformed Fathers sometimes made use of the profane–redemptive distinction, though he acknowledges that it was never their intent to make this a distinction between history and suprahistory: "Both the so-called 'sacred' history and the 'profane' history occur in the same realm, on earth, in our world, in time, among men of flesh and blood."[6] But Schilder even frowns upon a distinction between two kinds of history within the one realm: "All history is sacred history because all history is in reality God working toward his goal." Every date is therefore anno Domini, the year of our Lord Jesus Christ.[7] In Christ, God redeems, re-creates the world. His kingdom is coming into this world, into our "profane," fallen, history. "God's redemptive work does not make a separate history, detached from the 'profane,' but it enters history and comes about with and through history."[8] God realizes his plan of redemption on the horizontal plane of history. That is the first postulate.

Closely connected with this view of redemptive history are two other presuppositions: the unity of and the progression in redemptive history.

---

distinguish "heilshistorie" and "openbaringshistorie," but the result is rather confusing. Cf. *HC*, II (1949), 260 ff. We shall return to this in chapter V.

5   "Tijd en eeuwigheid blijven ook bij Barth uiteengerukt." Schilder, *Ref*, XIV (1934), 373.

6   *HC* (1939), p. 178.

7   (1942) *Preken*, III, 223 ff. In this sermon on the Heidelberg Catechism, L.D. XXI, Schilder continues by speaking of all history as church history. Cf. (1937) *Preken*, II, 174.

8   *Wat is de Hemel?*, p. 68. Cf. *'t Hoogfeest*, p. 108, and Holwerda, *Ibid.*, p. 49.

Redemptive History is a Unity

Schilder begins his articles "Concerning the Unity of 'Redemptive History' in Connection with Preaching" as follows: "Reformed people.... believe that the Counsel of God has planned all things according to his will, that God fulfills that Counsel, that he reveals himself in Christ to save the world; that it follows from this that history is a unity, and that this unity, which includes the unity of 'redemptive history,' is apparent (to faith) in Holy Scripture which relates of this history that which is necessary for us to become acquainted with the central thrust of its development and its factual turning points."[9] As to the thoughts expressed, Schilder's involved sentence is quite in line with the Reformed Fathers,[10] and in the controversy this conception of the unity of redemptive history is not challenged.

Both sides profess that *Christ* is *the center* of this one history.[11] In addition, both sides ultimately find the final support for this unity in the *Counsel of God*. "Behind that which once occurred stands God's will which drives all things from the decreed to the deed, from alpha to omega, from Genesis 1 to Revelation 22."[12] "History is the fulfilment of God's Counsel. The Counsel is eternal, but its unfolding is in time."[13] With this in mind, Schilder, in 1946, defines redemptive history as "the successive realization in time of God's thoughts of peace for us according to his fixed plan, and the fulfilment *in* time of this work-program which Father, Son, and Spirit decided upon *before* time."[14]

9 "Gereformeerden.... gelooven, dat de raad van God alle dingen gedacht heeft naar Zijn wil, dat Hij dien raad volvoert, dat Hij Zich in Christus openbaart tot behoud van de wereld; dat daarin de eenheid der geschiedenis gegeven is, en dat dan deze laatste weer, ook voorzoover zij de eenheid der 'heilsgeschiedenis' insluit, zich laat herkennen (voor het geloof) in de Heilige Schrift, die van deze geschiedenis datgene ons verhaalt, wat wij weten moeten, om haar ontwikkeling te leeren kennen naar de beheerschende gedachten en feitelijke wendingen." *Ref,* XI (1931), 365.

10 Cf. his *Zur Begriffsgeschichte,* p. 420, on Calvin's notion of God's decree, creation, providence, and fulfilment in history. In English, W. S. Reid, "Calvinism in Sixteenth Century Historiography," *Phil Ref,* XXX (1965), 178–197. At the turn of the century, we find the same emphasis in, e.g., J. Van Andel, *Handleiding Gewijde Geschiedenis* (1903), Intro. and pp. 1 ff.

11 "... dat heel de heilige historie 'door één gedachte gedragen wordt en Christus als middelpunt heeft.' Daarvan gingen alle Schriftgeloovigen onder ons uit." Van 't Veer, *GM,* XIX (1941), 57. Cf. Schilder, *Christus en Cultuur,* pp. 65 f.

12 "Van raad tot daad." Schilder (1927), *Om Woord en Kerk,* I, 248. Cf. *Ref,* XVI (1936), 290 f.; *Christus in Zijn Lijden,* I, 326 f., and 313: Gods raadsbestel "is een plan, dat alle eeuwen samenvat in één immens besluit."

13 Schilder, *'t Hoogfeest,* p. 106. Cf. *Wat is de Hemel?,* pp. 49 ff., 88, 264; and J. Kapteyn, *Van Hem, Die Is, Die Was en Die Komt* (1941), pp. 43, 214 f.

14 "... het in den tijd naar vast plan door God successief verwerkelijken van Zijn gedachten des vredes over ons, en het ten uitvoer leggen van wat Vader, Zoon en Geest, onderling met elkander te rade gaande, en dienaangaande besluitende,

The phrase "the successive realization in time" gives expression to the progression, the development in redemptive history. This progression should not be disconnected from the unity: it is a progression in unity and a unity in progression. "History," Holwerda says, "always means unity and advance simultaneously."[15]

In and through the one history God comes ever closer to his goal. Redemptive history consists of epochs, dispensations. "In every subsequent epoch there is a decisive entrance of something new, an inevitable increase in atmospheric pressure, a rise in temperature, a drawing near of Bethlehem."[16] "Revelation exists in God's counsel and, according to his plan, is imparted in time, progressing from strength to strength, from nucleus to periphery, from twilight to noontide."[17]

We have highlighted the three postulates underlying the redemptive-historical approach: redemptive history is real history, is a unity, and progresses. At the same time we have noticed that this one progressing history is centered in Christ and anchored in the eternal decree of God. We have further seen that redemptive history is valued so highly because it is revelation to us. The terms "redemptive history" and "revelational history" are used interchangeably and the features of the one apply equally well to the other. The same thing — to add one more new element to this intricate pattern — is true for *Scripture*, particularly for its historical texts. From the unity of redemptive history "it follows immediately that the Bible does not tell histories (plural) but history (singular)."[18] Reformed people "read the Bible not as a collection of stray fragments and books... but as a *unity*, as the one book of God's self-revelation in Jesus Christ.... In the Bible they see a *progression* of revelation from the O.T. to the N.T., from shadow to reality, from less light to more light, from prophecy to fulfilment, from type to antitype, from this age to the one to come...."[19]

On all these points no appreciable difference of opinion can be detected among the Reformed theologians.[20] But as soon as this common starting point

hebben vastgesteld als hun werkprogram, bedacht '*vóór*' den tijd, en uit te voeren *in* den tijd...." *Ref*, XXI (1946), 225. Cf. *HC*, II (1949), 263.

15 *Begonnen*, p. 89.

16 Schilder, *Ref*, XI (1931), 382.

17 Schilder, *Bij Dichters*, p. 135. Cf. *Wat is de Hemel?*, p. 253; *HC*, II (1949), 270 ff. *vs.* a cyclical view of history; and Van 't Veer, *Cursus*, I (1943), vii, 4, *vs.* Vischer: "Bij deze voorstelling is de gedachte van een openbaring Gods *in de geschiedenis* principieel opgeheven. Bij geschiedenis is immers een proces, een ontwikkeling, een voortgaan van minder tot meer."

18 Schilder, *Ref*, XI, 365.

19 Schilder, *Bij Dichters* (1927), p. 401.

20 See, e.g., Hoekstra, *Homiletiek* (1926), pp. 220 ff.; Dijk, *Dienst der Predi-*

is worked out more explicitly for the interpretation and preaching of historical texts, dissension arises.

Disputed Inferences

Although Grosheide accepts a decree by which "God has fixed all things from eternity," he warns that "one should not try to construct a history of revelation by reasoning from the decree of God."[21] Grosheide does not mention anyone in particular, but we may surmise that he has Schilder in mind. Schilder, of course, knows very well and even says explicitly that "God only spoke in part and the part He spoke we only know in part."[22] Nevertheless, the Counsel of Peace takes such a central place in his dogmatics — one of the "cornerstones," says Stellingwerff[23] — that his speculative reasoning in dogmatics also spills over into his considerations on redemptive-historical preaching. We shall enlarge on this in our own critique in the next chapter, but at this juncture we are concerned to bring out the objections raised during the controversy.

The various objections from the exemplary side center on this speculation (systematizing that which cannot be systematized), especially the speculation regarding progression in redemptive history. Grosheide says: "We may say that there is progression from the less clear to clarity, but that does not mean that we can put this progression into words or delineate it with any precision."[24] Schilder is not that cautious. From the postulates of the unity and progression of redemptive history he infers for the preaching of historical texts that "every 'point' in a 'line' must be seen in its immediate connection with all other 'points' of that 'line' [the unity], and, in order to know where one is at that certain 'point,' one must always determine its 'place' within the totality [the progression]."[25] "A sermon on a historical text," he asserts, "is a real sermon only if it shows God's progressing work of self-revelation unto redemption at the particular point of time described by the text, and if it establishes the connection of that one 'point' with the whole 'line' of God's progressing work (throughout the ages, throughout the Scriptures). A sermon which fails to do this does not minister God's

---

king (1955), pp. 199 ff.; also Berkouwer, *Het Probleem der Schriftkritiek* (1938), pp. 321, 382; Greijdanus, *Schriftbeginselen* (1946), pp. 127 ff.; and *RES Report* (1958), pp. 18 f.

21 "Uitgaande van het besluit Gods." *Heraut*, 1941, No. 3330.

22 *Wat is de Hemel?* (1935), p. 51. Cf. *Ref*, XXI (1946), 225: "Van deze heilsgeschiedenis is ons niet alles geopenbaard." "Onze kennis ... kan nooit verder gaan dan wat God geopenbaard heeft."

23 *Phil Ref*, XXVII (1962), 108.

24 *Heraut*, 1941, No. 3330.

25 *Ref*, XI (1931), 365.

Word as found in the historical (!) preaching-text."[26] Again: "Everything that happened in the Old as well as the New Testament had to happen, was the coming of the Logos;... here too there was progression, so that we may not get exactly the same information from the type Joshua as, e.g., from the type Joseph, nor as little from David as from Joshua."[27] Schilder likes to speak of history as "the one day of the Lord." Starting out dim in the morning (the O.T.), the light continues to gain intensity till it reaches its height at noon (the Incarnation). Today we live in the afternoon of God's single day. The day progresses steadily: God's clock keeps ticking off the time; it strikes when an epoch comes to a close, but the hands keep moving... till time runs out. It is all one and the same day, but there is a difference between morning, noon, and afternoon; it is one morning, but there is a difference between nine, ten, and eleven o'clock. This difference, Schilder insists, should be taken into account when interpreting and preaching historical texts.[28]

The exemplary side is not opposed to the unity and progression as such, but they do object to Schilder's requirement of the "exact determination of the place,"[29] or — to retain the figure of the clock — the exact determination of the time. Because the time (date) of many events recorded in Scripture cannot be determined precisely, they fear that Schilder's prerequisite disqualifies many historical texts for preaching purposes. Douma protests: "One gets stuck with large pieces of sacred history. As a result, more than one preacher admits that he can no longer preach many historical texts."[30]

Schilder does not answer this objection directly, but years earlier he did say that refraining from tackling a difficult historical text until the problems have been surmounted is "an expression of respect for the Word, the church, and one's office." He also pointed out that "Reformed authors are only just beginning to write about the history of revelation, and indirectly at that."[31] Perhaps a somewhat unwarranted optimism led to the belief that the difficulty of dating would be solved in due time.[32] However that may be, the question

26 *Ibid.*, p. 374.
27 *Ibid.*, p. 382.
28 *Ibid.* Cf. *Christus*, I, 313 f.; III, 123 f.
29 "Precise *plaatsbepaling.*" Schilder, *Ref*, XIX (1938), 59.
30 *Heraut*, 1942, No. 3338. Cf. Berkouwer, *De Persoon van Christus* (1952), p. 109 (E, p. 138) on the clock: "Daartegenover zal men echter moeten opmerken, dat het ons niet gegeven is de wijzers van de klok tot in de minuten toe te vervolgen, omdat de heilshistorie plaats vindt in de geschiedenis, waarvan ons de datering lang niet altijd bekend is."
31 *Ref*, XI (1931), 365. Cf. p. 381.
32 In 1925 Grosheide, too, expressed this optimism in *De Geschiedenis der Nieuwtestamentische Godsopenbaring*, p. 71: "We mogen gelooven, dat de tijd, waarop [een geschiedenis der openbaring] ook door een niet-genie geschreven kan worden, komen zal, en dat ze ons dan brengen zal een afsluiting van de Nieuwtestamentische studiën."

remains whether this exact dating is a valid prerequisite for preaching historical texts and whether Schilder's notion of progression is perhaps an all-too-logical pattern which does not fit the givens of Scripture.

Schelhaas objects to Schilder's "rectilinear progression which is in essence mechanical. Although the fact that God gives direct revelation in his Word is taken into account, the progression of revelation is presented as a sequence of evolution from lower to higher, from weaker to stronger. God's revelation does not offer us a *historia evolutionis*, however, but a *historia revelationis*."[33] One might question the propriety of the word "evolution" in this connection precisely because revelation is not conceived of as an internal development within mankind,[34] but this does not nullify Schelhaas' objection against a "rectilinear progression."

The basic question is: Does Scripture present such rectilinear progression? Schelhaas answers: No, "God's revelation gainsays a straight-lined process of development. The Messianic light shines clearly from the beginning. The major truths of God have always been known. Christ is already present even while He is coming."[35] Inasmuch as the latter is one of Schilder's major emphases, the question of the Messianic promise given in paradise does not decide the issue of progression one way or the other — particularly since Schelhaas, too, speaks of progression, be it, then, "organic" progression.

More to the point is Schelhaas' next remark: the progression in redemptive history cannot be rectilinear because "there are times of scarcity of revelation and of general relapse of faith."[36] In response Schilder points out that the discussion is about the progression of revelation, not the reaction of man to this revelation. Because these two should be distinguished, a relapse of faith does not necessarily mean a regression in revelation.[37] Schilder does acknowledge that God addresses people at their own level, that Paul, e.g., offers "milk" to a certain church, but this, says Schilder, is no regression in revelation, for "in so doing, Paul advances (progresses) as pastor of that

---

33 *GTT*, XLII (1941), 123.

34 Cf. Schilder, *Een Bloedgetuige* (1946), p. 99: "De groei [zit] niet in de (pseudo-)religieuze beseffen en uitingen van den mensch, doch in het openbarend en scheppend spreken en werken van den in Christus evangelisch tot de wereld komenden God.... Geen evolutie-theoreem ligt hier achter, doch juist de consequente loochening van alle evolutionisme." On the other hand, in *Wat is de Hemel?* (1935), pp. 122 ff., Schilder comes close to applying a biological theory of evolution, including both development and mutation, to the realm of history. And this is not entirely foreign to Schelhaas' thought either when he prefers to speak of "organic development" and seeks an analogy in the germination of a seed and growth of a plant. *GTT*, XLII, pp. 110 f.

35 (1939) *GTT*, XLII, 123.

36 *Ibid.*

37 *Ref*, XX (1939), 96 f. Note that Schilder replies to Schelhaas' 1939 version which has the reverse order: "Er zijn tijden van inzinking des geloofs, van schaarschte der openbaring."

church and as such presents more light than was presented earlier." Schilder makes a distinction here between God's "speaking" and his "coming." God's speaking is always dated and takes into account human sin and weakness. "Because man cannot hear and obey rectilinearly, God does not speak rectilinearly. But God does speak ever more powerfully: He does progress from strength to strength; He does come rectilinearly closer to his goal."[38]

The fact that Schilder must make this distinction indicates the complexity of concretely establishing throughout Scripture this progression in which God's rectilinear coming becomes a more powerful speaking — and this is only the beginning of difficulties. For Schelhaas notes that Isaiah presents the most powerful and extensive O.T. prophecies concerning the Messiah, while he was by no means the last O.T. prophet.[39] And what to do with those portions of Scripture which we cannot date precisely and the persons in redemptive history whose dates we cannot even conjecture?[40] Moreover, there is silence for several centuries after Malachi — then the Messiah comes. "In view of the absence of direct revelation for several centuries, the progression of Christ's coming during this time is certainly not manifest." All this leads Schelhaas to the conclusion that "Scripture has not been given us with the paramount goal of showing us the process of the coming of Christ."[41]

Unfortunately, Schilder does not see fit to meet these problems in his reply except to say that Schelhaas should distinguish the goal of a part (the historical books) and the goal of the whole (all of Scripture).[42] However true this may be, the problems regarding the historical books remain. Nor are they solved by Schilder's suggestion (following Aalders) that Joel may "possibly" have come after Malachi, that the books of Chronicles, including Ezra and Nehemiah, are the most recent O.T. books, and that Ecclesiastes, too, comes near the end, so that it is "very significant in connection with the revelation of God concerning Christ."[43] For, aside from the rather hypothetical nature of this rearrangement, to determine the meaning of a text (partly) on the basis of the date because of the prior assumption that revelation must necessarily progress, puts the text into a scheme which may or may not fit the text itself, and the danger is ever present that the text will be forced to say what it does not intend to say.

---

38 *Ibid*. But see *HC*, II (1949), 268: "Er is een *tweevoudig* geschieden: een voortschrijdend geschieden van het *heil*, èn een voortschrijdend geschieden van de *openbaring* van het heil. Héilsgeschiedenis alzoo, èn openbáringsgeschiedenis. En beide zijn, om zoo te zeggen: '*rechtlijnig*'; een van kracht tot kracht en van minder tot meer vóórtgaan . . . ."
39 *GTT*, XLII (1941), 125, n. 23.
40 *Ibid*., p. 112.
41 *Ibid*., p. 124.
42 *Ref*, XX, 97.
43 *Ibid*.

Grosheide warns against the "circular reasoning" which, by exegesis, develops a history of revelation and then uses the latter as the hermeneutic key for exegesis.[44] In reviewing Van den Born's book on Ecclesiastes, J. Ridderbos opines: "His interpretation has no basis in Ecclesiastes but is the result of infamous 'eisegesis.'"[45] Schelhaas says: "At times we are treated to good insights, but there is also a great deal of distortion, contortion, and arbitrariness."[46] Bavinck observes: "Sometimes things are read in Scripture which God certainly did not intend. The tendency to come up with ever new finds, to dig up new thoughts manifests itself at times...."[47] Overduin is of the opinion that "redemptive-historical preaching was squeezed into rather speculative and scholastic molds and embellished with all kinds of dating speculations."[48] And, to add but one more voice from the choir of critics, Dijk states: "He who supposes that in preaching redemptive history he can date every moment exactly and that he can plot the precise curve of the line of progression in God's revelation, leaves the area of God's Word and becomes entangled in his own constructions and conclusions."[49]

Lest these denunciations leave us with the wrong impression and preclude a fair hearing of the redemptive-historical approach, we ought to interject a few observations at this point.

First, no one, not even Schilder, claims that he can "plot the precise curve of the line of progression in God's revelation" or follow the one day of the Lord down to the minute. As a matter of fact, in 1946 Schilder states explicitly: "To follow redemptive history in *all* its phases always means to confront a mystery."[50] It is not our intention with this observation to gloss over the fact that Schilder, particularly in the early thirties, issued several extreme statements which would lead one to suspect that he considered

44 He calls this a "circelredeneering in optima forma." *Heraut*, 1941, No. 3333. Cf. *GTT*, XLVI (1946), 75.

45 *GTT*, XLI (1940), 88.

46 "Gewrongenheid, overspannenheid en gekunsteldheid." *Franeker Kerkbode*, XIII (1940), No. 633.

47 Followed by the untranslatable: "... dat ik het beste kan typeeren, door het den naam te geven van 'ik-zie-ik-zie-wat-jij-niet-ziet preeken.'" *De Toekomst* (1943), p. 15.

48 *Opdracht*, XXXIX (1964), 24.

49 *Dienst der Prediking* (1955), p. 110. Cf. Boerkoel, *Bazuin*, March 10, 1961: "De heilshistorische methode heeft voornamelijk in haar beginstadium tot een *kunstmatig geknutsel* gevoerd, waarbij een tekst van het O.T. gewrongen werd in een vooruit klaargemaakt schema, dat een tijdschaal presenteerde, waarop men precies kon aflezen, in welke fase der ontwikkeling van de openbaring een gebeurtenis plaats vond.... De historia sacra, de heilige geschiedenissen, werden geabsorbeerd door de historia revelationis, de heilsgeschiedenis."

50 "... het volgen van de heilshistorie in *al* haar phasen toch altijd weer doet stuiten op het mysterie." *Een Bloedgetuige*, p. 99.

a knowledge of the progression down to the "minute" a prerequisite for preaching historical texts.[51]

But, and this in the second place, the redemptive-historical side as a whole should not be saddled with Schilder's extreme pronouncements. It is true that Schilder may be called the originator of their approach, but, as on the exemplary side, we must be mindful of individual variations. The speculation we find in Schilder is not to be found, e.g., in Holwerda and certainly not in Veenhof. Moreover, there is much more to the redemptive-historical approach than the emphasis on progression. And even this emphasis can be seen as part of the battle against the frequent recourse to historical equation marks in the traditional practice of preaching. Consequently, the accent in the redemptive-historical approach falls, generally speaking, more on the progression as the obvious difference between "then" and "now" than it does on progression as minute by minute advance "then."[52]

Third, we must be well aware that the problems regarding progression in revelation pertain to both sides in the controversy, for the exemplary side does not reject the redemptive-historical approach but desires to combine it with the exemplary approach. It may seem that the dating of historical texts is not so essential for the exemplary side, but that is somewhat deceptive. Schelhaas may say: "The value of dating must not be exaggerated because the central truth is made known from the beginning, and this nucleus, which is further unfolded in a particular history, is, after all, the primary element in the interpretation."[53] But if he wishes to do justice to this further unfolding in his text, he cannot avoid a decision on the *previous* unfolding of this truth and hence the place of his text within the totality. Schelhaas' scheme of "organic progression" — in contrast to what he calls Schilder's "rectilinear progression" — may give him more latitude than Schilder,[54] but whether preceded by one adjective or another, it remains "progression," and as such the element of succession and hence dating (in the sense of knowing the order of the sequence) is an indispensable element also in his interpretation.[55] Given the presuppositions on both sides, the question of dating cannot be avoided by either side.

Finally, it is true, no doubt, that the redemptive-historical side is sometimes guilty of rather fanciful exegesis. Already in 1931 Schilder foresaw this

---

51 See the quotations of Schilder above, pp. 125 f.

52 See, e.g., Schilder, *Ref*, XI, 382.

53 "Nadere ontvouwing." *GTT*, XLII, 112.

54 "Organische ontwikkeling is niet iets, dat door ons begrip zoo maar te grijpen is." Schelhaas, *ibid*., p. 123, n. 20.

55 E.g., *ibid*., p. 109: "Men moet, om recht te verklaren, allereerst de stof zien in verband met de openbaring Gods, die tot op dien tijd geschonken was." Similarly Huyser, *GTT*, LI, 15: "Voorts zal de prediker... rekening moeten houden met de *stand der Godsopenbaring* in het betrokken tijdvak."

danger,[56] and yet, he did not avoid it himself. Holwerda acknowledges that "many sermons constructed according to the redemptive-historical method can be criticized. But," he continues, "that is not the point at issue. The discussion is not about practical results but about the *proper method* for reaching ever better results."[57] Although it is debatable whether the method can be so easily divorced from the results attained, it is true that a lucid discussion will have to concentrate on the *method* and not on results which may or may not be results of the method advocated. We turn next, therefore, to the proposed redemptive-historical method.

THE REDEMPTIVE-HISTORICAL METHOD OF INTERPRETING HISTORICAL TEXTS

Schilder contends: "It is clear that the Reformed view of the unity of God's decree, of history, of the Old and New Testament, has consequences for preaching, particularly for preaching historical texts."[58] What these "consequences" are hermeneutically, we shall see in this section.

The Foundational Function of Redemptive History

Redemptive history is the real, factual history God makes in this world. In Scripture we find a record of this history in the historical texts. Discussing the relationship between these historical texts on the one hand, and dogmatic, ethical texts on the other, Holwerda argues: "In my opinion it is beyond doubt that dogmatic texts rest on historical texts and not vice versa. The exodus from Egypt, the lawgiving at Sinai, etc. are presuppósed by the prophets; the work of Jesus Christ as told historically in the gospels and Acts is in its richness set forth in the epistles. But," Holwerda continues, "once one acknowledges that history lays the foundation for dogma and ethics, he can no longer look upon historical texts as illustrative material for dogma and ethics: the foundational function of redemptive history excludes an illustrative function, for if redemptive history should illustrate dogma and ethics by picturing it concretely, dogma and ethics would be presupposed by (prior to) the historical texts."[59]

The exemplary side objects (in my opinion for the wrong reasons) to this line of argumentation. They want to retain both the foundational function

---

56 *Ref*, XI, 381: "De een zou zijn hoofd schudden over zóóveel 'inlegkunde,' waarvan dan ook het gevaar inderdaad voor de deur ligt."

57 *Begonnen*, p. 80.

58 *Ref*, XI (1931), 365.

59 (1942) *Begonnen*, p. 88.

and the illustrative function. Huyser appeals again to the examples of exemplary preaching in the N.T.: Phil. 2:5ff. presents the humility of Christ Jesus "both as illustration and as foundation of dogma" — Christ's humility "is a lofty example for us and at the same time of value for dogmatics where it serves as a pillar in Christology." Similarly in Rom. 4: "Abraham's justification by faith is simultaneously a picture of and a ground for the doctrine of justification. It is both illustrative of and foundational to dogma. The father of all believers gives us an example to imitate."[60] We need not reopen the question whether the biblical "preachers" are normative examples for preachers today,[61] but Huyser does raise a point which brings us to the heart of the matter. He wonders whether there is a contradiction in the redemptive-historical approach: "First they posit: 'the foundational function of redemptive history excludes an illustrative function,' and immediately after this they say: a dogma may certainly be illustrated with a historical event. It seems, therefore, that the illustrative function is not nearly as objectionable as they first suggested."[62]

Unfortunately, Huyser somehow misses the point Holwerda is making, for there is no question of a contradiction here. Having argued that the foundational function of redemptive history excludes an illustrative function, Holwerda continues: "One may, naturally, illustrate a certain 'truth' with a historical text *when one is preaching on a text from the epistles or on one of the commandments.*" And as long as one is looking for illustrations anyway he need not confine himself to redemptive history: church history and other history could also be used. *"But when one has chosen a historical text as preaching-text, that text must be taken in accordance with its own nature and no longer as illustration."*[63]

Lest we misunderstand this part of the controversy and find contradictions where none exist, several interrelated factors should be kept in mind. First, Holwerda clearly limits his proposition — the foundational function excludes an illustrative function — to the historical text as *preaching-text*. Already in 1931 the debate is narrowed to this specific point. Schilder by no means denies that one can preach on conversion, penitence, covetousness, prayer, etc. But, he says, "if one wants to preach about those subjects, he should take a text which presents God's direct revelation on these matters." Historical texts have another purpose; in them God reveals "his coming to the world in Christ." So if one desires to preach about, e.g., the internal struggle of a Christian, he must select "another text, and then by all means use illustra-

---

60 *GTT*, L (1950), 170.
61 See above, pp. 103–119.
62 "Is hier geen tegenstrijdigheid?" *GTT*, L, 179, n. 93.
63 *Begonnen*, p. 88. Emphasis *sic* also in Holwerda's original article (*GTT*, XLIII [1942], 361) used by Huyser. Cf. Schilder, *Ref*, XVI, 290 f.

tions from history."[64] Hence, it is not considered improper for preachers to use historical texts for illustrative purposes. As a matter of fact, historical texts can be used profitably in any number of ways: the historian may use them to reconstruct ancient history, the archeologist to locate a site, the sociologist to trace the development of social structures, the ethicist to learn the morality of a past age.... Historical texts may be used in many ways, but when the historical text is the *preaching-text*, the preacher must concentrate on its unique nature, the specific purpose for which it was recorded in Scripture.

Second, in speaking of preaching-texts Holwerda assumes the necessity of *textual, expository preaching*. If the preacher reads a text before the sermon, it is no more than a matter of honesty that he try to do justice to that text in the sermon. Schilder is of the opinion that a preacher might better not preach a text when he has not caught its central thrust than to preach it anyway and end up with a series of "pious thoughts which could be tacked onto other Bible texts equally well or even onto profane literature."[65] Connected with textual preaching is the emphasis on strict thematic preaching, but we can save this for later. The point to note here is the necessity for textual preaching — a necessity which is affirmed by both sides.

Third, textual preaching of the historical text requires that one do justice to the text as *historical* text. Holwerda states: "Our concern at this point is the *special character* of historical texts.... Every genre of literature has its own law of interpretation.... The object, then, is to treat a historical text as a *fact* of history and not, e.g., as a *parable*."[66] The exclusion of an illustrative function must, therefore, be seen as an attempt to safeguard the special character of the historical preaching-text. It is not a parable, myth, or saga which illustrates (exemplifies) dogmatic or ethical truths; rather, the historical text relates historical facts and must be treated as such in the sermon.

The exemplary side does not disagree on this score; they only desire the freedom to add the exemplary (illustrative) element. But the result of this addition is that the special character of the historical text is slighted. Huyser does not deny that exemplary sermons on historical texts are essentially the same as sermons on parables, but he contends that "the same objection must also be leveled at Psalm 78, for this is an exemplary sermon in *optima forma*. As the poet himself claims in verse 2, he presents history as a parable.... Jesus uses O.T. history in the same way: pedagogico-illustratively."[67] Huyser thus considers himself to be in good company, but he has

64 *Ref*, XI, 373 and 374. Van 't Veer, *Van den Dienst* (1944), p. 146, stresses a point which Huyser also tends to overlook sometimes, namely, that the debate is about *historical* texts. Cf. above, III, n. 13.
65 *Ref*, X (1930), 218.
66 *Begonnen*, p. 87.
67 *GTT*, L (1950), 168.

overlooked that he is appealing to non-textual "sermons" in the Bible, while Holwerda is speaking about our textual, expository preaching.

In our textual preaching, Holwerda maintains, justice should be done to the specific intent, the special character of the preaching-text. When the preaching-text is historical, justice should be done to its factual character: it reveals the very foundation of dogma and ethics — a part of redemptive *history*. And "whoever speaks of history, speaks of something dynamic, of movement; history always means development, growth, progression. History always means unity and advance simultaneously."[68] The historical text requires, therefore, a historical method of interpretation which will do justice to both the unity and progression. This leads to two hermeneutic principles: (1) the organic interpretation, which views the text (event) in its connection with the totality of redemptive history, and (2) the synthetic interpretation, which views the text (event) in its uniqueness.

These principles as such are not new, of course: one can also find them advocated by Hoekstra[69] and Grosheide.[70] And yet there is a difference. Whereas Hoekstra applied these principles to every text in general but hardly emphasized them for historical texts, the redemptive-historical side, counteracting the fragmentary and atomistic interpretation in exemplary preaching, applies these principles to historical texts in particular, and that very strictly. Grosheide did apply these principles to historical texts, but in doing so, he perpetuated the dualism that made the fragmentary interpretation possible in the first place by taking every history "also in and by itself": "*Apart from* its place in and its meaning for the totality of divine revelation, it proclaims something to us."[71] The redemptive-historical approach, on the other hand, opposes this (latent or overt[72]) dualism: the text proclaims something to us not apart from, but *in* its meaning for the totality of revelation. The two principles cannot be separated in the hermeneutic process: the first does not point more to revelational history and the second to the application, as Grosheide would have it.[73] It is *one* procedure, which Holwerda describes in the following ways: one must consider both the connection of the text with its external context and the relationship of elements within the text, or

68 *Begonnen*, p. 89.

69 *Homiletiek* (1926), pp. 290 ff.; *Het Woord Gods* (1931), pp. 53 ff.; *GTT*, XXXII (1932), 512 ff.

70 *Hermeneutiek* (1929), pp. 193 f. Cf. *GTT*, XLVI (1946), 70, for his objection to Calvin's exegesis as "te atomistisch en te analytisch, zij doet ons niet zien het geheel der Schrift, evenmin, wat God ons op een bepaalde plaats, in onderscheiding van andere, openbaart." On Kuyper, see, e.g., Veenhof, *Predik het Woord*, pp. 15 f.

71 "Afgedacht van." *Hermeneutiek*, p. 193, emphasis added. See further above, pp. 45 and 60.

72 Note again that Grosheide, too, pleads for the unity of his approach. *Ibid.*, p. 194.

73 "Wel zal het eerste meer den weg wijzen naar de *historia revelationis*, het tweede naar de toepassing." *Ibid.*

again, one must view the text both longitudinally and transversely.[74] The oneness of this procedure should be kept in mind as we break it apart momentarily in our analysis.

The Organic Interpretation

In opposing the fragmentary interpretation which reads the Bible as a collection of biographies, the redemptive-historical side stresses the hermeneutic significance of the unity of redemptive history. If the common assumption of this unity is to function in preaching the historical text, that text must be interpreted organically, that is, it must be seen as a constitutive part of a larger whole. As Schilder formulates it: "For *every* historical text the A B C for a method of obedient ministry of the Word is this: one must view the text in immediate connection with one general scheme, namely the unity of redemptive history, the unity of God's grand, never shattered, never fragmented, single self-revelation in the Logos."[75]

The unity of redemptive history implies the *Christocentric* nature of every historical text. Redemptive history is the history of Christ: He stands at its center, but no less at its beginning and end. "History is not broken off after the fall but continues in and for the second Adam as the root of the new humanity."[76] Scripture discloses the theme, the scopus of its historiography right at the beginning. "Gen. 3 : 15," Van 't Veer says, "places all subsequent events in the light of the tremendous battle between the Seed of the woman and the seed of the serpent, between Christ coming into the world and Satan the ruler of this world, and it places all events in the light of the complete victory which the Seed of the woman shall attain. In view of this, it is imperative that not one single person be isolated from this history and set apart from this great battle. The place of both opponents and 'co-workers' can only be determined Christologically. Only in so far as they received their place and task in the development of *this* history do they appear in the historiography of Scripture. From this point of view the facts are selected and recorded."[77]

Van 't Veer thus proceeds from the unity and Christocentricity of redemptive history to the unity and Christocentricity of Scripture. As far as the interpretation is concerned, he sees an analogy between the organic interpretation of Scripture and the organic interpretation of any other work which we assume to be a unity. In a stage play, for instance,[78] one may never evaluate

---

74 *Begonnen,* pp. 88 and 91.
75 "... de eenheid van Gods groote, nooit in stukjes-en-beetjes, nooit in fragmenten uiteenvallende, ééne zelfopenbaring in den Logos." *Ref,* XI (1931), 373.
76 Schilder, *Wat is de Hemel?,* p. 144.
77 *Van den Dienst,* p. 149.
78 Schilder also uses the analogy of "een drama" or "een film" in his *College-*

the characters apart from the totality of the play. One can come to a proper evaluation only by viewing the characters and their conduct in the course of the entire play and in the scopus, the intent of the play. "If one disconnects an episode from the totality, the interpretation will fail or lead to pure fantasy. Applied to Scripture, this means that every part of the one redemptive history can be properly interpreted only when this interpretation is Christological, for Christ is the center in which all of redemptive history has its unity and in Whom it finds its interpretation. If one disconnects a part from this Center, he has robbed it of its Christological character and retains, at best, an edifying moral which contains nothing particularly Christian." If, subsequently, one wishes to make the sermon Christocentric after all, he is forced to use "some artifice or other," such as typologizing. That, however, is but a belated and unsuccessful attempt to salvage the Christocentricity that was lost in the beginning.[79] Van 't Veer feels that the loss of the unity of redemptive history (Scripture) means the irreplaceable loss of a Christocentric interpretation; only the organic interpretation which accounts for this unity makes a truly Christocentric sermon possible.[80]

The exemplary side, of course, does not reject the organic interpretation entirely: such interpretation is valuable in discovering the Christological element which the preacher should bring out in the explication. But Douma fears that some preachers, because of "too one-sided Christocentric preaching, tend to pay but little attention to what God says about the human beings." He feels that sermons on historical texts should also be "practical, aimed at life today."[81]

We mention the objection of irrelevance at this juncture to bring out one more implication of the unity of redemptive history. Holwerda is of the opinion that once "the over-all connection is neglected and the one history dissolved into a great many independent histories," one has cut off the

Verslagen (1939), p. 24: "Zoals elke figuur op de film heenwijst en teruggaat naar het spanningscentrum van de film, zo is er een lange weg en een lange studie voor nodig om goed te preken over historische stof en alles te betrekken op het spanningsvolle centrum. Hebben we weinig tijd voor een preek, dan kunnen we beter een tekst nemen met zware exegese uit de brieven, dan een gemakkelijk schijnend historisch verhaal."

79 *Van den Dienst*, pp. 153 f. Cf. Van Andel, *Handleiding*, p. 4: Christ is the key "met welken de heilige geschriften, die ons de gewijde historie brengen, te openen zijn."

80 Here, by the way, lies the reason for the switch in the name from "christo-centrische methode" to "heilshistorische methode." "Heilshistorisch" can better express the contraposition to the underlying cause for the lack of truly Christocentric sermons, which cause Holwerda detected in the fragmentation of redemptive history: "Men maakt al die geschiedenissen zelfstandig" (*GM*, XVIII, 27). In addition, "heilshistorisch," containing the notion of progression, can express the opposition to the historical equation mark.

81 *Heraut*, 1942, Nos. 3342 and 3346. Cf. Nos. 3336, 3339.

very possibility of preaching relevantly on these texts. Because of this fragmentation, he says, one loses not only the Christocentricity, but, "having severed the *historical* tie between David, Abraham and us (the tie of being involved in the one, ever growing redemptive work of God in Christ), one is subsequently forced to make another connection in order to get an application. This is usually done in such a way that, instead of recognizing the historical connection, the unity is sought in the psychical resemblance" between biblical personages and present-day people.[82] This parallel is another "artifice," however, a belated attempt to recover the unity that was lost in the beginning. If the unity of redemptive history is acknowledged at the outset, if it really functions also in the application, relevancy will not have to be fabricated as an afterthought. For the unity of redemptive history implies that the church today is part of this history; we are participants in the great battle waged in history; we are part of the new humanity of which Christ is the root. The unity of redemptive history vouches for the continuity between past and present.

This continuity may never lead to the employment of historical equation marks, however, for that would be to neglect the progression in redemptive history, the discontinuity between one text and another, and between then and now. A necessary complement of the organic interpretation is, therefore, the synthetic interpretation.

The Synthetic Interpretation

Holwerda chose the term "synthetic" as an antonym of "atomistic." The selection of this term is not a very happy choice because in hermeneutics "synthetic" has been linked with the "deep sense" of Scripture,[83] and in homiletics "synthetic" was used in contrast not to "atomistic" but to "analytic." Moreover, it was so abused by "motto preachers" that the term "synthetic method" fell into disrepute as being practically the antonym of textual preaching.[84] Nevertheless, if we can divest our minds of these various connotations, the word can be used here — all the more so because it links up with the emphasis on thematic preaching (the synthetic method in the good sense).

Holwerda, then, sets the synthetic interpretation over against the atomistic interpretation encountered in exemplary preaching. By "synthetic interpretation" he means that the interpreter should pay attention to the specific relationship (the synthesis) of elements within the text. A certain text may contain many of the same elements as other texts, but in the synthesis of these

---

82   *Begonnen*, p. 89.
83   E.g., Grosheide, *Hermeneutiek*, pp. 64 ff.
84   Cf. Hoekstra, *Homiletiek*, pp. 389 ff.

elements every text is unique. Consequently, every text has a unique message, for the preacher should preach the text as a unit and not as a collection of separate elements. "Actually, it is just like chemistry," Holwerda says. "When I want to speak of the significance and characteristics of water (H_2O), I should not speak about the merits of hydrogen (H), but rather about H as it forms a compound in synthesis with O. And when I speak about sulfuric acid, I should not speak about H, but about that entirely different compound H_2SO_4." Similarly, "every historical text is a unit, composed, indeed, of a variety of elements, but these elements have formed a very specific synthesis at this point. This special synthesis gives to every text a unique place within the totality of revelation. Thus every text has its own unique content and its own unique application."[85]

Schilder is particularly adroit in discovering the uniqueness of specific historical situations. He sees the suffering of Christ, e.g., as progressing through several stages; although he points out many parallels between one stage and the next, these only underscore the progressing intensity in the suffering from one stage to the next. "Gethsemane and Golgotha — separated by only a few hours — but what an immense distance between these two!"[86] If within a few hours of a person's lifetime there can be stages which are so markedly different that the parallels drawn from one point to the next underscore the discontinuity between the stages, how much the more will this be the case when one tries to draw a parallel from a person in Scripture to people several thousand years removed from that person. Schilder calls it "folly" and "blasphemy" to say that everyone should have his Gethsemane and Golgotha. God's clock strikes twelve just once. "Gethsemane is nothing without Christ in his specific work, his specific relation with God, and his specific task as Mediator.... Take the specific [the uniqueness] away from Gethsemane and it is utterly devoid of meaning."[87] To say that everyone should have his Peniel may not be blasphemy but it certainly overlooks the uniqueness of Jacob's Peniel which, as a specific historical event, occurred just once. Because of the progression in redemptive history every historical event is by its very nature unique, "einmalig" in the sense that it will never be repeated in exactly the same way.[88]

Many preachers will readily grant this and yet, somehow, desire to draw

85 *Begonnen*, p. 92.
86 *Christus*, III, 206. Cf., e.g., II, 302 f., III, 181 f. The titles of the three volumes give expression to the three major stages: "Aan den ingang-, in den doorgang-, bij den uitgang van Zijn lijden."
87 *Ibid.*, I, 314 f. (*E*, pp. 315 f.).
88 Though a German term, "einmalig" should not be identified with, e.g., Brunner's use of the term. As a matter of fact, it is against his usage that Schilder first introduces it. *Ref*, XI (1931), 382. See also " 'Absolute Eenmaligheid,' " *Ref*, XVII (1936), 81 f., 89 f. (= *Schriftoverdenkingen*, II, 201–211); *'t Hoogfeest* (1939), pp. 31–44; *HC*, II (1949), 329–339.

a parallel between the man in the text and the man in the pew. But awareness of the uniqueness combined with desire for a parallel usually adds up
to atomism, Holwerda contends. "The exemplary method forces one of
necessity into an atomistic treatment of the text," for, given the uniqueness
of, e.g., Thomas' doubt in that specific situation (the compound), the parallel
from his doubt to our doubt can be constructed only by isolating the atom
"doubt." "We must then speak of doubt in general, abstracted from its
synthetic combination with the main thought of the text."[89] In this way, the
uniqueness of both Thomas' doubt and people's doubt today is neglected.
The synthetic interpretation, on the other hand, seeks to do justice to the
uniqueness of each and every historical text by considering the specific
synthesis at that particular place in history of all elements within the text.
And in preaching the text, this uniqueness must be retained throughout.

The exemplary side does not object to this procedure for the explication[90]
but tends to become hesitant in carrying it through in the application. Would
it not eliminate a relevant application? Schelhaas says: "He who overlooks
the general applicability of the text and its message of God for everyone,
cuts off the very possibility of sound application."[91] He contends that Schilder
"has overlooked the fact that the absolute and general applicability expresses
itself in and through and with the 'einmalige'.... Though it is not their total
significance, the pious men and women in the O.T. are undoubtedly also
examples for us. They summon us to imitation in similar circumstances."[92]
But once one has accepted the principle of *progressive* history, those "similar
circumstances" constitute precisely the problem.

Douma agrees that "a historical event is 'einmalig' as far as time and
place are concerned, and yet," he says, "it repeats itself again and again.
There is really nothing new under the sun, for man always has the same
nature and, what's more, God is always the same unchangeable God."[93] If
Douma would mean by this the unity of and continuity in redemptive history,
he would find Holwerda on his side. In actuality, however, the discontinuity

---

89 *Begonnen*, p. 93.
90 Hoekstra also said: "Nu is het de taak van een goede bediening des Woords
bij de behandeling van elken tekst aan de gemeente op eenvoudige wijze duidelijk
te maken, op welke plaats in het proces der openbaring de te behandelen tekst
staat." *Het Woord Gods* (1931), p. 55. On the other hand, certain statements of
Huyser make one wonder in how far he is serious in accepting the "both-and."
He says, e.g., of James 5 (one of his normative examples): "Hij schijnt te vergeten, dat het met de openbaringsgeschiedenis precies eender staat als met de chemie....
Hij neemt het element 'waterstof' apart." *GTT*, L, 176.
91 "Het algemeen geldende." *GTT*, XLII, 127. K. J. Popma, too, speaks of
"algemene 'geldigheid'" in his defence of Saul as an example for us (*Levensbeschouwing*, VI [1963], 130; cf. pp. 121 ff.), though *vs*. Barth he also stresses the
historicity, "eenmalig, onherhaalbaar" (pp. 114 ff.).
92 "Soortgelijke situaties." *Ibid.*, p. 126.
93 "Toch herhaalt het zich telkens." *Heraut*, 1941, No. 3348.

is swallowed up by the continuity and the historical equation mark introduced. The synthetic interpretation, contrariwise, cannot permit an event to be abstracted from the "time and place" so that "it repeats itself again and again," for the time and place are part and parcel of the compound. "A sound application," Holwerda maintains, "requires taking the historical moment into account, even if this makes matters more difficult.... It will not do to take account of the historical moment in the explication, only to ignore it again in the application. If anything adds up to duplexity in preaching, it is this."[94] Holwerda would, therefore, carry the synthetic interpretation right through the application: "Every text has its own unique content and its own unique application."[95] The application depends on the explication, and both, as a unity, must do justice to the intent of the text.

* * *

Summarizing, the historical text reveals a historical event, a fact in redemptive history. For a correct interpretation, the text (event) must be seen as part of the totality of redemptive history. This brings out both the Christocentricity and the continuity of this event with all other events in the one redemptive history. This organic interpretation finds its complement in the synthetic interpretation which brings out the uniqueness of the text in the specific synthesis of elements at that particular place in history. The organic, synthetic interpretation is one indivisible procedure, and both the continuity and discontinuity are to be carried through in the explication as well as the application. In the next section we shall see more specifically what this means for preaching.

REDEMPTIVE-HISTORICAL PREACHING OF HISTORICAL TEXTS

Theocentric Preaching

The preacher who views the historical text as part of one, progressing redemptive history will preach that text in quite a different manner than will the preacher who sees here a biography of one or another person whose memory is embalmed "to serve for our profit and admonition."[96] In the latter case anthropocentric preaching is practically unavoidable. But whether he leans toward the redemptive-historical or exemplary side, anthropocentric preaching is anathema to any Reformed preacher. He is to preach Christ!

---

94 *Begonnen*, p. 86.
95 *Ibid.*, p. 92.
96 Burrell, see above, III, n. 50.

Hoekstra does not tire of emphasizing that *Christ* must be preached: "A sermon without Christ is no sermon. A sermon... which lacks all connection with the Christ who died and arose, is no ministry of the Word."[97] Hoekstra admits that it is not always easy to perceive the link with Christ in a text, and he singles out the historical texts as being particularly difficult in this respect. "When glittering subsidiary characters appear in redemptive history," he says, "the danger is undoubtedly present that the leading character will recede to the background, that Christ will remain in the darkness." But historical or otherwise, O.T. or N.T., the connection with Christ must be shown, or, as he often phrases it, the line must be drawn "from the periphery to the center."[98]

But how does one discover that connection with Christ? The exemplary side frankly admits that they are faced with a problem here. Huyser complains that, although Hoekstra gave some valuable directives, "on this extremely important point homiletics has achieved but precious little,"[99] and he calls upon the redemptive-historical side to produce a scientific study on how to preach Christ from historical texts, particularly O.T. historical texts.[100]

The exemplary preachers, generally speaking, seek the solution to this problem in what they take to be the redemptive-historical method. Here in particular the "both-and" enters in: the redemptive-historical method is valuable in that it provides for a Christocentric explication of historical texts. Schelhaas deems God's promise in Gen. 3 : 15 to be fundamental: "It is in this promise that the foundation for the Christocentric understanding of O.T. historical texts is to be found." "The point of departure for Christocentric preaching lies in the protevangel and in the Messianic prophecy which is presented throughout the O.T. as an organic unity."[101] Dijk says: "We are dealing with the history of revelation which leads to Bethlehem and Golgotha and finds its 'center' in the Christ of God." Consequently, one of the rules for preaching historical texts is: "To see in that history the coming of Jesus Christ and to preach this; to discover the lines which run to Bethlehem; to behold the figure of the Seed of the woman, the Shiloh, the great Prophet, David's Son, the Prince of Peace."[102] Douma seems to be one of the few

---

97 *Homiletiek*, p. 172. Cf. *GTT*, XXXII, 515 f.: "Zoowel het Oude als het Nieuwe Testament is christocentrisch.... Het is dus eisch van homiletische exegese, dat de bediening des Woords moet zijn theologisch en christocentrisch." Further references above, III, nn. 53, 54.

98 *Ibid.*, pp. 173 f.

99 *De Ouderling* (1959), p. 107.

100 *GTT*, LI (1951), 17.

101 *GTT*, XLII (1941), pp. 110 and 111. In similar vein, Grosheide, *Heraut*, 1941, No. 3331.

102 *Dienst der Prediking*, pp. 82 and 201.

who is not too enthusiastic about drawing lines to Jesus Christ, and that on the basis of Calvin. Although Calvin teaches "that without knowledge of Christ Scripture is a dead letter for us," Douma remarks, "this does not tempt him into a more or less haphazard 'drawing of lines' to Christ in each and every sermon."[103] But on the whole the exemplary preachers, though aware of the danger of allegorizing, seek the solution to making the sermon "Christocentric" in drawing a line from the text to Bethlehem or Golgotha, or presenting a parallel between the event in the text and an event in the life of Christ.[104]

It is a rather common misconception that the above expresses the redemptive-historical idea of "Christocentric preaching," but it is a misconception nevertheless. For the redemptive-historical side the Christocentric nature of a sermon does not hinge on a line drawn to Christ Incarnate. Holwerda calls this procedure "staurocentric," or, somewhat more inclusively, "Jesucentric." "Christocentric," however, denotes much more than the Cross or Jesus of Nazareth.[105] Schilder can say about the passion narratives (Jesucentric without equal): "In the entire passion narrative the only subject is God who reveals himself in and through Christ."[106] He is willing to use the term "Christocentric preaching" provided its relation with "theocentric" is properly perceived.[107] It is true that Christ Incarnate is the center of redemptive history, but Christ also stands at the beginning of this history. "'The Logos asarkos,' the pre-incarnate Logos (the Word, the Son), has worked in the world from the beginning," and therefore, says Schilder, "it doesn't make sense, strictly speaking, to talk about a 'before Christ' and an 'after Christ.'"[108] This is not just a clever remark, but it emphasizes once again the unity of redemptive history: our confession of Christ as "very God of very God" should function homiletically, too, so that we do not see the Incarnation as a foreign intrusion which divides the one history into a 'before' and 'after.' Christ does not intrude upon and break up the unity of redemptive history; on the contrary, in Him the unity is to be found. As the eternal Logos He stands above history and works in it from the beginning to the end of time.

---

103 *Heraut*, 1941, No. 3300. It goes without saying that Dijk and others also warn against allegorizing.

104 Cf. Huyser, *GTT*, LI, 17: "... een verbindingslijn naar Christus... dat is het Christologische." This customary solution may also be found in Gispen, *De Christus in het O.T.* (1952). On pp. 43-60 ("De Christus in historische teksten") the attempt is made to find "lijnen naar de Christus" (p. 59). "Zó wordt de Doorboorde... in het O.T. aanschouwd. Zo worden op Golgotha onze levensraadsels samengevat en opgelost" (p. 60). A more theocentric emphasis is to be found on p. 32.

105 *Begonnen* (1942), p. 84. Cf. *Hom*, VIII (1948), 141.

106 *Ref*, X (1930), 218.

107 *Ref*, XI (1931), 365.

108 *Ibid.*, p. 382. Cf. *Christus en Cultuur*, p. 41; *HC*, III (1950), 137-181.

"Everything that happened in the Old as well as in the New Testament had to happen, was the advent of the Logos, was in reality as 'einmalig' as when Christ was seen in the flesh. In this advent too," Schilder asserts, "there is progression."[109]

The Incarnation, then, should not be exalted as the one and all. "For the 'point' of the birth of Christ is nothing without that long road from creation to parousia upon which the God of history has placed it."[110] The Incarnation is part of the progressive coming of Christ. Seen in the light of the unity and progression of redemptive history, the birth of Christ is but another stage, be it ever so important, of the ongoing work of Christ throughout history. The progression in redemptive history is not so much a progression *to* Christ (the Incarnation) as the progression *of* Christ — a progression, indeed, *to* his incarnation, but also to his crucifixion, his resurrection, his ascension, his return in the Spirit, and his return at the end of time.

In Schilder's opinion a preacher cannot preach truly Christocentric sermons when he discovers only "tiny Messianic lights" here and there in the O.T. and all the while fails to see "the great evolution of the Messianic self-revelation and self-preparation of the Logos." He should see the eternal Christ himself marching through the O.T., revealing, redeeming, and preparing the way for his own coming in the flesh.[111] Christocentric preaching is preaching in which "Christ is the theme — not Christ and his work as summarized in dogmatics, but Christ as God's office-bearer reaching a certain 'point' of his work-program."[112]

Schilder considers it improper — except during the Advent season — for the preacher to draw a line in his sermon from the "point" disclosed by his text to the "point" of the Incarnation. First of all, he says, the preacher should have enough work passing on God's revelation at this one "point"; and second, there is no reason to place such emphasis on the birth of Christ. The "points" that come after the Incarnation — Good Friday, Easter, Ascension, Pentecost, Parousia — are even more important. "The whole O.T. and the whole N.T. concern God's coming in Christ, but the points along this road are different." The preacher should consider "his task (in the summer) fulfilled when he has presented the strict, unique meaning of that point of the road which his text discloses."[113]

In the foregoing it will have become evident that in Schilder's view "Christocentric preaching" is intimately related with "theocentric preaching."

109   *Ibid.*
110   *Ref,* XIX (1938), 59.
111   *Ref,* XI, 381, and XIV, 346.
112   *Ref,* XI, 373.
113   *Ref,* XIX (1938), 59. Note, however, that Schilder continues right after this quotation: "Dan zal meteen het verband tusschen elk ééne punt en àl de punten van A [schepping] tot en met X [wederkomst] zijn aangeduid in die grootsche conceptie, die een goedgereformeerde preek altijd worden kan ...."

"Christocentric" refers to Christ the eternal Logos who appears not only at the center of redemptive history but who is at work throughout history.[114] By virtue of this, the O.T. epoch in its entirety is Christocentric. "The whole O.T. is Christocentric," Holwerda says, and elsewhere: "The whole O.T. is Messianic."[115]

This Christocentric character is typical of the *New* Testament as well. We note this specifically because discussions on Christocentric preaching usually concentrate on the O.T. — as if the N.T. presented the preacher no problems in this respect. But one has to think only of the book of Acts — "the Acts of the *Apostles*" — to see that the preacher is confronted with similar problems in the N.T. And here, too, we must see Christ in action. "Christ, the glorified Lord, works in and through the apostles. It is He who travels with them through the world, who speaks through them, who establishes the churches."[116] "Christocentric," thus, encompasses both the Old and the New Testament. Every historical text is by nature Christocentric because it relates the work of Christ.

The essence of Christocentric preaching is not to be found, therefore, in a line drawn from the text to Christ Incarnate or in the discovery of a parallel event in the life of Christ on earth. As a matter of fact, Holwerda is quite opposed to this traditional habit of "magically producing a line from every text to the Cross or the Incarnation." He feels that this a priori assumption that every text speaks of Christ Incarnate leads inevitably to a schematism resulting in forced parallels. But, says Holwerda, Christ should be seen as "signifying the fulness of God's revelation." The assumption is "*that* there is revelation of Christ here, but *what* is said about him must still be determined."[117] Van 't Veer agrees: "No one should think that 'Christological' means that every text must point to Bethlehem or Golgotha or some incident in 'the life of Jesus'.... Rather, it signifies the Christ, the Anointed, the Mediator, and that not only as to his person but also as to his work. Viewed this way one can preach Christologically without making the text point to a certain part of Christ's life on earth — and, vice versa,

---

114 Calvin uses the term "the eternal Christ" in this sense. Cf. Veenhof in *Zicht op Calvijn*, pp. 73 ff. On Kuyper, see Veenhof, *Predik het Woord*, pp. 20 f.
115 *De Wijsheid*, pp. 159 and 35 f. In the latter place Holwerda also speaks of "mediate Messianic" (in distinction from "immediate") to indicate the progressive fulfilment of prophecy (Isa. 7:14, Hos. 11:1). Cf. *Populair*, pp. 105 f., and *Historia*, 65: "Men mag 'Messiaans' niet versmallen tot aankondiging van de geboorte van Jezus." In this connection see N. H. Ridderbos, "Christus in de Psalmen," *GTT*, XLIV (1943), 129–149, for the various ways Christ appears in the Psalms.
116 Van Dijk, *PE*, VII (1942), 149. Cf. Veenhof in *De Verborgenheid der Godzaligheid* (1941), pp. 268 f., and *Getuigend* (1947), pp. 8 ff. Also D. K. Wielenga, "De Plaats van de Handelingen der Apostelen in de Openbaringsgeschiedenis van het N.T.," *VT*, XI (1940), 155–167.
117 *Begonnen*, p. 112.

one can point to the Cross (as Vischer does on Esther) and completely miss the Christological character of the text."[118] The same emphasis is found in Van Dijk: "The Son of God does not initially become Christ at his incarnation; He has been anointed from eternity,... and commences his work as Mediator right after man's fall into sin."[119] It is true that the great battle announced in Gen. 3 : 15 culminates in the fulness of time in the struggle of the Word Incarnate with Satan, but, Van Dijk asks, how do we understand the ages before and after this culmination point? He feels that we too often see this period of time merely as a battle between the people of God and the unbelieving world and "lose sight of the fact that both before and after the Incarnation Christ himself, from heaven, is actively engaged in this battle. It is He who fights in and through his people." Christ is there in Moses, Joshua, the judges, David, etc.[120] Christ is at work in the flood, in Egypt, at Horeb, in Babylon, in Bethlehem, at Golgotha, at Pentecost, in Rome — always Christ.[121]

This conception of Christ as the eternal Logos actively at work throughout history removes the props from under the traditional insistence that every sermon must somehow point to Christ Incarnate in order to be Christocentric. It bursts the confining mold which has caused so many aberrations throughout the history of preaching; it creates more room for the text itself to speak. The preacher is no longer required "to land with an acrobatic leap at Golgotha"[122] in order to *make* the text and the sermon Christocentric, for Christ is already present at that point of redemptive history which the text relates.[123]

This feature of redemptive-historical Christocentric preaching seems to have escaped the attention of the exemplary side. Huyser complains about the "complicated, long-winded themes,"[124] but he fails to see that these themes — indeed, sometimes awkwardly- and even mis-formulated — are attempts to express precisely how Christ was at work in that part of history, centuries before He was born. Dijk objects to the term "Christocentric preaching" because: (1) "in this way the work of God so easily recedes to the background"; (2) it overlooks the revelation of God in nature, outside the Word

118 *Cursus*, I, iii, 4.
119 *PE*, VII (1942), 149.
120 *Ibid.*, p. 161.
121 *PE*, VI, 287.
122 Holwerda, *GM*, XVIII (1940), 55.
123 See, e.g., Holwerda's sermons in *Een Levende Hoop*: "Gideon heeft het adventswonder gezien" (II, 110); "Juda's zonde was:... ze hebben de *Christus* verworpen" (IV, 8); "Christus kwam verder, ook toen het volk in ballingschap ging" (IV, 15); "Nebucadnezar's aanval is gericht tegen ... de Christus" (IV, 28).
124 Huyser selects, e.g., "Christus' worsteling met David om de erkenning van Gods recht in Absalom's dood," and "Christus volbrengt zijn verlossingswerk door in te gaan tot de zonden zijns volks en zich zo te geven in de macht hunner vijanden." *GTT*, LI, 14.

Incarnate; and (3) it tends to neglect the work of the Spirit.[125] But these objections are valid only after one has first divorced Christ from the Father and the Spirit and limited Christ, moreover, to Christ Incarnate.[126] But this, we have seen, is not the intent of redemptive-historical "Christocentric preaching"; on the contrary, the emphasis falls on Christ as the eternal Logos, *one* with the Father and the Spirit. Christocentric preaching is theocentric preaching.[127]

Sola Scriptura

In one of his sermons Schilder states that many people overlook Christ while reading the Bible because they focus their attention solely on the "Bible saints." "But happily," he says, "we need not treat of Jacob's 'soul.' We are not even allowed to do this, for in the history of the Bible the concern is with *God* — God who reveals himself in Christ Jesus. Every point of time on the long road of redemptive history represents a milestone which God has reached in coming ever closer to his goal."[128] The intent of the historical text is to show this advent of God, and "when God tells us something about *his* work, *his* coming to the world in Christ (from the beginning to the end), then we ought to speak about that and nothing else."[129]

The question remains, however, whether this redemptive-historical preaching, this theocentric-Christocentric preaching, does not overlook the *men* in the text; as Schelhaas says: "The text is most certainly also about them."[130]

The redemptive-historical side can hardly deny, of course, that the preacher is confronted with various people in the historical text, but Holwerda feels that we too often begin at the wrong end. "We often begin by immediately concentrating on the *men* and are busy drawing a line from these men to the application before we know it. Naturally we may not neglect the people in the text; every detail — this too — requires our attention. Nevertheless, we must always see these human deeds as a reaction to *God's* action." For that reason Holwerda considers it "extremely important to determine first of all exactly what *God* is doing in any given section" of Scripture. The

---

125   *Dienst der Prediking*, pp. 82 f.

126   This seems to be Dijk's assumption *in his use of the term* "Christocentric preaching." He sets "Patrocentrische, Christocentrische én Pneumacentrische prediking" side by side as each covering a part of the truth, and in his trinitarian approach he proceeds so much from the three Persons, each with his own distinct work, that to my mind the *one* work of the *triune* God is in danger of being slighted. See *ibid*, pp. 83 f., 87; and on the restriction of "Christ" to Christ Incarnate, e.g., p. 201.

127   Cf. Kapteyn, *Van Hem*, p. 244.

128   (1934) *Preken*, II, 5 f.

129   *Ref*, XI, 373.

130   *GTT*, XLII, 128.

men described in the text may never, for the sake of the application, be viewed in isolation from God's acts at that particular stage of redemptive history. The murmuring of Israel in the desert, for instance, is not just the general sin of dissatisfaction as we see it all around us today; "it is Israel's unbelieving rejection of God's redemption which it witnessed in the water springing from the rock: 'the rock was Christ.' "[131]

In addition, Holwerda suggests that "one should explore whether the men concerned act in their capacity as office bearers. The discovery of loyalty or disloyalty in office helps us in the right direction and at the same time offsets the tendency to staurocentric preaching. With Elijah, for instance, one need not be bent on drawing a line to the Cross; it suffices to see him as bearer of the Word, as a person on whom the Spirit of Christ rests."[132] God, Christ, is at work in and through his people. The people we meet in Scripture are not included because they are so pious or impious, nor because they are such good or deterring examples for us; rather, they appear in Scripture because they have a specific task in redemptive history, a specific office, and hence, "a *specific* significance for the appearance of Christ and his work."[133] As Van Dijk puts it: All that was written was indeed written for our instruction; "it was recorded, however, not as actions of pious or ungodly people, but as human deeds through which the Lord God makes the history of his Kingdom. Only when seen in this light can those deeds become bearers of comfort and warning to us."[134]

It is not so much a question, then, of God *and* man appearing in the historical text as two factors which must each receive their due in preaching (the first mainly in the explication and the second as prerequisite for the application), but rather *God*, one factor, working in and through man.[135] If we must speak of *two* factors, we should speak of God and Satan. "On either side men come into action, but the real parties in the battle are God and Satan."[136] The men described in the text may never be isolated from this great battle and their specific historic place in it. "The place of both opponents and 'co-workers' can only be determined Christologically."[137] The Koran, the Book of Mormon, and other literature may mention the same persons, but only in the Bible do they appear in this context of the great battle initiated by the triune God to redeem his people and to advance his Kingdom till God shall be all and in all. *Sola Scriptura.*

131 *Begonnen*, p. 104.
132 *Ibid.*
133 Schilder, *Ref*, XI, 374. Cf. *Ref*, XIV, 18.
134 *PE*, VI, 303.
135 See, e.g., Holwerda's sermons on Gideon with their emphasis on: "De Geest des *Heeren* toog Gideon aan, Hij trok hem aan, zoals je een jas aantrekt." *Een Levende Hoop*, II, 70. Cf. pp. 17, 86, 109; and on Daniel, *ibid.*, IV, 4 ff., 26 ff.
136 *Ibid.*, II, 81.
137 Van 't Veer, *Van den Dienst*, p. 149.

More must be said about the men appearing in historical texts. As historical figures they are part of the one redemptive history. We, too, are part of this one redemptive history, be it at a later date. There is, therefore, continuity because we are all part of the same history; there is a connection between these figures of the past and us today. "This connection does not lie in the area of common faith experiences, however, but *in Christ*, in being included in the same great struggle."[138] "Only because the events in the desert belong to the one redemptive history, only because the communications about Abraham, etc. are Christocentric — only for that reason is this history significant for us. We stand with Abraham and Moses in the one history of God. That is why we are involved when God appears to Abraham; that is why Israel's murmuring is significant for us: Scripture says they tempted Christ in the desert."[139] "In Christ lies the unity of the history in which Elijah stood and prayed and in which we stand and pray. But with that we have also said that Elijah's prayers and our prayers are *dated*."[140]

Dated — that is the other side of the coin: unity but also progression, continuity but also discontinuity. The unity of redemptive history may never lead to placing historical equation marks between people then and people now. Then is *not* now. This is most obvious, of course, when one considers the persons appearing in the O.T., but it is equally true for the persons appearing in the N.T.[141] The progression in redemptive history did not come to a halt with the closing of the Canon but continues throughout history to the end of time. The church today is not the church of Pentecost and the preacher may not act as if the two can simply be identified for purposes of application. "Let there be no anachronism, especially not in the history of salvation, which is always progressive, which always wants to advance from the potential to the deed, from latent power to patent development, from bud to flower, from morning to day." "We may not abuse the fact that God's revelation in Scripture virtually puts a period behind the chapter on Pentecost and then leaves us alone. For the Bible itself teaches us that God with his revelation in Scripture brings us no further than the morning and that we ourselves, guided by this light, must now proceed to the full afternoon."[142] The progression in redemptive history is not to be slighted. The people we

---

138 *Ibid.*, p. 155.

139 Holwerda, *GM*, XVIII, 27.

140 Van 't Veer, *Van den Dienst*, p. 161. For a detailed exposition on Elijah, see Van 't Veer's *Mijn God is Jahweh*.

141 "Dat historisch verschil is ook in rekening te brengen bij stoffen uit het N.T." Holwerda, *Begonnen*, p. 111.

142 Schilder, "Niet terug naar Pinksteren!" (1920), *Om Woord en Kerk*, II, pp. 41 and 42.

address today live not only in an entirely different situation[143] but also at a different stage of redemptive history: after Easter, after Pentecost — by almost twenty centuries. The historical gap must be taken into account whether one preaches on the O.T. or the N.T., and no preacher should try to get around it by psychologizing, spiritualizing, or moralizing.

The Psychical as a Constituent Part

The people mentioned in the historical texts live at different stages of redemptive history. Everyone is "einmalig," says Schilder: "Everyone has a different office, is a different person, has a different responsibility, acts in a new situation." This uniqueness is to be brought out in preaching historical texts. But sermons which concentrate on the soul do just the opposite, Schilder contends. "As often as one delivers 'psychological' sermons, he is occupied with something that is not 'einmalig'.... Psychology tries to describe certain universal traits. Consequently, when one presents in his sermons a 'soul-analysis' of Melchizedek, Joseph, Joshua I, David, Joshua II, etc., and allows that to be the leading motif, he has eliminated precisely that one thing which is 'einmalig.'"[144] This does not mean that the psychical should be eliminated, but it should be seen as an element which is meaningful only as a component of the totality revealed in the text. "When we preach a historical text, the psychical moment, if present, must certainly receive its due in the exposition of the concrete situation," Schilder says, "but the biotic no less, if that plays a role, and the social, the political, the ecclesiastical, etc."[145]

We are back at the "synthetic interpretation": not one element may be neglected, but neither may any element be abstracted from the synthesis, the compound formed by all these different elements in the preaching-text. Though the details may not be slighted, each and every detail must be seen as part and parcel of the central thrust of the historical text. If, as Schilder contends, the thrust of these texts is the progressive redemptive history of Christ,[146] then the psychical element may never be set apart from this history for the sake of a relevant application.

As a matter of fact, one can gain a proper perspective on the psychical element only in terms of redemptive history. Take, for instance, the psychical element of doubt. John the Baptist's doubt occurred when Jesus had just begun to preach; Thomas' doubt arose, on the other hand, after Jesus died. Both

---

143 "Wie heeft risico's als Abraham bij Abimelech; wie heeft in zijn tent moeilijkheden als hij had met Sara en Hagar?" Holwerda, *Begonnen*, p. 90.

144 *Ref*, XI (1931), 382.

145 *Ref*, XVIII (1938), 336.

146 *Ibid.*: "Maar de openbaringshistorie moet in preeken over historische stoffen de eigenlijke stof zijn."

are "doubt," and yet each has its own unique stamp. The difference is in no small measure due to the fact that John's doubt arose at a stage of redemptive history earlier than that of Thomas' doubt. These two different kinds of doubt may not simply be isolated and made to parallel the (unique) doubt of contemporary people; rather, each doubt should be seen as but one of many elements which combine to form the message of the text in this unique setting. Seen synthetically in this way, Holwerda understands Matthew 11 : 1-6 (the Baptist) to be speaking of "the crisis in preaching, while John 20 : 24-29 is about the specific *Easter* confession: My Lord and my God."[147] The psychical element does play a role, but it is completely integrated in and subservient to the central thrust of the text.

The Events as Concrete Historical Facts

It is hardly necessary to repeat that the redemptive-historical approach views the events recorded in historical texts as down-to-earth, concrete historical events. And this, we have seen, is a postulate common to both sides. But then the consequences of this assumption must be borne: as concrete historical events they are dated, past, and "einmalig" — they do not recur today in exactly the same way.

For example, God does not ask anyone today to offer his son as he asked Abraham to offer Isaac, and no one becomes mute today as punishment for his unbelief as Zechariah did. "It is possible to spiritualize these events, but," Van 't Veer asserts, "that is an all-too-easy solution. Everyone feels that they cannot be simply transferred, for we live in a different historical dispensation. It is necessary, therefore, always to take account of the special meaning of such a fact in connection with the calling and task of that certain person on that particular date of redemptive history. And only when we have thus seen the special meaning are we able to understand the 'divine teaching' that comes to us who live in another dispensation, at a different stage of history."[148] Once one has seen the redemptive-historical meaning of the text, Holwerda adds, "there is no longer any need to spiritualize."[149]

The historical understanding is an absolute requirement for interpreting historical texts. To bypass the historical gap via spiritualizing amounts to falsification of these texts. There is no deeper, spiritual sense to be found behind or above the historical, for that deep sense can be found only *in* the historical. "The spiritual sense can never be exegetical (historical) nonsense."[150]

---

147 *Begonnen*, p. 92. Cf. Holwerda's meditation on Matt. 11 : 1–6 in *De Wijsheid*, pp. 74–77 (= *Ref*, XIX, 409).
148 *Cursus*, I, iii, 4.
149 *GM*, XVIII, 28.
150 Holwerda, *Begonnen*, p. 103.

The Intent of the Text

The redemptive-historical side has nothing positive to offer on the question of moralizing. To explain this void, at least three reasons suggest themselves. First, the man in the pew is not conceived of as consisting of three faculties, each of which — but especially the will — must be stimulated in every sermon. Second, the persons described in the text display a conduct which only underscores the historical discontinuity. It will hardly do to transfer only those actions which we deem suitable for imitation in our age and to ignore the rest. Third, and this we take to be the major reason, the sermon must be a proclamation of the content of the preaching-text and must do justice to the intent of that text. The historical text itself does not moralize and hence should not be used for moralizing. The purpose of historical texts is not to offer us human models for proper conduct but to show the progressive coming of *Christ* in history.[151]

Typology

Finally, as to typology, the redemptive-historical side — strange as it may seem — both curtails and enlarges the use of types of Christ. Both are connected with their view of the historical text, of history, and of Christ. The restrictions are intended to curb the unbridled fantasy in discovering types, to call a halt to the arbitrary parallels drawn between biblical personages and Jesus of Nazareth. We are not to *make* types but must confine ourselves to the types God has given.[152] Mere discovery of a parallel with the life of Jesus does not make a sermon Christocentric. Schilder writes: "We are overjoyed when we discover, e.g., that the name Othniel may have meant 'lion of God.' That sounds much like 'Lion of Judah.' The fact that Othniel was from the tribe of Judah clinches it. Another picture of Christ, thank goodness! But the Bible says: Christ was already present; He was there himself, and He would have been there no matter what Othniel would have been called."[153]

In this quotation we find both the restriction and the expansion of typology. The presence of Christ in the text does not hinge on a rather "accidental" detail — a name, character trait, or experience — which we subsequently also discover in Jesus; rather, the eternal Christ himself is at work in and through that person. As Van Dijk phrases it: "The figures in the O.T. are

---

151 Cf. Koole, *Hom*, XIX (1960), p. 49: "Ook hier moraliseert de Historia Sacra niet, omdat het daar niet gaat over een Historia Sacrorum Hominum, maar om een Historia Revelationis Dei."

152 See above, pp. 84 f.

153 *Ref*, XI (1931), 382.

not modeled after the figure of Christ, but Christ himself, working through them from the inside out, so to speak, causes the resemblance." It is only in this sense that Van Dijk wishes to speak of "types." "But then," he says, "it is also clear that this 'typicalness' is not found in just a few people but in every man and woman who contributed to the building of the Church of God during the O.T. epoch."[154]

And why should typology in this sense be restricted to the O.T. epoch? Do we not see men and women in the N.T. epoch building the Church, the Kingdom of God? Schilder does not hesitate to speak of John the Baptist and Mary as types of Christ,[155] but there, inexplicably, he stops. Well, not quite inexplicably, for then Christ appears in the flesh as the fulfilment of all the foregoing types: "When the Sun of righteousness appears, all types can be blown out, and that is exactly what God does."[156] The uniqueness of the O.T. types is thus honored: here too there is progression;[157] here too there is discontinuity. On the other hand, the eschatological perspective, so typical of the redemptive-historical approach, also breaks through. The culmination point, says Schilder, lies not so much between the Old and New Testament dispensations as at the Last Day. For that reason "we, too, are children of advent; there are still 'shadows' today" awaiting their final fulfilment.[158] Here we discern the continuity again. "What God did before the Incarnation He can also do after it.... The Christ who took form in Joshua also takes form in me today; I, too, am an antitype of Christ."[159] Here we see the eternal Christ again, marching through the N.T. as well as the O.T., the twentieth century as well as the first century, manifesting himself in and through his people, and all the while advancing ever closer to his goal: the completed Kingdom of God.

* * *

The objections raised by the exemplary side to exclusive redemptive-historical preaching center on the lack of application. Douma says: "Every Reformed person in the past thought it quite normal for historical texts to

---

154 *PE*, VII (1942), 161. Cf. Schilder (1936), *Preken*, II, 119: "Ik kan nooit weten, waarom Christus achter David aankomt naar het vlees, of ik moet ook hebben gezien, dat Hij naar Zijn godheid aan David is vooruitgegaan en dat door Hem David kon gemaakt worden type van Christus, zodat Hij later als antitype kon verschijnen, niet door David, die Hem verwekte, maar door Zichzelf."

155 *Capita Selecta*, III (1951), pp. 38 and 48.

156 *Ibid.*, p. 38. Cf. p. 59.

157 *Ibid.*, p. 48.

158 *Ibid.*, p. 45. Cf. p. 46 on the Sunday as type of the great day of the Lord.

159 *Ibid.*, p. 35, with references to L. D. XII and II Cor. 3 : 18. Schilder uses the word "*anti*type" because we live after the Incarnation. See also *College-Verslagen* (1939), p. 31: "Elk mens waarin de werkingen van den Geest zich openbaren, is vertoning van den Christus."

be presented in a practical and relevant manner." "The two subjects, Sacred History and History of Revelation, may not dominate to such an extent that every sermon on a historical text would, in effect, have to describe merely a moment in the process of the development of God's revelation."[160] Dijk writes: "I agree... that the application can be corrupted in all sorts of ways, but this misuse does not give us the liberty to abolish the application and restrict ourselves to mere explication."[161] And Bavinck, to call upon only one more critic, complains: "In many a new sermon the application is not much more than a 'dud.' Many sermons in our time are splendid discourses, profound lectures about some redemptive-historical thought, but they are not sermons in the true sense of the word.... They are discourses which, however brilliant and deep, do not really move us.... These preachers have forgotten the man in the pew."[162]

In all these quotations we detect the charge that exclusive redemptive-historical preaching is not sufficiently relevant, that it is too objective, that the application is offered up on the altar of pure explication, that, in fact, it is no preaching. Before we make up our mind on the correctness of these accusations, it would be well to hear out the redemptive-historical side on the nature of preaching.

PREACHING THE WORD

Earlier we heard Veenhof claim that the objective–subjective dilemma cannot be overcome by any possible combination of the two poles: both the objective preacher and the subjective preacher stand in need of a fundamental change in their attitude towards and their view of Scripture.

Those influenced by the Calvinistic Philosophy (WdW) tried to overcome the objective – subjective dilemma by speaking of Scripture as *norm*. As Spier put it: "The Bible is neither objective nor subjective.... The gospel is the power of God unto salvation (I Cor. 1 : 18). 'For the Word of God is living and

160 *Heraut*, 1941, Nos. 3292 and 3300.
161 *OB*, XXII (1944), 3004.
162 *De Toekomst* (1943), p. 20. ("Dud" is our translation for "een lam handje, waarmee niemand een gevoelige tik ontvangt.") See also, e.g., Schelhaas, *GTT*, XLII (1941), 127: "... die snijdt de mogelijkheid van gezonde toepassing af en bouwt misschien wel een gewrocht van openbaringsconceptie, maar houdt geen preek"; J. Ridderbos, *GTT*, XLIII (1942), pp. 274 f.: "...men loopt gevaar, in plaats van het levenvernieuwende Godswoord te geven een theoretische beschouwing of speculatie, die, ook al kan ze sommigen behagen, de gemeente niet genoegzaam biedt wat ze tot haar opbouw in het geloof van noode heeft"; and Overduin, *Opdracht*, XXXIX (1964), 24: "Het objectieve werd al heel gauw objectivistisch en de preek een theologisch referaat. Dan is het heilshistorische uit het Schriftklimaat, het verkondigingsklimaat en het beslissingsklimaat gevoerd in het klimaat van de beschouwing."

active...' (Heb. 4 : 12). Thus the Word of God is the dominating *norm* for our lives. And because the ministry of the Word derives its character from the Word on which it depends, preaching must be normative. The proclamation of the Word must be neither objective nor subjective but *normative!*"[163] Put into more familiar terms: Scripture is the Word of the living God; it is not a theory, a collection of doctrines, a number of loci; rather, "Scripture is *kerygma*, address, appeal.... Scripture itself lays hold of life; better, in it God lays hold of life. Thus Scripture itself is pertinent to human existence in its entirety."[164]

Scripture may never be divorced from the speaking God: it is *his* Word. "Christ is present in the Word; He stands behind it as the divine Logos; the Word is never without his Spirit." "Word and Spirit always go together."[165] The same eternal Christ whom we saw earlier marching through both the Old and New Testament epochs is speaking in Scripture. Through the Scriptures He addresses his people today. Seen in this light, the preaching-text, as Van Dijk puts it, is "not a piece of dogmatic, historical, religious, or ethical truth, but a living, warm Word of the God who comes to his people in speaking this Word to them."[166]

The Sermon as God's Word

Redemptive history did not stop with the closing of the Canon. The eternal Christ who marched then, marches on even today; the Logos who spoke then, speaks today through his ministers of the Word. Veenhof says: "The church's preaching is *the* means by which Christ makes his spoken and subsequently written Word into a living present.... In the proclamation Christ comes and calls and warns and conquers." "Preaching is not merely a story *about* one or more moments of redemptive history — no, preaching is itself a moment *in* the redemptive history made by Christ. Jesus Christ continues his work of redeeming and liberating the world in and through pro-

---

163 *Wijsbegeerte*, p. 57. Cf. *CB*, I (April, 1936), 1: "Prediking is noch objectief, nòch subjectief.... Wat gepredikt dient te worden is het Woord Gods. Maar dat is niet object, doch wet." So also Popma, *Psychologie*, p. 38. Cf. Veenhof, *Prediking en Uitverkiezing*, pp. 167 ff. on Kuyper and the WdW on this point.

164 Veenhof, *Bondsboekje 1940*, p. 58.

165 Spier, *Wijsbegeerte*, pp. 58 and 48. Cf. *PE*, VI (1941), 159. On the relation of Word and Spirit, see Veenhof, *Bondsboekje*, pp. 32, 48 ff.; Holwerda, *Populair*, pp. 11 ff.; Schippers, *Van den Dienst*, pp. 46 ff.; and, more recently, Berkouwer, *Heilige Schrift*, I, 73 ff.

166 "Een levend, warm Woord, van de daarin tot Zijn volk komende, tot Zijn volk sprekende God." *Hom*, XXI (1962), p. 83. Cf. Schilder, *College-Verslagen* (1939), p. 31: "De Bijbel geeft geadresseerde waarheden." This emphasis can also be found in, e.g., Dijk, *Dienst der Prediking*, p. 81: "De Schrift is een levend boek, waarin God tot ons spreekt, waarin Christus Zijn stem doet horen."

clamation; in it He works out his Easter, Ascension, and Pentecost."[167] Preaching, then, is the continuation of God's redemptive activity. As such it is itself a *redemptive event*. "Wherever preaching takes place in accord with Christ's command, it becomes a redemptive event and the Kingdom of God forges ahead.... It is Christ himself who leads the way.... He it is who comes along in Spirit and in power."[168]

As a redemptive event the sermon itself is a moment in the ever *progressing* redemptive history. That is why Schilder can say: "A look in the manger in Bethlehem is less than listening attentively to a sermon"; and again: "Every Sunday in 1927 announces greater things than does the hour in which Christ was born."[169] As a redemptive event the sermon stands right in the midst of the eschatological drive of redemptive history. It opens and closes the gates of heaven.[170] It drives history to its consummation. "Up-to-date preaching is not to let the latest events pass in review as on a newsreel," Holwerda says, "for current events do not control the course of history. Preaching is to intervene in history,... to impel to the radical choice, to intensify the antithesis, to propel to life or otherwise to death...." "Only that sermon is up-to-date which is preached in the awareness that the time for preaching becomes shorter with each sermon, in the awareness that every sermon brings the end nearer."[171]

Every sermon brings the consummation closer because Christ marches on in the church's proclamation, because the sermon is the Word of the triune God. Every scriptural sermon partakes of the nature of Scripture. "The real ministry of the Word has the authority and glory of the Word itself."[172] The sermon is the Word of God! This is not a careless use of pregnant words, but it emphasizes once again that God enters the horizontal plane of history and uses men to accomplish his goal. God's Word and man's word are not mutually exclusive; preaching is not "to create room for the Word of God"; it is not an "impossible possibility," a "venture."[173] On the contrary, "the

167 *Bondsboekje 1940*, pp. 33 and 35. Cf. Veenhof's sermon on II Cor. 2 : 14–17 (*Een Drietal Predicaties* [1946], p. 23): "Gods triomfmarsch geschiedt in de prediking!" Cf. Schippers, *Van den Dienst*, p. 33, on Luke 24 : 46 f.: "Het is niet voldoende, dat Christus geleefd heeft en geleden, gestorven is en opgestaan. De heilsfeiten moeten worden uitgeroepen.... Door *kèrugma* te heeten wordt dus de dienst des Woords getypeerd als de prediking, die zegt, dat het heil er is.... Wanneer deze prediking wordt vernomen, breekt het heil zich baan in de wereld."

168 Van den Born, *Van den Dienst*, p. 84. Cf. Spier, *ibid.*, p. 102: "Daar gebeurt het in de prediking! Daar wordt het beslist! Daar scheurt Gods stem de wereld, ook vandaag!"

169 (1927) *Om Woord en Kerk*, I, 251, and II, 125.

170 Cf. Schippers, *Van den Dienst*, pp. 44 ff.; Veenhof, *Een Drietal Predicaties*, pp. 35 f.; Hoekstra, *Het Woord Gods*, p. 61.

171 (1943) *Een Levende Hoop*, I, 92.

172 Schippers, *Van den Dienst*, p. 30.

173 As Miskotte claims in *Het Waagstuk der Prediking* (1941), p. 41. Cf. p. 44:

preacher ventures nothing. In faith he fulfils his calling to bring the Word of God."[174]

We shall see later that not every sermon is glibly identified with the Word of God, but the point to note at this juncture is that any sermon which (ad)ministers the Word of God is truly the Word of God. Though this emphasis may have been lost in the Orthodoxy of post-Reformation times, in itself it is not radically new: one can find it, e.g., in Calvin and the Reformed confessions.[175] What was new, and that only relatively, was the firm reassertion of this confession[176] and its utilization to break through the objective – subjective dilemma.[177] Preaching is bringing the gospel, the good news, the message of salvation. "It is not merely telling about salvation," Veenhof says, "but the well-meant offering, the presentation of salvation. It is not merely a narration of a historical event,... much less a presentation and analysis of all kinds of dogmas,... and least of all a description of what one has experienced or hopes to experience. No, preaching is a powerful happening that is pertinent to all of human existence. It puts into operation a living power which always gains effect for good or ill."[178]

This means that preaching can be neither objective, nor subjective, nor a combination of both. Holwerda states: "We can overcome the defect of the objective – subjective scheme only when we fully recognize that preaching is a moment of living intercourse between the Lord and his people. Then the preacher is no longer the expert in theological questions, an expert who enters the pulpit with popularized objective and subjective theology; he is only a minister of the Word." "Preaching is possible only when the Word

To require that the preacher speak the Word of God "ware waanzin." A rejection of the Barthian view of the sermon is found in, e.g., Dijk, *Dienst der Kerk*, pp. 14 ff., 93 ff. Cf. Hoekstra, *Het Woord Gods in de Prediking*: Een Beoordeeling van Barths Woordtheologie. We note this specifically to indicate that one cannot simply identify the Reformed and Barthian solutions to the objective – subjective dilemma, or string together quotations from J. H. Bavinck, D. Ritschl, K. Dijk, and H. Ott as Müller does in *Die Lewende Woord*, p. 201, n. 203.

174 Van den Born, *Van den Dienst*, p. 87.

175 On Calvin, see Veenhof, *Zicht op Calvijn*, pp. 63–101; Van der Vegt, *Het Gepredikte Woord*, pp. 3–12; Kromminga, *Man Before God's Face in Calvin's Preaching*. As to the confessions, see the *Helvetica Posterior*, I: "Praedicatio verbi Dei est verbum Dei"; *The Belgic Confession*, XXIV, XXXV; *The Heidelberg Catechism*, XII (31), XXV (65); *The Canons of Dort*, I, 7; III/IV, 6–17; V, 14.

176 Also to be found in H. Bavinck, *Gereformeerde Dogmatiek*, IV (1901), 213 (4th ed., p. 439); and J. C. Sikkel, *Dienst des Woords* (1923), pp. 8 ff.

177 Also to be found in Kuyper. Cf. Veenhof, *Predik het Woord*, pp. 135 ff.

178 *Bondsboekje*, p. 34. Cf. p. 37: "Wat verkondigd wordt... is niet een 'leer,' die men 'aanneemt'; of een 'beschouwing,' waarmee men het 'eens' wordt; of een 'overtuiging,' waartoe men 'geraakt'; of een 'theorie,' waarin 'het denken' 'rust' vindt; of een 'moraal,' waarvoor men 'gewonnen' wordt! Niets van dat al! Wat gepredikt wordt is een Goddelijke realiteit, die geopenbaard wordt." Similarly Schippers, *Van den Dienst*, p. 37.

is seen as God's address to his people, as the glad tiding and proclamation of the kingdom of heaven.... A message is never an objective truth outside us.... It is always addressed and directed at our life. That is why one can hardly say that the Word must be applied lest it remain outside us. It *is* applied. God speaks to us in all the relationships and circumstances in which we live."[179]

The Sermon as Applicatory Explication

Because the Word *is* applied, because Scripture is kerygma, it is incorrect to see the sermon as an objective explication of this Word to which an application must be added to make it relevant. "Scripture *is* applied," Veenhof asserts; it is only necessary, therefore, "to pass on its message in its 'applicatory' character."[180] Instead of defining the sermon as "the explication and application of God's Word," Van Dijk favors: "the applicatory explication of God's Word."[181] To avoid even the suggestion that the application is an independent additional element, Holwerda prefers to drop the word "application" altogether and speak instead of "making the content of the text *concrete* for the church here and now. Accordingly, the whole sermon from A to Z is explication, while from the very first sentence it is also addressed in an applicatory way. Thus the whole sermon remains ministry of the Word."[182]

At times the impression is given that this emphasis on the applicatory character of the preaching-text solves all problems connected with relevant preaching, but the practice of preaching shows clearly that this is not the case. Although the explication – application problems have been taken out

179 *Populair*, pp. 26 and 24. Cf. *Een Levende Hoop*, I, 113. Note the similar emphasis of Bavinck (*De Toekomst*, p. 20) in rejecting the "objectivism" of redemptive-historical preaching: "Gods Woord ... is altijd een oproep, een verkondiging, het is altijd tot den mensch gerichte en naar den mensch gekeerde Godsopenbaring."

180 Veenhof, *Bondsboekje*, p. 58. Cf. p. 59: "Een *prediker* is dus niet 'verklaarder,' niet 'toepasser,' niet 'verklaarder + toepasser,' maar *dienaar* des Woords."

181 *De Preektrant* (1935), p. 7: "Prediken is: het toepasselijk verklaren van Gods Woord." Note that this terminology is also found in Hoekstra, *Homiletiek*, p. 226. Spier, *Cursus*, I, v, 12, suggests: "De ambtelijke ontsluiting van het Woord Gods in de gemeente van Christus."

182 "Concretisering." *Begonnen*, p. 108. Cf. Schilder, *College-Verslagen* (1939), pp. 31 f.; and Spier, *PE*, VI (1941), 159: "Daar behoeft geen toepassing bij gemaakt te worden, want ... het is één en al toepassing. En steeds actueel!" Cf. already Kuyper in Veenhof, *Predik het Woord*, pp. 170–197. Note that this is Hoekstra's ideal too — "een ideaal waarnaar ieder prediker moet streven. De preek verliest dan elk karakter van een verhandeling, wordt, zoals het wezen moet, een toespraak, en richt zich van het begin af rechtstreeks tot de gemeente." But for Hoekstra this is not given so much with the character of the Word that is preached as in "homiletische aanleg en voldoende oefening" which enables one "de explicatie zóó te bewerken, dat zij applicatief van karakter wordt." *Homiletiek*, p. 418.

of the objective – subjective sphere, they reappear, be it in a different context, in the sphere of redemptive history. This is evident in Holwerda's substitution: "making the content of the text concrete for the church here and now," for the church here and now is not the church there and then, and historical equation marks may not be employed. As Holwerda says elsewhere: "The task of the minister of the Word is to pass on concretely to the church here and now the Word which God spoke to a church in another place and another time, in another language and in connection with other circumstances."[183] The sermon, therefore, still consists of explication and application — not because the Word is objective, but because the Word is addressed to the church at one stage of redemptive history while the preacher must address this Word to the church at another stage of redemptive history. The Word, to be sure, is addressed to the church of all ages, but this confession should not cause us to lose sight of the fact that it is first of all directed to a particular church at a certain stage of redemptive history. There is, certainly, continuity in redemptive history; there is continuity in the church of all ages; but the discontinuity between then and now should not be overlooked. That is why Holwerda must also say: "Whoever makes an application draws a parallel between then and now."[184]

Huyser is astonished at this "switch in Holwerda's argumentation" and speaks of a "contradiction."[185] At first glance it does seem rather strange that the unrelenting opponent of historical equations now speaks of drawing parallels as a matter-of-course. The question may be asked, however, whether Huyser and Holwerda mean the same thing when they speak of drawing a parallel. Holwerda's sermons will prove instructive in this respect. We shall focus our attention particularly on his series of six sermons on Judges 6-8.

The story of Gideon, Holwerda says in one sermon, "is not a meaningless story from the distant past, but the Word through which the Lord addresses us, saying: See, here is your God." And in another sermon: "From A to Z it was the work of the Lord.... You say: Gideon is no longer around today. But what of it?... Christ is still here, and the Spirit, and the Lord — the same yesterday and today, then and now and always."[186] That is the first and basic parallel: the same God, then and now. The theocentric explication, therefore, is the first step of the application. The unity and continuity of history is given in God: He is one; the history He makes is one; the Kingdom

183 *Populair*, p. 26.
184 *Begonnen*, p. 112.
185 *GTT*, L (1950), 217 f.
186 *Een Levende Hoop*, II, 25 and 91 f. Cf. p. 105: "...niet een verhaal van vroeger, doch een belofte voor vandáág"; and p. 110: "Het was het verhaal van het verlossingswerk van God, die toen leefde en die vandaag nog leeft. Het was het verhaal van zijn messiaanse wonderwerken." On Daniel, cf. IV, 28 f.: "...niet de *mens* Daniël, maar wel de *naam* Daniël typeert het hele boek. 'Mijn Rechter is God'.... *God* overwint! Hij handhaaft de Christus en verplettert de antichrist."

He establishes is one; the Church He creates is one — one throughout the ages. And so it is possible to establish parallels between what God did then and what God does today, and even between the people through whom God worked then and the people through whom the same God will work today: "Gideon then and we today — together we stand in the one history of God's works.... We are called to continue the same battle Gideon waged, the one campaign which God carries on in this world."[187] The parallel is drawn even in the details: "In the appearance of the Angel of the Lord and in his summons, Gideon was placed before a decision in which the lot of the church and the world was at stake. And the same thing holds today now that the Lord calls us.... If only we don't look at the overwhelming odds and say: It is hopeless!"[188] The parallel is sought, therefore, in the continuity of the one redemptive history. But as soon as one says redemptive history, he is also face to face with the progression, the discontinuity: "Naturally, we need not grab a sword and take on the Midianites as Gideon did. But he worked for the Church, and the Lord extends this call to us also — everyone in his *own* place."[189]

The parallel may never degenerate into a historical equation mark; it must always be drawn *within* redemptive history so that the discontinuity is reflected along with the continuity. While the exemplary parallel means identity or similarity, for Holwerda the very parallel may underscore the contrast between then and now: "You are much richer than Gideon, for you will never see the Angel of the Lord as he did. To us has been proclaimed the man Jesus Christ, God revealed in human flesh, in whom the Lord has established continuous contact with his people. Gideon saw him once,... but to us He appears every Sunday."[190] The progression in redemptive history must be taken into account. That is why Holwerda, immediately after saying, "Who-

187 *Ibid.*, p. 67. Cf. p. 44: "Deze God komt nu zijn volk roepen; Gideon toen, ons vandaag; ons machtelozen. Hij roept ons om zijn instrumenten te zijn bij zijn grote werk van kerkverlossing." Cf. IV, 32 and 47, on the continuity of the spirit of the antichrist (Babylon) throughout history.

188 *Ibid.*, p. 38.

189 *Ibid.*, emphasis added.

190 *Ibid.*, p. 32. Cf. IV, 20: "Wij leven niet in die tijd.... Dit is thans voorbij. Want tusschen Daniël 1 en ons staat Christus *Jezus*.... Dat maakt, dat onze zonde vandaag duizendmaal erger is dan die van de Joden toen.... Aan de andere kant is nu ook de vertroosting voor alle geloovigen grooter." IV, 76: "Of God ons aldus verlossen zal? Natuurlijk is ons dat niet beloofd. Maar dit is ons gezegd, dat we voor geen enkel dreigement behoeven te zwichten. Vreest niet degene, die het lichaam kan doden." Cf. IV, 33 f., 38. Cf. V, 57 f. on a Psalm: "Zullen wij vandaag maar niet naast Ethan gaan staan, nu onze omstandigheden aan de zijne gelijk zijn geworden? ... Wij kunnen dat niet doen en wij mogen dat niet doen.... Wij mogen de psalmen toch nooit ongewijzigd zingen, we moeten ze altijd nieuwtestamentisch zingen. Wij kunnen Ethans gebed niet overnemen.... En toch moet ik bidden. In de lijn van Ethan en toch als geloovige van 1944 boven Ethan uit."

ever makes an application draws a parallel between then and now," warns not only against various illegitimate parallels but also against that "parallel which is proper as such but which neglects the historical difference."[191]

Continuity and discontinuity, a parallel and yet a contrast — both must be brought out if one is to do justice to the text in its historical setting as well as to the church today in a farther advanced setting of the same history. The contrast is greatest, of course, when the text is taken from the O.T., but whether the text is from the O.T. or the N.T., the contrast should not entice any preacher into adding an application by way of a non-historical parallel. The preacher's task is not to *add* applications to the Word, but to proclaim that Word today in all its relevance — a relevance which is already contained in the theocentric explication. The preacher is a minister of the Word, a herald for the King.

The Preacher as Herald

"The minister of the Word," Spier says, "is called by Christ to interpret in Christ's name and on his authority the living Word in his church in the midst of the world. As representative of Christ, as ambassador of God, he appears with special authority."[192] The preacher is a herald, and a herald does not *add* to the message entrusted to him by the king. As Schippers says: "A herald never comes with his own authority or with his own message. He is backed by a higher power; he is the mouth-piece of his lord. In like manner Christ stands behind the preachers of his Word with his authority." "God speaks through them. They have an official task; they are ambassadors of Christ. It seems as if *they* speak, but in reality *God* speaks."[193]

In reverting to the conception of the sermon as the Word of God, we observe in this context the major qualification: "The sermon is normative only in so far as the ambassador does not deviate from his Sender; the sermon requires unconditional submission only in so far as it correctly interprets the normative, infallible Word of God."[194] Far from raising the sermon beyond

191 "Nivellerende parallelisering." *Begonnen*, pp. 112 f.
192 *Cursus*, I, vi, 11.
193 *Van den Dienst*, pp. 17 and 19. Cf. Van den Born, *ibid.*, pp. 87 f.
194 Spier, *Cursus*, I, vi, 11. Cf. Schippers, *Van den Dienst*, p. 27: "Binding aan het Woord alzoo zal de garantie en het kenmerk zijn van die prediking, waarmee Christus heden ten dage tot zijn gemeente en tot de wereld komen wil." J. M. Spier speaks of the sermon as a "*secundaire* geloofsnorm" because it is "menselijke positiveringsarbeid, die als zodanig een subjectieve geloofshandeling is, die in gehoor-zaamheid aan de primaire geloofsnorm van het Woord Gods behoort verricht te wor-den." "De normativiteit van de prediking ontspringt nooit bij de persoon, die als instrument van Christus de verkondiging verricht, maar bij de Heilige Schrift, die als

the reach of critique, therefore, the conception of the sermon as the Word of God points instead to the preacher's responsibility not to stray from that Word.

It is this conviction that lends such a highly charged character to the criticism of exemplary sermons. A subjective application added to an objective explication is not preaching the Word; subjective preaching is not preaching the Word; using the historical preaching-text to present certain traits for self-examination is not preaching the Word. The preacher is a *herald*. If the intent of the historical text is to reveal God in his coming to the world, the preacher should not turn it into an analysis of souls. He is to proclaim what Christ proclaims in the Word without any additions. For the Word is "kerygma, the message of redemption, appeal, admonition" — always directed. "Reformed preaching struggles to transmit, to urge, to elucidate Scripture as it is. It clears up obstacles that might hinder the understanding and acceptance of Scripture.... It shows that the people who hear *are* involved in it — and that is quite different from trying *to* involve people in it."[195]

In order to speak the Word of God, then, the preacher must tie himself to Scripture and as herald of Christ proclaim only that which Scripture proclaims. "He may not force a message upon Scripture but must let it say what it really wants to say."[196] The latter, of course, is a common Reformed conviction. Hoekstra, too, affirms: "The source for the material of the ministry of the Word is *Scriptura sola et Scriptura tota*." "The preaching [of that Word] comes to the church with divine authority; the Lord speaks to the church through the mouth of the minister."[197] And elsewhere: "The office bearer speaks in the name of Christ and can ask absolute subjection to this Word of Christ, but he can do this only when he adheres strictly to Holy Scripture and brings nothing else but the Word of the Lord."[198] In the controversy, one can find this emphasis on the exemplary[199] as well as the redemptive-historical side — and yet, what a multitude of reciprocal criticism regarding each other's preaching of historical texts! How does one preach the Word in such a way that it really conforms to the intention of the Word, that it is truly the Word of God?

---

eigen Woord van God de enige inhoud van de prediking behoort te zijn." *Wetenschappelijke Bijdragen* (1951), pp. 87 f.

195 Veenhof, *Bondsboekje*, p. 61.
196 Holwerda, *Begonnen*, p. 103.
197 *Homiletiek*, p. 219.
198 *Het Woord Gods*, p. 47.
199 Cf. the quotations of Huyser, above, II, n. 124; and Dijk, *Dienst der Kerk*, pp. 107 f.

In his "In Memoriam Prof. Dr. T. Hoekstra" Schilder wrote: "The preaching technique taught by Hoekstra does justice to the text in all its parts; it avoids motto-preaching; ... it compels the preacher not to bring his own ideas but to let the text speak; it prevents the basically sacrilegious and un-Reformed experiments in which the text is used as a peg on which to hang one's own thoughts."[200] The contribution of Hoekstra which Schilder singled out for praise was thematic preaching — a procedure which we shall discuss at some length.

Hoekstra asserts that "a theme is necessary for every sermon" because, first, "the sermon must be an organic unity," second, people will be able to understand it better, and third, "the preacher can construct a good address only when one major thought grips him from beginning to end."[201] This, of course, is but an ancient rule of rhetoric, which in itself cannot guarantee proper textual preaching. Hoekstra himself points out the abuse that was made of thematic preaching when, under the influence of Scholasticism and later Rationalism, thematic preaching turned into a motto-preaching which was the very antithesis of textual preaching. If the theme merely gives expression to the unity of the subject matter without establishing the connection with the text, the sermon can turn into a grand oration which has little or nothing to do with the text. To ward off this danger, Hoekstra adds two prerequisites. The first firmly links the theme to the preaching-text: "The theme is the precise formulation of the main thought of the text; it is the summary of the text. It is the description of the specific, characteristic thought which is revealed in the preaching-text, and at the same time the unifying bond which holds together all the thoughts of the text and therefore all the thoughts of the sermon. From this it follows that a text can have only *one* theme.... Unless one wishes to choose the disastrous path of motto-preaching, he cannot deduce more than *one* theme from one and the same text."[202] The second prerequisite concerns the formulation of the theme — a formulation which should give expression to the fact that the text presents a *message*. The theme is not a topic to be discussed, not a concept such as love, righteousness, faith, hope, etc., but an assertion, a positive declaration, "a combination of concepts." "The text *says* something; it is a communication of God, a message for us. Such a message or communication can never be couched in one concept (word) but finds expression in an assertion (a subject and a predi-

---

200 *Ref*, XVI (1936), 130. Cf. *Jaarboek Geref. Kerken*, 1937, p. 427: "Doch wat Hoekstra over de techniek der preek, over thema en verdeeling gezegd heeft, dat zal niet zonder groote schade voor de kerk van Christus kunnen worden genegeerd door onze predikanten ...."

201 *Homiletiek* (1926), pp. 397 f.

202 *Ibid.*, pp. 398 f.

cate) in which the one concept predicates something of the other." Reduced to a bare minimum, the theme could conceivably consist of two nouns linked by a verb, or even one noun and a verb, or a noun with a modifying adjective. But one solitary noun cannot be a theme; neither can a question (unless rhetorical) be a theme, for a theme is by definition an *assertion*, the positive declaration proclaimed by the preaching-text.[203]

All this is directly in line with the redemptive-historical conception of the nature of the preaching-text and textual preaching. Hoekstra, however, is not completely consistent in his presentation. He weakens his first prerequisite considerably by writing: "Every text has, stricto sensu, only *one* main thought (and hence *one* theme), but because of the abundance of material the main thought can be exhibited from different points of view." And so, Hoekstra suggests (p. 296), one can preach on I Kings 18 : 20ff. (Mount Carmel) from the viewpoint of God's goodness in giving such a glorious revelation, or the necessity to serve the Lord whole-heartedly, or again, from the viewpoint of the faith of Elijah. "Because of the unity of the sermon one of these viewpoints must dominate."[204] The unity of the sermon may thus be safeguarded, but one can hardly claim that the main thought of the text thus becomes the theme of the sermon, nor that through that main thought all elements in the text are seen in their proper perspective. On the contrary, the theme is determined not by the text but by the viewpoint from which the viewer looks at the text; and since there are at least three viewpoints, there is not one but three possible themes for this one text. The inconsistency is underscored when Hoekstra later (p. 410) suggests as "theme" for the same text: "The Great Decision at Carmel," and subsumes under that "theme" two of the above-mentioned "viewpoints."[205] It would appear, therefore, that Hoekstra has made viewpoints and themes (p. 296) of that which he subsequently (p. 410) takes to be mere subdivisions of the actual "theme."

We have put "theme" in quotation marks, for according to Hoekstra's own second prerequisite "The Great Decision at Carmel" hardly qualifies as a *theme*. This is merely a topic; it may be an assertion, but it does not express what the text proclaims; it does not declare the message, the communication of God in this text. And what to say of "The History of Man's Fall" and "The Praying Isaac" — "themes" listed on the very pages where Hoekstra speaks of a "communication of God" and a "message to us"?[206] Hoekstra thus weakens the second prerequisite which a few pages earlier he so pointedly described as: "The theme contains the core of the

203 *Ibid.*, pp. 399 f.

204 *Ibid.*, p. 296. Cf. p. 322.

205 *Ibid.*, p. 410: "1. de geloofsmoed van Elia; 2. de machtdaad des Heeren; 3. de belijdenis des volks."

206 *Ibid.*, pp. 399 f.

message of redemption which the preacher must proclaim to the church."[207]

Hoekstra's inconsistency has broad repercussions for the thematic preaching of historical texts. He writes: "The minister of the Word should retain the main thought of the narrative from beginning to end. While he narrates the history he has opportunity to make comments, to give lessons on life, by attaching to the persons or events observations which are important to the hearers."[208] Hoekstra can be so casual about these excursions because, besides the main thought, which becomes the theme, he works with "subsidiary thoughts," which are supposedly subordinated to the theme[209] but which, in fact, function quite independently. For when the question is asked, "What is to be applied?" the answer is: "First, the main thought of the text which is expressed in the theme.... Second, applicatory comments must be deduced from the subsidiary thoughts. Especially historical texts give the minister of the Word countless opportunities to make practical observations and apply the subordinate points of the explication to life." Somewhat belatedly Hoekstra adds: "One should not spin this out too broadly lest the main thought of the text be overshadowed."[210]

Dijk makes an excellent correction when he states: "The preacher should restrict himself to the special message which God gives in his preaching-text and should stick to the *main thought*. I don't deny that subsidiary thoughts can often give occasion to practical remarks, but the big question is whether Scripture was given us for all these practical asides."[211] Unfortunately, Dijk later weakens his point in much the same way Hoekstra did. He calls the notion of one main thought — and hence one theme — per text "one-sided," for I Sam. 18 : 1-4, e.g., can be treated from the point of view of David, Jonathan, friendship, or God. These four different viewpoints give the preacher a choice of four themes for this one text: "David Honored by Jonathan," "The Crownprince Bows before the Anointed King David," "Friendship," and "God Paves the Way for David's Kingship." "These are not just different formulations," Dijk adds explicitly, "but definitely different points of view."[212] He maintains, moreover, that the theme *can* consist of one solitary noun (e.g., "Friendship") and even a question.[213] In this way Dijk in effect eliminates both of Hoekstra's prerequisites for textual-thematic preaching.

---

207 *Ibid.*, p. 395.
208 "... levenslessen te geven, door aan personen of gebeurtenissen beschouwingen vast te knoopen, die voor de hoorder van belang zijn." *Ibid.*, p. 362.
209 *Ibid.*, p. 290.
210 *Ibid.*, p. 301.
211 *OB*, XXII (1943), 2996. Cf. p. 3020: "Wat mogen we ons gelukkig prijzen, dat de oude toepassingen, die bij iedere preek vrijwel gelijk waren ... verdwenen zijn, en dat wij beter verstaan hebben, dat de applicatie ten nauwste zich bij de explicatie moet aansluiten."
212 *Dienst der Prediking* (1955), p. 177.
213 *Ibid.*

Grosheide, too, declares that "there is not always one synthesis [read: theme]. Because it must be constructed from the details, it is possible to combine the details differently and to combine different details." Take, e.g., Matt. 8:23-27 (the storm on the sea): the theme could be either "The Power of Christ," or "The Apostles Rescued," or "The Warning against Little Faith." "These are three main thoughts, each of which can be made central. This," Grosheide claims, "shows the richness of Holy Scripture as the Word of the infinite God."[214]

One may well ask, however, whether all these "themes" disclose the richness of Scripture or whether they display the versatility of the preacher. To rephrase Dijk's own words, we don't deny that these different viewpoints are possible, but the big question is whether Scripture was given us for all these different points of view. Schilder writes: "If prof. Hoekstra is right that the Bible writer has let his historical account be dominated exclusively... by the significance which the content of his account has for the Christological line of revelation,... then every additional element brought in 'in connection with the text,' even if it is mentioned there, is a subsidiary element. Such an element may be mentioned but should never dominate the sermon; it may never become the theme."[215]

The proponents of redemptive-historical preaching are much more consistent in advocating thematic preaching than either Hoekstra, Grosheide, or Dijk.[216] Of the above-mentioned themes, the anthropocentric are summarily dismissed as being contrary to the intent of historical texts. The various elements of the text may not be combined according to the good pleasure of the preacher: the Bible writer has already combined them. Who are we to "improve" the Bible writer's synthesis? to break apart that which he has joined together? to look at the text from different viewpoints so that we come up with three, four, or more themes per text? The text may be viewed from only one point of view: that of the writer. The various elements in the text "have formed a very specific synthesis in every text," Holwerda says. "This special synthesis gives to every text a unique place within the totality of revelation. Thus every text has its own unique content and its own unique application."[217]

---

214 *Hermeneutiek* (1929), pp. 68 f. Cf.: "Aangezien de boodschap van een bepaalde 'tekst' doorgaans zo rijk is, dat ze niet in één preek uitputtend kan worden weergegeven en het daarom mogelijk is, dat verschillende preken dezelfde tekst uit verschillend aspect behandelen, moet Hoekstra's mening, dat 'uit dezelfde tekst niet meer dan één thema kan worden afgeleid,' onjuist worden geacht." G. E. Meuleman, *De Ontwikkeling van het Dogma* in de Rooms Katholieke Theologie (Kampen: Kok, 1951), Stelling XIX.

215 *Ref*, XI (1931), 374.

216 Cf. Boerkoel, *Bazuin*, CIV (Feb. 17, 1961), No. 7, on Schilder's preaching: "Zijn preken waren een ordelijke uitbouw van een centrale gedachte.... En naar Hoekstra's aanwijzingen bevatte het thema altijd een assertorisch oordeel."

217 *Begonnen*, p. 92.

Van Dijk recommends that, in making the sermon, the preacher should first discover the specific meaning of the text, "the message which God gives to his people in the text." "This message becomes the theme of the sermon. Next, paying attention to every part of the text, the *full* content of that message must be found and ordered."[218] This means that every part of the text, every element, will be seen in the perspective of the theme, the main thought — and not the reverse, that every element may conceivably become a perspective for another theme. There can be only one theme to a text.[219] This theme is "the special Word of God that comes to us in every text — the Word which we must transmit to the church."[220] No element in the text should be treated independently of this theme; no element should occasion a treatise on some dogmatic subject or other;[221] no element should be applied separately. Rather, all elements should be viewed in the light of their specific combination in the given text, in the light of their subsidiary and contributory role to its theme. And throughout the sermon this theme must be driven home as the specific message of God in this particular text.[222]

One message throughout the sermon — this also implies that a multiple application which would address a separate word to different categories of people is out of the question. The preacher is bound from beginning to end to his chosen preaching-text; the application should not be considered an opportunity for adding to the explication, for changing the message of the text at some point.[223] The preacher is to proclaim to all alike the Word of God as given in his text. It is one Word that is spoken, but this Word has a dual effect: it calls up faith here, hardens hearts there; it equips for greater service here, increases resistance there; it saves here, condemns there — the Keys of the Kingdom,[224] the Word of God.

---

218 *Van den Dienst*, pp. 190 f.

219 Cf. Holwerda's evaluation of a sermon outline in *Hom*, VIII (1949), 142: "Schets onhelder; feitelijk permanent hinken op twee thema's .... Daaraan is de schets mislukt. Zodoende is 't geheel brokkelig en verward; ook teveel uitstapjes buiten den tekst; en de 'toepassing' werd noodwendig onzeker."

220 Van Dijk, *De Preektrant*, p. 32.

221 As Van Dijk found in the sermons of the "oude afgescheiden dominé's." *Ibid.*, pp. 8 ff.

222 "Een preek moet 'enkelvoudig' blijven. Het is niet goed, telkens van de hoofdweg af te dwalen, dingen er bij te halen die wel in enig verband staan met de hoofdgedachte, maar toch slechts in zijdelings verband." Van Dijk, *Hom*, XXI (1962), p. 85.

223 Note that Dijk also makes this point in *OB*, XXII (1943), 2996: "De applicatie grijpe niet verder dan de tekst reikt.... De goede applicatie sluit *uit*, dat elken Zondag de verzekerden en bekommerden, de verblijden en bedroefden een beurt krijgen."

224 Cf. Kapteyn, *Van Hem*, pp. 250, 286; Schippers, *Van den Dienst*, pp. 42 ff.; Veenhof, *Een Drietal Predicaties*, pp. 32 f.

This Word of God that is preached is directed at the heart of man. Spier remarks: "The ministry of the Word should not merely stir the emotions of man or stimulate his will, but, much deeper, in the absolute seriousness of God's speaking, it must grip the heart of man."[225] The Word is not addressed to a part of man, or various parts consecutively; man is addressed as a unity. "Typical of man is that he is called to serve the Lord with his heart and therefore with his whole life," Veenhof says. "Man must and shall choose for or against God. He must do the one or the other. With all that he is and has... he either serves God or rejects him. That is central in the being and life of man. In short, man is a religious being."[226] And the Word addresses man as the religious being he is. This includes undoubtedly the intellect, the will, and the emotions, but not as component parts which must each receive their due: "Preachers are not learned people who must convince others with their knowledge. They are not moralists who try to elevate the virtues of their hearers.... They are heralds. They bring a message.... That message does not call for a discussion, an 'I'll-think-about-it'; rather, it calls for the total man all at once; it calls for faith."[227]

The conception of the sermon as a word addressed to the heart of man should not be misconstrued. Preaching is not merely concerned with some internal sector of a person's life; on the contrary, through the heart the whole of a person's life comes into view. "From the heart, rooted in Christ, reborn through his Spirit, our whole life is being renewed and the communion with God is extended into all the relationships and functions of life."[228] "The entire scope of Christian living flows from the pulpit," Holwerda says, "not because a clergyman happens to occupy the pulpit, but because there the Word is proclaimed — the Word that re-creates and renews. The church is not in politics; it does not touch the school; it is not a clinic for marital problems; and yet, because of the preaching of the Word, the fount of life is in the church: from this common source the streams run in different directions."[229] The preacher, then, is not the expert on social and economic problems, the man who has the answers to problems of state, labor, and

225 *Wijsbegeerte*, p. 47.
226 Veenhof, *Bondsboekje*, p. 41.
227 Schippers, *Van den Dienst*, p. 34.
228 Spier, *Wijsbegeerte*, p. 47. Cf. p. 52: "Wij erkennen dus geen dualiteit, alsof de prediking maar een beperkt gedeelte van ons leven aangaat, en het andere deel buiten z'n invloed vallen zou. Al treedt de prediking nimmer buiten z'n eigen sfeer, hij beheerst krachtens de door God geschapen orde van ons leven, met het geloof als leidende functie, ons gehele veelzijdige bestaan."
229 Holwerda, *De Betekenis*, p. 150. Cf. Van der Vegt, pp. 21 ff. on "De Eere-positie der Prediking" in Calvin's thought.

management. But he does preach the Word, and that Word has much broader implications than merely for the internal "soul-life"; as the Word addressed to the heart, it takes hold of the central religious core of life and thus has implications for all of life. As Holwerda says: "Preaching does not mean that one can busy himself with spiritual things at the expense of politics. Preaching means that in speaking his Word God causes the light of his revelation to illuminate all things, politics included, and discloses to us the meaning and end of all things."[230]

The preacher who subscribes to this broad view of preaching is to be even more wary than the subjective preacher that he does not lose the message of the text under an avalanche of so-called "practical remarks." As minister of the Word he must bring the one message of the text. If this stringent thematic preaching seems to neglect the specific needs of the particular church being addressed, it should not be forgotten that the preacher as pastor has both the freedom and the responsibility to select a text according to the needs of his congregation. Veenhof strikingly asserts: "The only application which the minister of the Word must make is the *choice of the text*."[231] But this, then, is extremely important.[232] For "once the preacher has chosen his text (and this must certainly be done with an eye to the conditions of the time, the nature of the local church, its sins, its struggles, etc.) he is tied hand and foot. Then it is his only to speak, to show, to plead the message which God gives in his text."[233]

TEXTUAL, EXPOSITORY PREACHING

In the preceding section we have seen that the sermon is conceived of as the Word of God, provided the preacher is truly a herald for the King. The preacher must transmit the specific message of the preaching-text. Because every preacher so easily adds his own thoughts to the text or encases it in his own framework, strict thematic preaching is necessary. By way of summary, and to pick up a few loose threads, we conclude our presentation

---

230 *Een Levende Hoop*, IV, 42. Cf. "Pasen en de Politiek," in *De Wijsheid*, pp. 182 ff. Cf. Spier, *Wijsbegeerte*, p. 50: "De Evangelieverkondiging blijft steeds *geloofs*arbeid, en daarom kennen wij geen sociaal evangelie, geen economische prediking, geen politieke Woorddienst, geen staatkundige of aesthetische verkondiging. Doch aan elke actie van de gelovigen op elk gebied moet de bediening van het Woord *leiding* geven."

231 "De enige toepassing, die voor rekening van den dienaar des Woords komt, is de *tekstkeus*." *Bondsboekje*, p. 58.

232 Cf. Hoekstra's objections against "een pericopensysteem," which usurps the pastor's responsibility to select the text (*Homiletiek*, p. 245) and which cannot take into account the special situations and needs of the local congregation (p. 248).

233 Veenhof, *Bondsboekje*, p. 58.

of the redemptive-historical approach by considering the selection, the scopus, and the exposition of historical texts.

The Selection of the Historical Preaching-Text

Textual preaching is required to do justice to the text. The selection of the preaching-text is often taken for granted, but the importance of this selection is underscored by Veenhof's statement (above): "The only application which the minister of the Word must make is the *choice of the text*." Because every text does not fit every situation, the preaching-text must be carefully selected if one is to do justice to both the text and the needs of the local congregation.

Historical texts in particular are easily distorted in their very selection as preaching-texts. John 2 : 2a ("Jesus also was invited to the marriage") may seem ever so appropriate as preaching-text for a wedding, I Kings 19 : 7b ("Arise and eat, else the journey will be too great for you") may seem suitable for the celebration of the Lord's supper, Matthew 17 : 8b ("They saw no one but Jesus only") may seem fitting for a minister's installation service — but Holwerda has no better term for this manner of reducing texts to fit the occasion than "superficial parallels."[234] In all these instances a few words are plucked from the historical text in order to serve as preaching-text for the occasion at hand. This procedure can be carried even further by selecting a single word as "preaching-text." One preacher selects from Acts 23 : 30 the word "farewell" (K.J.V.) as "text" for his farewell sermon; another uses "a record" from Ezra 6 : 2 as "text" for his New Year's eve sermon.[235] If this is a legitimate selection, the possibilities are almost limitless.

The above-mentioned selections are, no doubt, some extreme instances of the distortion historical texts suffer in their very selection as preaching-texts. Perhaps no one today would think of preaching on one word just because it happens to be in the Bible, but the point to note is that the rather common practice of brief preaching-texts is often the first step in distorting historical texts. "The ever-present danger in selecting too short a text is that the preacher and the sermon obscure the Word," Holwerda says.[236] According to Hoekstra "the very short text is a left-over from the time when motto-preaching took its toll,"[237] but a magical conception of the words of Scripture

---

234   *Begonnen*, p. 90.
235   On the latter, the Dutch Statenvertaling's "gedachtenis" may clarify the connection. I have not been able to find in any English version at my disposal the equivalent to the words someone used as "text" for a New Year's day sermon: "Wat zal het ook nu zijn?" (I Kings 14 : 14 c). These "preaching-texts" are mentioned by Van Dijk, *De Preektrant*, pp. 14 f.
236   " . . . dat de dominee en de preek zich plaatsen voor het Woord." *Hom*, III, 39.
237   *Homiletiek*, p. 234.

is perhaps an equally plausible explanation of this phenomenon. However that may be, the redemptive-historical side insists that the preaching-text be a complete unit, not a word, phrase, or sentence. To isolate as preaching-text some phrase or some experience of a Bible "saint" makes a Christocentric sermon a virtual impossibility. Moreover, isolating an element from its context is in itself an act which precludes doing justice to the historical text.

The selection of a preaching-text which is a complete unit is easier to insist upon than to achieve, however, for even when a paragraph or an entire chapter is selected, the preaching-text is part of a still greater unit. In view of this, Holwerda suggests that a series of sermons is particularly appropriate for historical texts.[238] But whether they preach one sermon on a text or a series of sermons on a number of consecutive chapters, in general the redemptive-historical preachers tend to select longer texts than their exemplary colleagues. The first step towards doing justice to the historical text is to select a complete unit as preaching-text.

The Scopus of the Historical Preaching-Text

The second step towards doing justice to the historical preaching-text is to determine its intention, its scopus. Everyone feels that a preacher who uses Balaam's donkey for a tirade against cruelty to animals, or Elijah's coat for a discourse on Christian fashion, is not doing justice to his text. By the same token, says Holwerda, to use the doubt of Thomas to preach on doubt is also to do an injustice to one's text.[239] The historical text is made up of many elements; it can provide us with information on geography, politics, ethics, psychology, etc., but one may not detach any element from its textual connection and present a discourse on that element. In the words of Spier: "The interpreter must pay attention to the goal at which the text itself aims, the direction in which it looks, its intention, its scopus."[240]

The great problem, of course, is to determine this scopus. Detailed exegesis in and by itself is not sufficient: witness the different themes Hoekstra, Grosheide, and Dijk deduce from one and the same text.[241] The text will give us different answers, depending on the standpoint from which we view the text, depending on the questions we ask. At this point the redemptive-historical presupposition enters the picture: "All narratives in Scripture have one tendency that links them together.... All history is *one* history in virtue of the belief that when the Bible narrates history, it only intends to narrate

238 "Het lukt niet zonder meer een pericoop te nemen uit een grotere cyclus." *Begonnen*, p. 104.
239 *Begonnen*, p. 93.
240 *Van den Dienst*, p. 109.
241 See above, pp. 163–165.

one history: God revealing himself in Jesus Christ."[242] As Van 't Veer puts it more concretely: "Scripture... designates the theme and hence the tendency of its historiography as the battle between the Seed of the woman and the seed of the serpent (Gen. 3 : 15)."[243] Van 't Veer sees a confirmation of this in Revelation 12 and continues: "Consequently, Scripture itself gives us the key to a correct interpretation: it can be nothing other than redemptive-historical and/or Christological. When one disconnects a small part to view it separately... he loses all certainty that this part (or that person and his conduct) has been properly interpreted."[244]

The redemptive-historical approach, accordingly, takes this over-all Christo-centric scopus to be *the* perspective in which to view historical texts. Only from this standpoint can one direct questions to the historical text and receive answers in accordance with its intention. One can, of course, raise questions concerning politics, ethics, psychology, the order of salvation, etc., but the specific purpose of the historical text is to reveal the ever-progressing redemptive history of Christ, Christ in his coming.

Expository Preaching

The identical scopus of all historical texts might lead to a sterile monotony in preaching, were it not for the insistence on strict textual, expository preaching:[245] the unique message of the selected preaching-text must be proclaimed and nothing else. Although "Christ in his coming" is the over-all scopus of historical texts, one must go on to determine the unique theme of the selected text.[246]

---

242 "...één tendenz, die ze samenbindt." Schilder, *College-Verslagen* (1939), p. 23. Cf. (1933) *Preken*, I, 479: "Want het bijbels geschiedverhaal, dat is ook hier [Thomas] een beschrijving van Gods zelfopenbaring in Christus, van Christus' komen tot zijn volk"; and (1936) *Preken*, II, 94: "De Schrift spreekt ons niet over de *mensen*,... doch zij verhaalt ons de grote werken *Gods*; zij verhaalt, wat *God* gedaan heeft en nog doet tot openbaring van zichzelf als Schepper en Herschepper in Jezus Christus, en tot behoudenis der wereld door den Zoon, dien Hij gezonden heeft."

243 *Van den Dienst*, p. 148.

244 *Ibid.*, p. 150.

245 Mickelsen, *Interpreting the Bible*, p. 365, perpetuates a rather unfortunate distinction between textual and expository preaching: "In a textual sermon a particular text provides the main points, but the subpoints depend on the logical analysis by the minister of the subject and text. An expository sermon is one in which both the main points and the subpoints of the sermon are derived from the text or textual passage." Only the latter – at least the way we have used it – comes close to being a textual sermon, though some criticism of all those (logical) "points" may be in order. The same distinction can be found in Koller, *Expository Preaching*, p. 22.

246 Holwerda, *Begonnen*, p. 112: "Men gaat er slechts van uit, dát hier openbaring van Christus is; maar wát hier van Hem wordt gezegd, moet nog worden vastgesteld."

Schilder seeks this uniqueness primarily in the progression in redemptive history, in the coming of Christ. Since this progression makes every historical text different, Schilder calls for the "exact determination of the place," that is, the date, of the textual event.[247] For Holwerda, too, the date is important, but for him it functions more as part of the synthesis of the various elements in the text. The specific synthesis of elements in a text makes up the unique message of the preaching-text.[248]

In preaching the text, the preacher should not stray from this unique message (theme). He should not balance a truth in the text against a truth expressed elsewhere (as is often done in dogmatic preaching under the adage of comparing Scripture with Scripture): "A Word of God is thus made colorless and powerless by one's reasoning," Van Dijk remarks.[249] Neither should the preacher draw an artificial line from the text to Christ Incarnate: as the message of God's work the text is already Christocentric. Nor should he add a subjective application: as the Word addressed to the heart the exposition of the text is already relevant.

The preacher's responsibility to preach the Word of God requires textual, expository preaching in the strictest sense. Even though the preachers in the Bible do not fulfil this requirement, that is their prerogative, not ours today. We do not honor their "sermons" as the Word of God by copying whatever we can recover of their method of preaching but by making their "sermons" preaching-texts for our expository preaching today. Whether the text be historical or otherwise, respect for the Word of God requires that one do justice to the intent of the text.

247 "Preciese *plaatsbepaling.*" *Ref*, XIX, 59. Cf. *Ref*, XI, 374.
248 *Begonnen*, p. 92.
249 *Persoonlijk Onderzoek van de H.S.* (1949), p. 13: "Als hij leest, dat de Heere eerst tegen Hiskia zegt: 'Gij zult sterven,' en later na Hiskia's gebed hem nog 15 jaren geeft, dan begint hij niet te redeneeren en zegt niet: 'Hoe kan dat nu? Kan God terugnemen wat hij eerst zegde?'" The point is more clearly made on Eph. 4 : 30 where the dogmatic preacher will play off God's grief against God's immutability: "Dan gaat hij trachten dit woord 'bedroeven' zoo te behandelen, dat het toch eigenlijk geen bedroeven meer is; en de kracht van dit Woord is gebroken."

Chapter V   *Critique*

In the two foregoing chapters we have collected and arranged the various strands which together make up the redemptive-historical approach. Looking back upon this collected material, one must acknowledge that the "new direction" not only scrutinized and evaluated but at many points also criticized and re-formed the homiletical tradition. This examination and re-formation was motivated, as we saw time and again, by a zeal for the Word of God. In preaching the Word, preachers must permit the *Word* to speak; the text must be allowed to say what it intends to say; no arbitrary parallels should blunt the point of the text, divert its thrust, weaken its message. In the very process of criticizing the traditional way of preaching historical texts, the redemptive-historical school was motivated by the Reformation's *sola Scriptura*.[1]

The same motive drives us as we, in turn, critically examine the redemptive-historical approach. We agree with this approach at many crucial points: we can only appreciate the fact, e.g., that it freed historical texts from the confining framework imposed upon them by the many well-meaning preachers who insisted on reading them in a biographic, moralistic, Jesucentric, dogmatic, subjectivistic, or other manner. The question arises, however, whether the redemptive-historical method does not imprison historical texts in an equally confining framework, a framework which prevents these texts from saying what they intend to say. Was it merely a misunderstanding when the redemptive-historical preachers were themselves accused of speculation? Was it a misunderstanding when they were accused of objectivism? They, after all, were precisely the ones who broke through the objective – subjective dilemma in such an admirable way. We can hardly get around the fact that there exists a tension within the redemptive-historical approach — a tension which manifests itself in our presentation as a tension between the first and last parts of the foregoing chapter; a tension, in terms of persons, between Schilder and, e.g., Veenhof.[2]

---

1 "Het 'sola Scriptura' functioneert in de Reformatie als een gericht zijn op het Woord Gods en als beginsel van alle vertolking tegenover menselijke willekeur." Berkouwer, *Heilige Schrift*, II, 357.

2 We are referring to the fact that despite our attempt to include quotations of all authors in every section, Schilder figures prominently in IV A and B where Veenhof

Instead of presenting a long list of points at which we agree or disagree with the redemptive-historical method, we shall concentrate our critique on its inner tension. We can best penetrate to the heart of this approach — and extend our evaluation to the exemplary approach as well — by focussing our attention on two major areas: (1) the hermeneutic use of the progression in redemptive history, and (2) the characterization of historical texts.

THE HERMENEUTIC USE OF THE PROGRESSION IN REDEMPTIVE HISTORY

This section will deal mainly with the foundation of the redemptive-historical approach as blueprinted and laid by Schilder.

The idea that God's revelation takes place in concrete history and that redemptive history is a unity and progresses is thoroughly biblical: God's Kingdom is coming into this world; He leads history to its consummation. The acknowledgement of the eschatological drive of history does not mean, however, that one can pinpoint that progression,[3] nor that one should interpret historical texts in terms of the progression advocated by Schilder. To attempt the latter is to become entangled in a host of insurmountable problems — problems in determining this progression in concrete instances when, e.g., revelation is addressed to people who regressed, when its date is unknown, when there are extended periods of silence, etc.[4] Schilder's grand scheme is not without appeal, and yet it must be rejected because it does not do justice to historical texts. We shall try to demonstrate this concretely in terms of three related points: schematism, speculation, and objectivism.

Schematism

We saw earlier that Schilder bases his conception of redemptive history on the Counsel of God: the unity of the diversity in history is guaranteed by God's decree. Although this idea itself is scriptural, Schilder works with God's decree in quite another way than Scripture does: he uses it as an a priori for making (logical) deductions concerning the course of history.[5]

is not represented, while Veenhof figures prominently in IV D and E where Schilder's contribution is negligible. Holwerda bridges and combines the two, as it were.

3 Cf. J. Veenhof's critique of H. Bavinck's "belichting van de openbaringsgeschiedenis als een geleidelijk voortschrijdend proces." *Revelatie en Inspiratie*, p. 639. N. Ridderbos, *VT*, XXXI (1961), 157, wonders "of het toentertijd zo machtige evolutie-geloof daar niet op de een of andere manier invloed op geoefend heeft."

4 We need not repeat the problems which came to light during the controversy. See above, pp. 125 ff.

5 See, e.g., *Zur Begriffsgeschichte*, pp. 420 ff.; and *Christus*, II, 361: "... dat

Berkouwer detects a "strong logicistic element" in some of Schilder's views and speaks of "a schematization of the content of Scripture."[6] Though Schilder vehemently denies this charge,[7] he can hardly deny that he reasons from God's decree to history, while Scripture proceeds in the opposite direction, namely, from history to God's decree.[8]

In reasoning from God's decree, Schilder tends to interrupt historical texts when they have hardly begun to speak. This is most easily demonstrated with those texts which speak of God's grief (Gen. 6 : 6, 7), his repentance (Ex. 32 : 14; I Sam. 15 : 11, 35; II Sam. 24 : 16), his being moved to pity (Judg. 2 : 18), etc.[9] Schilder contends that this is only "the language of observation," for "the revelation of Hos. 13 : 14, Ezek. 24 : 14, Num. 23 : 19, I Sam. 15 : 29, Ps. 110 : 4, Zech. 8 : 14, and Heb. 7 : 21 ultimately excludes all anthropomorphic speaking.... God knows all his works from eternity."[10] For some penetrating questions on this subject we refer the reader to Holwerda and others;[11] we only wish to point out here that Schilder overrules the speech of many historical texts by reasoning from God's decree, or, if one prefers, that he plays off one series of texts against another. In either case he contradicts the redemptive-historical emphasis on strict textual-thematic preaching, and the words of his colleague Van Dijk apply to his method: "A Word of God is thus made colorless and powerless by one's reasoning."[12]

Schilder's schematism is particularly evident in the hermeneutic use he makes of the progression in redemptive history for interpreting historical texts. Redemptive history, we have seen, is "the successive realization in time

God, dat de Logos, de dingen, welke chronologisch achter elkander aankomen, *van den aanvang* reeds geschikt heeft en geplooid naar den wil van Gods verkiezing en verwerping, ja, dat de Logos en de Geest al wat de historie baart tot schouwtooneel en werkterrein gekozen heeft voor de wet van verkiezing en verwerping ...."

6   *De Voorzienigheid* (1950), p. 83 (E, 72). Cf. pp. 82 ff.

7   See *HC*, IV (1951), pp. 172 f., n. 37.

8   See J. Douma, *Algemene Genade* (1966), p. 342. This, by the way, is another J. Douma than the one involved in the controversy.

9   A larger summation is given by Schilder, *HC*, IV, 99.

10   *Ibid*. Cf. *HC*, III, 85 ff.

11   Holwerda, *Exegese O.T. (Deuteronomium)*, pp. 133 f.; and especially *Historia Revelationis*, pp. 251 f., e.g.: "Welke maatstaf hanteert men als men uitmaakt welke teksten naar de letter moeten worden genomen, om dan van daaruit de anthropomorfe gedeelten aan te wijzen en eigenlijk krachteloos te maken? Het gevaar is in ieder geval heel groot, dat men hierbij opereert vanuit een filosofisch Godsbegrip, en daarmee toch feitelijk alles wegsnijdt wat niet in eigen theologische kraam te pas komt; de vraag kan ook gesteld worden: als wij in staat geacht moeten worden om anthropomorfe gedeelten in feite te corrigeren, door ze hetzij buiten beschouwing te laten, hetzij ze te transponeren in niet-anthropomorfe taal, waarom heeft dan God aldus gesproken?" See further, G. Visée, "Over het 'anthropomorphe' spreken Gods in de H.S.," *Ref*, XXVIII, Nos. 34-43 (May 30 – Aug. 1, 1953); and Kuitert, *De Mensvormigheid Gods*, pp. 21 ff. *et passim*.

12   See above, IV, n. 249.

of God's thoughts of peace for us according to his fixed plan."[13] This progression, according to Schilder's avowed presupposition, *must* come to expression in historical texts.[14] We shall have occasion later to examine this notion of progression and to see concretely how Schilder works with it. At this point we observe only that even though redemptive history seems to be a more suitable framework for interpreting historical texts than a biographic or moralistic framework, Schilder's scheme, too, imprisons historical texts. Our objection is not against a framework as such — the text, after all, does not come to us in a vacuum but in the framework of its context. We do object to Schilder's framework, however; we doubt that the rich variety of Scripture's historical texts can be caught in one, all-encompassing scheme, as Schilder would have it. Moreover, even a history of redemption (revelation) painstakingly deduced from the givens of Scripture itself, remains a theoretical construction which, though it may aid interpretation, should never rule over the text. Grosheide warns, not without reason, against using the "historia revelationis" as an a priori scheme with which to exegete a text.[15] It is our contention that Schilder's particular redemptive-historical method comes into conflict with the motive of *sola Scriptura*. As we shall demonstrate below, he superimposes on historical texts his rigid scheme of necessary progression in such a way that they can no longer say what they intend to say; the result is speculation.

Speculation

To substantiate the charge of *speculation* as well as that of *schematism*, we shall consider in some detail Schilder's three-volume *Christus in Zijn Lijden*, his most elaborate expository work on historical texts. Since two volumes of the 1930 edition were revised in 1949/51, this work also enables us to take into account any "corrections" Schilder deemed necessary after the twenty year interval.

Schilder, as might be expected, continually warns against speculation.[16] Ironically, it is often on the very pages where he voices these warnings that

13 See above, IV, n. 14.
14 "Wij binden ons ... in vol-bewust vóóroordeel aan het thema der *openbarings-geschiedenis* in het lijden, wanneer wij voorop stellen, dat Christus in de verloochening van Petrus *dieper is getreden in Zijn isolement." Christus*, II, 184.
15 "Men moet niet met de historia revelationis als met een soort vooropgezette idee gaan exegetiseren en dat doet men als men heilshistorisch uitlegt, dat beteekent aan ieder Schriftgedeelte een plaats wil geven in de geschiedenis van (de openbaring van) het heil, zooals men meent, dat die is verloopen. *GTT*, XLVI (1946), 75. Similarly, *Heraut*, 1941, No. 3333. The latter is quoted by Holwerda, *Begonnen*, p. 83, with the comment: "Volkomen mee eens."
16 "Een sluier, dien de Heilige Geest werpt, mogen wij niet optillen." *Christus*, I, 151 (E, 157; rev. ed., 181).

we encounter what we consider to be speculation.[17] Schilder is continually on guard against any form of speculation which would posit more historical detail or credit the figures around Jesus with more knowledge than the gospel accounts reveal. "That would be 'eisegesis' and arbitrary distortion of the sparse historical givens we have," he says. Closing the door to one kind of speculation he opens it to another, however, for he continues: "Whether the *people* understood little or nothing of the Passover amnesty does not affect the issue; the important question is, What did *Christ* understand of it?"[18] Via the consciousness of Christ, Schilder arrives at a whole new vista of Christ's suffering and is able to interpret the gospels in what we consider to be a speculative way. Christ *knew* of the priestly idea of reconciliation and peace expressed in the ceremony of the Passover amnesty, says Schilder; and that he takes to be sufficient grounds for interpreting Luke 23 : 17 and John 18 : 39 in that light.[19] Again, Christ was *aware* of "his personal property rights" as the soldiers raffled off his clothes;[20] and that Schilder takes to be sufficient grounds for linking together — in his exposition of John 19 : 23f. — the magi bearing gifts (Matthew 2), the question of the temple tax (Matthew 17), and the raffling soldiers. "No," he says, "we are not establishing a connection between things too far removed from each other; we are simply doing our *duty* when we link together those things which Christ's Spirit brought together!"[21]

The question arises, however, whether there are any limits to this use of "Christ's consciousness" for interpreting N.T. historical texts. Can it not become a sanction for boundless fantasy? Schilder stakes everything on the progression in the suffering of Christ.[22] Even Matthew's statement that Judas hanged himself must fit this scheme lest it be used for a biographical treatise on Judas. "The question is this," Schilder contends, "What is the significance of Judas' death...for sacred history? As we lead our thoughts in that direction, we see Jesus Christ confronted by the corpse of Judas."[23] If one should object that Scripture nowhere mentions this encounter, Schilder would

---

17 See, e.g., *Wat is de Hemel?*, p. 64: "Wij zijn hier bang voor fantasie, en voor gedachtenspinsels, die aan fantasie ontsproten zijn," followed by speculation. (Note that Schilder considers this to be legitimate deduction.) In connection with another publication of Schilder, Berkouwer writes: "Hier bespeurt men de zuigkracht van de speculatie, die zich van de Schrift distantieert *direct na de theoretische verwerping der speculatie.*" *De Voorzienigheid*, p. 83, n. 157 (not in E ed.), emphasis added.

18 *Christus*, II, 425 f. (E, 441 f.; rev. ed., 487 f.).

19 *Ibid.*

20 *Ibid.*, III, 161 (E, 179).

21 *Ibid.*, III, 162 f. (E, 180 f.).

22 See, e.g., *ibid.*, II, 463 (E, 481; rev. ed. 519).

23 *Ibid.*, II, 232 (E, 244). The rev. ed., p. 280, is changed slightly: "De vraag is... wat Judas' dood beteekend heeft voor Christus' dood, en voor diens plaats in open-barings- en heilsgeschiedenis. Want wij zien Christus geconfronteerd worden met het lijk van Judas ...."

reply: "We may assume that Jesus, who saw Nathanael sitting under a fig tree, and who always perceives the deadly end of the ways of sin, *knew* that Judas committed suicide."[24] Accordingly, this chapter is entitled: "Christ Confronted with the Dead Judas." This is paralleled in the succeeding volume with an exposition of Luke 23 : 42f. under the title: "Christ Confronting the Dead Judas with the Dead Criminal."[25] With all due appreciation for Schilder's warning against biographical preaching, does not he himself end up reading the gospels as a "biography of Jesus"? With all appreciation for the warnings against psychologizing, does not Schilder himself base his expositions on a "psychology of Jesus," and a very hypothetical psychology at that?

It cannot be denied that in many ways Schilder's trilogy on the suffering of Christ is a theological masterpiece. Each volume deals chronologically with a major stage in the suffering of Christ: volume I with the period from the "beginning" of the suffering to Gethsemane, volume II with the trial, and volume III with the crucifixion and burial. By means of the chronological development Schilder tries to accentuate the progression in Christ's suffering, a progression from stage to stage as well as within each stage. This progression is highlighted by the intricate parallels drawn between each of the stages (volumes) and between the parts of each stage (volume). Christ's isolation progressed from his abandonment by the disciples in Gethsemane through Peter's denial of him during the trial to his utter desolation in the darkness of Golgotha.[26] Christ's suffering progressed as his blood was shed in Gethsemane, at the trial, and finally on the cross.[27] Christ's suffering increased as He was progressively stripped of his freedom: freedom of action (bound in Gethsemane), freedom of speech (condemned by the judge), and finally freedom of thought (cast outside the gates).[28]

Schilder is ever on the lookout for the "new moment," the "new phase."[29] This is not necessarily wrong, but it can become an obsession leading to speculation, especially when every text must fit this scheme. Dealing with Peter's denial (John 18 and Matt. 26), Schilder frankly states his presupposition: "He who would preach Christ.... must take his starting point in Christ and proceed from the presupposition that Christ's suffering enters a new

24   *Ibid.*, II, 247 (E, 257; rev. ed., 295).
25   "Het verwondere niemand, dat wij hier nog van Judas spreken: wij 'halen' hem niet 'uit zijn graf,' want hij tuimelt juist erin.... Terwijl nu eenerzijds, *ook voor Christus' eigen besef*, de Heiland *wordt* geconfronteerd met den dooden Judas, daar kan Hij nu van Zijn kant Judas met dezen bekeerden moordenaar confronteeren...." *Ibid.*, III, 314 (E, 329).
26   *Ibid.*, II, 183 f. (E, 199; rev. ed., 216).
27   *Ibid.*, II, 497 f. (E, 519 f.; rev. ed., 549 f.).
28   *Ibid.*, III, 186 ff. (E, 206 ff.). See also III, 237 ff. on "Christus' priesterschap," and III, 160 ff. on Christ's "requisitie-recht" and "Zijn eigendomskwesties."
29   *Ibid.*, II, 473 (E, 494) and 210 (E, 222). The rev. ed., pp. 528 and 249, omits these words, mainly, it seems, for stylistic reasons.

phase in what is told us concerning Peter."[30] Consequently, the major issue has been decided *before* the text is heard; to the text falls the subsequent task of disclosing the specific line (parallel) of progression and its extent. But even concerning this secondary task we cannot help wondering to what extent the *text* decides which line of progression it describes. Because Schilder already knows two "points" on the line of isolation (the disciples' flight in Gethsemane and the darkness of Golgotha), he can neatly fit Peter's denial between these "points" on the progressing line of isolation. Although this is quite natural, the attempt to fit Judas' death into a progressing line is much more problematic, and Schilder's solution (see above) can only be called a forced construction.

Schilder is so enthralled by the lines of progression that on occasion he does not hesitate to lengthen such lines on the basis of an argument from silence.[31] He tries to lay bare the divine *necessity* of every mentioned (and sometimes unmentioned) detail. The blood *had* to flow in each of the three stages;[32] the privilege of freedom of thought *had* to be taken away from Christ;[33] He *had* to appear before Herod.[34] It is "the wise Counsel of God,"[35] "the compelling logic of justice,"[36] whose structure Schilder tries to lay bare; he wishes to "discover the pattern, the design of God's architecture in every detail of His perfect building" of "justice and grace,"[37] the "harmony of ultimate *necessity*, the connection of divine *logic*."[38]

With all respect for the genius manifested in these volumes, it is impossible to shake the impression that Schilder's expositions are too schema-

---

30 *Ibid.*, II, 183 (E, 198 f.; rev. ed., 216).

31 An argument from silence is used to establish the progressing line of Christ's silence: "*Jezus zweeg stil.* Neen, dat is dezen keer nu eens geen 'bijbel-tekst'; het 'staat' er met zooveel woorden niet.... Maar het zou wel eens kunnen zijn, dat de bijbel *dit maal* het 'zwijgen' van Christus daarom niet opzettelijk vermeldt, omdat het hier – op Golgotha, 'buiten de poort' – iets '*vanzelfsprekends*' is te achten." On the basis of this "het zou wel eens kunnen zijn" Schilder then proceeds with a lengthy exposition of the significance of this silence of Christ. *Ibid.*, III, 239 f. (E, 257).

32 "Moest." *Ibid.*, II, 497 f., (E, 519 f.; rev. ed., 550).

33 "Bij Hem *moest*, behalve de vrije daad, en het vrije woord, ook de vrije gedachte inzinken, wegvluchten, Hem ont-gaan. Indien God Hem de vrije gedachte niet bestrijdt, dan is Hij *niet* ter helle gevaren." *Ibid.*, III, 187 (E, 207).

34 "Indien de stem van Ezau [Herod] zou ontbreken in het slotkoor van al de krachtige zangmeesters in het oratorium des doods..., dan zou het oordeel van de wereld en van het vleesch over deze Verkorene Gods niet volkomen ["volledig" (rev. ed. 415)] zijn geweest." *Ibid.*, II, 352 f. (E, 369 f.).

35 "De wijze raad van God." *Ibid.*

36 "Dwingende rechtslogica." *Ibid.*, III, 188 (E, 208).

37 "...trachten weer te vinden de groote lijnen van Gods architectuur, ook in dit détail van Zijn volmaakte bouw...." *Ibid.*, I, 333 (E, 333 f.). The rev. ed. omits "van Zijn volmaakte bouw" on p. 395 but retains on p. 394: "het gebouw van Gods recht en genade" (first ed., p. 332).

38 "Harmonie van uiterste *noodzakelijkheid*, een verbinding van goddelijke *logica*." *Ibid.*, III, 293 (E, 308).

tic, too speculative, too forced. He undoubtedly deserves credit for uncovering many scriptural insights, but the warning against drawing arbitrary parallels is applicable to his own expositions as well. For he frequently takes the texts out of their scriptural context, combines them, places them in a redemptive-historical framework, draws parallels, and thus establishes their meaning. Despite his lofty aim of calling attention to "the impressive parallelism which was so logically constructed by God,"[39] after reading these expositions one is left with the distinct impression that he has received a taste of the logical parallelism of Schilder's dogmatics.[40]

Objectivism

Earlier we called it an oversimplification to attach the label "objectivism" to the "new direction." The latter, after all, attacked objectivism as well as subjectivism and must be credited with overcoming the objective – subjective dilemma.[41] Nevertheless, the charge of objectivism is not entirely without foundation, particularly where Schilder is concerned. Boerkoel remarks that Schilder's sermons were not much different from his lectures, that they were "intellectualistic in character" and "preponderantly objective," and that often the application merely consisted of "He who has an ear, let him hear what the Spirit says to the churches."[42] This characterization resembles the charges of objectivism leveled at redemptive-historical sermons during the controversy. Even Van Reest, a great admirer of Schilder, makes a similar evaluation when he observes: "His [Schilder's] sermons were always dominated by stringent objectivity; he was averse to all subjectivism and mysticism.... He also disliked applications because he realized their worthlessness."[43] While sharing the same aversion to subjectivism and mysticism, we hardly share Van Reest's enthusiasm about Schilder's "stringent objectivity" and dislike for applications. It seems to us that a minister of the Word neglects his duty when he fails to *ad*minister the Word. As Holwerda put it so cogently: "The task of the minister of the Word is to pass on concretely to the church

---

39 *Ibid.*, II, 330 (E, 344). "De ijzingwekkende, door God zo logisch geconstrueerde parallelie" is changed in the rev. ed., p. 391, to "de ijzingwekkende, door God zoo stijl-getrouw geconstrueerde parallelie."

40 Holwerda's words hit closer home than he himself probably realized at the time: "'t Groote gevaar bij Schriftstudie is, dat we de deelen der Schrift losrukken uit hun eigen verband om ze te persen in een door ons geconstrueerd raam." *GM*, XVIII (1940), 21.

41 See above, pp. 33 ff. and 153 ff.

42 *Bazuin*, CIV, Feb. 24, March 3, and June 2, 1961.

43 *Opdat Zij Allen*, I, 131. Cf. Vanden Born's advice: "Het Woord Gods moet bediend worden zóó, dat het alleen is uitlegging van het Woord Gods, *met* de ambtelijke verkondiging, dat wie gelooft het leven heeft, en wie het Woord Gods verwerpt, het leven niet zien zal." *Ref*, XVIII (1938), 413.

here and now the Word which God spoke to a church in another place and another time...."[44] That rules out anything resembling objective preaching.

In this section we would like to get to the bottom, the root(s) of Schilder's objectivism. We can best do this by digging more deeply into his notion of the progression in redemptive history. It soon becomes apparent that this progression moves along two parallel lines. We already came across these lines in Schilder's distinction — introduced in his exchange with Schelhaas on "rectilinear progression" — between God's "speaking" and God's "coming."[45] God's speaking, being adapted to human sin and weakness, does not progress rectilinearly, but "God does speak ever more powerfully," and "He does come rectilinearly closer to his goal." Schilder maintains the progression along both lines — speaking as well as coming, words as well as facts.[46] We shall follow Schilder a distance along either line by discussing in turn progressive revelation and progressive redemptive history.

Progressive Revelation

In order to understand what Schilder means by progressive revelation, it is necessary to have some idea of his concept of revelation. It is quite beyond our scope, of course, to work this out in detail. Central, we may say, is the idea that revelation unveils the hidden things of God. "As to content and effect," says Schilder, "revelation can be likened to instruction by God, our great Pedagogue and Teacher. Because He created our mind and causes his Word to enter that mind, He himself accommodated his revelation... to our creatureliness, our humanity, our limited capacity." Whereas, on the one hand, we are never able to comprehend (all of) God's thoughts, on the other hand, we are able to understand what He has *revealed*.[47] In the process of redemptive history this revelation unfolds more and more. "The farther revelation advances and progresses, and the more the boundaries ('metae') between the hidden and revealed things recede,... the clearer will be (from the Word) the picture of that which has been (and is and shall be) in God's thoughts from eternity. It is a coherent picture, whose perspective becomes

44 See above, IV, n. 183.
45 See above, IV, nn. 37, 38. See also Kuyper, *Encyclopaedie*, III (1909), pp. 174 f. on the "Historia idearum" and the "Historia rerum gestarum"; and Vos, *Biblical Theology*, p. 14 on "revelation" and "objective redemption," p. 15 on "word revelation" and "act revelation," p. 24 on "Biblical Theology" and "Sacred History." Regarding H. Bavinck's view of the relationship, see J. Veenhof, pp. 334 ff.
46 In 1949 Schilder speaks of both the history of revelation and the history of redemption as "rechtlijnig." See above, IV, n. 38.
47 *HC*, II (1949), p. 105. Cf. p. 107: "Dat geopenbaarde deel is dan geen 'afdruk' van goddelijke kennis, doch inhoud van een met paedagogische wijsheid ingekleede en aan onze bevattingsmogelijkheden aangepaste *mededeeling*." Cf. *Zur Begriffsgeschichte*, p. 454.

ever deeper."[48] Accordingly, Schilder conceives of the history of revelation as a process in which revelation grows both in *quality* and in *quantity*.[49]

This brief résumé is sufficiently comprehensive to warrant the question whether or not Schilder proceeds from an *intellectualistic* concept of revelation. The fact that he speaks of progressive revelation does not in itself, of course, constitute sufficient grounds for answering this question in the affirmative. Over against Van Ruler, Berkouwer correctly maintains: "It is not true that the idea of progressive revelation is *necessarily* intertwined with an intellectualistic concept of revelation. On the contrary, one should rather say that the idea of progressive revelation is charged with the thought of God's acts in the encounter with his people. These acts include communication, but that has nothing to do with intellectualism."[50] This statement should caution us against any hasty deductions. Nevertheless, the idea of progressive revelation *may* be intertwined with an intellectualistic concept of revelation and such, we feel, is the case with Schilder.[51] His way of speaking about progressive revelation tends to reduce revelation to the progressively clearer disclosure of (some of) the eternal truths which exist in God's "mind" and which, through God's accommodation in revelation, can be perceived by our minds.

Every Word which God utters, Schilder says, "always has a very specific content and that content is always coherent. Now, these separate internally consistent Words, which are mutually coherent as well, can be viewed as '*doctrine*,' as '*teaching*' — a teaching which is preached, which is understood, which can also be formulated scientifically...."[52] We must add immediately

---

48 *Ibid.*, p. 108.

49 *Zur Begriffsgeschichte* (1933), p. 459: "...weil Christus in die Welt kommt als Mittler und als Kyrios auch der 'metae' (die Er durch qualitativ pleromatisierende und quantitativ vervollkommnende Erkenntnismitteilung setzt und versetzt) unser Erlöser ist...." Cf. *Bij Dichters*, pp. 401 ff.; and *HC*, II (1949), p. 260: "Die groei, en die trapsgewijze zoowel in qualiteit als in quantiteit toenemende licht-uitzending Gods, Gods steeds *méér* aan ons zeggen, en zijn steeds verder terugnemen van de grenspalen, die het niet- en het wèl-geopenbaarde van elkander scheiden, dat is de *groei* der openbaringshistorie, die parallel gaat met de heilshistorie."

50 *De Persoon van Christus*, p. 105 (E, 133).

51 J. Veenhof's (pp. 639 f.) criticism of the "intellectualism" in H. Bavinck's view of progressive revelation is to the point and all the more applicable to Schilder. Cf. Stellingwerff, *Phil Ref*, XXVII (1962), p. 121: "Zo vinden we bij Schilder veel erfgoed dat niet uit de bijbel afkomstig is. Onder invloed van het humanistisch motief van de mens als autonoom-kennend subject en God als transcendent kennis-object was het mogelijk dat Schilder dit erfgoed in zijn dogmatiek opnam." Cf. p. 118: "De mens [is] bij Schilder primair kennend. En ook God is primair zichzelf kennend...." Cf. K. J. Popma's evaluation, above, p. 35, n. 86.

52 *HC*, II, 267, Cf. *ibid.*: "Omdat God, die groote Paedagoog, tot ons spreekt in *ònze* taal, en zich bedient van *ònze* begrippen en kategorieën, en omdat voorts al zijn openbaringsinhouden uit zijn ééne goddelijke wijsheid opkomen, en van één-zelfden vasten en onveranderlijken raad de ontvouwing zijn, en nimmer elkander

that here, as elsewhere, Schilder is reacting to "Barthians who claim that revelation is an event and that *therefore* it cannot be doctrine."[53] This opposition is certainly legitimate. In some circles revelation is considered to be so dynamic that it is practically devoid of content and a new kind of mysticism results. We need only mention Bultmann who, adopting the nature – freedom dualism of existentialism, has so deformed the meaning of "kerygma" that it becomes the very opposite of "didache."[54] In the face of such impoverishment (not to say: elimination) of revelation and kerygma, one can only stress that "*didache* is not secondary but part of the proclamation,"[55] that "'kerygma' is also 'didache' and faith is also knowledge."[56] At the same time, one should not overreact — as Schilder tends to do with his emphasis on doctrines — by conceiving of revelation as a number of (theo)logical propositions which can be fitted neatly into a dogmatic system. Schilder's "doctrine" and Scripture's "didache" are quite distinct categories of knowledge. "Didache" in Scripture is not theoretic knowledge but "torah" — practical instruction.[57] It is an impoverishment of revelation to reduce Scripture's concrete, religious language to a number of dogmatic truths.[58] Revelation, after all, is much

tegenspreken, daarom kan die immer wassende, en toenemende inhoudenreeks op allerlei wijze worden *verstaan*. Verstaan kan ze worden door den eenvoudige,... ook door den man, die wetenschappelijke uitdrukkingsvormen zoekt, en daarom den geopenbaarden inhoud in den vorm eener wetenschappelijk uitgedrukte 'doctrine' straks begint samen te vatten en weer te geven."

53 *Ibid.* Cf. *Wat is de Hemel?* (1935), p. 201: "Het beeld, dat van Christus in de Schriften ons gegeven wordt, neemt voor ons geen vaste vormen aan zonder het medium van leerbegrippen, die Kierkegaard, als 'objectief,' tenslotte ijdel achten moet."

54 Because Bultmann proceeds from a "Natur – Geschichte" dualism (cf. Trimp, *Om de Oeconomie*, pp. 112-143; and Frör, pp. 34-44, 91 ff.), all objective statements are qualified as myths and must be demythologized (cf. Frör, pp. 69 f.). As a result, "kerygma" and "didache" turn into opposites (cf. Bakker, *Kerugma en Prediking*, pp. 20 ff.), and Bultmann's "kerygma" would be devoid of all content if he were consistent with his own premises (cf. Kuitert, *De Realiteit*, p. 52; see Zuidema, *Van Bultmann naar Fuchs*, pp. 21, 45 f., 57 f., 62, on the antinomy in all existentialistic philosophies: "Zij verwoordt het h.i. onverwoordbare.").

55 Clowney, p. 58, *vs.* C. H. Dodd.

56 H. Ridderbos, *Heilsgeschiedenis*, p. 140. Cf. *Paulus*, pp. 266 ff. on "het kenniselement in het paulinische geloofsbegrip."

57 "Het woord 'leer' is dus iets anders dan wetenschap. Het heeft practische zin." Von Meyenfeldt in *Gereformeerden, Waarom?*, p. 80. In view of this, Dijk rightly rejects the term "dogmatische teksten" as being a misnomer for a certain category of texts. *Dienst der Prediking*, p. 116. On "torah" and "didache" see Firet, pp. 72 ff. Specifically on the N.T. use of "didache" cf. H. Ridderbos, *Heilsgeschiedenis*, pp. 134 ff., and Schippers, *Van den Dienst*, pp. 26 f.

58 Cf. Holwerda (1945), *Een Levende Hoop*, III, p. 95: "De theologie riekt altijd naar de studeerkamer, en ze ontdekt dan wel mooie dingen, en ze legt haar vondsten wel vast in mooie termen; maar het leven is altijd meer dan de wetenschap. En het Woord Gods spreekt tot zijn volk midden in het leven. En daarom is de taal der Schrift ook altijd zo vloeiend en bewogen en veranderlijk als het leven zelf..., daarom is haar taal ook altijd veel directer en meer op de man af; de bijbel spreekt daarom

183

more than logical propositions, just as faith is much more than logical assent.[59]

Schilder knows this too, of course,[60] and yet his dogmatics is such an integral part of his whole approach that we cannot help but characterize it as "logicistic." In his expositions Schilder continually couples the progress in redemptive history with a progress in doctrinal content. When the text gives a "historical supplement," Schilder insists on reading it as a "dogmatic complement."[61] When the text speaks in concrete, down-to-earth language, Schilder speaks of progression in the "legal state" of Christ,[62] progression of "the idea of Christ exlex," "the idea of Christ's priesthood," Christ's offices of prophet, priest, and king, etc.[63] These dogmatic terms and distinctions function not merely as abbreviated, technical ways of expressing the revealed truth but as the very lines along which revelation progresses. Sometimes the doctrinal development even supplants the historical order.[64] In other words, for interpreting historical texts Schilder not only uses his dogmatic system as a framework in *addition* to the redemptive-historical framework, but at times also allows the former to overrule and even to *replace* the latter.[65] From here it is but a small step to

---

veel meer spontaan en fris en concreet en warm en echt, dan de theologie." On the language of Scripture see also Kuitert, *De Mensvormigheid*, pp. 290 ff. Vos, *Biblical Theology*, p. 17, also distinguishes the hellenistic concept of knowledge from the semitic one: "The circle of revelation is not a school, but a 'covenant.'" Cf. Wright, *God Who Acts*, pp. 33 ff. on the difficulties encountered in writing a biblical theology "by adopting the rubrics of dogmatic theology."

59 "When ... the element of knowledge inherent in all faith is isolated from the other analogies [love, justice, harmony, frugality, fellowship, etc.], faith invariably becomes a form of intellectualism." De Graaff, *The Educational Ministry*, p. 139. See this whole section on "the knowledge of faith," pp. 138 ff. Cf. Runner's description of a "logicistic thinker": "For him the central personal experiencing of truth has come to be reduced to one (logical) mode of this experiencing." *CP 1961*, p. 36.

60 See, e.g., the section on knowledge and trust in *HC*, II, 481 ff.

61 On John 18 : 28b: "Het is een zuivere historische *aanvulling* ... en het geeft een dogmatische *afronding* ...." *Christus*, II, 268 (E, 280). Note the different wording in the rev. ed., p. 321: "Een *aanvulling* ... en ook wel een pijnlijke illustratie ...." Cf. III, 92: "Wij eerbiedigen Gods wil, die onze gedachten zich niet laat hechten aan – niet geopenbaarde – historische bizonderheden, maar aan de idée, de profetie, de openbaringsgedachte ...."

62 "Rechts-staat." *Ibid.*, II, 303 (E, 314; rev. ed., 361).

63 "De idée van den Christus exlex," "de idée van het priesterschap van Christus." *Ibid.*, II, 411 (E, 427 f.; the rev. ed, 473 f. omits "de idée"). Cf. III, 237, 258.

64 In at least two places, *ibid.*, I, 72, 206 (rev. ed. 85; omitted on p. 186), Schilder states that he is aware of changing the "chronological order," but (unawares?) he changes the order quite frequently. Having treated John 12 in Chapter III, Schilder goes back to John 11 in Chapter IV with the particularly strange introduction: "Thans gaat de Schrift verder ...." *Ibid.*, I, 40 (retained in rev. ed. 50).

65 In another connection, Jager, *Het Eeuwige Leven* (1962), p. 403, comes across the same incongruity in Schilder: "Hoewel Schilder het tegenover vele theologen opneemt voor de waarde van de geschiedenis, beheerst hem toch telkens een logicistisch en systematiserend en speculatief denken dat hem o.a. brengt tot een devaluatie van de tijd en van Gods spreken in de tijd." See also Bakker, *Coram Deo* (1956), pp. 213 f.:

the objective, dogmatic sermons which the redemptive-historical side first rejected.[66]

Dogmatics, however, should never be used as a framework for interpreting historical texts (or any other text for that matter). To change the figure, dogmatics should never occupy a place between Scripture and the hearer. Filtering the message of Scripture through dogmatics not only frequently alters the message as to content[67] but also changes the direct speech of Scripture into an objective exposition of certain truths. As Seerveld says, it "removes the reader half a step away from existential confrontation with the living Word of God and asks him to comprehend these realities for codified, propositional dogmas."[68] Then, indeed, a gap has been created between the Word and the hearer and the relevance of the Word becomes problematic. In fine, we feel that Schilder's propensity for logicistic treatment of revelation is one of the roots of his objectivism.

In this connection we must mention one more crucial question. Schilder, we noted, speaks of revelation as "instruction" and of God as "the great Pedagogue and Teacher." Discussing the progression of revelation, he extends the figure even further: "God acts like every pedagogue: with continued education the old teaching aids are superseded; they make themselves superfluous. The weaker conceptions make room for better, stronger ones, and they do that in an organic manner."[69] Clearly, this way of speaking about progressive revelation involves another problem. Kuitert, for one, observes: "One of the questions which the advocates of progressive revelation must answer is: What is to be done with 'the old teaching aids' (Schilder) when a new phase has commenced?" He calls to mind several theologians who pleaded for abolishment of the old teaching aids and sees this drastic solution as well as the problem itself "as a warning not to embrace the notion of progressive revelation uncritically."[70]

"Tracht Schilder niet steeds weer boven de historie uit te komen en dan vanuit het schema verkiezing – verwerping heel de geschiedenis, ook de openbaring te doorlichten?"

66 See above, pp. 35 f.

67 It is obvious that, notwithstanding good intentions, a dogmatic system would then rule over (stand above) Scripture and the text would not always be able to say what it intends to say. See, e.g., above on Schilder's speculation.

68 *CP 1969*, p. 75, in criticism of the "scholastic, Christian orthodox reading" of Scripture.

69 *Bij Dichters*, p. 410. Hence, p. 406: "Zij [de preek] heeft ook de roeping om alle anthropomorphe beelden uit te werken in een zin, die van het lagere denk-standpunt opvoedt en opvoert naar het hoogere."

70 *De Mensvormigheid*, p. 177. Cf. Frederikse, *Wegen der Prediking*, p. 66: " 'Voortschrijdend' vat men [vanuit een Grieks-idealistisch waarheidsbegrip] dan niet op als een voortgaande concrete ontmoeting tussen God en zijn volk, maar als een steeds helderder worden van bepaalde waarheden, die in zichzelf tijdloos zijn. Aannemende, dat men in het n.t. de betrokken christelijke waarheden in hun volle ontplooiing en zuiver-

It hardly needs saying that Schilder would never seriously consider abolishing the O.T. or any part of it. But how can he escape the force of this question? Dogmatically he could, perhaps, seek the solution in the *quantitative* (as distinguished from qualitative) progression[71] and in the *organic* nature of progression: the seed is no less perfect than the fruit.[72] But homiletically the question would only return with more force: Why preach the "seed" when we have the fully developed "fruit"? Why preach the shadows when we have the reality? Why preach the *Old* Testament when we have the *New* Testament?[73] If progressive revelation is conceived of as the progressive revelation of truths, the only way out of the dilemma seems to be to eliminate much of the O.T. for preaching purposes, that is to say, to eliminate as preaching-texts all those O.T. texts containing truths which the N.T. repeats and develops further.[74] But it is inconceivable that Schilder would ever entertain this "solution" as a live option. As far as we can see, the only course open to him at this point is to switch from the truths to redemptive *history* — or better, to link progressive revelation firmly to progressing redemptive history. Since revelation is also revelation of a progressing redemptive history, no part of revelation, no matter how ancient, can ever become obsolete, and no historical text can ever become redundant or subject to elimination. And indeed, in Schilder's articles on redemptive-historical preaching the emphasis does fall on this progression in God's coming, on redemptive *history*. Whether this solves the problem of objectivism remains to be seen, however.

heid bezit, blijft het bij deze visie steeds problematisch, waarom wij als christelijke kerk nog wezenlijk en noodwendig aan het o.t. vasthouden." Similarly, *Klare Wijn*, pp. 103, 118.

71 See above, V, n. 49. Cf. *HC*, II (1949), 268: "De openbaring...begon met een eerste samenvattende openbaring in het paradijs; en zij ging daarna in quantitatieve en steeds meer détailleerende uitbreiding der stof al verder. Steeds meer en steeds fijner ging zij spreken."

72 *HC*, II, 260 on the O.T.: "Vergelijkenderwijs, relatief genomen, is het minder licht.... Maar *licht*, openbaringslicht, was het altijd." Cf. *Christus*, I, 77 f. (rev. ed., 94): "Openbaring is altijd zuiver...nooit volkomen...altijd groeiend.... Is de openbaring zuiver, dan moet hij ze aannemen."

73 These questions also apply to Van Dijk when he says: "Alweer, dezelfde waarheid, die bij het voortschrijden der openbaring al duidelijker in het licht treedt, staat hier, nog in nevelen, toch reeds voor ons." *PE*, VII, 149. Frederikse, *Wegen*, p. 66, says: "Het preken uit het o.t. krijgt dan iets van een overtollig goed werk, of van een extra kunststuk om ook daar reeds de christelijke boodschap uit te pellen."

74 This problem, by the way, must be faced also by those who see revelation as the progressive disclosure of *ethical* truths and by those who speak of the *development* of Israel's faith. When, e.g., Rowley, *The Faith of Israel*, p. 80, speaks of "outgrown beliefs" without considering the intent of the text, he does not solve but only aggravates the problem. Cf. the evaluation of Rowley's *The Relevance of the Bible* by Oosterhoff, *Het Openbaringskarakter van het O.T.*, pp. 8 ff.; e.g., p. 10: "Rowley gaat, om onderscheid te maken tussen wat in het O.T. werkelijk openbaring Gods is en wat niet, vrij subjectief te werk."

In Schilder's articles on redemptive-historical preaching, we said, the emphasis falls on redemptive history, on the *facts*. These facts must be preached. Schilder says, for example: "When one has selected a historical preaching-text...he is duty-bound to preach nothing else but the historical fact, or sequence of facts, revealed in that particular Bible passage."[75] Elsewhere he states: "In regular (summer) sermons on O.T. historical texts the real goal is...exact determination of the place. One must know what God *did*, there and then, in the process of the coming of his Son...."[76] Summarizing the intention of his earlier articles, Schilder adds: "Tell *exactly what happened*...." This should not be construed as a recommendation to preach the "bare facts" in a positivistic sense — only "the eyes of faith, enlightened by the Word and Spirit" can perceive the true significance of these facts.[77] Nor should the quotations above be construed as a recommendation simply to narrate the story told in the text — Schilder enjoins: "Let the sermon be a masterpiece."[78] The facts must be preached not as isolated facts but as interconnected facts which speak only in the context of the entire process of redemptive history.[79]

In this emphasis on preaching the facts we detect yet another root of Schilder's objectivism. The first observation we would make is similar to the one made above regarding doctrines. Schilder calls for sermons "which open the treasures of the Word and disclose the glories of Reformed dogma and of redemptive history," in a word, sermons which are "masterpieces."[80] The question arises whether Schilder wants sermons which are *theological* masterpieces.[81] His ideal is to preach the facts in their significance for the

75 *Ref*, XVI (1936), 290. The words omitted are: "met name op feestdagen." These words are a remnant of the strategic role the church calender played in Schilder's earlier articles against anthropocentric, biographic preaching: during Advent and Lent, at Christmas and Easter, the facts of Christ must be preached, not the facts of Peter, etc. In stressing the feastdays, Schilder often leaves the impression in these articles that he condones anthropocentric, biographic preaching "in de 'feestlooze helft van het kerkelijk jaar.' " *Ref*, X (1930), 204. Cf. *Ref*, XI (1931), 365, and *Christus*, II (1930), 183, 184 (E, 198; rev. ed., 215 f.).

76 *Ref*, XIX (1938), 59. Cf. *Ref*, XVIII (1938), 336: "De *openbaringshistorie* moet in preeken over historische stoffen de eigenlijke stof zijn. We kunnen... slechts daaruit bepalen, wàt er nu *eigenlijk* gebeurd is."

77 *Ibid.*: "Vertel *precies, wat er gebeurd is*, zooals zich dat voor de door het Woord en den Geest geopende en gescherpte oogen van het geloof heeft voltrokken." Cf. *Christus*, I, 43 (rev. ed., 53): "Een 'feit' is en blijft altijd een verborgenheid, tenzij de God der openbaring den zin zelf ervan ontdekt uit al de Schriften."

78 *Ref*, XVIII (1938), 415.

79 "Rechte in-verband-zetting." *Ref*, XIX, 59.

80 *Ref*, XVIII (1938), 415.

81 *Ibid.*: "Laat de preek een wèrkstuk blijven, en niet een opstelletje worden dat ieder ontwikkeld gemeentelid ook zonder theologischen studiegang, even goed zou

course of redemptive history. The danger in trying to attain this goal is that the congregation will not hear a *sermon* but a *lecture* on redemptive history.[82] Just as dogmatics, the discipline of biblical theology can so rule over the text that the direct speech of Scripture is changed into an objective, theoretical account of certain facts of redemptive history — and the hearer would again be "half a step away from existential confrontation with the living Word of God." Preachers should remain preachers of the Word, however, and should not become "dogmaticians or redemptive historians." The last words, quoted from Schilder, indicate that he himself was not wholly blind to this danger.[83]

Our second observation concerns the way in which Schilder speaks of the "objective facts" which together form "the building" God erected.[84] We shall come to the "objective facts" in a moment, but first we should consider "the *building*." Schilder conceives of redemptive history as the building which was designed and constructed by God, "the great Architect." It is "the building of God's justice and grace" — an edifice which displays "its pure and exalted style not only in its broad, general outlines but also in its details."[85] Holwerda makes use of the same metaphor: "The important question is whether the preacher views the biblical histories (plural) as building blocks with which he himself constructs the building, or whether he views that history (singular) itself as the building which he must describe."[86] This figure serves a useful purpose in clarifying the principle that the preacher may not proceed as an architect by placing the facts in a historical, dogmatic, psychological, or other structure of his own contriving, for in the historical texts God has already fashioned, joined, and patterned the facts according to his own design.[87] Nevertheless, we question the felicity of this expression because

kunnen leveren." Cf. *Ref*, XI (1931), 381: "De kansel zal geven, wat de man, die erop staat, in qualiteit van wetenschappelijk mensch heeft geleerd."

82 Cf. Boerkoel, *Bazuin*, CIV, June 2, 1961: "Zijn [Schilder's] preken hadden veel gemeen met redevoeringen...."

83 *Ref*, XVIII, 415: "...de schatten des Woords opendoen en de heerlijkheden van het gereformeerde dogma, en van de heilsgeschiedenis...zonder daarmee dogmatisten of openbaringshistorici...te worden, doch predikers blijvende...." Cf. Holwerda, *Begonnen*, p. 83: "Natuurlijk is het wel mogelijk, dat deze of gene op dit punt [het geven van een college over historia revelationis] eens uitgegleden is...." Cf. Popma, *De Psychologie*, p. 40. Hoekstra also argues continually "dat de kansel geen katheder is." *Homiletiek*, pp. 286 ff., 327 f. Similarly Veenhof on Kuyper, *Predik het Woord*, pp. 126 f.: "Niet een docent met zijn leerlingen zijn in het kerkgebouw aanwezig. Neen, de dienaar des Woords brengt Gods boodschap...in de 'vergadering der geloovigen.' En 'de vergadering der geloovigen' moet geen convent van kleine theoloogjes worden...." Cf. Spier, "De Theologie en de Preek," *Van den Dienst*, pp. 91-115.

84 *Ref*, XI, 381.

85 *Christus*, I, 332 f. (E, 333; rev. ed., 394).

86 *GM*, XVIII (1940), 26. Cf. Van 't Veer, *GM*, XIX, 66, on "het gebouw van Gods openbaring."

87 "God zelf heeft in de historische stoffen het feitenmateriaal al *verwerkt*; die

historical texts are viewed as parts of a building out there[88] and because the preacher is assigned the role of "a guide" who "merely has to search out God's design and point that out to others."[89] Does this not lead to objective sermons? If the goal in preaching historical texts is, as Schilder puts it, "exact determination of the place" of the related fact in the total structure, if the goal is "to show the beauty of the building,"[90] what is left of the overpowering Word of God? And does this goal not lead to timeless sermons which, except for a deepening insight into the design of the building, could be preached equally well a hundred years from now?[91] Need people still come to church for this? Would reading a decent commentary at home not fill the bill? We wonder, in other words, whether such sermons describing the beauty of the redemptive-historical building do not lack precisely that character which makes a sermon a sermon: the Word of God addressed to this particular congregation.

A third indication that redemptive-historical preaching easily leads to objectivism lies in the insistence on preaching the *facts*. A "fact," after all, is a thing out there, *extra nos*, and as such its contemporary relevance is problematic. Luther already struggled with this problem when he tried to express the relationship between Christ's suffering (the facts) and the church in terms of "the Augustinian schema 'sacramentum – exemplum'" — a formulation which he later replaced with the distinction between "factum" and "usus facti."[92] The distinction between and inseparability of "factum" and "usus facti" is still being advocated by some as the solution to the problem,[93] but

---

feiten in elkaar gezet en die gegevens onderling verbonden krachtens zijn eigen plan." *Ibid.*, p. 27.

88 Would this view not be included in the "fundamentally false view of Scripture" (Veenhof) which was rejected both as objectivistic and, philosophically, as subjectivistic? See above, pp. 90 f., esp. n. 202, and pp. 153 ff. Cf. Popma, *De Psychologie*, p. 35: "Ook kan ... het historisch gewordene tot absolute norm worden gemaakt. Uit den aard der zaak is het subjectivisme rijk gevarieerd."

89 Holwerda, *GM*, XVIII, 27: "We hebben slechts naar het bestek Gods te vragen en dat aan elkaar te wijzen."

90 Cf. J. G. Feenstra, "Exemplarisch of Openbaringshistorisch," *De Wachter*, XXXIX, No. 38, July 18, 1941: "Het gebouw, dat God ons in de Schrift heeft gegeven, is een architectonisch geheel. God Zelf is de opperste Bouwmeester en Kunstenaar .... God heeft Zelf het gebouw van de heilige geschiedenis doen verrijzen. Wij moeten dus alleen maar vragen naar het bestek, dat Hij ons heeft gegeven. Zo willen wij ... alleen het werk doen van een gids, die het gebouw beziet en daarvan dan spreekt. Die, wat hij gezien heeft, anderen laat zien: de schoonheid van het gebouw."

91 Cf. Ritschl, *A Theology of Proclamation*, p. 178, on sermons that "could be preached in any congregation": "A sermon that can endure this treatment is a polished theological lecture rather than a sermon."

92 See Bakker, *Eschatologische Prediking bij Luther*, pp. 41-53. Also, *Kerugma en Prediking*, pp. 17 f.

93 E.g., Frör, p. 101: "Hier wird man am besten in der Richtung weiterdenken, die durch Luthers Unterscheidung von factum und usus facti gewiesen wird."

others have given up trying to overcome the objective character of the facts and either want to demythologize all facts (Buri) or retain merely the "Dass" of Christ's coming as a fact (Bultmann).[94] The central question in contemporary discussions on this problems is: "How can...a historical text be meaningful for me in a sense more than merely historically interesting?"[95] Since N.T. texts, relating the central redemptive events, are generally considered to be so problematic, there seems to be but little hope for O.T. texts. Not surprisingly, many theologians have practically abandoned the search for the relevance of O.T. facts except in so far as they are preparatory to the Incarnation of Christ[96] and in so far as they can serve as negative or positive examples.[97]

We have called to mind some of the contemporary discussion to indicate the tremendous problems one faces in the requirement to preach the *facts*. The redemptive-historical side rightly maintains that historical facts are "einmalig": they are past and can never become present. But what, then, is the relevance of, say, the fact that Ehud killed Eglon, that David captured Jerusalem, that Elijah prayed for rain? Schilder wants to "place" these facts in the course of redemptive history and thus see Christ in his coming. But that hardly overcomes the *extra nos*. How does that coming of Christ in the O.T. involve the church today? How does that past fact, that detail in the building affect us existentially? Holwerda seeks the solution in the unity and hence continuity of redemptive history: it is the same Christ who works in the same history, now as well as then; we are participants in the same great battle waged in history.[98] This perspective is not without value, but does it solve the problem of preaching relevantly? Does the information about a battle in the past touch the hearer any deeper than, say, the information on his own birth certificate? In both cases the facts described have to do with him and would seem to be extremely relevant, but neither fact will move him existentially. For even though they take place in the same history, as historical facts they are past; though they have shaped the present, past facts can as little become present as the hearer can return to the past.[99] All these problems, we feel, are warnings that Schilder is on the wrong track when he insists on preaching

94 Cf. *ibid.*, p. 38, n. 25; and Fuller, *The N.T. in Current Study*, pp. 27 f.

95 Kuitert, *De Realiteit*, p. 41. See pp. 196 ff. for his attempt at a solution.

96 We find this emphasis, e.g., in Cullmann: "Inasmuch as the history of the people of Israel finds its fulfillment in the cross, it too affects my individual salvation" (p. 219).

97 See above, pp. 11 ff. *et passim*.

98 See above, pp. 137, 148. Cf. Trimp, *Petah-Ja*, XV (1961), 86: "De continue historie van het heil, waarin Christus, die gisteren en heden dezelfde is, regeert, *die* historie verbindt de Oud-testamentische verhalen met óns leven vandaag ...."

99 One should not make the problem easier than it is by pointing out the immediate relevance of the facts of Christ's death and resurrection. Although this is often done in contemporary discussions, if one wants to speak about facts, he should consider all the facts recorded in Scripture.

"nothing else but the historical fact." This must lead to objective preaching, which is, strictly speaking, no preaching. As Veenhof says: "Preaching is not merely a story *about* one or more moments of redemptive history — no, preaching is itself a moment *in* the redemptive history made by Christ."[100]

Schilder, in our opinion, is trapped in the same dilemma in which the exemplary side finds itself. Notwithstanding differences, both sides ultimately view Scripture's historical texts as objective presentations of facts. Preaching historical texts is therefore the same as preaching historical facts, and this, in turn, leads to preaching objective sermons. It is to the *exemplary preachers'* credit that they keenly feel the poverty of such objective sermons. They seek to compensate for this deficiency by combining the objective pole (the redemptive-historical fact) with the subjective pole (the exemplary element which can be deduced from the fact). It is to *Schilder's* credit that he is among the first to expose the poverty of such exemplary sermons and the schematism and speculation they produce.[101] He rejects the subjective and seeks to solve the problem by stressing the objective pole: "Tell exactly what happened...."[102] The exemplary side can respond only by reasserting the legitimacy of the subjective element. Holwerda, Spier, and Veenhof correctly perceive that neither side can escape the dilemma as long as the pendulum keeps oscillating between the objective and subjective pole. Moreover, neither side can be exonerated from the charge of schematism and speculation in interpreting and preaching historical texts. Notwithstanding their earnest desire to be *subject* to Scripture, both the redemptive-historical and the exemplary method actually *rule over* Scripture and hence fall short of their ideal of *sola Scriptura*. The cause for this failure we would seek in the fact that neither method is in tune with the nature of historical texts.

THE CHARACTERIZATION OF HISTORICAL TEXTS

In the foregoing we have concentrated our critique mainly on Schilder's views. The fact that we were able to contrast these views at various points

100 *Bondsboekje 1940*, p. 35.

101 We purposely use the same words we used for Schilder to indicate that the same weaknesses, be it in a different context, are found on the exemplary side, particularly in their insistence that every person described can function as a positive or negative example. See chapter III.

102 There are a few indications that Schilder himself is not entirely satisfied with merely the objective pole, for more than once he introduces an exemplary parallel in his own expositions. See, e.g., *Christus*, I, 12, 70 f., 197, 462 (rev. ed., 17, 82 f., 259, 547). Note that the rev. ed. does give a redemptive-historical expansion on pp. 82 f. but does not eliminate the original exemplary parallel. On the remote possibility of anthropocentric, biographic preaching, see above, V, n. 75.

with opposing views of other members of the redemptive-historical school should have made sufficiently clear that one cannot generalize: Schilder's schematism, speculation, and objectivism are not to be found in the same measure among his colleagues. In this section, where we shall discuss the *nature* of historical texts, we enter upon more commonly held ground.

The Foundational Function of Historical Texts

We have seen that one of Holwerda's major arguments against exemplary preaching of historical texts is that the foundational function of redemptive history excludes its illustrative function. Holwerda applies this foundational function of redemptive *history* to historical *texts* as a matter of course. "In my opinion," he says, "it is beyond doubt that dogmatic texts rest on historical texts and not vice versa."[103] But this statement is clearly fallacious: inasmuch as Paul's epistles were written prior to the gospels, his "dogmatic texts" cannot possibly rest on the gospels' "historical texts." Holwerda means, of course, that Paul's "dogmatic texts" rest on the redemptive history which was later recorded in the gospels, but here, as elsewhere, he simply identifies historical texts with historical facts. This identification is an illegitimate short cut, however, which does not do justice to the nature of historical texts.

For a start, one could point out that redemptive history is the foundation of *all* of Scripture — the foundation of its historical texts no less than of its "dogmatic texts." It will not do, therefore, to describe the peculiar character of historical texts in terms of their being foundational to dogmatic texts. Neither will it do to say that the preacher must "treat a historical text as a *fact* of history,"[104] and build one's hermeneutics on that basis. Even though historical texts relate historical facts, as *texts* they are of a different order than the facts. To state the obvious: all texts are literature; all texts have an author; all texts are addressed to certain people. The difference, then, between preaching a "historical text" and preaching a "dogmatic text" is not nearly as great as was often assumed in the controversy. The gospel of Luke is as much an epistle of Luke to Theophilus as Romans is an epistle of Paul to the church in Rome.[105] We must save the implications of this easily overlooked feature of historical texts for later. We wish to observe here only that by insisting on treating historical texts as facts (Holwerda), by insisting on preaching the facts (Schilder), the redemptive-historical method moves at a

---

103 See the entire quotation above, p. 131.
104 Holwerda, *Begonnen*, p. 87.
105 This is not to deny, of course, that Romans is different from Luke. Whether that difference should be expressed as a difference between didache and kerygma (cf. H. Ridderbos, *When the Time*, pp. 94 f.) is debatable, however.

level which might be described as *sub Scriptura*. Holwerda and Schilder try to go behind the text to the original facts, to God's original word and act revelation, to the persons whom God used in making his redemptive history: Abraham, Jacob, Joseph, etc.[106] One of the most revealing statements on this score is found in Schilder's sermon on Gen. 14 : 18ff. Abraham meets Melchizedek, says Schilder, "because Abraham must learn the true meaning of the book Genesis which is still to be written."[107] In this descent to the "fact-level" below the text, we feel, lies the origin of the redemptive-historical method's deficiencies: the problems of recovering the precise date, the schematism and speculation, the objectivism. Moreover, this emphasis on the original facts, on the foundation, easily causes the preacher to look right past the most important redemptive-historical fact for preaching: the *text*.

It is striking that the exemplary side does not point out the fallacy in Holwerda's argument. This neglect is significant because it indicates that the exemplary preachers, notwithstanding differences, proceed from the same basic assumption: *characteristic* of the historical text is that "it relates what once happened";[108] historical texts are the foundation. The exemplary preachers, too, seek to go behind the texts to the original facts. They agree that historical texts disclose part of redemptive history, but, aware of its objective

---

106 This, as we see it, is one of the major problems of biblical theology when it is described as "the study of the actual self-disclosures of God in time and space which lie back of even the first committal to writing of any Biblical document." Vos, *Biblical Theology*, p. 13. This necessitates for the O.T. documents that "two elements should be clearly distinguished": "The Pentateuch records retrospectively what unfolding of revelation there was from the beginning, but it also contains much that belongs to the chapter of revelation to and through Moses." *Ibid.*, p. 24. The same procedure is required for the N.T. historical books: "In het algemeen zullen we dus bij de geschiedenis der openbaring eerst als bron hebben te gebruiken, hetgeen in de evangelien en ten deele ook hetgeen in de Handelingen der Apostelen staat opgeteekend, dan volgen de brieven en daarna komen de evangelien en de Handelingen zelf, nu niet naar hun inhoud maar als geschriften." Grosheide, *De Geschiedenis der Nieuwtestamentische Godsopenbaring* (1925), p. 21. We would ask just two questions: Is the relationship between the original facts and the later texts as simple as Vos and Grosheide here assume? And can one separate that easily the retrospectively recorded previous revelation from the later revelation pervading the same document?

107 (1941) *Preken*, II, 356; "...omdat Abraham leren moet vandaag, welke de ware zin is van het nog te schrijven boek Genesis. Verwonder u niet, dat ik Genesis er bij haal, ofschoon het nog geschreven moet worden; want juist omdat God de Heere vandaag Zijn openbaring kent van Zichzelf in Melchizédek aan Abraham en omdat God één is van plan en één is van zin, daarom gaat God een paar eeuwen voor Mozes het boek Genesis begint te schrijven, den zin van het boek reeds duidelijk maken aan Abraham, opdat Abraham zonder schriftuitleggers, die nog komen moeten, den zin des Heeren toch verstaan kan."

108 Grosheide, *Hermeneutiek*, p. 193. Cf. Schelhaas, *De Val van Assen* (1968), p. 31, on the genre of Gen. 1-11: "Hier moet...worden gedacht...aan het genre van eenvoudige mededeling van feiten en zaken, aan het genre van historiebeschrijving in werkelijke zin."

character, they desire to add the exemplary element. The latter, too, is sought in the original facts. "One must penetrate to the inner life, to the psychical condition of the 'Bible characters,' who are subject to like passions as we are," Dijk says. "Only in this way can the historical fact be understood as *history* which is still relevant today...."[109] Hence, the combination of the redemptive-historical and exemplary approach leaves the text behind on both counts.

A rereading of the foregoing chapters will make clear that a large part of the controversy rages at this "fact-level." A central question turns out to be: Is the significance of the facts strictly redemptive-historical, or may they also be used to deduce exemplary elements? This is a dilemma which must be rejected as false because it overlooks the specific nature of historical texts. The dilemma is placed at a level where it ought not to be placed: the level of *facts.*

It must be granted at once that the text is not entirely overlooked and that many worthwhile perspectives are opened by the redemptive-historical approach. But all too often the text is used so *emphatically* as a window through which to view the panorama of unfolding redemptive history that the text itself is no longer perceived. We, on the contrary, would place the emphasis on the text. The historical text, as any other Bible text, springs from the solid foundation of God's redemptive acts in history but may not, on that account, be identified with redemptive history. We have only the text, and the preacher's task is to proclaim that text in conformity with the intention of its inspired author.

The Identification of Historical Texts and Historical Facts

We claimed above that both sides involved in the controversy seek to go behind the texts to the original facts. In all fairness, it must be observed that because of their ready identification of historical texts and historical facts, this procedure is not really problematic for them. The words "redemptive history" and "historiography" are used practically interchangeably (the one word "history" denoting both "history" and "historiography" further confuses matters); the characteristics of redemptive history are applied directly to Scripture's historical texts;[110] preaching historical texts is virtually equated

109 "Alleen op deze wijze wordt het historisch feit verstaan als een stuk *geschiedenis,* dat ook nu nog betekenis heeft en een bepaalde boodschap brengt." *Dienst der Prediking,* p. 200. Cf. p. 110 on "de verschillende 'openbaringspersonen.'" In *De Bijbel: het Boek der Ontmoetingen,* Bavinck similarly wishes to go back to the "directe ontmoeting" (p. 13) of God's Word with the various persons in the Bible. "Wij willen menschen ontmoeten ... tot wier leven God is doorgedrongen met zijn heilig en machtig Woord" (p. 55).

110 See above, pp. 124, 135.

with preaching historical facts. However customary the identification of texts and facts may be, one should not fail to notice that such identification prejudges Scripture's own testimony regarding the nature of the historical text and in so doing neglects the text's essential characteristic. In this section we shall try to uncover the reason(s) for this ready identification.

Historical and Normative Authority

In the controversy we can see reflected the traditional struggle to gain the proper perspective on the authority of Scripture. We have in mind the distinction between *auctoritas historiae* and *auctoritas normae*. The redemptive-historical side insists correctly that one cannot present a person as a normative example merely because he is mentioned in Scripture. The exemplary side grants this point immediately but wishes to retain the normative examples nevertheless. They seek the solution in the direction indicated by Hoekstra: "The history related in Scripture lacks normative authority.... 'Is' (Sein) is not identical with 'ought' (Sollen). Historical texts have historical authority, that is, the narrated history has indeed happened as recounted by Scripture. Though this history can and must be the subject of sermons, it can be preached only on condition that the words and deeds of the mentioned people are tested by those sections of Scripture which have normative authority...."[111] The redemptive-historical side is not satisfied with this answer, however. They reply that this amounts to carrying a truth from another text back into the preaching-text and that thus the historical text itself is not preached. Following this procedure one could equally well preach on Napoleon or even on an imaginary figure. "Whoever reads the texts in an exemplary fashion," Holwerda says, "no longer has to be concerned about their historicity."[112] We might say that the redemptive-historical side demands that Scripture's historical authority be upheld in the practice of preaching historical texts. The exemplary side is interested in this also but desires to complement the merely historical with some normative elements "borrowed" from other sections of Scripture. We are putting it somewhat crudely to set into bold relief the fact that whatever the differences, both sides are agreed that historical texts

111 *Homiletiek*, p. 231. Cf. Grosheide, *Hermeneutiek*, p. 95: "... historisch en normatief gezag. Alles wat het N.T. ons mededeelt, is waar in dien zin, dat het aldus gebeurd is, gelijk het wordt beschreven. Hier heeft de kritiek te zwijgen. Maar niet alles is voor ons voorschrift of navolgenswaardig voorbeeld ...." Cf. Greijdanus, *Schriftbeginselen*, pp. 28 f., 55 f., 118 f.; also H. Bavinck, *Gereformeerde Dogmatiek*, I, 419, 427 ff.

112 *Historia Revelationis*, p. 21. Cf. p. 115: "Dat is de tragiek van Aalders en vele anderen: ze maken zich druk om de historiciteit, vanuit hun gereformeerd Schriftgeloof .... Doch een gelijkenis kan dezelfde religieuze functie vervullen .... Het is niet in te zien, waarom we ons dan zo druk moeten maken over de historiciteit."

have only historical authority and that the normative authority is to be found elsewhere in Scripture.[113]

Although the distinction between historical and normative authority is legitimate in so far as it calls attention to the fact that Scripture is neither a picture gallery with normative examples nor a codex with timeless dogmatic and moral truths, it is hardly capable of adequately describing the authority of Scripture. This becomes evident when we notice that the distinction turns into a dualistic notion of Scripture's authority — formal (historical) and material (normative) authority[114] — and that it creates a dualism *within* Scripture between historical texts and normative texts.[115] According to this conception, historical texts lack normative authority, and the battle concentrates itself on the question whether or not the preacher in preaching these texts should take the liberty of borrowing some normative elements from other texts. The question arises, however, whether this whole distinction is not geared too much to an is – ought, information – obligation, description – prescription dualism. Here, it seems to us, lies the cause of the predicament: normative authority is seen too much in terms of ethical (moral) authority, while historical authority is equated with inerrancy in the description of the facts.

If this analysis is correct, it becomes understandable why such great emphasis is placed on inerrancy: the latter is the final bastion of protection for the authority of historical texts. Grosheide declares: "If any lie, any error be found, all authority perishes."[116] In the same vein, Schilder cries out: *"Everything or nothing!"*[117] "We admit," he says, "that there are contradictions in

113   See above, pp. 59, 71 f., 80 ff.

114   E.g., Grosheide, *Schriftgezag* (1918), p. 26: "De Schrift heeft formeel of historisch gezag, d.w.z. alles, wat in haar staat, is daarom alleen reeds zoo geschied en zoo gezegd." Cf. H. Bavinck, I, 428: "Deze quaestie.... bracht het eerst duidelijk tot bewustzijn, dat er onderscheid is tusschen woord Gods in formeelen en woord Gods in materiëelen zin, en dwong tot nadenken over de verhouding, waarin beide tot elkander staan. Nu werd die verhouding zeer zeker door de meesten der bovengenoemde theologen [e.g., Voetius] al te dualistisch opgevat." See further on Bavinck, J. Veenhof, pp. 471 f., and Berkouwer, *HS*, II, 110 f.

115   In addition to the quotation from Hoekstra above, V, n. 111, and the references in n. 113, see, e.g., Van Dijk, *PE*, VI (1941), 295: "Ik vind in den Bijbel aan den eenen kant beschreven de Geschiedenis van het Koninkrijk Gods, aan de andere zijde de normen, die gelden voor het leven binnen dat Koninkrijk. Wie exemplarisch de geschiedenis bespreekt, laat deze beide elementen niet op zijn plaats, maar verwart ze; hij tracht immers wat historie-gevend is bedoeld, norm-gevend te maken.... Dat is een zonde tegen het organisme der Schrift...."

116   "Dan mag geen leugen, geen fout kunnen voorkomen, of het gezag vervalt." *Schriftgezag* (1918), p. 2. This reminds one of some of the statements of C. Hodge, A. A. Hodge, Warfield, Machen, and E. Young which make the authority of Scripture dependent on its inerrancy. See Runia, *CTJ*, IV (1969), pp. 176 ff., for references and criticism. Note that in 1956 (*GTT*, LVI, 19) Grosheide clearly distinguishes between "geschiedenis" and "geschiedenisbeschrijving" and even speaks of "de subjectiviteit van het Bijbelverhaal."

117   (1919) *Om Woord*, III, 94. Cf. p. 59: "De hele Schrift is hem [een Gerefor-

196

Scripture. But we add immediately ... that we do not accept the notion that the *original* manuscripts contained these errors. Our admission of contradictions which can be solved by textual criticism does not in the least diminish the *authority* of the Bible."[118]

In the booklet we are quoting (*Tegenstrijdigheden in den Bijbel?*), Schilder is engaged in a fierce battle with critics who ridicule the Bible by "making a sport of hunting out contradictions."[119] Schilder agrees with these Bible critics on one crucial point: if the inerrancy of Scripture falls, its authority falls. Hence every available weapon is mustered in defence of Scripture's inerrancy. The first weapon is common sense: "One should level out the seeming discrepancies as long as one can without using text critical findings."[120] The second and major weapon is textual criticism: "The greatest enemy of Bible criticism is sound textual criticism."[121] Schilder would solve the seeming contradictions in Bible content in terms of Scripture's anthropomorphic way of speaking[122] and the progression in revelation: "What is called contradictory is nothing but further development."[123] Another weapon, employed particularly to explain the differences in the gospels, is the intention, the purpose of the author: "The gospel writers often combine the facts according to a certain system to show the development of things; they were motivated to relate matters as they did not by concern for historical order but for material content."[124] And finally, completing the circle: "Reformed people have always distinguished between *normative* and *historical* authority; Scripture itself is always true, and because it is true — even when it recounts the lies or errors of people, of false prophets, of Satan — it guarantees that the things said were said in the way they are related in the Bible. That means that the words of people who were not inspired by God's Spirit do not have to be correct.... Luke *was* inspired when he recounted Stephen's speech, but Stephen was not inspired when he spoke. Whereas Stephen, therefore, could make a mistake in his speech, Luke could not make a mistake in recounting the facts."[125]

---

meerde] het Woord van God. Valt zij [door tegenstrijdigheden] dan valt ook zijn geloof...."

118 *Ibid.*, p. 65, emphasis added on "authority." Cf. p. 67: "...zonder ook maar in iets de autoriteit der Schrift prijs te geven," and p. 93: "Dit meenen we wel aannemelijk gemaakt te hebben, dat van den kant der tegenstrijdigheden-vernuftelingen het geloof in de Schrift en haar autoriteit geen gevaar heeft te duchten."

119 *Ibid.*, p. 70.

120 "Vereffenen." *Ibid.*, p. 64.

121 *Ibid.*, p. 66. Similarly Holwerda, *De Wijsheid*, p. 38: "De overschrijvers van het origineel hebben blijkbaar ten aanzien van de getallen meerdere fouten gemaakt."

122 *Ibid.*, pp. 68 f. See above, p. 175.

123 *Ibid.*, p. 92.

124 *Ibid.*, p. 83. Cf. pp. 75, 84 f.

125 *Ibid.*, p. 88. Cf. n. 101: "Had men deze onderscheiding van normatief en histo-

We said that the latter completes the circle because, as we see it, the distinction between historical and normative authority is partly responsible for causing the crisis in the authority of historical texts, while the distinction is used, in turn, to bolster their authority. Runia has well said:

> Although we do not wish to deny the relative right of this and similar distinctions, yet there is a serious danger looming here which already became a reality in Voetius' formulations. We mean the danger of approaching the Bible as if it were an ordinary book of history. In Voetius' formulation the historical aspect becomes too "massive." There is no indication of the fact that the Bible is an historical book *sui generis*. No doubt this is closely linked with Voetius' mechanical conception of inspiration....[126]

Schilder's view of inspiration, to be sure, is not identical with Voetius' mechanical notion (inspired vocal points, etc.); yet he accuses Augustine of not doing justice to the inspiration of Scripture because the latter thought that Matthew made a mistake in speaking of the prophet Jeremiah instead of Zechariah.[127] Schilder fails to mention that the same charge should then be leveled at Calvin who wrote without embarrassment: "The passage plainly shows that the name of Jeremiah has been put down by mistake."[128] We only mention this as one example of the difference in temper between Schilder and Calvin. H. Ridderbos' general observation is quite pertinent to the prevailing view of inspiration during the controversy: "With regard to the *effect* of the inspiration... it permits itself altogether too much to be guided by theological and dogmatic postulates and takes too little into account the factual content of Scripture and the manner in which it came into existence." "In this manner the organic nature of inspiration... is robbed of its significance and the 'mechanical' view is brought in again through the back door."[129]

It may seem strange that we apply Runia's remark concerning "the danger of approaching the Bible as if it were an ordinary book of history" to the

---

risch gezag vastgehouden, dan zouden vele 'tegenstrijdigheden' nooit moeite opgeleverd hebben."

126 *Karl Barth's Doctrine of Holy Scripture*, p. 182.

127 *Om Woord*, III, 62, n. 29, on Matt. 27 : 9.

128 Mickelsen, p. 40, n. 41, mentions this and several similar examples from Calvin's works. See also J. A. Cramer, *De Heilige Schrift bij Calvijn* (1926), esp. pp. 116-138.

129 *IRB*, XI, Jan., 1968, p. 34. The last sentence, which is not found in this English version, is the concluding sentence of that paragraph in the Dutch version: *Het Woord*, p. 67. Cf. Hartvelt, *Over Schrift*, pp. 61 and 71: "Velen, met name in ... de Gereformeerde Gezindte lieten onder de dekmantel van het woord 'organisch' hun eigenlijke voorstellingen die 'mechanisch' waren, doorlopen." Cf. C. Augustijn, "Kuypers rede over 'De Hedendaagsche Schriftkritiek' in haar Historische Context," *GTT*, LXIX (1969), pp. 18-31, 81-108.

redemptive-historical school. The latter, after all, leveled this charge at the exemplary way of preaching historical texts (Why not preach on Napoleon?). In their tenacious defence of the historical authority and inerrancy of Scripture, however, *both* sides are in danger of overlooking the unique character of Scripture's historical texts. It is true, of course, that the defence of inerrancy is an attempt to guard the unique character of Scripture's historiography, but this kind of defence easily leads to wrong implications.[130] It is true that Schilder had good reason to refute the arguments of those wishing to ridicule Scripture, but he should never have agreed with these critics that one error would deflate the authority of Scripture. He thereby placed himself on the same rationalistic footing as that of the Bible critics.[131] The authority of Scripture far transcends historical and normative authority, however; historical authority cannot possibly be the final line of defence for the authority of Scripture's historical texts. To sense the relative "poverty" of this historical authority one has only to place it next to historical faith. It is historical faith that "makes" of revelation ordinary history, says H. Bavinck. "If Scripture were nothing but a narration of past events, it could be accepted by historical faith solely on historical grounds." But Scripture is much "more than a historical account; it is God's Word which even now comes to man to call him to faith and repentance."[132]

Some have tried to give expression to this unique authority with the term *auctoritas salutis*.[133] Runia speaks of "revelatory authority":

In Scripture we have to do with the revelation of God and His great saving acts in Jesus Christ. Scripture is "a kerygma and not a history lesson; a message calling to faith and conversion and not only a pro-

---

130 E.g., Hoekstra uses inerrancy as basis for his argument that it is better to use the persons described in Scripture as examples than other persons, for, in distinction from church history, Scripture "teekent ons de menschen zooals ze inderdaad zijn." *Homiletiek*, p. 342. Cf. Huyser on the primacy of Scripture as source of sermon illustrations, above, p. 57. Quite to the point, Holwerda quotes Kuyper: "Dan toch is er uit de gewone en uit de vaderlandsche geschiedenis allerlei stof te nemen van personen, omtrent wie we veel meer bijzonderheden weten ....". *Begonnen*, p. 107.

131 Cf. Bromiley in *Revelation and the Bible* (ed. Henry), pp. 213 f., on the concession to rationalism in the post-Reformation view of inerrancy. Cf. Rogers, *Scripture in the Westminster Confession*, pp. 448 ff. on the difference between the Westminster Divines and the Princeton Theology. Cf. Rossouw, p. 321, n. 108: "Juis in hierdie leer van die wetenskaplike feilloosheid van die Skrif blyk dit duidelik hoedat die gesag van die Skrif getransponeer is op 'n vlak wat vreemd was aan die *sola scriptura* van die reformasie."

132 Quoted by J. Veenhof, p. 342. Cf. Berkouwer, *HS*, I, 68 f., and H. Ridderbos, *Heilsgeschiedenis*, p. 132: "Een zgn. 'historisch geloof' kan in geen enkel opzicht als correlaat van het Nieuwtestamentisch getuigenis gelden."

133 Bijlsma, *Schriftuurlijk Schriftgezag*, pp. 386 ff., for whom the *auctoritas salutis* encompasses the historical authority which in turn encompasses the normative ("paraenetisch") authority.

clamation communicating certain historical facts." Of course this must not be interpreted to mean that in the Bible historical facts are unimportant, or that there is a contrast between the kerygma and the historical facts....The above-mentioned distinctions intend only to say that history has its place and function *in* the kerygma. It finds its correct accent only within the structure of the kerygma. In all its necessity and indispensability the history is "subordinate" to the proclamation of salvation, and serves the proclamation in its own peculiar way.[134]

Here we receive a glimpse of the real nature of historical texts. Both "historical authority" and "inerrancy" — in so far as they lead to the identification of historical texts and historical facts — fail to give expression to the kerygmatic nature of historical texts.

Inspiration and Inerrancy

More needs to be said about inspiration and inerrancy. We can appreciate the fact that the postulation of inerrancy was motivated by the desire to defend the authority of Scripture against its many detractors. At the same time, we should not close our eyes to the fact that the doctrine of inerrancy, no less than the schemes discussed previously, can function as an a priori scheme which confines historical texts and chokes their witness. De Graaff remarks: "To ask...whether or not these stories actually happened in every detail and in the order in which they are presented is to ask the wrong question. The Bible is not a source book for the historian, that is not its purpose. Its purpose is to proclaim, to preach...by telling us the true stories of God's mighty acts."[135] It must not be overlooked that "inerrancy is but an inference drawn from the fact that all Scripture is inspired of God."[136] The Christian Reformed committee on infallibility pointedly observes: "We may not bring

134 *Karl Barth's Doctrine*, p. 184. The words in quotation marks are from H. Ridderbos, *Heilsgeschiedenis*, p. 128. Cf. *CRC Report*, p. 74 (*Agenda 1961*, p. 191): "It is not as a history book that the Bible speaks to us. It is a book of revelation."

135 *CP 1969*, p. 10. Cf. Oosterhoff, *Feit of Interpretatie*, p. 29: "Daarbij ontvangen we niet altijd een exakte weergave van wat gebeurd of gesproken is. De vraag of het meisje van zoëven alles precies zo heeft gezegd als het ons wordt voorgesteld, is een vraag, die alleen maar het mooie bederft en [het] de lezer of luisteraar ontoegankelijk maakt." Cf. Koole, *Verhaal en Feit*, pp. 29 f.: "Daarom vraagt men aan de tekst voorbij, wanneer men zou willen weten of zulke gesprekken in deze vorm gehouden zijn, en, zo ja, langs welke weg de geschiedschrijver, na zoveel eeuwen, van deze bewoordingen in kennis gekomen is. Men miskent dan het karakter en de bedoeling van zulke verhalen."

136 *RES Report*, p. 37. Cf. Harrison in *Revelation and the Bible*, p. 238: "One must grant that the Bible itself...says nothing precise about its inerrancy." Cf. H. Ridderbos *IRB*, Jan., 1968, p. 29 (D, 59).

to the Scripture criteria of infallibility, inerrancy, reliability or accuracy...
which are foreign and alien to Scripture's expressed intent and purpose. We
do violence to Scripture when we demand that it comply with any and every
conceivable criterion of infallibility; when, for example, we require it to meet
criteria of pedantic precision which it is not intended to meet."[137] And again:

> By "accuracy," "inerrancy" and "consistency" we should not in the first
> instance mean that the historical, psychological or phenomenological
> statements of Scripture conform precisely — as we today understand
> precision — to event, or circumstance or nature or parallel statement,
> but that they completely fulfil the Spirit's purpose for making these
> statements. This purpose, one must hasten to add, can only be dis-
> covered by a diligent and believing exegesis of Scripture. *It is not to
> be posited before interpretation begins, but is to be learned solely from
> the Scripture itself.*[138]

Having written his gospel, John gives us a fine pointer to the purpose of his
historical texts: "These [signs] are written that you may believe that Jesus
is the Christ, the Son of God, and that believing you may have life in his
name."[139] The purpose "that you may *believe*" can be ascribed to all of
Scripture's historical texts — *auctoritas salutis*. Only within that framework can
historical authority and inerrancy function biblically. Once that is seen,
one will no longer be forced into a position where he must with all available
means rationally prove the historical inerrancy of Scripture's historical texts
and, as Schilder, almost as a last resort appeal to the intention of the authors
to account for the obvious differences. Rather, he will *begin* with the intention of the authors. How they handled the facts in presenting their message
remains to be seen subsequently. At any rate, one may not by a doctrine
of inerrancy curtail the liberty of the inspired authors to present the facts in
the way they see fit.

H. Ridderbos poses the questions "whether there is a necessity for the
concept of inerrancy beside that of infallibility" ("Can anything better be
said than that which has already been expressed in the concept of infallibility?"),

---

137   CRC Report, p. 65 (*Agenda 1961*, p. 182). Cf. *RES Report*, p. 37: "The
concept of inerrancy...must be derived from the Scripture itself....We may
not subject the Scripture to preconceived notions of inerrancy." See already Kuyper,
Encyclopaedie (1909), II, 518 ff., and III, 68 on "het verschijnsel dat geheel de Openbaring kenmerkt, t.w. het volstrekte gemis aan mechanische, notarieele precisiteit."
Similarly H. Bavinck, *Gereformeerde Dogmatiek*, I, 415 ff.

138   *Ibid.*, p. 40 (*Agenda*, p. 157), emphasis added. Cf. pp. 73 f. (190 f.) on the many
questions that "can not be solved by mere appeal to the doctrine of Scriptural infallibility." See also Bandstra, "Infallible in What it Intends to Teach," *Reformed Journal*,
IX (Oct., 1959), 11-16, with frequent references to N. Ridderbos, "Schriftbeschouwing en Schriftgezag," *VT*, XXIV (1954), 93-105.

139   John 20 : 31.

and "whether this concept of inerrancy does not lead us to an inadequate approach to the Scripture, in so far as it concerns itself more with the details than with the whole of Scripture and its purpose."[140] However one may think about these questions, it is clear that if one wishes to use the term "inerrancy," he should define it in such a way that its content is not merely a logical inference from the doctrine of inspiration but does indeed do justice to all the givens of Scripture. In other words, "inerrancy" will have to be so defined that it can encompass, e.g., the different ways in which the facts are presented in Scripture. This has nothing to do with an inductive approach to Scripture.[141] It is simply to say that the doctrine of inspiration and its inferences should not be based merely on the witness of a few isolated texts but on the total witness of Scripture.[142] Although this will make the task of the systematic theologian much more difficult, it is only by taking account of the totality of Scripture that our doctrine of Scripture will be completely *subject* to Scripture.

Berkouwer says: "It may well be that Holy Scripture's empirical reality provides a more profound vision of God's redemption than would be provided by the ideal of exactitude."[143] Homiletically there can be no question about it. The fact that Scripture's "reporting of redemptive history" does not "always reflect the precise correspondence to event and circumstance which is often demanded by modern historiography"[144] should not be grudgingly admitted but gratefully accepted. It demonstrates that God's Word has entered history and meets the church in its specific needs. Moreover, what could preachers possibly do with sterile, objective, precise reproductions of facts such as modern historiographers might try to produce? Is not, in the final analysis, the demand for this kind of precision positivistic?[145] Does this demand not oversimplify

---

140   *IRB*, Jan., 1968, p. 40 (D, 75). Cf. Berkouwer, *HS*, II, 94 f.

141   For the meaning of this term, see above, p. 54.

142   "Men kan wel op grond van bepaalde uitspraken een fraaie inspiratie-theorie opbouwen, maar indien deze niet klopt met notoire, onweerlegbare feiten [the phenomena which are part of Scripture], kan men haar niet als de bijbelse inspiratieleer aandienen." J. Veenhof, p. 429. Cf. p. 642: "...dat de verschillen bv. tussen de synoptische evangeliën niet altijd kleinigheden betreffen, die men met de constatering: 'geen notariële exactheid' kan afdoen."

143   *HS*, I, 215. Cf. pp. 19, 39. Also *Verontrusting en Verantwoordelijkheid*, pp. 111 ff., and *Vatikaans Concilie*, p. 161: "De interpreterende 'tusseninstanties' hebben in het wordingsproces der evangeliën het uitzicht op het *historische* heil niet verduisterd, maar verrijkt."

144   *CRC Report*, p. 67 (*Agenda*, p. 184).

145   See Richardson, *History Sacred and Profane*, pp. 109 ff., on "Positivist History." Cf. p. 190: The historian (let alone the preacher) "never gets at the uninterpreted facts, 'what really happened' ...." Cf. Van der Laan, *Spanningen*, p. 18: "Zuiver geschiedschrijving is niet alleen onmogelijk, maar is een positivistische idee van geschiedschrijving geworteld in een religieus grondmotief, namelijk dat van het subjectivistische neo-rationalisme."

the complexity of history, the complex nature of facts and their multiform meaning? And does it not completely misjudge the role of the Bible writer by viewing him as if he were some neutral reporter who merely recounts what happened?

It is striking that the historiographies in the N.T. received the caption: "The Gospel According to ...." They are written not by some neutral historiographers but by inspired preachers who are completely involved in the history they relate. And the product of their pen is not some precise, objective account of the facts but the *gospel*, the glad tidings. Similarly, the first five historical books in the O.T. were called "the law," *torah* — a word, someone suggested, which had the same ring for the Israelite as the word "gospel" has for us.[146] The books Joshua, Judges, Samuel, and Kings "were not called historical but prophetic books. They are not modern historiographies but books which proclaim and confront us with the great acts of God — *prophecy*, therefore."[147] These words — "gospel," "torah," "prophecy" — are external witnesses, as it were, to the fact that the historical texts of the Bible are unique: no modern historiographer would or could write this way. It is illegitimate, therefore, to impose on these writings standards which proceed from a modern, western mentality, whether that be the positivistic ideal or an unbiblically defined concept of inerrancy.[148] The historical texts of the Bible can be preached relevantly only because they are unique, because in proclaiming the acts of God they far transcend the modern ideal of exactitude.

The Harmonization of Historical Texts

The preaching of the facts behind the texts — based on the identification of texts and facts — results in the harmonization of parallel historical texts. This harmonization, too, can be found both on the exemplary and the redemptive-historical side. Dijk states: "Each of the gospel writers reports what happened from his own viewpoint and angle.... This manner of reporting compels the preacher always to check the parallel texts in the other

---

146 Frederikse, *Klare Wijn*, p. 12: "*Torah* .... 'wegwijzer,' of 'heilsbericht.' Het klinkt de Israëliet in de oren als ons het woord 'evangelie.'"

147 Oosterhoff, *Feit of Interpretatie*, p. 25. See N. Ridderbos, *De Canon van het O.T.*, pp. 14 f., on this and another ancient classification of the O.T. books. Runia, *Karl Barth's Doctrine*, pp. 9 f., 97 ff., prefers to speak of all historical texts as "prophetic historiography."

148 Cf. Van Elderen, *CTJ*, I (1966), p. 174: "We have no right to impose extrabiblical and twentieth-century standards on these ancient writings." Cf. Runia, *Karl Barth's Doctrine*, pp. 187 f., and the quotation from H. Sasse: "What we have to learn again is to measure Biblical history by its own standards."

gospels in order to gain a view of what actually happened."[149] Elsewhere he criticizes the text choice of a sermon on Mark 15 : 26 because John 19 : 19ff. gives a more detailed description of the facts. Dijk asserts: "In dealing with parallel passages, I deem it homiletically more correct to select as preaching-text that passage which describes the event in most detail...."[150] We agree that one should check the parallel passages — not so much, however, to see what actually happened or to select the text with the most detail but rather to gain a better understanding of the intention of the author whose text is to be preached.

Grosheide, it must be noted, is opposed to any "exegesis of the gospels that results in harmonizing. A large share of the blame for this harmonizing," he says, "must go to the method of interpreting the three Synoptics together — as if God gave us some kind of harmony instead of four gospels. We can only be grateful that this method belongs to the past and that at present [1929] the effort is being made to exegete each gospel in such a way that full justice is done to its special character."[151] In order to avoid harmonizing, however, Grosheide seems to see no other solution than to exclude the comparison of parallel texts from the field of exegesis proper by relegating that task to biblical theology ("historia sacra").[152] "It is not the business of exegesis," he says, "to determine whether two or more passages differ."[153] This, we feel, is an unwarranted restriction of the task of the exegete (preacher); it sets aside a valuable tool for determining the author's intention with a particular text. Often it is precisely the difference between parallel texts that provides helpful clues to the specific intention of the author concerned. Ultimately, Grosheide arrives at the same point as Dijk, namely, the fact behind the text which can be preached in different ways depending on one's viewpoint.[154] We, in contrast, would like to stress, even more than did Grosheide, that the only legitimate viewpoint in preaching a text is the viewpoint of the particular gospel writer.

We have seen that the redemptive-historical side is opposed to viewing a

---

149 "...zó te komen tot een inzicht in de juiste toedracht der dingen." *Dienst der Prediking*, p. 254.

150 *Hom*, III (1942), 69 f.

151 *Hermeneutiek*, p. 101. Cf. p. 195: "De evangeliën geven blijkens en door hun vorm prediking, zendingsprediking en prediking voor de gemeente, ze zijn tendenz-geschriften, wil men stichtelijke lectuur....Uit dat oogpunt is de stof gekozen, voorgesteld en ook – men lette daarop – geordend...."

152 "De *historia sacra* kan pogen de twee of meer verhalen met elkaar in overeenstemming te brengen." *Ibid.*, p. 197. Cf. p. 101. In *De Eenheid der N.T. Godsopenbaring* (1918), he considers it necessary – strangely – to get at the main thought by stripping off the *hic et nunc* ("ontdoen van het *hic et nunc*," p. 18; "af te trekken het *hic et nunc*," p. 21) in order "in de historia revelationis, in de dogmatiek te komen tot de hoogere eenheid" (p. 32).

153 *Ibid.*, p. 101.

154 See above, p. 165.

text from different viewpoints, that it settles for one perspective: "the Christological line of revelation." Although this is a vast improvement over considering a certain fact from different angles (its significance for Peter, John, the Pharisees, Christ, etc.), it makes harmonization of historical texts unavoidable. To arrive at one progressing line of redemptive history, the differences between the gospels, especially their discrepancies in chronology, must be harmonized.[155] The date and sequence are of primary significance for determining the meaning of a certain fact; the "new moment" in the development of redemptive history must be discovered. Whether the text is taken from Matthew, Mark, Luke, or John seems to be of little significance. Schilder indiscriminately selects and combines texts from each gospel and places the textual facts on the progressing line of redemptive history.[156] The "new moment" in the development of redemptive history must be brought out even at the expense of the specific witness of the gospel writer. What counts, after all, is the *fact*. "The significance of Christmas," Schilder asserts, "lies not in what Luke relates, not in what Matthew says, but in the unity of the message of both." "Matthew next to Luke — that, truly, is the sermon."[157]

We would say just as categorically: Matthew is one sermon; Luke is another! Even though the attempt to harmonize the gospels has a long history and ranges in scope from the transcribers' textual emendations to Tatian's *Diatessaron*,[158] it should not be forgotten that harmonization, however understandable, does not do justice to Scripture as God has entrusted it to us. Baarda may overstate the case somewhat when he says that reversing John 5 and John 6 amounts to "criticizing the scheme of John,"[159] but it can hardly be denied that harmonization imposes a structure on the gospels in which they can no longer speak their own language. Schippers observes that harmonizing the gospels is equivalent to "denaturizing" them. "They lose their real and essential nature.... Everything is turned topsy-turvy: John is no longer John and Matthew is no longer Matthew." "Careful reading of the gospels makes one more and more aware of the fact that each tells its own story,

155 See, e.g., Schilder, *Christus*, II, 486 f. (E, 508f.; rev. ed., 538, n. 1).

156 See all three volumes of *Christus in Zijn Lijden*. Some examples are given above, pp. 177 ff. See also, e.g., Van Dijk in *'t Hoogfeest*, p. 122.

157 *Schriftoverdenkingen*, I, pp. 333 and 334 (= *Ref*, X, Jan. 2, 1931).

158 Cf. Baarda, *De Betrouwbaarheid*, pp. 35 ff., 78 f., and 11. Berkouwer, *HS*, II, 208, mentions in addition to Tatian, the *De Consensu Evangelistarum* of Augustine, the harmony of Osiander, and Calvin's *In Harmoniam ex Mattheo, Marco et Luca Compositam Commentarii*. See also Grosheide, *Chr. Encyclopedie*, II (1957), p. 674, and especially Baarda's survey of attempted harmonizations, *Vier = Een*: Enkele Bladzijden uit de Geschiedenis van de Harmonistiek der Evangeliën (Kampen: Kok, 1970).

159 *Ibid.*, p. 16. Cf. p. 22: "Deze harmonistische oplossing betekende een motie van wantrouwen tegenover de ordening van Jh." Cf. Berkouwer, *HS*, II, 224: "Feitelijk gaat elke poging tot harmonistiek uit van een *kritische* vooronderstelling omtrent de wijze, waarop de evangelisten van Christus' leven en werken het best en het meest zuiver en betrouwbaar hadden kunnen (en mòeten) getuigen ...."

which fits beautifully within its own framework. But that story loses its power, its potency to be proclamation, gospel, the power of God for deliverance, when one... tries to compose a fifth story which contains 'everything' in a sequence and form which eliminates the 'lacunae' and 'irregularities.' "[160]

The differences between the gospels should not be considered a drawback which the preacher must somehow overcome by harmonizing or by excluding the parallel texts from his consideration.[161] Rather, the differences should be used to full advantage to discern the particular point of the preaching-text. It is only because the gospels are what they are — proclamations in specific historical situations — that they can be preached relevantly today. Commenting on the epistle to the Hebrews, Holwerda states: "The full significance of this verse can be perceived only when the situation of the first readers of this epistle is taken into account. This chapter is not a paragraph from a textbook in dogmatics but the Word of God addressed to common church people according to their needs in that particular situation."[162] The same observation holds for Scripture's historical texts. They are not paragraphs from a textbook in history but the Word of God addressed to specific people according to their needs.

It is only natural, then, that differences occur in the gospels. It is only natural that the authors selected, combined, changed, and shaped the available material in such a way that it would speak to their addressees. The changes they made "did not, to their mind, in the least constitute a threat against the authority and trustworthiness of their message."[163] On the contrary: "He who saw it has borne witness — his testimony is true, and he knows that he tells the truth — that you also may believe" (John 19:35). It is striking that this testimony is given by the writer of the gospel which perhaps more than any of the others bears the marks of the specific situation to which it is addressed. This should not be considered a handicap; it is "the truth." Because the Word of God entered history and addressed specific people, it is by its very nature intensely relevant — first of all to those people in the past, but no less so to us.[164] Because historical texts are proclamation of God's mighty acts to

---

160 *Jezus Christus in het Historisch Onderzoek*, I, pp. 31 f., and 35 f. Cf. Berkouwer, *HS*, I, 120: "Deze harmonistiek miskent het zo duidelijke relief en de zo grote gedifferentieerdheid der Heilige Schrift en is altijd een vorm van Schrift-docetisme, dat al deze gevarieerdheid vanuit de goddelijkheid der Schrift maar moeilijk kan honoreren en daarom nauwelijks geïnteresseerd is voor verschillende blik-richtingen, voor concrete polemiek in de Schrift, voor andere dimensies, waarin gedacht en gesproken wordt over dezelfde Heer." See also Bakker, *Hom*, **XXV** (1966), 7.

161 Nor can one say with Harrison, p. 245: "Generally speaking, there is no such thing as an inspired order of narration." If the author is inspired, what biblical reason could there be to exclude the order of narration from inspiration?

162 *De Wijsheid*, p. 161. Cf. p. 169.

163 Berkouwer, *HS*, II, 223.

164 Cf. *ibid.*, pp. 101 ff. on the "evidente tijd-betrokkenheid (tegenover tijdloosheid)" which is so easily denied because it is conceived of as "relativering." "Daar-

specific people, these same texts can be proclamation to us. They are not objective descriptions of facts which once occurred and which the preacher must put into a certain framework to make them meaningful. Scripture has already taken up the facts into the only suitable framework: proclamation. Historical texts take up the facts of the past and project them forward pertinently toward future generations. The written Word, Berkouwer asserts, is like an arrow aimed at the heart of man.[165]

Earlier we called attention to the words "gospel," "torah," and "prophecy" as external witnesses, as it were, to the special character of Scripture's historical texts. This unique nature of historical texts is confirmed by the *internal* witness of the texts themselves — a witness which becomes most audible when one compares parallel texts. The gospels are particularly instructive because they provide us with four accounts of the same facts. Having made a comparison, Van Elderen comes to the following homiletically significant conclusion:

> The *Sitz im Leben* in the Gospels is that of the Evangelist, and it is in that perspective that the Gospels should be interpreted. The *Sitz im Leben Jesu* can elucidate details, but the interpreter must always realize that he is seeing the event or saying through the eyes of the Evangelist — in the *Sitz im Leben des Verfassers*. The Gospels are not journal accounts nor diary records of the life of Jesus, but they are the witnesses of individuals who wrote about events which had taken place thirty or more years earlier. They are written to interpret certain events and sayings of Jesus of Nazareth, to meet certain needs in the Church, to defend the message of Jesus against certain errors, to correct certain misconceptions, and to advance the Christian Church in her enlarged environment with its concomitant problems. A concern for the *Sitz im Leben des Verfassers* will preclude the submerging of the emphasis of one Gospel in favor of another in order to harmonize them. Each account stands in its own right as a legitimate emphasis and interpretation. Such a concern will prevent the interpreter from ignoring the historical and environmental context, for it will compel him to reckon with these factors which provide important keys to the understanding of the passage. Thus the fragmentation of a given Gospel will be avoided, and

tegenover zal men moeten erkennen, dat juist het ingaan van het Woord Gods in de talloze gevarieerde situaties de *virtualiteit* van het Evangelie in de geschiedenis omvat."

165 "Dit geschrevene is als een pijl op de boog, die de mens in het hart zoekt te raken .... Men kan het geschreven woord niet verstaan, wanneer men deze gerichtheid niet in het oog vat en er alleen maar 'een oud verhaal' in leest." *HS*, I, 177. Cf. H. Ridderbos, *Heilsgeschiedenis*, p. 110: "Het N.T. richt zich niet tot de 'historicus' of de 'theoloog' in de mens, maar heeft een veel meer practisch-existentiële bedoeling, wanneer daaronder verstaan wordt, dat het de mens in zijn diepste wezen, zijn hart, het centrum van zijn zelfbepaling aangrijpt ...." Cf. *Zelfopenbaring*, p. 29: "historische tendenzgeschriften," "overwegend kerugmatisch." Similarly, *Mattheus*, I (1952), 14, 17 f. See also C. Bouma, *Johannes*, I (1950), 5 ff.

the unity of the work will be highlighted as presenting a certain portrait of the life and ministry of Jesus.[166]

We call this a homiletically significant conclusion not only because it under-scores the fact that N.T. historical texts are already proclamation before they are used for that purpose, but also because it shows that each gospel has its own unique message even when it makes use of the same facts as the other gospels. To quote Van Elderen again:

> That unique message must be proclaimed — not a forced and watered-down harmonization. In some cases where an event is recorded in the triple tradition, three distinct, although related, interpretations are possible. The homilete must choose that interpretation which meets the needs of his audience, just as the Gospel writer interpreted the event to meet the needs of his readers. Or the preacher may use all three interpretations in successive messages to unfold the riches of the multiple Gospel tradition the Church has received.[167]

Slightly modified, the same observations hold for the O.T. historical texts. Although the O.T. does not have as many parallel accounts as the N.T., the books of Kings (including Samuel) and Chronicles cover the same period of history. Everyone recognizes that these two historiographies are different. Von Rad, in fact, thinks that "the two works are so very different in pur-pose," that it is "difficult" even to make a comparison.[168] Others have tried to describe the difference in various ways, such as: "In Kings we have the

---

166 In *Jesus of Nazareth*, p. 115. Cf. *CTJ*, I, 174 f. Baarda, *De Betrouwbaarheid*, presents a more extensive comparison – a comparison which makes clear that his frequently repeated question: "Wat is er nu in werkelijkheid gebeurd?" (e.g., pp. 12, 29, 31, 35, 38, 40) is, as asked, out of order. This question must be seen against the background of his earlier article in *GTT*, LXVI, 82-106. "Kerygma en Historie," *Ministerium*, III (1969), 154-160, further clarifies Baarda's position. Cf. H. Ridderbos, *When the Time*, p. 91: "They were not notaries, they were not distinguished historians, they were preachers of the gospel of Jesus Christ, proclaimers and heralds of the fulfillment of God's promises in His Son." Cf. *Heilsgeschiedenis*, pp. 129 ff., and *Zelfopenbaring*, pp. 32 f.: "Het was hem er niet om te doen precies weer te geven wat Jezus bij een bepaalde gelegenheid gesproken heeft, maar zijn woorden als verkondiging van den Christus tot het nageslacht te doen spreken .... Het christologisch-kerugma-tisch belang domineert. Dit bepaalt en beperkt het resultaat, dat de historicus van professie hier kan behalen." Cf. Schippers, *Jezus Christus*, to the effect that (p. 38) "iedere evangelist zijn verhaal brengt door de feiten, die hij uit zijn bronnen kent, zó te interpreteren, dat zijn verhaal een eigen dimensie, een typische dynamiek, een aparte boodschap over Jezus brengt ...."

167 *Ibid.*, p. 119.

168 *Old Testament Theology*, I, 352. Goslinga, *GTT*, LXI (1961), 111, says: "De verhouding tussen Samuël en Koningen enerzijds en Kronieken anderzijds is wellicht te vergelijken ... met die tussen de Synoptische Evangelieboeken en het Evangelie naar Johannes."

facts of history; in Chronicles we have God's thoughts and words about these facts."[169] The latter view will readily grant that Chronicles is prophetic historiography, but Kings, at least, is equated with "the facts of history." It has been pointed out, however, that the writer of Kings certainly does not merely describe the facts. Omri, for example, was an able and successful king who expanded the kingdom of Israel considerably, and yet the writer covers his reign in eight short verses and mainly disapprovingly at that. This is only one of many indications that the author of Kings, too, has structured his account with a certain goal in mind. "Old Testament historiography," N. Ridderbos concludes, "is tendentious; its character is kerygmatic."[170] This applies to O.T. historiography in general. The writers do not want to present what R. H. Pfeiffer calls "objective history"[171] (an impossibility, in any case, considering the nature of facts), but they select, rearrange,[172] and mold the material to serve their immediate aim: proclamation to the O.T. church.[173] In other words, O.T. historical texts have basically the same nature as those in the N.T. "Even before they are 'used' for preaching," Frör says, "the O.T. texts themselves are already proclamation and appeal to the church."[174]

169 Hartill, p. 96. Cf. Harrison, p. 239: "The annalistic accounts of the kings of Judah found in the books of Kings take us into the realm of history as ordinarily understood. Here the customary standard of truth may fairly be applied. But in Chronicles the same period is presented from quite a different standpoint."

170 *GTT*, LVII (1957), 118, with a few other examples and a rejection of R. H. Pfeiffer's premises (see p. 116) which lead to the latter's view that the author of Kings accepted "the two standard devices which inevitably mar objective history: *suppressio veri* and *assertio falsi.*" Von Rad, *O.T. Theology*, p. 337, n. 8, remarks aptly: "Those who want information about the secular exploits of the kings are expressly directed to the sources." See, e.g., I Kings 16:27: "Now the rest of the acts of Omri... are they not written in the Book of the Chronicles of the Kings of Israel?" See also Van Gelderen, *De Boeken der Koningen*, I (1926), 15 ff., on "het zakelijke indeelingsprincipe" ("en daar heeft natuurlijk de *chronologische* orde onder geleden") and "de pragmatische beschouwing van onzen hoofdredactor."

171 See the foregoing note. "Het is duidelijk dat het in de bijbel om een heel andere vorm van geschiedschrijving gaat dan een waarbij het gaat om exakte historische gegevens in een juiste chronologische samenhang." Oosterhoff, *Feit of Interpretatie*, p. 28. See there for other examples. Also Koole, *GTT*, LXV (1965), pp. 81 ff., and *Verhaal en Feit, passim.*

172 "Zonder de lezer te 'waarschuwen,' wijkt hij [de Bijbelschrijver] van de chronologische volgorde af en gaat hij zijn stof kunstmatig – wat iets anders is dan: willekeurig – groeperen." N. Ridderbos, *Beschouwingen*, p. 59.

173 Cf. De Graaff, *CP 1969*, p. 11: "The story of the creation must not be read as a scientific, abstract systematic account of how the world came into being. Rather, this story must be read as a proclamation that demands our response." Cf. Stek, *CTJ*, IV, 34 on the book Jonah: "It is *interpreted* history, the prophetic writer himself providing the interpretation, and so disclosing its inner meaning .... All historical narrative in the Bible must be so understood ...." In view of this, Mickelsen, p. 65, gives a fitting definition of present-day interpreters: "those who set forth by exegesis and exposition *an* interpretation of *the* interpretation."

174 P. 123.

What we have said so far seems to be right in line with the redemptive-historical emphasis on the intention of the author. Holwerda, too, states that Kings is not ordinary "history," not even simply "sacred history": "The Books of Kings can be accepted as 'sacred history' only when we reckon with their unique character and the writer's unique purpose." "Driven by the Spirit the Bible writers select, arrange, and sort the material according to their own viewpoint and method."[175] Holwerda says of Genesis that it is "a highly tendentious book," and he typifies it as a "well-devised, rounded off composition."[176] Schilder says similarly: "The whole book of Genesis is one large tendentious narrative.... It is turned towards Christ's redemption."[177] Even though the emphasis falls on the intent of the authors, the problem is that the intent of the different authors is identified to such an extent with that of Genesis 3 : 15 that there is hardly room for individual variations. When the ultimate concern is to place the facts on the progressing line of redemptive history, it makes little difference whether one preaches on Kings or Chronicles because the facts are the same. It is undoubtedly true that there is one progressing redemptive history, but the fact that the O.T. contains *two* major historiographies (both commencing with Adam) should caution us against trying to fit the intent of the authors into *one* grand design.

The variety of Scripture's historical texts becomes all the more evident when we consider in addition the four historiographies of the N.T. Schilder furnishes a fine description of the gospels: "Every gospel manifests a specific tendency; it places certain facts from the life of Christ on a specific track.... If the Bible were not a tendentious narrative, it would be a poor book."[178] On occasion he makes some use of this insight,[179] but on the whole it is neglected in favor of tracing the progression in redemptive history. Quite typical of Schilder's approach is the saying we quoted earlier: "Matthew next to Luke — that, truly, is the sermon."

Like Schilder, Holwerda certainly has an eye for the "goal" of the writer: "John desires to show Jesus to us from a very special point of view";[180] "Luke selects, sorts, and arranges the material of his Christmas story according to its significance for Christ's ascension";[181] Matthew writes to Jews, Luke

---

175 *GM*, XVIII (1940), 21.

176 *Historia*, pp. 13 and 14. Cf. p. 247 on the "anachronistic" use of the name Yahweh: "Dan heeft Mozes dus God woorden in de mond gelegd, die Hij niet zelf bezigde en de patriarchen een aanspraak op de lippen gelegd, die zij niet kenden." Holwerda sees an analogy here with the N.T. which does not give us Jesus' exact words.

177 (1941) *Preken*, II, 357.

178 *College-Verslagen* (1939), pp. 21 f.

179 See, e.g., *Christus*, I, 212 ff. (E, 212 ff.; rev. ed., 192 ff.), and on Matthew 1, pp. 399 ff. (E, 403 ff.; rev. ed., 475 ff.).

180 *De Betekenis*, p. 57.

181 *'t Hoogfeest*, p. 50.

to gentiles.[182] This sounds fine, but it hardly functions homiletically. The differences in the gospels cause the attention to be riveted on the original factual situation where these differences did not exist: "Matthew and Luke complement each other"; "It is a foregone conclusion that Matthew means the same thing as Luke."[183] The fact that Matthew wrote to Jews and Luke to gentiles is only used to get back to the original meaning of Jesus' words, while the specific messages of Matthew and Luke to these post-Easter communities is neglected. The fact that "John desires to show Jesus to us from a very special point of view" does not induce Holwerda to raise his sights from the historical Jesus to the historical situation of the post-Easter community which John addresses with the gospel of the living Christ.[184] Typical of the prevalent view is Van 't Veer's assertion: "The witness disappears entirely behind the history he relates."[185] Historical texts are seen in only one dimension: a description — be it "tendentious" — of the facts. The depth dimension of historical texts — the historical setting of the *texts* — does not function. In spite of the redemptive-historical side's frequent emphasis on doing justice to the intention of the author, its exclusive concentration on the original facts results in a grand harmonization of parallel historical texts. In this way, however, justice is done neither to the intention of the authors nor to the kerygmatic nature of historical texts.

* *
*

In this chapter we have shown concretely how the redemptive-historical approach (Schilder's in particular) leads to schematism, speculation, and objective preaching. The cause for this must be sought primarily in the attempt to impose upon Scripture's historical texts the features of redemptive history: unity and progression. Although historical texts arise from and relate redemptive history, the redemptive-historical framework confines historical texts in an unnatural way. The unsuitability of this framework is most easily perceived in terms of the following three considerations: first, Scripture contains several different and overlapping historiographies which cannot with impunity be reduced to one; second, many of the related facts cannot be dated precisely; and third, these texts, thus framed, can hardly be preached in a relevant manner. This lack of relevancy, in turn, gives rise to the search for examples by the exemplary side. Thus the controversy is mired in an insolvable dilemma because both sides fail to pay sufficient attention to the unique nature of historical texts. They seek to preach the original facts behind the texts — the redemptive-historical side stressing the orginal acts of God, the

---

182 *De Wijsheid*, p. 66.
183 *Ibid.*, pp. 54 and 66.
184 See, e.g., Holwerda's remarks above, pp. 71, 77.
185 *Cursus*, I (1943), vii, 1.

exemplary side adding the conduct of the people described. Because of an unwarrantable identification of historical texts and historical facts, neither side considers this descent to the "fact-level" below the texts problematical. The resultant harmonization (as well as the schematism, speculation, and objectivism) shows clearly, however, that this procedure does justice neither to the historical text as text nor to the specific intentions of the various authors addressing different churches.

In contrast, we have emphasized that historical texts cannot simply be identified with the facts; they do not merely relate past facts but proclaim these facts in a relevant manner to the church at various stages of redemptive history. The nature of the historical text can best be described, therefore, as proclamation, kerygma. For the preacher this perspective entails several important advantages. In this context we shall mention only three. First, it eliminates the need to determine the precise date of the original facts. If the author did not consider that date of sufficient importance to make it known, he could hardly have wanted his readers to be overly concerned about it. More important than the date of the original facts is the situation to which the author addresses himself. This was known to the first readers, of course, because they lived in it. Although a reconstruction of that situation may involve problems for us, the author himself often gives sufficient information of the general situation to enable us to understand what, specifically, he is driving at.[186] Second, seeing the historical text as proclamation to a church in a specific historical situation provides an invaluable link for relevant preaching today. One does not have to turn to another category of texts ("normative") or fall back on examples to find warning, comfort, and admonition. All of this is already contained in the historical text which is the relevant proclamation of God's acts to the church in its particular needs. The task of the preacher is to make the same message concrete for the church here and now. He must preach the facts, indeed, but only as they are projected forward by the Bible writer. Third and most important, viewing historical texts as distinct historical proclamations eliminates the need to harmonize these texts and allows one to do full justice to the specific intent of each and every author.

It will be clear that our critique of both the redemptive-historical and the exemplary method involves much more than inconsequential peripheral questions. Our emphasis on historical texts as historical proclamations leads to a different approach in interpreting and preaching historical texts. We feel that this will not only overcome the dilemma(s) of the controversy but also do more justice to *sola Scriptura*. We shall try to demonstrate this briefly in our concluding chapter.

---

186 The precise date of "publication," though helpful, is not a *sine qua non* for understanding the message of the author either. "The historical situation is more important than the precise historical date." Mickelsen, p. 161.

Chapter VI

Principles for Preaching Historical Texts

One may have received the impression from the foregoing chapters that preaching historical texts is extremely problematic: the weaknesses inherent in the traditional exemplary approach were clearly exposed by the redemptive-historical side (chapter III), while some of the latter's principles (chapter IV) called forth our criticism (chapter V). It may have appeared that every principle, upon closer analysis, turned into a problem. Although historical texts are certainly not as easy to preach as is often supposed, it would be tragic if, on that account, they were no longer preached. As we tried to indicate in the last chapter, the problems we have with historical texts are often of our own making because we try to fit these texts into schemes which clash with their basic character. By attempting to fit historical texts into a progressing line of redemptive history we create innumerable difficulties and, moreover, thwart their purpose. The identification of historical texts and historical facts is quite understandable in the face of the hypercritical and a-historical tendencies among many modern theologians; nevertheless, in preaching historical texts we must seek our point of departure not in redemptive history but in the historical *text*.

Naturally, one cannot eliminate redemptive history: if there were no redemptive history, there would be no historical texts; as Paul says: "If Christ has not been raised, then our preaching is in vain...."[1] Redemptive history is the very foundation of historical texts: the *extra nos* of redemptive history is the basis for the *pro nobis* proclamation of historical texts.[2] Even so, one should not identify the foundation with the superstructure. Historical

---

1 I Cor. 15 : 14.
2 Cf. H. Ridderbos, *Heilsgeschiedenis*, pp. 111 ff., e.g., p. 114: "Het openbarings-karakter van het Nieuwtestamentisch kerugma kan dan alleen zijn absolute betekenis behouden, wanneer het gegrond is op de feitelijkheid van het in dit kerugma geproclameerde historische heilsgebeuren." Cf. Bakker, *Kerugma en Prediking*, p. 26, on the "totale afhankelijkheid van de verkondiging ten opzichte van het funderende werk Gods in de heilsgeschiedenis." Also his *Eschatologische Prediking*, pp. 46 f., n. 11, and his article in *De Bijbel in het Geding*, pp. 148 f. See further, Müller, p. 182; and Kuitert, *De Realiteit*, pp. 133 f., 177 ff.

texts are literary compositions and must be interpreted as such.[3] Though they witness to God's acts in history, the nature of their witness is not objective description but proclamation: their aim is kerygmatic.[4] A comparison of parallel historical texts shows that the biblical preachers (writers) have a liberty similar to that of painters: the authors of Scripture do not present precise photographic accounts (an impossibility for any historiographer, certainly for one who proclaims *God's* acts in history) but compositions, word-paintings. Placing all these different paintings in one redemptive-historical frame amounts to the irreplaceable loss of the distinctiveness of each composition. We would, therefore, take as our starting point not redemptive history but the historical text.

Although we take our departure from the redemptive-historical approach at this important fork in the road, we should not lose sight of the many worthwhile insights and helpful suggestions it offered. We are not going to repeat all that been said earlier, but, linking up with the contributions made during the controversy, we shall conclude our study by formulating positively a few principles (guidelines) for preaching historical texts. It is not at all our intention to make a complete list of rules but merely to suggest a few principles which should point the way *out* of the dilemma(s) of the controversy and *toward* a proclamation which is both scriptural and relevant.

THE SCOPUS OF HISTORICAL TEXTS

Taking historical *texts* as one's starting point influences the way their general scopus is formulated.[5] Instead of describing that scopus entirely in terms of progressive redemptive history, we would define it in terms of the *nature* of historical texts: historical texts are and intend to be *proclamations*

---

3 See J. Ridderbos, *Bijbelsch Handboek*, I (1935), 381 ff., on "het theologisch – litterair karakter van schriftuitlegging." Cf. Stek, *CTJ*, IV, 35: "The Biblical words are inspired, but Biblical literature is still *literature*, and must be interpreted as such." One consequence is: "The interpretation of such an historical narrative has much in common with the interpretation of a parable" (n. 25).

4 Cf. Berkouwer, *HS*, II, 211: "...een *bewust* procédé van beschrijving in een variatie, die gestructureerd is door een onweersprekelijk kerugmatische gerichtheid." On the use of the word "kerygma," see *HS*, I, 211: "Het zou zeer te betreuren zijn, wanneer men...het woord 'kerugma' zou gaan hóren als een bijna 'haeretisch' woord, terwijl het toch in het N.T. zulk een centrale betekenis heeft." Cf. H. Ridderbos, *Heilsgeschiedenis*, pp. 102 ff., and *When the Time*, pp. 90 ff.

5 Ritschl, p. 138, sets the "scopus of the text" over against its "message" and rejects the former ("a dogmatical presupposition which is brought to the text from the outside") in favor of the latter. It will be clear that we use the word in the original sense of the intention, the purpose, the aim of the text. Thus "scopus" cannot be the opposite of "message": recognition of the one leads to the other. Cf. Berkouwer, *HS*, II, 95 ff.

of God's acts in history. This designation is sufficiently broad to cover all historical texts without confining them and has the additional advantage of including both the proclaimed history and the historical proclamation (the look backward and the projection forward). As we shall see shortly, the more specific scopus of each historical text can be determined only after a detailed study of the particular book in which the text is found. Here, however, it is sufficient to note the general kerygmatic scopus of all historical texts. This scopus is the only proper basis for developing a hermeneutic method.[6] It is a first guideline, derived from the nature of Scripture's historical texts, that should ensure that we approach these texts with the proper questions. One can, of course, approach historical texts with questions arising from one's interest in dogmatics, ethics, (redemptive) history, political science, psychology, etc. Although one will undoubtedly receive interesting answers to questions of this sort, in asking them he will miss the central religious thrust of the historical text. Our questions must be in tune with the scopus of the text.

We have defined the general kerygmatic scopus of all historical texts as *proclamation of God's acts in history*. One cannot detail the specific scopus of a particular text until he has listened attentively to that text. One cannot make the a priori assertion that this scopus must necessarily be progressive redemptive-historical or exemplary or both. We do agree with the redemptive-historical side, however, that it must be *theocentric*, for historical texts intend to proclaim the acts of *God*. The kerygma proclaimed to the church cannot be the exemplary conduct or acts of man; it can only be the acts of God. This does not mean that the people we meet in historical texts should be neglected; on the contrary, it is only through these people that God's acts are shown to be concrete historical acts. The theocentric viewpoint would underscore, however, that these people have been taken up into the scriptural narrative not for their own sake but for the sake of showing what God is doing for, in, and through them. The Bible does not present, as Koole puts it, "a *Historia Sacrorum Hominum* but a *Historia Revelationis Dei*."[7] This theocentric quality of the scopus must be kept in mind when interpreting historical texts. It judges as inadequate all questioning of the text which stops short of the acts of God. Historical texts do not intend to give biographies of men but to proclaim the redemptive acts of God for man.

With the exemplary side we agree that this proclamation must be *relevant*.

---

6 Holwerda uses the *factual* character as basis, but — to apply his own analogy to another area — this is as insufficient as building up a theory on the use of water (H_2O) on the basis of either H or O.

7 *Hom*, XIX (1960), 49. Cf. *Verhaal en Feit*, p. 37: Het gaat "om het handelen van Israël's God in deze gebeurtenissen," and p. 46: "De hoofdinhoud van de bijbelse geschiedschrijving is het zichtbaar worden van Gods handelen in de geschiedenis." Cf. p. 63. See also Aalders, *De Geschiedschrijving in het O.T.* (1928), p. 16; further, Frederikse, *Wegen der Prediking*, pp. 81 ff., on "het theologisch gehalte," "de profetische visie," "het kerugma."

Schelhaas states that the historical books of the Bible were written "with the primary object of making us wise unto salvation."[8] This is the *auctoritas salutis* of which we spoke earlier. The theocentric scopus of historical texts should in no way be seen as opposed to their soteriological purpose:[9] God's acts are proclaimed with the goal of saving men. Huyser has perceived something of the concrete relevance of historical texts when he speaks of "the pragmatic view of history" apparent in Deuteronomy: "The preacher is not at all interested in presenting a pure chronology of the facts but aims at practical ends."[10] Once this is seen, however, there is no longer any need to *add* relevance to the historical text by means of the questionable exemplary method. Historical texts are relevant by their very nature because they are proclamations directed to specific people.

In addition to theocentricity (God's acts) and inherent relevance (proclamation), we must call special attention to a third implication of the general scopus: historical texts are proclamations *directed to specific churches* at various stages of redemptive history. There can be no proclamation without specific hearers, no address without addressees. Real proclamation is always historically conditioned: it enters the historical situation and meets the hearers where they are. The historical text is no exception to this: it bears the marks of the time in which it was first proclaimed, as is apparent from its language, imagery, patterns of thought, polemical thrust, etc.[11] This state of affairs should not be considered a deficiency of historical texts; on the contrary, it is evidence of the concrete relevance of the Word of God in a particular historical situation. This same Word can again become relevant in another historical situation, for, as part of Scripture, it transcends its own historical boundaries and is proclamation to the church of all ages.[12] A proper understanding of the text requires, however, that it be heard first of all as proc-

8 *Franeker Kerkbode*, XIII (Feb. 10, 1940), No. 633.

9 Cf. Berkouwer, *De Voorzienigheid Gods*, pp. 36 f.; *De Mens het Beeld Gods*, pp. 395 ff.; *HS*, II, 99 f.

10 *GTT*, XLII (1941), p. 169. Cf. p. 170: "De grepen, die hier gedaan worden uit het volksverleden, verraden kennelijk de bedoeling, de historie dienstbaar te maken aan de paraenese."

11 "De Bijbel, zo zegt Bavinck, 'is eene verzameling van boeken, die niet uit de lucht zijn komen vallen, maar die, onder de leiding des Geestes, door verschillende personen in verschillende tijden en omstandigheden geschreven zijn, en die daarvan op iedere bladzijde het merkteken dragen. Het zijn altemaal historische boeken, dat is, boeken, die in een bepaalden kring en tijd zijn ontstaan.' In de Schrift komt altijd een woord Gods tot ons, 'maar ingegaan in het woord der menschen, en dus steeds in zooverre een menschelijk, historisch, plaatselijk, tijdelijk karakter dragend.'" J. Veenhof, p. 447, quoting Herman Bavinck.

12 "Dat is het eigenaardige van de Schrift, dat God Zijn verleden woord niet laat liggen, maar dat God er mee werkt." Zuidema, *De Christus*, p. 31. Cf. Koole, *Hermeneutische Orientatie*, p. 5: "Door middel van deze verduurzaming [in de Schrift] wil de verkondiging, die eenmaal geschied is, worden tot verkondiging die opnieuw geschiedt."

lamation to the particular historical church to which it is specifically directed.[13] In other words, one must take into account whether the proclamation is addressed to the pre- or post-exilic O.T. church, or — in the case of Matthew, Mark, Luke, and John — to the post-Easter Jewish, Roman, Greek, or Christian community.

The conception of historical texts as historical proclamations of God's acts in history thus lays the groundwork for an approach to Scripture's historical texts which is attuned to their nature and scopus. In the following sections this approach will be worked out in a little more detail.

THE SELECTION OF THE HISTORICAL PREACHING-TEXT

The nature and general scopus of historical texts has several implications for their selection as preaching-texts. First, we are able to maintain more consistently than either the exemplary or the redemptive-historical side that a preaching-text from Scripture is *indispensable* for proclaiming the Word. Even though this indispensability is undoubtedly the common conviction of both parties in the controversy, their methods ultimately contradict that conviction. Schilder and Van Dijk already observed that the exemplary method does not really need a preaching-text from the Bible — an observation finding confirmation in other circles where the exemplary method leads to the supposition that "the use of the text is purely conventional."[14] But, as we pointed out, the redemptive-historical approach is liable to similar consequences in that it, too, seeks to preach the facts behind the texts to the detriment of the preaching-text.[15] The latter is indispensable, however, when one views the texts of Scripture as the only authoritative proclamations which, directed specifically at various churches, are intended for the church of all ages.[16]

A second implication flowing from the nature of historical texts is that the selected preaching-text should be a *unit*. This is already implied in the word

13 Cf. Müller, p. 187: "Die Woord mag slegs gehoor en verstaan word met betrekking tot dít wat gesê *wil* word in die verbande en struktuur waarin dit gesê *is*. Die *grondbeginsel vir die verklaring* is dat dit die *ontsluiting* van die ware inhoud van die Skrif moet wees (d.i. die *teks* moet aan die *woord* kom) . . . ." Cf. Berkouwer, *HS*, II, 106 ff., on "tijdbetrokkenheid" and "blijvende actualiteit," and pp. 248 ff. on the necessity of "vertolking." See also *CRC Report*, p. 37 (*Agenda 1961*, p. 154): "A true exegesis of Scripture gives due weight to this necessary adaptation ["to the conditions and the culture" of the addressees]."

14 See above, pp. 59, 69. Cf. Perry, *A Manual for Biblical Preaching* (1965), p. 107: "A wealth of Biblical material exists for the purpose of biographical preaching, and this type of subject matter also includes the possibility of bringing messages on the lives of men and women whose names are not found in the Scriptures but who lived for God and contributed much for the cause of His Kingdom."

15 See above, pp. 192 ff., 198 f.

16 "Preken is het Woord aan het woord laten." Jonker, *Actuele Prediking*, p. 101.

"text," which, as Hoekstra observes, is derived from the word "texere," to weave, and therefore signifies "an interwoven unit."[17] More important is the consideration that the historical text speaks only as an interwoven unit. For that reason one cannot with impunity isolate, e.g., a saying from the text. One will have to consider both the original historical background of the saying and the historical situation to which it is directed by the writer. Consequently, it can only be advantageous to select the text in such a way that it includes these factors. In general, therefore, a complete pericope would seem to be most suitable as preaching-text.[18] If this, for some reason, turns out to be impracticable, a shorter section can be selected. Frederikse's point is well taken, however, that in the latter case, too, the whole narrative must be taken into account and that a specific verse should be chosen only after the exegesis of the entire pericope has been completed.[19]

A third implication, already implied in the second, is that the preaching-text should not be a combination of sections from various books. In other words, one should not combine a verse from Mark with one from Luke, or a text from the O.T. with one from the N.T.[20] This does not mean, of course, that in one's preparation and preaching one may not consider parallel texts or move from an O.T. promise to the N.T. fulfilment. But it is confusing, to say the least, to make one preaching-text of several texts which are directed to different historical situations. In that way one can hardly do justice to the unique context and historical situation of each text. The requirement that the preaching-text be a unit implies that it ought to be selected from *one composition*.

THE HISTORICAL INTERPRETATION

Under "historical interpretation" we would include what Holwerda calls "synthetic interpretation." The latter carries over into the interpretation the idea that the historical text is and speaks as a unit and not as a collection of

---

17 *Homiletiek*, p. 223.

18 Except for the fact that we meet two historical horizons in historical texts, this is analogous to Frör's advice (p. 227) "dass die eigentlich fruchtbaren Texte für Predigt ... nicht die blossen Prophetensprüche sind, sondern die Perikopen, in denen das Wort eng mit der einmaligen geschichtlichen Situation verbunden ist, in der es gesprochen wurde."

19 "Anders exegetiseert men van een bepaald gezichtspunt uit, waar men zelf graag wil uitkomen." *Wegen der Prediking*, p. 62.

20 Although Hoekstra, *Homiletiek*, p. 235, leaves room for some exceptions, he asserts: "De homileet blijve altijd *dienaar* des Woords en verbinde niet wat God in zijn Woord gescheiden heeft." Cf. Berkouwer, *Geloof en Openbaring* (1932), Stelling XVII: "Het is ongeoorloofd, bij de tekstkeuze voor de bediening des Woords teksten uit Oud- en Nieuw-Testament te combineeren."

loose elements (recall Holwerda's graphic H_2O analogy).[21] This is also the place to determine the specific scopus of the text, to discover the goal at which it aims, the specific purpose of the author for proclaiming this narrative in the way he does.[22] The purpose of the different authors is much more varied, however, than the redemptive-historical approach assumes. One must raise his sights to the historical situation to which the author directs his proclamation. To give expression to this expanded horizon, we prefer to speak of *historical* rather than synthetic interpretation.[23]

The historical interpretation, then, seeks to determine, with all the proper means at its disposal, the meaning of the text in its *historical context*. The interpreter must try to hear the text as its first readers heard it. This will make him aware of the distance which separates the church today from those first readers. Nevertheless, the historical gap[24] — arising from the difference in time and place and the progression of redemptive and revelational history — should not be ignored for the sake of instant application.

Even while accentuating the historical gap, the historical interpretation will make one aware of the intense relevance of this Word for the people in that particular situation. Although the redemptive-historical method discovers many valuable clues for determining the meaning of historical texts — these texts, after all, frequently came to the readers in the form of a redemptive-historical composition (think, e.g., of Genesis) — it tends to overlook this immediate relevance for the first readers. In its justified opposition to the exemplary method, it fails to see, e.g., that some of the figures in the narratives function as representatives for the first hearers. The Israelites recognized themselves in such figures as Abraham, Isaac, Jacob, David.[25] What God did for these men, he did for the O.T. church which heard these narratives.

21　Above, p. 138.

22　"We hebben dus te vragen, wat de bijbelschrijver *zelf bedoelde*, toen hij een bepaald 'verhaal' aldus beschreef en mogen het niet hanteeren naar een *anderen* maatstaf." Holwerda, *GM*, XVIII, 21. See further, above, p. 170. This question is more complex than may appear at first sight: cf. N. Ridderbos, *Beschouwingen*, pp. 21 f., n. 3.

23　"De historische, de 'zeitgeschichtliche' verklaring is dus onmisbaar," says H. Bavinck. Although he makes this statement in connection with the book of Revelation, its general applicability is indicated by the way he speaks elsewhere of, e.g., the gospels as "gelegenheidsgeschriften." See J. Veenhof, p. 450. Cf. L. Berkhof, *Principles of Biblical Interpretation*, pp. 113 ff., on "Historical Interpretation."

24　By "historical gap" we mean something quite different from what Noth describes as the "fatal chasm" that "yawns between a 'historico-critical' exegesis which feels obligated to fix its eye rigidly on the given facts and a concern for relevance." *Essays*, p. 77. That "fatal chasm" seems to be the result of an unscientific approach to Scripture — unscientific because it fails to take into account the nature of its object of study.

25　"Men zou in al deze gevallen kunnen spreken van een zekere identifikatie met de persoon, wien 't verhaal geldt; in zulke volksverhalen verstaat het volk (de groep) zichzelf." Koole, *Verhaal en Feit*, p. 29.

Concerning a figure like Jonah, Stek writes: "There is no reason to doubt that, in Jonah's attitude toward the Assyrians, all Israel would identify itself with him and would know itself to be rebuked in him. And there is equally no reason to doubt that this is exactly what the writer intended."[26] The interpreter must have an open eye for this possible intention of the author to sketch certain personages in the narrative in such a way that the addressees are immediately drawn into and involved in the story. Historical texts are not objective descriptions of facts from the distant past but relevant proclamation.

In its concentration on the facts, the redemptive-historical approach fails to see that the facts are taken up into various literary forms and projected forward to speak relevantly to the church in a particular time and place. Besides the representative function of certain figures, one can see this relevance very concretely in the polemical thrust of certain passages.[27] For example, it has been pointed out that Genesis 1 : 14-19 (the creation of sun, moon, and stars) contains "a polemical thrust against all veneration of heavenly bodies."[28] Because God created these "lights," the worship of sun, moon, and stars is not only idolatrous but ridiculous. For the first readers, tempted as they were to follow the pagan practices of their neighbors,[29] the relevance of this passage was obvious. But as soon as one sees this, he becomes aware of the historical gap which seems to block any attempt to carry this polemical thrust into the twentieth century. For who would venerate the sun and moon in an age when we fly circles around them? Modern man does not consider the sun and moon to be gods, nor is he tempted to do so as Israel was. That does not mean, however, that this passage is obsolete and can no longer be preached relevantly. To modern man the sun and moon may only be things, but these "things" turn out to be just as autonomous and independent of the Creator God as the sun and moon were in the pagan view. Even today, then, this passage retains its polemical thrust and its warning to God's people not to be tempted by the modern world view which, looking upon the universe as a closed continuum, ignores God the Creator. We have followed this example through somewhat because it shows so concretely that the historical interpretation does not only bring one face to face with historical discontinuity but also opens up a perspective for relevant preaching precisely by way of the relevance the text had in another time and place. The historical interpretation is not out to relativize the message of the text but to listen to it in the context in which it was first heard as the revealing, promising, comforting, admonishing Word of God.

26 *CTJ*, IV, 39.

27 See, e.g., H. Ridderbos, *Mattheüs*, I, 18, on the polemical thrust of the gospel of Matthew.

28 N. Ridderbos, *Beschouwingen*, p. 93. Cf. Gispen, *Schepping en Paradijs*, p. 59.

29 See the passages mentioned by Ridderbos: Deut. 4 : 19; II Kings 23 : 11; Job 31 : 26-28; Is. 47 : 13; Jer. 10 : 2. Deut. 17 : 2-7 prescribes the death penalty for this sin.

THE ORGANIC INTERPRETATION

The organic interpretation concerns itself with the *literary context* of the text. It is not an additional, a second way of treating the text, but is of one piece with the historical interpretation. This is already implied in the historical interpretation itself. Although Koole states that "the folk tale forms a complete unit," he must also admit that these narratives shift their emphasis in being "joined together into a more or less continuous history."[30] The preacher has to do not with the isolated units but with narratives which are joined together in the Canon. We cannot agree with Frör who, however guardedly, allows for the possibility of preaching the traditions behind the text in their own "Sitz im Leben."[31] This approach — no less than preaching the facts — involves one in unwarrantable sub-textual preaching. Whatever oral and written traditions may lie behind historical texts, the preacher's concern is with these texts *as parts of the Canon.*[32] "Neither Israel nor the church listen to these sub-layers of the O.T.," says Kuitert, "but to the O.T. as the selection, redaction, and composition of these layers from one specific point of view."[33] Gispen remarks: "When one interprets the Pentateuch, he has to do with the intention of the author who constructed the totality."[34] The same observation may be made regarding the N.T. historical texts: the preacher's primary concern is not with the traditions behind the gospels but with the gospels in their final, canonical form. Thus the historical interpretation already includes the organic interpretation to a certain extent, for it is as a unit, as a totality that a certain composition is addressed to a specific church. The organic interpretation, then, requires one to take account of the text's literary context.

---

30 *GTT*, LXV (1965), 89 and 90: "Het is waar, nadat deze vertellingen onderling verbonden zijn tot een min of meer doorlopende geschiedenis, is het accent op de Goddelijke leiding komen te liggen."

31 See pp. 151, 174, 250 ff. Note also his criticism (p. 246), however, of "die formgeschichtliche Untersuchung" which considered the gospel writers to be mere compilers: "Darin wirkte noch das Urteil aus den Anfängen des historischen Arbeit nach: Nur das Ursprüngliche ist wertvoll!" Richardson, pp. 238 f., goes one step further in rejecting this presupposition: "St. Luke's 'own ideas' may represent a more satisfactory historical interpretation of the Gospel story than do the 'sources,' which are, after all, only earlier and necessarily more limited interpretations of that story."

32 This is not to deny, of course, that source studies may shed additional light on the meaning of a text.

33 *De Mensvormigheid*, p. 29. Cf. p. 30, n. 18 on "de voorzichtigheid van Eissfeldt... die zijn bronnentheorie 'weithin hypothetisch' noemt," and the reference to Kraus.

34 *Israëls "Verhaaldwang"*, p. 21. Cf. p. 26 on "de tendenz tot het vormen van grootere eenheden." Also *GTT*, LXVIII (1968), 245 (a book review): "Men zal dan aan de vraag, waar de stof vandaan komt, niet behoeven voorbij te gaan. Maar wel zal men alleen aan wat de laatste redactie heeft vastgesteld gezag toekennen." Further, "het bouwen van hypothese op hypothese" which "zelfs indien zij juist was, nooit de plaats zou kunnen innemen van het geheel."

The historical text must be seen in an *expanding* context: its immediate context, the book, the Testament, the Bible[35] — in that order. "No axiom is better known and more frequently disobeyed," says Mickelsen, "than the oft quoted: 'A text without a context is only a pretext.' "[36] Holwerda observes similarly: "One of the most important rules of hermeneutics is that every text must be seen in its context.... It is striking, however, how frequently this rule is ignored in the interpretation of historical texts."[37] The fragmentary interpretation leading to anthropocentric, biographic, character preaching certainly ignores this rule. One of the bluntest recommendations for transplanting the text into a context of one's own design is Perry's recipe for character sermons: "Buy two cheap Bibles and clip out all the passages related to this character. Paste them together in chronological sequence."[38] In our opinion, this mutilation of Scripture — not the clipping but the transplanting — should be avoided at all cost. We stress, therefore, the *order* of the expanding context lest the unity of Scripture be used as a pretext for shifting the material to suit one's own purposes. The text should be left in its own context: it must be heard in its immediate context, next in the context of the book, then in the context of the Testament, and finally in the context of the entire Bible.

Observing this expanding order will also serve as an antidote against the practice of using the unity of Scripture as a pretext for harmonizing. Scripture is undoubtedly a unity, but within this unity the differences should be respected as expressive of God's progressive revelation which confronts people in relevant ways in different times and places, at different stages of redemptive history. Smoothing over the differences in a grand harmonization attempt is detrimental to both Scripture and its relevant proclamation today. On the other hand, it must also be observed that the practice of playing off, say, the O.T. against the N.T. is equally detrimental. "The preacher will... fulfil his task best," says Vriezen, "if, instead of looking upon O.T. and N.T. as two different entities, he considers the Bible as a unity, historical and organic, the parts of which, however different in date of origin, in form and in life-setting, are one because of the eschatological perspective they offer on the Kingdom of God, and because of the fact that in them the same Spirit speaks of the same God, however widely they may differ in their manner and in the character of their authors."[39]

---

35 Cf. Kapteyn, p. 11: "De pericoop laat zich niet uit het hoofdstuk losrukken, het hoofdstuk niet uit het boek, het boek niet uit het gehéél der boeken." Cf. Packer, p. 101.

36 P. 113.

37 *Begonnen*, pp. 88 f.

38 *A Manual for Biblical Preaching* (1965), p. 108.

39 *An Outline of O.T. Theology*, p. 115. The most important connections between O.T. and N.T. are for Vriezen: typology (including parallelism), preparation, similarity, and contrast (p. 111). Note, however, Kuitert's criticism of Vriezen's view of "een 'inwendige, materiële, theologische kritiek' van het NT op het Oude .... Daarmee

Because the organic interpretation views the text in the context of the whole of Scripture, it shows even more clearly than the historical interpretation that the interpretation must be *theocentric*: God's acts proclaimed in the N.T. are seen as the fulfilment of God's acts proclaimed in the O.T.; God's acts proclaimed in the O.T. find their climax in God's acts proclaimed in the N.T. Provided it is not (mis)understood in a "Christomonistic" or "Jesucentric" sense,[40] we can also, along with the redemptive-historical side, speak of *Christocentric* interpretation. At this point the organic interpretation moves us beyond the historical interpretation by reading the O.T. texts in the light of the N.T. fulfilment. As Stek says: "The fact of progression in salvation history demands an ever new hearing of the word of the Lord spoken at an earlier moment in salvation history. The hearing must be new because it is a hearing in the context of the later events and circumstances in salvation history, and in the light of the word of the Lord spoken later in salvation history."[41] From our vantage point in redemptive history it is possible, therefore, that we see more in a text than the author himself realized.[42] Here, obviously, the danger that matters will be read *into* instead of out of the text lurks just around the corner. As far as we can see, arbitrariness can be precluded only by beginning with and taking seriously the historical interpretation, so that the "new hearing" becomes an extension of the original hearing.

A case in point of reading foreign matters *into* the text is the typologizing to which the redemptive-historical side rightly objected.[43] Although the O.T. contains types of Christ Incarnate, one does not have to consider his interpretation incomplete if he fails to discover such a type in his text. The whole O.T., after all, witnesses to Christ.[44] The N.T. teaches us that Christ is active from the beginning as the Logos.[45] "Nowhere," says Cullmann, "has

---

wordt het NT tot kriterium verheven voor hetgeen waardevol in het OT mag heten." *De Mensvormigheid*, pp. 48 f. On the relation O.T. – N.T., see further, e.g., Van 't Veer, *Cursus*, I (1943), lessons v to ix; Berkouwer, *De Persoon van Christus*, pp. 87-123 (E, 113-152); Koole, *Hermeneutische Oriëntatie*, pp. 7-28; N. Ridderbos, "De Verhouding van het O.T. en het N.T.," *GTT*, LXVIII, 97-110; L. Berkhof, pp. 134 ff.

40 Cf. Berkouwer, *Algemene Openbaring*, pp. 82 ff., *vs.* Brunner: "Hier ... wordt alle Openbaring Christologisch of beter nog: Jesucentrisch versmald" (p. 83). Cf. *De Persoon van Christus*, pp. 96 ff. (E, 123 ff.), *vs.* Vischer and Hellbardt. See also Troost, *Phil Ref*, XXXIV (1969), 14, on "de tragiek van het zgn. 'christomonisme,'" and pp. 21 f. on "Christus als 'nieuwe wortel' van de kosmos."

41 *CTJ*, IV, 47 f.

42 Cf. Kuyper, *Encyclopaedie*, III (1909), 96 ff.; and J. Ridderbos, *Bijbelsch Handboek*, I (1935), 395 ff.

43 "Often typology becomes an excuse for sensationalism in interpretation," says Mickelsen, p. 263. "De moderne 'typologische exegese'" reminds Koole of "de allegorische vernuftigheden van weleer." *Hermeneutische Oriëntatie*, pp. 19 f.

44 Cf. Schilder, *HC*, II, 308 ff. Cf. Veenhof, *Zicht op Calvijn*, p. 77: "Christus, zo horen we van Calvijn, is de *scopus* – het doelwit, het beheersend gezichtspunt – en daarom ook de *summa* – de hoofdsom van de Schrift."

45 John 1. See further, e.g., I Cor. 8 : 6; Col. 1 : 15-19; Heb. 1 and 2.

the unity of the entire revelatory process as a Christ-process... found more powerful expression than in the prologue of the Gospel of John, where creation and redemption appear as a single process in which Christ and revelation are active."[46] It will not do, therefore, "to speak of Christ only at some fixed point part way along the line, as though previously one could speak only of God, without reference to Christ."[47] Christ acts from the very beginning. From the N.T. perspective, therefore, the theocentric interpretation is by its very nature Christocentric.

THEOCENTRIC-CHRISTOCENTRIC PREACHING

The redemptive-historical side rightly insists on Christocentric preaching. "Christocentric," we have seen, should not be confined to the person of Christ or narrowed down to "Jesucentric." The tri*une* God allows of no division. Christocentric preaching is as broad as theocentric preaching.[48] When Paul says, "I decided to know nothing among you except Jesus Christ and him crucified," he contrasts his way of preaching not with theocentric preaching but with preaching "in lofty words or wisdom."[49] Commenting on the former part, Berkouwer observes: "For Paul this does not mean — as his preaching shows — a quantitative reduction... of the many 'truths' to the one 'truth,'" but a concentration on this central redemptive event.[50] If an O.T. text contains a type of Christ Incarnate, one may certainly work this out from the N.T. perspective, but one need not feel constrained to find such types in order to fulfil the requirement of Christocentric preaching. The witness to Christ does not hinge on a typological parallel.

Baumgärtel makes a point worth considering in this connection when he says: "From the standpoint of the N.T., the introduction of a typological parallel of itself accomplishes nothing at all. It must be demonstrated to what extent the *parakalein* dwells within the typological parallel."[51] In so far as he questions the purely formal parallel which only addresses itself to the intellect, his point is well taken. A typological parallel in and by itself

46 *Christ and Time*, p. 24. Cf. pp. 25 f., 50.

47 *Ibid.*, p. 108. Cf. p. 113 for his criticism of "the sharp separation of the three articles" in the later creeds.

48 Even of the N.T. Friedrich says: "Im Mittelpunkt des nt.lichen Kerygmas steht die Gottesherrschaft." *TWNT*, III, 710. Cf. II, 728, concerning Paul: "Object und Subject der Predigt ist Christus, und der Irdische und Erhöhte sind für ihn eins." See further, above, pp. 142 ff.

49 I Cor. 2 : 2 and 1. Cf. vss. 4 ff.

50 *HS*, II, 79. See also H. Ridderbos, *Paulus*, e.g., p. 287: "Het theocentrisch gezichtspunt – zo mogen wij concluderen – vormt het grote uitgangspunt van de paulinische paraenese."

51 *Essays*, p. 143, n. 10. Cf. *Verheissung*, p. 125. On *parakalein*, see Firet, pp. 91 ff.

makes the sermon neither relevant nor, as was observed, Christocentric.[52] Christocentric preaching does not hinge on the discovery of a type of Christ Incarnate but on the discovery of Scripture's all-pervasive witness to Christ as we see it from the N.T. perspective. Historical texts proclaim the acts of God. To hear the proclamation of the acts of God is to hear the proclamation of the acts of Christ. This means that the Christocentricity of a sermon cannot be measured in terms of the typological parallels rightly or wrongly deduced from the text. It also means that the Christocentricity of a sermon cannot be measured by counting the number of times the name of Christ is mentioned.[53] "In many of Calvin's sermons Christ is not mentioned at all," Veenhof observes. The reason for this "lacuna" (as some would consider it) is not only that he shrinks from allegory and that he feels that every sermon need not say everything but especially that "Christ is for Calvin so radically and totally the scopus of Scripture that this need not be repeated over and over again."[54]

Christocentric preaching, as here used, takes issue not only with strained typological preaching but also with anthropocentric, biographic preaching. The redemptive-historical side correctly exposed the untenability of anthropocentric preaching but tended to overreact occasionally by virtually dismissing the men in the text. Despite the theocentric emphasis, however, the men in the text continue to resurface: they just cannot be kept down. Neither can every person mentioned be seen as an office bearer preparing the coming of Christ or advancing the Kingdom of God.[55] If one takes his starting point in historical texts as proclamation of God's acts, however, the stark alternative — either God or man — disappears, and the men in the text can receive a legitimate place in the sermon — as legitimate a place as they have in the historical text itself. The Bible writer can — indeed, he must — use these men to proclaim the acts of God to posterity, for these acts are the historical acts of the *covenant* God for and with men. The preacher who, in turn, takes up these texts can and must use the same figures to transmit to the church at a later stage of redemptive history this message of the God who keeps covenant. The pitfall of using these human figures for spiritualizing, psychologizing, and moralizing can be avoided by leaving them at all times in their scriptural context and doing full justice to the intention of the author.

Perhaps a concrete illustration will clarify our proposal somewhat. In Judges 3 we read the narrative of Eglon's victory over Israel and his subsequent, ghastly death at the hand of Ehud. Several suggestions have been made for reading and preaching this narrative in a relevant manner. Vischer, e.g., understands Ehud's action as a "cogent contribution of the Bible to the

---

52 See above, pp. 84, 144 f.
53 Cf. N. Ridderbos, *GTT*, LVI (1956), 149.
54 *Zicht op Calvijn*, p. 80. Cf. Jonker, pp. 122 f.
55 See above, pp. 146 f.

right of killing a tyrant" — a positive example, therefore. Baumgärtel, on the other hand, discovers only a negative example: "We are Ehud" — murderers by nature.[56] Both theologians query the text in a moralistic, anthropocentric, exemplary manner, thereby, in our opinion, completely missing the intention of the author. For the (final) author has cast this whole narrative in a theocentric framework: "the Lord strengthened Eglon" (vs. 12), and "the Lord raised up for them a deliverer, Ehud" (vs. 15). Clearly, then, the author's point is not to give moral examples but to reveal that *God*, through Eglon and Ehud, is at work in history judging and redeeming his people; his message to the O.T. church is the admonition (cf. vss. 7, 12): Do not forget the Lord your God! The theocentric perspective, thus, can take in both the ethical thrust of this passage and the men in the text — not in isolation, however, but in the light of the author's theocentric framework. The ultimate concern of the authors of Scripture's historical texts is not to present biographies or character sketches of men; they do not describe these men for their own sake or for their value as moral examples but for the sake of proclaiming the acts of God.[57] By using the same men in the same way, present-day preachers can achieve truly theocentric sermons.

TEXTUAL-THEMATIC PREACHING

Although the term "thematic preaching" is used at times to indicate the very opposite of "textual preaching,"[58] the two terms as such are not mutually exclusive. It all depends on how one defines them.[59] Hoekstra made a fine contribution in showing the correct relationship between textual and thematic preaching. He posited two prerequisites for the formulation of the theme,

---

56 See above, p. 12.

57 Cf. Stek, *CTJ*, IV, 36, on Jonah: "Throughout the narrative, Yahweh is the leading actor who completely dominates the scene.... The narrative, then, is first of all a narrative of the acts of Yahweh." Cf. Koole, *GTT*, LXV, 99, on David's history that "de auteur het geheel, even subtiel als subliem, onder hoger licht plaatst.... de ontsluiting van de zin van de geschiedenis." Cf. H. Ridderbos, *Zelfopenbaring*, p. 37, on the gospels: "Jezus als den van God gezonden Christus-koning.... Hierin ligt de 'kern' en eenheid van heel de Christus-prediking van het evangelie."

58 So, e.g., Karl Barth in 1933: "Das ganze Elend des modernen Protestantismus ... lässt sich auch dahin zusammenfassen: seine Verkündigung ist Themapredigt geworden." Quoted by Müller, p. 230. See further p. 229 with many quotations from German works.

59 Cf. Thielicke, *Leiden an der Kirche*, pp. 91 ff. on "zwei sehr verschiedene Rassen von Themen" (p. 94). Of the kind he rejects he writes: "Noch heute kann man in Amerika solche Themen ["Man and Society," "The Ethical Problem of the Sermon on the Mount," "The Essence of Love," etc.] auf den Anschlagtafeln unitarischer Kirchen lesen" (Only in America? Only in Unitarian churches?). To avoid confusion, we would designate this kind of preaching as topic or motto preaching.

prerequisites which would firmly link theme to text. First, because the text is "a communication of God, a message for us," the theme cannot be a topic but must be an assertion. Thus the kerygmatic nature of the text — proclamation — is carried over into the formulation of the theme. Second, the theme is "the specific, characteristic thought which is revealed in the preaching-text, and at the same time the unifying bond which holds together all the thoughts of the text and therefore all the thoughts of the sermon."[60] Thus the one message of the text — first taken into account in selecting the textual unit and further worked out in the interpretation — comes to expression in the theme. Although these two requirements should be adequate, our previous discussion has shown that somehow there remains a loophole allowing for arbitrary formulations of the theme, a loophole allowing for the practice of looking at the text from different viewpoints. We would explicitly add the requirement, therefore, that the theme must be formulated from the viewpoint of the author: the message he proclaims in the text must be the theme of the sermon. Hence, the nature of the text, the unifying thought of the text, the intention of the author — all come together in formulating the theme of the sermon. Text and theme are thus insolubly joined together.

Because thematic preaching in this sense is strict textual preaching, the sermon will be limited in scope: it has one focal point, one message to drive home. "Every text," says Dijk, "contains one specific message of God to us. The preacher must administer, transmit, and *limit himself* to that specific message."[61] Thielicke remarks: "No person can say everything at once without running the danger of saying nothing at all."[62] The thematic sermon will not scatter like buckshot but drive home the one message of the text. Emphasis on the one message is necessary not only to counteract the hearer's inclination to select from the sermon whatever suits his predisposition,[63] but also to do justice to the text. The sermon, in other words, must be as one-sided as is the text. The text must be permitted to speak without being interrupted by systematic theology[64] or other texts which contain dif-

---

60 See above, pp. 162 f.

61 "Daartoe beperke hij zich." *Dienst der Prediking*, p. 82 (=*Dienst der Kerk*, p. 104), emphasis added.

62 P. 82. Cf. p. 90: "Man muss aber, um plastisch zu sein, den Mut zur Schwerpunktbildung und also zur Unvollständigkeit haben."

63 Cf. Firet, p. 333: "In de voorbeelden die wij gaven betekende het selecteren: een elimineren van de kern van de boodschap." But even concentration on "de kern" cannot guarantee that the message comes across as intended. "Wie in een preek ... niet meer doet dan de boodschap die hij te brengen heeft bij het gemeentelid deponeren, bereikt niet alleen niets, maar bereikt in veel gevallen zelfs het omgekeerde van wat hij bedoelde" (p. 334). Driving the message *home* entails more than a concern with the message alone.

64 Cf. Hoekstra, *GTT*, XXXII (1932), 516: "... dat de homiletische exegese hierin bestaat, dat de dienaar des Woords den tekst concreet benadert en dezen niet met zijn kennis van dogmatiek en ethiek gaat bewerken .... De woorden der H. Schrift

ferent accents. Other passages may be mentioned, of course, but this should not be done with the intent to harmonize different messages but to bring out more clearly by similarity and contrast the specific point of the preaching-text. "The preacher will have to make up his mind very clearly," says Ritschl, "whether he will preach Mark's or Luke's account or Matthew's report when he preaches on a synoptic passage, for the different accounts will create different sermons. Balancing one text with the other would lead, if it were properly done, to a theological lecture."[65] Preaching, however, is not presenting a lecture in theology but permitting the text to speak as concretely and as one-sidedly in the new situation as in the old one. Provided the preacher is not one-sided in his choice of texts, the congregation will still receive a well-balanced diet.

The theme having been formulated, the question can still be raised whether the sermon should be developed by the analytic or by the synthetic method. Because of the confusion surrounding these terms,[66] we would like to avoid them entirely. We can do so by rephrasing the question: Should the preacher develop the theme of the text and sermon by following the order of the text, or should he follow a more logical order of sub-points of his own making? The choice will depend largely on the chosen text and on the preacher's judgment as to how he can best get its message across. We personally prefer to follow, where feasible, the order of the text. Sub-points often have a way of becoming independent points, whereas the sermon should drive home the one point of the text. Sub-points have a way of circling around a subject, whereas the sermon should have forward movement, reaching for the climax. Sub-points have a way of putting the text into a logical scheme which, if it does not fit the text, ends up distorting the textual message. Historical texts in particular do not easily lend themselves to a logical restructuring, for the author makes his point by relating the narrative in a certain order. It seems that preachers could do worse than follow the development of the narrative

---

moeten niet verabstraheerd worden, maar als vloeibare, als concrete grootheden ge-exegetiseerd." Cf. Spier, *De Bijbel in Tegenspraak* (1967), p. 9: "Laten wij niet proberen alles wat er in de bijbel een beetje uitspringt, dadelijk glad te strijken of te systematiseren." Cf. pp. 12, 93.

65 *A Theology of Proclamation*, p. 161. Cf. Bakker, *Hom*, XXV (1966), 7. See further, above, pp. 205 ff.

66 Often the terms are applied without distinguishing between the interpretation of the text and the way the sermon is developed. Hence, our position would look roughly like this: analytic-synthetic-synthetic-analytic, that is to say: analytic in exegesis, synthetic in interpretation, synthetic in theme, analytic in following the textual order where feasible. The interaction of analytic and synthetic makes the distinction quite unsatisfactory. For the pros and cons of each method and their combination, see Hoekstra, *Homiletiek*, pp. 389 ff.; Dijk, *Dienst der Prediking*, pp. 168 ff.; Jonker, *Actuele Prediking*, pp. 134 ff. On Calvin (analytic) and Kuyper (synthetic), see Veenhof, respectively, *Zicht op Calvijn*, pp. 56 f., and *Predik het Woord*, pp. 219 ff.

as given by the original preacher. One could state the theme early in the sermon and show how it comes to expression in the consecutive parts of the text, or one might follow the textual order by gradually working up to the theme and reaching the climax along with the text. Numerous variations are possible even when one structures his sermon in accordance with the order of development in the text. And as far as the congregation is concerned, when it can see the sermon outline in the text itself, it will certainly be able to follow and remember that sermon as well as one which is developed by means of several logical sub-points. But again, this is largely a matter of personal preference. Every preacher is personally responsible for bringing the message of the text in such a way that justice is done both to the text and to the congregation.

RELEVANT PREACHING

In conclusion we must say a word about "relevant preaching" — actually a tautological expression, which we employ to indicate that here we shall consider explicitly the sermon as it is addressed to a specific congregation. The fact that this is our last point does not mean, of course, that the application is the last point in the sermon, nor that the congregation is the preacher's last consideration. On the contrary, the church which is to be addressed functions in the homiletical process from the very beginning: its needs guide the preacher in selecting a suitable preaching-text; its place in redemptive history is the place from which the preacher interprets the text; its situation and make-up determine to a large extent the structure of the sermon. Throughout the interpretative process the preacher will have his congregation in mind and search for the message which the text has for this church here and now.[67]

The redemptive-historical side showed the way toward overcoming the objective – subjective dilemma by stressing the fact that Scripture is address, appeal, kerygma. More so than was done during the controversy, we would emphasize that this is the essential characteristic also of historical texts: they are kerygma, proclamation to the church at a certain stage of redemptive history. In transmitting this proclamation to the church here and now, the preacher must take into account both the continuity and discontinuity between "then and there" and "here and now." Relevant preaching of past proclamation is possible only because of the underlying continuity.[68] The latter is to be

---

67 Cf. Firet, p. 342: "O.i. moet de kwestie van de toepassing primair ter sprake komen ... onder het aspekt van het *hermeneutisch* moment."

68 Cf. Frör, p. 153: "Diese Arbeit des Übersetzens und Nachsprechens in einer anderen Situation ist aber doch nur sinnvoll und möglich, weil in ihr die Kontinuität

found, first of all, in the triune God who, then as well as now, works in history, bringing his Kingdom, establishing his covenant, promising salvation, demanding obedience. It is to be found, secondly, in the one Church which throughout redemptive history lives by and under the same Word of God, fighting the same battle, possessing the same faith, living in the same hope.[69] The reality of continuity should not, however, lead to the identification of the church first addressed by the text with the church to be addressed today. Much less should it lead to the exemplary identification of individuals mentioned in the text with today's hearers.[70] The progression in redemptive history, the discontinuity must be taken into account: the churches today are not identical with the churches first addressed by the texts of Scripture.[71] "The Christian proclamation of an O.T. text is not the preaching of an O.T. sermon," Clowney says.[72] By extension, we must also say that twentieth-century proclamation of a N.T. text is not the preaching of a first-century sermon. The preacher must address the past proclamations relevantly to his particular congregation in the twentieth century.

Instead of speaking of the sermon as explication *and* application, there is much to be said for Van Dijk's suggestion that we speak of the sermon as "the applicatory explication of God's Word."[73] There is no tension between the Word and the church because the Word is addressed to the church; the Word need not be *made* relevant because it *is* relevant. Hence, the application is not an independent element added to the explication of the text.

We must not think, however, that solving in *theory* the problems connected with the application means that they are thereby solved for the *practice* of

des Handelns des dreieinigen Gottes in Bund und Erwählung, in Verheissung und Erfüllung erfahren wird."

69 See, e.g., H. Ridderbos, "Verbond en Koninkrijk Gods," *GTT*, XLIV (1943), 97-121, and *De Komst van het Koninkrijk* (Kampen: Kok, 1950). Further, N. Ridderbos, *GTT*, LVI (1956), 148 ff., and *VT*, XXXI (1961), 154 f., on the "herhaling van de geschiedenis, die toch geen herhaling is"; also H. Berkhof, *Christus de Zin der Geschiedenis*, pp. 102 ff. See H. Ridderbos, *Paulus*, pp. 364 ff. on the one church; and Schippers, *Gereformeerde Zede*, p. 134, and Troost, *IRB*, X, Oct., 1967, p. 56, on the abiding love commandment.

70 We find this identification also in Wingren (e.g., pp. 84 f., 271), particularly where he takes over C. H. Dodd's notion that the stories in the Bible are "the story of everyman" (pp. 61, 106).

71 In addition to the different historical situation in which today's church exists, the task of the church institute has also changed because of the process of cultural differentiation. See Von Meyenfeldt, *Kerkelijk Vooruitzicht*, pp. 59 ff., extensively quoted by De Graaff, *The Educational Ministry*, pp. 60 f.

72 P. 75.

73 See above, IV, n. 181. Cf. Jonker, p. 138: "De toepassing is niet een stuk aansprekende prediking, dat volgt op de uitleg, maar de gehele prediking vanaf het begin is toepassing op de gemeente, zo, dat de uitleg erin is opgenomen." Cf. Trillhaas, *Evangelische Predigtlehre* (1936), p. 101: "Es darf in der Predigt keine explicatio geben, die nicht zugleich applicatio wäre und umgekehrt."

preaching. Even though the Word is applied to the church and therefore intensely relevant, it is applied to a different church than the one addressed by the preacher. Sometimes the discontinuity may be so great (think of the example of Genesis 1 mentioned earlier) that it is advisable to present first the relevance of the text for the church at that time and then for the church here and now. The historical context of the text is not to be neglected in the interest of preaching a sermon which is application from A to Z. As a matter of fact, it is usually through the perception of the text's relevance in the past that it begins to speak all the more relevantly in the present. Even the presentation of the past relevance of the text aims, therefore, at disclosing its present relevance. In that sense the whole sermon is applicatory explication. This is further underscored by the fact that the preacher, as Volbeda says, "should not be a mere speaking tube or trumpet or phonograph record, reproducing perfectly but mechanically the message of God's written Word. Before one can preach in the true sense of the term, he must have taken up in his heart the message that he must bring...."[74] In other words, the message of the text passes through the preacher. Provided he knows his congregation and is one with them, the dialogue between the text and this particular congregation will already take place in the preacher's study, and the present relevance of the text will be an integral part of the sermon when it is delivered.

Because the Word is directed at man's heart — the "religious centre and radix of temporal existence"[75] — its relevance is as broad as life itself. The sermon must meet man where he is and address him concretely. The relevance of the Word can come to expression in any area of life, for no area is off-limits to the renewing Word. This does not mean, however, that the preacher should superficially cover the broad range of life and current events, making applications here, there, and everywhere. The relevance of the text is not enhanced by a host of practical asides.

Even though the Word is relevant for all of life, the preacher must observe certain limitations in making the message of the text concrete for his hearers. First, in making the application the preacher should not range far and wide but stick to the specific point of the text. Second, as Troost observes, the purpose of preaching is to build up the congregation in the faith (Eph. 4: 11-16), which means that the preacher's sphere of competence, though all-encompassing, is limited to the perspective of faith.[76] Third, as Firet points out, the

---

74 Pp. 26 f. On this "witnessing element of preaching," see further: Müller, pp. 196 ff.; Jonker, p. 141; J. Waterink, *De Prediking en de Geestelijke Volksgezondheid* (1957), pp. 6 f.; J. Thomas, *Ministerium*, I (1967), 97.

75 Dooyeweerd, *New Critique*, I, 65. Cf. Runner, *CP 1960*, pp. 103, 136 f., and *CP 1962*, pp. 165 f.; Von Meyenfeldt, *CP 1964*, pp. 49 ff., and "Enige algemene beschouwingen gegrond op de betekenis van het hart in het O.T.," *Wetenschappelijke Bijdragen*, pp. 52-67.

76 *Casuïstiek*, p. 123: "Ten eerste blijkt de ambtelijke bevoegdheid zich uit te

preacher's task is not to push his private solutions but to open perspectives so that the hearers themselves will personally work with and live out of the Word.[77] Finally, as Hoekstra remarks: "In preaching — in the application, too — the minister of the Word must always be able to say: This is the Word of God!"[78]

We have mentioned these limitations not in order to detract from the relevance of the sermon but to safeguard its real relevance for the congregation. For the sermon's true relevance is embodied in its unique authority — its relevance is that in its totality it is the Word of God to his people here and now. Every proclamation of the Word is "a link in the chain of God's acts" in history;[79] the sermon extends "the lines of God's redemptive history to contemporary man";[80] it is itself a redemptive event.[81] It pleases God to advance his Kingdom through the preaching of the Word. "In the proclamation God himself acts, distributing Christ's redemption."[82] The triune God himself addresses his people. In short, the biblical sermon is truly the Word of God.[83] This conviction can never be the preacher's boast, however, for it

---

strekken over het *gehele* leven, maar dan *onder één bepaald* gezichtspunt.... Steeds zal deze ruime competentie *innerlijk begrensd* zijn door het dienst-karakter in de geloofs-gemeenschap. De prediking, ook in haar 'toepassingen,' moet blijven een 'prediking des geloofs,' dienstbaar aan het 'in liefde heengroeien naar Christus,' door de doorwerkende macht van Gods Woord en Geest." See this whole section, pp. 117-133. Also his *Kerkelijke Verantwoordelijkheid voor de Politiek* (1967). Cf. De Graaff, *The Educational Ministry*, pp. 77-86, 149.

77 *Het Agogisch Moment in het Pastoraal Optreden*, p. 285: "Gerichtheid op het *zelfstandig* geestelijk funktioneren betekent: de ander voor de zaak plaatsen, hem helpen de zaak goed in het oog te vatten – en dan de zelfbepaling in die zaak *zijn zaak* te laten zijn." P. 344: "Het ideale effekt van de prediking is niet, dat men 'er wat van meeneemt,' maar dat men ermee aan het werk gaat en er vanuit gaat werken." See pp. 343 f. on the question whether the application should be explicit or implicit. Cf. J. H. Bavinck, *GTT*, LVII (1957), 151: "De toepassing is iets dat elk hoorder thuis moet gaan doen, hij moet de tekst toepassen in zijn eigen leven, hij moet gaan doen wat er staat, een dader des Woords worden. Dat is toepassing. Maar dat kan de predikant op de preekstoel niet gaan beginnen, die kan hoogstens aanwijzingen geven."

78 *Het Woord Gods*, p. 60: "Deze eisch dwingt den dienaar des Woords tot groote zelfbeperking." Cf. *Homiletiek*, p. 314, on the "concrete moeilijkheden" where the preacher cannot give "voorschriften" and is "onbevoegd."

79 Wingren, p. 47, n. 4. Cf. pp. 48, 77, 127 f., 142.

80 Frederikse, *Klare Wijn*, p. 193: "Een doortrekken van de lijnen van Gods heilsgeschiedenis naar de mens in het heden.... Van de Bijbel uit op ons toe; niet omgekeerd!"

81 See above, pp. 154 ff., 160 f.

82 "Dat was het eigenlijke wat de reformatoren over de prediking beleden...." Bakker, *Kerugma en Prediking*, p. 26. Cf. pp. 11 ff. on the "nauwe samenhang tussen het heil en de verkondiging ervan" (p. 15). Cf. De Jong, *The Well-Meant Gospel Offer*, pp. 102 ff., 129, 135 ff.; Von Meyenfeldt, *Kerkelijk Vooruitzicht*, p. 131; Firet, pp. 25, 41, 57.

83 Cf. Volbeda, pp. 59 ff., 67 f.; Müller, pp. 328 ff.; Schrotenboer, *IRB*, XII, July, 1969, pp. 21-26. On the "is" ("est"), see Berkouwer, *HS*, II, 397 ff.

points to God, to duty and responsibility, to the preacher's calling as minister of the Word to minister, to *ad*minister the Word of God aright.[84] Here as everywhere our final word must be: *sola Scriptura.*

<hr>

84 Cf. the "Form for the Ordination of Ministers of God's Word": "The office of pastors or ministers of God's Word is: First: That they thoroughly and sincerely present to their people the Word of the Lord, revealed by the writings of the prophets and the apostles, and apply the same, as well in general as in particular, for the benefit of the hearers ...." The following words are addressed, significantly, not to the preacher but to the congregation: "Receive the Word, which he, according to the Scripture, shall preach unto you, *not as the word of men, but, as it is in truth, the word of God.*"

List of Abbreviations

CB	*Correspondentie-Bladen* van de Vereniging voor Calvinistische Wijsbegeerte
CP	*Christian Perspectives Series*
CRC	Christian Reformed Church
CTJ	*Calvin Theological Journal*
D	Dutch edition
E	English edition
GM	*Gereformeerd Mannenblad*
GTT	*Gereformeerd Theologisch Tijdschrift*
HC	Schilder's *Heidelbergsche Catechismus*, I (1939), I-IV (1947-1951)
Hom	*Homiletica* and *Homiletica en Biblica*
HS	Berkouwer's *De Heilige Schrift*, I, II
IRB	*International Reformed Bulletin*
Med	*Mededelingen* van de Vereniging voor Calvinistische Wijsbegeerte
OB	*Het Ouderlingenblad*
PE	*Pro-Ecclesia*
Phil Ref	*Philosophia Reformata*
Ref	*De Reformatie*
RES	Reformed Ecumenical Synod
TWNT	*Theologisches Wörterbuch zum Neuen Testament*
VT	*Vox Theologica*

235

Selected Bibliography

For ease of reference, the selected books and articles are listed alphabetically by author and under each author chronologically by the first date of publication.

AALDERS, G. CH. De Geschiedschrijving in het Oude Testament. Kampen: Kok, 1928.

Acta (en Bijlagen) der Generale Synode van de Gereformeerde Kerken in Nederland, 1936, 1939, 1967/68. Kampen: Kok.

BAARDA, TJ. De Betrouwbaarheid van de Evangeliën. Kampen: Kok, 1967.

BAKKER, J. T. Coram Deo: Bijdrage tot het Onderzoek naar de Structuur van Luthers Theologie. Kampen: Kok, 1956.

———— Kerugma en Prediking. Kampen: Kok, 1957.

———— Eschatologische Prediking bij Luther. Kampen: Kok, 1964.

———— "Wezen en Actualiteit der Prediking," Homiletica en Biblica, XXIV (1965), 253–255, XXV (1966), 6–8, 25–28.

BANDSTRA, A. J. "Infallible in What It Intends to Teach," Reformed Journal, IX (October, 1959), 11–16.

BAUMGÄRTEL, D. F. Verheissung: Zur Frage des evangelischen Verständnisses des Alten Testaments. Gütersloh: Bertelsmann, 1952.

———— "The Hermeneutical Problem of the Old Testament," Essays on Old Testament Hermeneutics, pp. 134–159. Trans. M. Newman. Richmond: John Knox, 1964.

BAVINCK, H. Gereformeerde Dogmatiek. 4 vols. 4th ed. Kampen: Kok, 1928–1930.

BAVINCK, J. H. Mensen Rondom Jezus. 3rd ed. Kampen: Kok, 1948. (1st ed. 1936.)

———— De Bijbel: Het Boek der Ontmoetingen. Wageningen: Zomer & Keuning, [1942].

———— De Toekomst van onze Kerken. Bruinisse: Van der Wal, 1943.

———— "Exegese en Preek," Gereformeerd Theologisch Tijdschrift, LVII (1957), 147–151.

BERKHOF, H. Christus de Zin der Geschiedenis. 5th ed. Nijkerk: Callenbach, 1966.

BERKHOF, L. Principles of Biblical Interpretation. Grand Rapids: Baker, 1950.

BERKOUWER, G. C. *Geloof en Openbaring in de Nieuwere Duitsche Theologie.* Utrecht: Kemink, 1932.

—— *Karl Barth.* Kampen: Kok, 1936.

—— *Het Probleem der Schriftkritiek.* Kampen: Kok, [1938].

—— *De Voorzienigheid Gods.* Kampen: Kok, 1950. (*The Providence of God.* Trans. L. B. Smedes. Grand Rapids: Eerdmans, 1952.)

—— *De Persoon van Christus.* Kampen: Kok, 1952. (*The Person of Christ.* Trans. J. Vriend. Grand Rapids: Eerdmans, 1954.)

—— *De Heilige Schrift.* 2 vols. Kampen: Kok, 1966, 1967.

—— *Verontrusting en Verantwoordelijkheid.* Kampen: Kok, 1969.

BIJLSMA, R. *Schriftuurlijk Schriftgezag.* Nijkerk: Callenbach, 1959.

BOERKOEL, J. D. Series of articles on the Gereformeerde Kerken since 1920 and especially on K. Schilder, *De Bazuin,* CIII, No. 19–CIV, No. 26 (May 6, 1960–June 30, 1961).

BULTMANN, R. *Glauben und Verstehen*: Gesammelte Aufsätze. Vols. I (2nd ed.) and II. Tübingen: Mohr, 1954, 1952.

—— *Theologie des Neuen Testaments.* Tübingen: Mohr, 1953.

—— "Prophecy and Fulfillment," *Essays on Old Testament Hermeneutics,* pp. 50–75. Trans. J. C. G. Greig. Richmond: John Knox, 1964.

BURRELL, D. J. *The Sermon*: Its Construction and Delivery. New York: Revell, 1913.

Christian Reformed Church Report: "Infallibility and Inspiration in the Light of Scripture and the Creeds." Grand Rapids: Christian Reformed Publishing House. (*Agenda 1961,* Supplement No. 24, pp. 119–194.)

CLOWNEY, E. P. *Preaching and Biblical Theology.* Grand Rapids: Eerdmans, 1961.

CULLMANN, O. *Christ and Time*: The Primitive Christian Conception of Time and History. Trans. F. V. Filson. 2nd ed. rev. London: SCM, 1962.

DAVIS, H. C. *Design for Preaching.* Philadelphia: Fortress, 1958.

DE GRAAF, S. G. *Het Woord Gods en de Kerk.* Zutphen: Van den Brink, 1935. (A compilation and partial revision of three articles dating from 1925, 1934, and 1935.)

—— *Verbondsgeschiedenis*: Schetsen voor de Vertelling van de Bijbelse Geschiedenis. 3rd ed. Kampen: Kok, 1952. (1st ed. 1936.)

DE GRAAFF, A. H. *The Educational Ministry of the Church*: A Perspective. Delft: Judels & Brinkman, 1966.

—— *Understanding the Scriptures*: How to Read and not to Read the Bible, pp. 1–40. *Christian Perspectives 1969.* Toronto: A.A.C.S., 1968.

DE JONG, A. C. *The Well-Meant Gospel Offer*: The Views of H. Hoeksema and K. Schilder. Franeker: Wever, 1954.

DEN HARTOGH, G. M. *In de Lijn der Afscheiding.* Groningen: Niemeijer, 1945.

238

DE WOLFF, I. *Verbondsmatige Zelfbeproeving.* Enschede: Boersma, 1936.

————— and VAN DOOREN, G. (eds.) *De Geschiedenis der Godsopenbaring* in Hoofd-lijnen Beschreven. Enschede: Boersma, 1947–1955.

DIJK, K. *De Dienst der Kerk.* Kampen: Kok, 1952. (A compilation and partial revision of articles dating from 1937–1950.)

————— "Over de Prediking," *Het Ouderlingenblad,* XXII, Nos. 254–261 (November, 1943–June, 1944), 2986–3047.

————— *Het Gericht Gods* in de Prediking des Woords. Delft: Van Keulen, 1952.

————— *De Dienst der Prediking.* Kampen: Kok, 1955.

DOOYEWEERD, H. *A New Critique of Theoretical Thought.* 4 vols. Trans. D. H. Free-man and W. S. Young. Amsterdam: H. J. Paris; Philadelphia: Presbyterian and Reformed, 1953–1958. (A revision and translation of *De Wijsbegeerte der Wetsidee.* 3 vols. Amsterdam: H. J. Paris, 1935–1936.)

————— "Wat de Wijsbegeerte der Wetsidee aan Dr Kuyper te danken heeft," *De Reformatie,* XVIII (October 29, 1937), 63–65.

————— "Kuyper's Wetenschapsleer," *Philosophia Reformata,* IV (1939), 193–232.

DOUMA, J. "Calvijn over Historische Stoffen," *De Heraut,* 1941, Nos. 3292–3297, 3299–3300.

————— "Exemplarische Prediking," *De Heraut,* 1941, Nos. 3333–3335, and 1942, Nos. 3336–3343, 3345–3349.

DOUMA, JOCHEM. *Algemene Genade*: Uiteenzetting, Vergelijking en Beoordeling van de Opvattingen van A. Kuyper, K. Schilder en Joh. Calvijn over 'Algemene Genade.' Goes: Oosterbaan & Le Cointre, 1966.

EICHRODT, W. "Is Typological Exegesis an Appropriate Method?", *Essays on Old Testament Hermeneutics,* pp. 224–245. Trans. J. Barr. Richmond: John Knox, 1964.

ELLIS, E. E. *Paul's Use of the Old Testament.* Edinburgh: Oliver and Boyd, 1957.

FEENSTRA, J. G. "Exemplarisch of Openbaringhistorisch," *De Wachter,* XXXIX, No. 38 (July 18, 1941).

FIRET, J. *Het Agogisch Moment in het Pastoraal Optreden.* Kampen: Kok, 1968.

FREDERIKSE, TH. C. *et al.* (eds. C. W. Mönnich and F. J. Pop). *Wegen der Prediking.* Amsterdam: Holland, 1959.

————— *et al. Klare Wijn*: Rekenschap over Geschiedenis, Geheim en Gezag van de Bijbel. (Aangeboden door de Generale Synode der Nederlandse Hervormde Kerk.) Den Haag: Boekencentrum, 1967.

FRÖR, K. *Biblische Hermeneutik*: Zur Schriftauslegung in Predigt und Unterricht. 2nd ed. München: Kaiser, 1964.

FULLER, R. H. *The New Testament in Current Study*: Some Trends in the Years 1941–1962. London: SCM, 1963.

GISPEN, W. H. *Israëls "Verhaaldwang".* Assen: Hummelen, 1947.

239

———— *De Christus in het Oude Testament. Exegetica*, I, 1. Delft: Van Keulen, 1952.

———— *Schepping en Paradijs*: Verklaring van Genesis 1–3. Kampen: Kok, 1966.

GOSLINGA, C. J. "De Parallelle Teksten in de Boeken Samuël en Kronieken," *Gereformeerd Theologisch Tijdschrift*, LXI (1961), 108–116.

GRAAFLAND, C. *Verschuivingen in de Gereformeerde Bondsprediking*. Woerden: Zuijderduijn, 1965.

GREIJDANUS, S. *Schriftbeginselen ter Schriftverklaring* en Historisch Overzicht over Theorieën en Wijzen van Schriftuitlegging. Kampen: Kok, 1946.

GROSHEIDE, F. W. *De Eenheid der Nieuwtestamentische Godsopenbaring*. Kampen: Kok, 1918.

———— *Schriftgezag. Schild en Pijl*, I (1918), 1–29.

———— *De Geschiedenis der Nieuwtestamentische Godsopenbaring*. Kampen: Kok, 1925.

———— *Het Belang van de Historiciteit der Bijbelsche Verhalen* voor het Onderwijs op de Zondagsschool. Amsterdam: Bosch, 1926.

———— *Hermeneutiek*: Ten Dienste van de Bestudeering van het Nieuwe Testament. Amsterdam: Van Bottenburg, 1929.

———— *Leerverschillen* in de Gereformeerde Kerken. Amsterdam: Bakker, [1941].

———— "De Geschiedenis der Openbaring," *De Heraut*, 1941, Nos. 3327–3333.

———— "Heilshistorische Exegese," *Gereformeerd Theologisch Tijdschrift*, XLVI (1946), 69–78.

———— "Iets over de Geschiedschrijving in den Bijbel," *Gereformeerd Theologisch Tijdschrift*, LVI (1956), 17–21.

HARRISON, E. F. *et al.* (ed. C. F. H. Henry). *Revelation and the Bible*: Contemporary Evangelical Thought. Grand Rapids: Baker, 1958.

HARTILL, J. E. *Biblical Hermeneutics*. Grand Rapids: Zondervan, 1947 (10th printing 1960).

HARTVELT, G. P. *Over Schrift en Inspiratie*. Kampen: Kok, 1967.

HOEKSTRA, T. *De Tegenwoordige Critiek op onze Preeken*. Kampen: Kok, 1918.

———— *Gereformeerde Homiletiek*. Wageningen: Zomer & Keuning, [1926].

———— *Het Woord Gods in de Prediking*: Een Beoordeeling van Barths Woordtheologie. Kampen: Kok, 1931.

———— "Homiletische Exegese," *Gereformeerd Theologisch Tijdschrift*, XXXII (1932), 505–519.

HOLWERDA, B. *De Wijsheid die Behoudt*. Comp. D. Holwerda. Goes: Oosterbaan & Le Cointre, 1957. (A compilation of Scripture studies dating from 1938–1952.)

———— *Een Levende Hoop*: Een Serie Prekenbundels van B. Holwerda. 5 vols. Enschede: Boersma, 1953–1954. (A compilation of sermons dating from 1939–1950.)

———— "Bijbelse Voorbeelden," *De Betekenis van Verbond en Kerk* voor Huwelijk, Gezin en Jeugd, pp. 23–65. Goes: Oosterbaan & Le Cointre, 1958. (First published in *Samen het Leven In.* Ed. J. H. Scheurer. Amsterdam: Bottenburg, 1939.)

———— "Hoe Lezen we de Heilige Geschiedenis?", *Gereformeerd Mannenblad*, XVIII (1940), 20–21, 26–28, 35–36, 54–55.

———— "De Heilshistorie in de Prediking," "...*Begonnen Hebbende van Mozes*...", pp. 79–118. Terneuzen: Littooij, 1953. (First published in *GTT*, XLIII (1942), 349–370, 381–403.)

———— "Beoordeeling van de Preekschets over Jozua 7 : 4," *Homiletica*, III (1942/43), 38–43.

———— "Evenwichtsconstructies met Betrekking tot de Prediking," *Populair–Wetenschappelijke Bijdragen*, pp. 9–33. Goes: Oosterbaan & Le Cointre, 1962. (First published in *Cursus* tot Ontwikkeling van het Gereformeerd Kerkelijk Denken, vol. II, 39–42, 55–56, 61–68. Eds. R. Schippers and H. J. Spier. Rotterdam: "De Valk," 1944.)

———— "Enkele Notities bij de Schets over Jozua 9 : 3–23," *Homiletica*, VIII (1948), 140–142.

———— *Tot de Dag Aanlicht.* Goes: Oosterbaan & Le Cointre, 1950.

———— *Dictaten Historia Revelationis* Veteris Testamenti. Kampen: Comité voor de uitgave van de college-dictaten van wijlen Prof. B. Holwerda, 1954, 1961.

HULST, A. R. *Hoe Moeten wij het Oude Testament Uitleggen?* Wageningen: Veenman, 1941.

HUYSER (HUIJSER), PH. J. "Prediking in het Oude Testament," *Gereformeerd Theologisch Tijdschrift*, XLII (1941), 165–182, 193–208, 241–255.

———— *De Paraenese in de Prediking.* Franeker: Wever, 1941.

———— " 'Exemplarische' Prediking," *Gereformeerd Theologisch Tijdschrift*, XLIX (1949), 232–249; L (1950), 163–182, 205–219; LI (1951), 1–18.

———— *Het Exempel in de Prediking.* Groningen: Niemeijer, 1952.

———— *De Reformatie der Prediking.* Den Haag: Willem de Zwijgerstichting, 1955.

———— *De Ouderling en de Prediking.* Kampen: Kok, 1959.

———— "De Dominee, de Preek en de Politiek," *Homiletica en Biblica*, XXII (1963), 73–82, 97–102.

IMPETA, C. N. *Zelfonderzoek Noodzakelijk!* Kampen: Kok, 1936.

JAGER, O. *Het Eeuwige Leven*: Met Name in Verband met de Verhouding van Tijd en Eeuwigheid. Kampen: Kok, 1962.

JANSE, A. *Lourens Ingelse*: Een Episode uit het Godsdienstig Leven op Walcheren omstreeks 1780. Goes: Oosterbaan & Le Cointre, 1932.

JONKER, H. *Actuele Prediking.* Nijkerk: Callenbach, [1965].

241

KAMPHUIS, J. "Critische Sympathie (Over den Dogmatischen Arbeid van Dr K. Schilder)," *Almanak* van het Corpus Studiosorum in Academia Campensi "Fides Quadrat Intellectum" *1953*, pp. 73–108. Kampen: Zalsman, 1953.

KAPTEYN, J. *Van Hem, Die Is, Die Was en Die Komt.* Goes: Oosterbaan & Le Cointre, [1941].

KIEVIT, I. *Voorwerpelijke Onderwerpelijke Prediking*: Eisch der Heilige Schrift. 2nd ed. Baarn: n.n., 1939.

KOLLER, C. W. *Expository Preaching without Notes.* Grand Rapids: Baker, 1969.

KOOLE, J. L. *De Overname van het Oude Testament door de Christelijke Kerk.* Hilversum: Schipper, 1938.

———— "Het Oude, Testament in onze Prediking," *Homiletica en Biblica*, XIX (1960), 14–17, 49–52.

———— *Hermeneutische Oriëntatie.* Oration held at the Theologische Hoogeschool, Kampen, December 13, 1962.

———— "Het Soortelijk Gewicht van de Historische Stoffen van het Oude Testament," *Gereformeerd Theologisch Tijdschrift*, LXV (1965), 81–104.

———— *Verhaal en Feit in het Oude Testament.* Kampen: Kok, [1966].

KROMMINGA, C. G. *Man Before God's Face in Calvin's Preaching.* Grand Rapids: Calvin Theological Seminary, 1961.

KUITERT, H. M. *De Mensvormigheid Gods*: Een Dogmatisch-Hermeneutische Studie over de Anthropomorfismen van de Heilige Schrift. Kampen: Kok, 1962.

———— *De Realiteit van het Geloof*: Over de Anti-Metafysische Tendens in de Huidige Theologische Ontwikkeling. Kampen: Kok, 1966.

KUYPER, A. *Encyclopaedie der Heilige Godgeleerdheid.* 3 vols. 2nd ed. rev. Kampen: Kok, 1908–1909.

MICKELSEN, A. B. *Interpreting the Bible.* Grand Rapids: Eerdmans, 1963.

MISKOTTE, H. H. *Sensus Spiritualis*: De Verhouding tussen het Oude Testament en het Nieuwe Testament in de Rooms-Katholieke Hermeneutiek sinds het Verschijnen van de Encycliek 'Divine Afflante Spiritu' in 1943. Nijkerk: Callenbach, 1966.

MISKOTTE, K. H. *Het Waagstuk der Prediking.* Den Haag: Daamen, 1941.

———— *Als de Goden Zwijgen*: Over de Zin van het Oude Testament. 3rd ed. Haarlem: Holland, 1966.

MÜLLER, B. A. *Die Lewende Woord aan die Mens van die Hede*: 'n Bespreking van die Vrae rondom die Aktuele Woordverkondiging. Zaandijk: Heijnis, 1961.

NIXON, L. *John Calvin, Expository Preacher.* Grand Rapids: Eerdmans, 1950.

NOTH, M. "The 'Re-presentation' of the Old Testament in Proclamation," *Essays on Old Testament Hermeneutics*, pp. 76–88. Trans. J. L. Mays. Richmond: John Knox, 1964.

OLTHUIS, J. H. *Facts, Values and Ethics*: A Confrontation with Twentieth Century British Moral Philosophy in Particular G. E. Moore. Assen: Van Gorcum, 1968.

242

OOSTERHOFF, B. J. *Het Openbaringskarakter van het Oude Testament*. Alphen aan den Rijn: "Holland," 1954.

———— *Feit of Interpretatie*. Kampen: Kok, 1967.

OVERDUIN, J. Letters to the editor on "Gereformeerde Prediking en Heilsgeschiedenis," *De Reformatie*, XVIII (1937/38), 311 (partial reprint of article in *Credo*), 335, 350–351.

———— "De Bijbel: Het Boek der Prediking!", *Opdracht en Dienst*, XXXIX (1964), 22–24.

PACKER, J. I. *'Fundamentalism' and the Word of God*: Some Evangelical Principles. Grand Rapids: Eerdmans, 1964.

PANNENBERG, W. "Redemptive Event and History," *Essays on Old Testament Hermeneutics*, pp. 314–335. Trans. S. Guthrie. Richmond: John Knox, 1964.

PERRY, L. M. *A Manual for Biblical Preaching*. Grand Rapids: Baker, 1965.

PHELPS, A. *The Theory of Preaching*. Rev. F. D. Whitesell. Grand Rapids: Eerdmans, 1947.

POPMA, K. J. *De Vrijheid der Exegese*. Goes: Oosterbaan & Le Cointre, 1944.

———— *Levensbeschouwing*: Opmerkingen naar Aanleiding van de Heidelbergse Catechismus. 7 vols. Amsterdam: Buijten & Schipperheijn, 1958-1965.

POPMA, S. J. "Een Situatieteekening"(?), extensively quoted by C. Veenhof, *Om de "Unica Catholica,"* pp. 153–167. Goes: Oosterbaan & Le Cointre, 1949. (A stencilled brochure, Amersfoort, 1943.)

———— *De Psychologie van een Schisma*: Een Poging tot Begrijpen. Groningen: Niemeijers, 1945.

PRAAMSMA, L. *Het Dwaze Gods*: Geschiedenis der Gereformeerde Kerken in Nederland sinds het Begin der 19de Eeuw. Wageningen: Zomer & Keuning, 1950.

PUCHINGER, G. *Is de Gereformeerde Wereld Veranderd?* Delft: Meinema, 1966.

Reformed Ecumenical Synod Report by the Committee on Inspiration, 1958. (Stencilled.)

REU, M. *Homiletics*: A Manual of the Theory and Practice of Preaching. Trans. A. Steinhaeuser. Chicago: Wartburg, 1922.

RICHARDSON, A. *History Sacred and Profane*. Philadelphia: Westminster, 1964.

RIDDERBOS, H. N. *Zelfopenbaring en Zelfverberging*: Het Historisch Karakter van Jezus' Messiaansche Zelfopenbaring volgens de Synoptische Evangeliën. Kampen: Kok, 1946.

———— *Heilsgeschiedenis en Heilige Schrift van het Nieuwe Testament*: Het Gezag van het Nieuwe Testament. Kampen: Kok, 1955.

———— *When the Time Had Fully Come*: Studies in New Testament Theology. Grand Rapids: Eerdmans, 1957.

———— *Paulus*: Ontwerp van zijn Theologie. Kampen: Kok, 1966.

—————— "An Attempt at the Theological Definition of Inerrancy, Infallibility, and Authority," *International Reformed Bulletin*, XI, No. 32 (January, 1968), pp. 27-41. (First presented at Gordon College, Boston, Mass., June, 1966. A slightly revised version in Dutch: "Feilloosheid, Onfeilbaarheid, Autoriteit (Over de Aard van het Schriftgezag)," *Het Woord, het Rijk en onze Verlegenheid*, pp. 57-77. Kampen: Kok, 1968.)

RIDDERBOS, J. *De Beteekenis van het Oude Testament voor de Christelijke Religie.* Kampen: Kok, 1913.

—————— *Het Oude Testament in onze Prediking.* Kampen: Kok, 1922.

—————— "Over de Uitlegging der Heilige Schrift," *Bijbelsch Handboek*, I, 365–422. Kampen: Kok, 1935.

—————— Recensie (*De Wijsheid van den Prediker* door Ds E. Th. v. d. Born), *Gereformeerd Theologisch Tijdschrift*, XLI (1940), 86–92.

—————— "Iets over Heilshistorische Schriftverklaring," *Gereformeerd Theologisch Tijdschrift*, XLIII (1942), 261–275.

RIDDERBOS, N. H. "Christus in de Psalmen," *Gereformeerd Theologisch Tijdschrift*, XLIV (1943), 129–149.

—————— "Het Oude Testament in de Prediking," *Gereformeerd Theologisch Tijdschrift*, LVI (1956), 142–153.

—————— "Het Oude Testament en de Geschiedenis," *Gereformeerd Theologisch Tijdschrift*, LVII (1957), 112–120.

—————— "Typologie (Speciaal de Typologie naar Von Rads Conceptie)," *Vox Theologica*, XXXI (1961), 149–159.

—————— *Beschouwingen over Genesis I.* 2nd ed. rev.. Kampen: Kok, 1963.

RITSCHL, D. *A Theology of Proclamation.* Richmond: John Knox, 1960. (The German preliminary study: *Die homiletische Function der Gemeinde.* Zollikon: Evangelischer Verlag, 1959.)

ROGERS, J. B. *Scripture in the Westminster Confession*: A Problem of Historical Interpretation for American Presbyterianism. Kampen: Kok, 1966.

ROSSOUW, H. W. *Klaarheid en Interpretasie*: Enkele Probleemhistoriese Gesigspunte in Verband met die Leer van die Duidelikheid van die Heilige Skrif. Amsterdam: Van Campen, 1963.

ROWLEY, H. H. *The Faith of Israel*: Aspects of Old Testament Thought. London: SCM, 1961.

RUNIA, K. *Karl Barth's Doctrine of Holy Scripture.* Grand Rapids: Eerdmans, 1962.

—————— " 'New' Views of Scripture," *Torch and Trumpet*, XVII, No. 8 (October, 1967), 10–13.

—————— "The Authority of Scripture," *Calvin Theological Journal*, IV, No. 2 (November, 1969), 165–194.

RUNNER, H. E. "The Relation of the Bible to Learning," *Christian Perspectives 1960*, pp. 83–159. Pella: Pella, 1960.

—————— "Scientific and Pre-Scientific," and "Sphere-Sovereignty," *Christian Perspectives 1961*, pp. 9–87. Hamilton: Guardian, 1961.

244

———— "Scriptural Religion and Political Task," *Christian Perspectives 1962*, pp. 133–257. Hamilton: Guardian, 1962.

SCHELHAAS, J. "Christus en de Historische Stoffen in de Prediking," *Gereformeerd Theologisch Tijdschrift*, XLII (1941), 107–128. (A slight revision of articles originally published in the *Franeker Kerkbode*, XII, Nos. 620–621, 623–626, and XIII, Nos. 630–631, 633 [November 11, 1939 – February 10, 1940].)

———— *De Val van Assen*. (With appendix: "Minderheidsrapport over Assen 1926.") Vlaardingen: Bolland, 1968.

SCHILDER, H. J. *Rachels Troost*: Vrouw en Vrouwen in de Heilshistorie. Goes: Oosterbaan & Le Cointre, 1960.

SCHILDER, K. *Preken*. 3 vols. Eds. W. G. De Vries and Others. Goes: Oosterbaan & Le Cointre, 1954–1955. (A compilation of sermons dating from 1914–1952.)

———— *Schriftoverdenkingen*. 3 vols. Eds. C. Veenhof and Others. Goes: Oosterbaan & Le Cointre, 1956–1958. (A compilation of Scripture studies dating from 1915–1952.)

———— *Om Woord en Kerk*. 4 vols. Comp. C. Veenhof. Goes: Oosterbaan & Le Cointre, 1948–1953. Specifically:

"Rhetorica en Eerbied," Vol. II, 29–30. (First published in *Gereformeerde Kerkbode* Classis Gorinchem, November 8, 1919.)

"Tegenstrijdigheden in den Bijbel?", Vol. III, 50–95. (First published in *Ons Arsenaal*, II, Nos. 3–5. Zutphen: Van den Brink, [1919].)

"Niet terug naar Pinksteren!", Vol. II, 41–43. (First published in *Gereformeerde Kerkbode* Classis Gorinchem, June 12, 1920.)

"Kerktaal en Leven," Vol. III, 96–227. (First published separately. Amsterdam: Holland, [1923].)

"Het Feest en Wij," Vol. II, 124–126. (First published in *Leidsche Kerkbode*, January 28, 1927.)

"Kerstfeestviering en Heilshistorie," Vol. I, 246–252. (First published in *Op den Uitkijk*, December, 1927.)

———— *Bij Dichters en Schriftgeleerden*: Verzamelde Opstellen. Specifically: "De Paradox in de Religie" (pp. 65–147), and "Anthropomorphe Prediking" (pp. 392–411). Amsterdam: Holland, 1927.

———— *Tusschen "Ja" en "Neen"*: Verzamelde Opstellen. Specifically: "Over Ware en Valsche 'Mystiek'" (pp. 165–232), "Calvijn over de Geloofsparadox" (pp. 233–305), "'Alsof' of 'Nochtans'" (pp. 307–328), "'In de Crisis?'" (pp. 329–359), and "Iets over Prediker contra Psychoanalyticus" (pp. 379–426). Kampen: Kok, 1929.

———— *Christus in Zijn Lijden*: Overwegingen van het Lijdensevangelie. 3 vols. 1st ed. Kampen: Kok, 1930. (English edition: *Christ in His Suffering*; *Christ on Trial*; *Christ Crucified*. Trans. H. Zijlstra. Grand Rapids: Eerdmans, 1938–1940. 2nd Dutch ed. Vols. I and II revised. Kampen: Kok, 1949–1952.)

———— "Iets over het Gereformeerd Karakter der Lijdensprediking," *De Reformatie*, X (1929/30), 203–204, 211–213, 218–219.

———— "Iets over de Eenheid der 'Heilsgeschiedenis' in Verband met de Prediking," *De Reformatie*, XI (1930/31), 365–366, 373–375, 381–383.

245

———— "Over het 'Skandalon,'" *Gereformeerd Theologisch Tijdschrift*, XXXII (1931/32), 49–67, 97–130.

———— *Christus en Cultuur*. 2nd ed. rev. Franeker: Wever, 1948. (Revision of "Jezus Christus en het Cultuurleven," in H. L. Both *et al.*, *Jezus Christus en het Menschenleven*, pp. 225–285. Culemborg: De Pauw, 1932.)

———— *Zur Begriffsgeschichte des "Paradoxon"*: Mit besonderer Berücksichtigung Calvins und des nach-kierkegaardschen "Paradoxon." Kampen: Kok, 1933.

———— "'Punten van Overeenkomst,'" *De Reformatie*, XIV (1933/34), 18–19, 27–28, 34–35, 42, 50–51, 59.

———— "De Logos asarkos 'Roept' den Vader van den Logos ensarkos," *De Reformatie*, XIV (1933/34), 346.

———— "Iets over de Geschiedenis en haar Waarde of Waardeloosheid," *De Reformatie*, XIV (1933/34), 365–366, 373–374, and XV (1934/35), 1–2, 25–26, 33–34, 41–42, 49–50, 57–58.

———— *Wat is de Hemel?* Kampen: Kok, 1935.

———— "In Memoriam Prof. Dr T. Hoekstra," *De Reformatie*, XVI (January 24, 1936), 130–131.

———— "Paschen in de Prediking," *De Reformatie*, XVI (1935/36), 235–237.

———— "Pinksterfeest in de Prediking," *De Reformatie*, XVI (1935/36), 290–291.

———— "De Mystiek ter Tafel," *De Reformatie*, XVIII (1937/38), 226–227.

———— "Gereformeerde Prediking en Heilsgeschiedenis" (Schilder's reply to J. Overduin), *De Reformatie*, XVIII (1938), 311–312, 335–336, 351.

———— "Versobering of Verarming?", *De Reformatie*, XVIII (1937/38), 414–415.

———— "Adventsprediking," *De Reformatie*, XIX (1938/39), 58–59.

———— "Waar ik Niets van Begrijp" (Schilder's reply to Schelhaas), *De Reformatie*, XX (1939/40), 96–97.

———— and VOLLENHOVEN, D. H. TH. *Van "Oorzaken" en "Redenen"*: Minderheidsnota inzake: Algemene Genade, Genadeverbond, De onsterfelijkheid der ziel, Pluriformiteit der kerk, Vereeniging der twee naturen van Christus, en Zelfonderzoek. Comp. C. Veenhof. Kampen/Amsterdam: (stencilled), 1939.

———— *College-Verslagen* der door Prof. Dr. K. Schilder in Amerika Gehouden Lezingen April '39–Juni '39. Kampen: (stencilled), 1939.

———— *Heidelbergsche Catechismus*. Vol. I (Zondag 1–3). Goes: Oosterbaan & Le Cointre, 1939.

———— B. HOLWERDA, S. GREIJDANUS, J. A. VINK, D. VAN DIJK, E. TH. VAN DEN BORN, C. VEENHOF, J. KAPTEYN, A. JANSE, M. B. VAN 'T VEER, *'t Hoogfeest naar de Schriften*: Studies over de Vleeschwording des Woords. Goes: Oosterbaan & Le Cointre, [*ca.* 1939].

———— "'De Spits' der Paaschprediking: Geen Openbarings-, doch Heils-historie," *De Reformatie*, XXI (1945/46), 225–226.

246

———— "De Theoloog," in R. Van Reest, *Een Bloedgetuige der Kerk*: Het Leven en Sterven van Johannes Kapteyn, pp. 93–113. Groningen: De Jager, 1946.

———— *Heidelbergsche Catechismus*. 4 vols. Goes: Oosterbaan & Le Cointre, 1947–1951.

———— "Type en Antitype in de Openbaringshistorie," *Capita Selecta III*, pp. 33–64. Kampen: Brever, 1951.

SCHIPPERS, R. "De Dienst des Woords en het Woord Gods," *Van den Dienst des Woords*: Een Boek over de Prediking naar Gereformeerde Belijdenis, pp. 9–53. Goes: Oosterbaan & Le Cointre, 1944.

———— *De Gereformeerde Zede*. Kampen: Kok, 1954.

———— *Jezus Christus in het Historisch Onderzoek*. Vol. I: Van het Verhaal naar de Feiten. Kampen: Kok, 1969.

SCHRAMM, W. (ed.) *The Science of Human Communication*: New Directions and New Findings in Community Research. New York: Basic Books, 1963.

SEERVELD, C. *Understanding the Scriptures*: How to Read and not to Read the Bible, pp. 41–92. *Christian Perspectives 1969*. Toronto: A.A.C.S., 1968.

SIKKEL, J. C. *Dienst des Woords*. Haarlem: Verleur, 1923.

SMIT, J. W. "Iets over de Heilshistorische Prediking," *Ons Kerkblad* (Zeeland), April 27–June 8, 1946.

SPIER, H. J. "Schriftuurlijke Woordbediening!", *Pro-Ecclesia*, VI (1940/41), 159–160.

———— "Objectiviteit en Subjectiviteit in de Prediking?", *Cursus* tot Ontwikkeling van het Gereformeerd Kerkelijk Denken, vol. I, lesson i, 9–12. Rotterdam: "De Valk," 1943.

———— "De Woorddienst," *Cursus*, I (1943), lessons v, 11–13; vi, 11–14; vii, 10–14; viii, 10–14; ix, 7–11.

———— "De Theologie en de Preek," *Van den Dienst des Woords*, pp. 91–115. Ed. R. Schippers. Goes: Oosterbaan & Le Cointre, 1944.

———— "Wijsbegeerte en Prediking," *Wijsbegeerte en Levenspractijk*: De Betekenis van de Wijsbegeerte der Wetsidee voor velerlei Levensgebied, pp. 40–59. Eds. H. J. Spier and J. M. Spier. Kampen: Kok, 1948.

———— *De Bijbel in Tegenspraak*. Kampen: Kok, 1967.

SPIER, J. M. "De Norm voor ons Geloven," *Wetenschappelijke Bijdragen* door Leerlingen van Dr D. H. TH. Vollenhoven, pp. 72–89. Ed. S. U. Zuidema. Franeker: Wever, 1951.

STECK, K. G. *Die Idee der Heilsgeschichte*: Hofmann - Schlatter - Cullmann. Zollikon: Evangelischer Verlag, 1959.

STEK, J. H. "The Message of the Book of Jonah," *Calvin Theological Journal*, IV, No. 1 (April, 1969), 23–50.

STELLINGWERFF, J. "Kritiek op K. Schilder als Filosoferend Dogmaticus," *Philosophia Reformata*, XXVII (1962), 106–125.

STEVENSON, D. E. *Preaching on the Books of the Old Testament*. New York: Harper, 1961.

STREEFKERK, N. "Exemplarische Prediking," partly reprinted in *Pro-Ecclesia*, VI (1940/41), 349. (First published in *Gereformeerde Kerkbode* voor Wolvega en Om-streken, August, 1941.)

―――― "'Heilshistorische' en 'Exemplarische' Methode," partly reprinted in *Pro-Ecclesia*, VII (1941/42), 39. (First published in *Gereformeerde Kerkbode* voor Wolvega en Omstreken, October, 1941.)

THIELICKE, H. *Leiden an der Kirche*: Ein persönliches Wort. Hamburg: Furche, 1965.

TRIMP, C. *Om de Oeconomie van het Welbehagen*: Een Analyse van de Idee der 'Heils-geschichte' in de 'Kirchliche Dogmatik' van K. Barth. Goes: Oosterbaan & Le Cointre, 1961.

―――― "De Sleutel der Kennis," *Petah-Ja*, XV (June, 1961), 83–91.

TROOST, A. *Casuïstiek en Situatie-Ethiek*: Een Methodologische Terreinverkenning. Utrecht: Libertas, 1958.

―――― *Kerkelijke Verantwoordelijkheid voor de Politiek*: Overwegingen bij "De Poli-tieke Verantwoordelijkheid van de Kerk" (Uitgave Nederlandse Hervormde Kerk). Kampen: Kok, 1967.

VAN ANDEL, J. *Handleiding Gewijde Geschiedenis*. Leiden, Donner, 1903.

VAN DEN BORN, E. TH. "Iets over de Methode der Prediking," *De Reformatie*, XVIII (1937/38), 397–398, 405–406, 413–414.

―――― "De Methode der Prediking," *Van den Dienst des Woords*, pp. 75–89. Ed. R. Schippers. Goes: Oosterbaan & Le Cointre, 1944.

VAN DER LAAN, H. *Spanningen in de Gereformeerde Kerken*. Amsterdam: Buijten & Schipperheijn, 1965.

VAN DER VEGT, W. H. "Inleiding," *Het Gepredikte Woord*: Preeken van Johannes Calvijn, vol. I, 1–73. J. Douma cotranslator. Franeker: Wever, [1942].

VAN DIJK, D. *De Preektrant* van de Dominé's in de Kerken der Afscheiding in de Jaren 1834–1869. Aalten: De Graafschap, 1935. (First published in part in *GTT*, XXXV [1934], 451–480).

―――― *Verbond en Belijdenis*. Kampen: Kok, [1939].

―――― "Tot onze Leering," *Pro-Ecclesia*, VI (1940/41), 271–272, 279–280, 287, 295, 303, 307.

―――― "Openbaringshistorisch-Christocentrisch Preeken," *Pro-Ecclesia*, VII (1941/42), 137, 141, 149, 153–154, 161–162.

―――― "Over Preeken Maken en Preeken," *Van den Dienst des Woords*, pp. 179–204. Ed. R. Schippers. Goes: Oosterbaan & Le Cointre, 1944.

―――― and FRANCKE, JOH. *Persoonlijk Onderzoek van de Heilige Schrift*. Utrecht: Ned. Bond van (vrijgemaakte) Jongelingsvereenigingen, 1949.

―――― "Hoe Maak ik mijn Preek?", *Homiletica en Biblica*, XXI (1962), 80–86.

VAN ELDEREN, B. "New Perspectives in Biblical Research," *Calvin Theological Journal*, I, No. 2 (November, 1966), 165–181.

—— "The Teaching of Jesus and the Gospel Records," *Jesus of Nazareth*: Saviour and Lord, pp. 109–119. Ed. C. F. H. Henry. Grand Rapids: Eerdmans, 1966.

VAN REEST, R. [K. C. Van Spronsen] *"Opdat Zij Allen Één Zijn"*: Prof. Dr. K. Schilder in zijn Strijd om Woord en Kerk. 2 vols. Goes: Oosterbaan & Le Cointre, 1962–1963.

VAN SCHELVEN, A. A. *De Bewerking van eene Piëtistisch-getinte Gemeente.* Goes: Oosterbaan & Le Cointre, 1914.

VAN TEYLINGEN, E. G. *Aard en Achtergrond* van het geschil in de Gereformeerde Kerken. N.p.: n.n., [1944].

—— *Tussentijdse Balans* van het Heroriëntatieproces in de Gereformeerde Kerken. Kampen: Kok, 1964.

VAN TONGEREN, H. *Bewaard Bevel*: De Vrijmaking in Kort Bestek. 4th ed. rev. Enschede: Boersma, 1962.

VAN 'T VEER, M. B. *Mijn God is Jahweh* (Elia). Franeker: Wever, 1939. (A second volume was published posthumously; Groningen: De Jager, 1949.)

—— "Iets over de Heilshistorie," *Gereformeerd Mannenblad*, XIX (1941), 57–58, 65–66, 73–74, 81–82, and XX (1942), 1.

—— "Nog eens: Christocentrisch of Exemplarisch," *Pro-Ecclesia*, VII (1941/42), 59–60.

—— "Christologische Prediking," *Cursus* tot Ontwikkeling van het Gereformeerd Kerkelijk Denken, vol. I, lessons i, 1–3; ii, 1–5; iii, 1–4. Eds. R. Schippers and H. J. Spier. Rotterdam: "De Valk," 1943. (Reworked to form part of "Christologische Prediking over . . . ," below.)

—— "De Beteekenis van het Oude Testament," *Cursus*, vol. I (1943), lessons v, 1–4; vi, 1–4; vii, 1–5; viii, 1–4; ix, 1–4. (Reworked to form part of the following article.)

—— "Christologische Prediking over de Historische Stof van het Oude Testament," *Van den Dienst des Woords*, pp. 117–167. Ed. R. Schippers. Goes: Oosterbaan & Le Cointre, 1944.

VEENHOF, C. *In Kuyper's Lijn:* Enkele Opmerkingen over den Invloed van Dr A. Kuyper op de "Wijsbegeerte der Wetsidee." Goes: Oosterbaan & Le Cointre, 1939.

—— "Wereldcrisis en Prediking," *Bondsboekje 1940*, pp. 16–63. Zwolle: "De Gereformeerde Mannenbond," 1940.

—— *Predik het Woord*: Gedachten en Beschouwingen van Dr A. Kuyper over de Prediking. Goes: Oosterbaan & Le Cointre, [*ca.* 1943].

—— "Het Goddelijke Wonder der Prediking," *Een Drietal Predicaties* door Prof. C. Veenhof en Ds. H. J. Schilder, pp. 17–41. Enschede: Boersma, [1946].

—— *Getuigend de Wijde Wereld In!*: Hulpboekje bij het Lezen van "de Handelingen der Apostelen." Utrecht: Nederlandsche Bond van (vrijgem.) J.V. op G.G., 1947.

——— *Om de "Unica Catholica"*: Een Beschouwing over de Positie van de Bezwaarden onder en over de Synodocratie. Goes: Oosterbaan & Le Cointre, 1949.

——— "In Memoriam Benne Holwerda," *Almanak* van het Corpus Studiosorum in Academia Campensi "Fides Quadrat Intellectum" *1953*, pp. 169–180. Kampen: Zalsman, 1953.

——— *Prediking en Uitverkiezing*: Kort Overzicht van de Strijd, Gevoerd in de Christelijk Afgescheidene Gereformeerde Kerk tussen 1850 en 1870, over de Plaats van de Leer der Uitverkiezing in de Prediking. Kampen: Kok, 1959.

——— "Calvijn en de Prediking," *Zicht op Calvijn*, pp. 47–101. Ed. J. Stellingwerff. Amsterdam: Buijten & Schipperheijn, 1965.

VEENHOF, J. *Revelatie en Inspiratie*: De Openbarings- en Schriftbeschouwing van Herman Bavinck in Vergelijking met die der Ethische Theologie. Amsterdam: Buijten & Schipperheijn, 1968.

VOLBEDA, S. *The Pastoral Genius of Preaching*. Comp. and ed. R. Evenhuis. Grand Rapids: Zondervan, 1960.

VOLLENHOVEN, D. H. TH. *Het Calvinisme en de Reformatie van de Wijsbegeerte*. Amsterdam: Paris, 1933.

——— and SCHILDER, K. *Van "Oorzaken" en "Redenen"*: Minderheidsnota inzake.... See under Schilder, 1939.

——— *Geschiedenis der Wijsbegeerte*, I. Franeker: Wever, 1950.

——— "In Memoriam K. Schilder," *Philosophia Reformata*, XVII (1952), 149–150.

VON MEYENFELDT, F. H. "Enige Algemene Beschouwingen, Gegrond op de Betekenis van het Hart in het Oude Testament," *Wetenschappelijke Bijdragen* door Leerlingen van Dr D. H. Th. Vollenhoven, pp. 52–67. Ed. S. U. Zuidema. Franeker: Wever, 1951.

——— "Dominee," *Gereformeerden, Waarom?*, pp. 56–84. Ed. S. U. Zuidema. Delft: Van Keulen, 1951.

——— *Kerkelijk Vooruitzicht*. Wageningen: Zomer & Keuning, [1959].

——— *The Meaning of Ethos. Christian Perspectives 1964*. Hamilton: Guardian, 1964.

VON RAD, G. *Old Testament Theology*. 2 vols. Trans. D. M. G. Stalker. Edinburgh: Oliver & Boyd, 1962–1965.

VOS, G. *Biblical Theology*: Old and New Testaments. Grand Rapids: Eerdmans, 1959. (First printing 1948.)

VRIEZEN, TH. C. *An Outline of Old Testament Theology*. Trans. S. Neuijen. Oxford: Basil Blackwell, 1962.

WATERINK, J. *De Prediking en de Geestelijke Volksgezondheid*. Rotterdam: Donner, 1957.

WESTERMANN, C. "Remarks on the Theses of Bultmann and Baumgärtel," *Essays on Old Testament Hermeneutics*, pp. 123–133. Trans. D. Ritschl. Richmond: John Knox, 1964.

250

WETERMAN, J. A. M. "De Verkondiging van het Woord 'Gods," *Levende Zielzorg*, pp. 174–205. Utrecht: Het Spectrum, 1954.

WINGREN, G. *Die Predigt*. Göttingen: Vandenhoeck & Ruprecht, 1955.

WRIGHT, G. E. *God Who Acts*: Biblical Theology as Recital. London: SCM, 1964.

ZUIDEMA, S. U. *Van Bultmann naar Fuchs*: Een Studie over de Studeerkamer van de Predikant. Franeker: Wever, [1964].

———— *De Christus der Schriften en Oecumenische Theologie*. Amsterdam: Buijten & Schipperheijn, 1965.